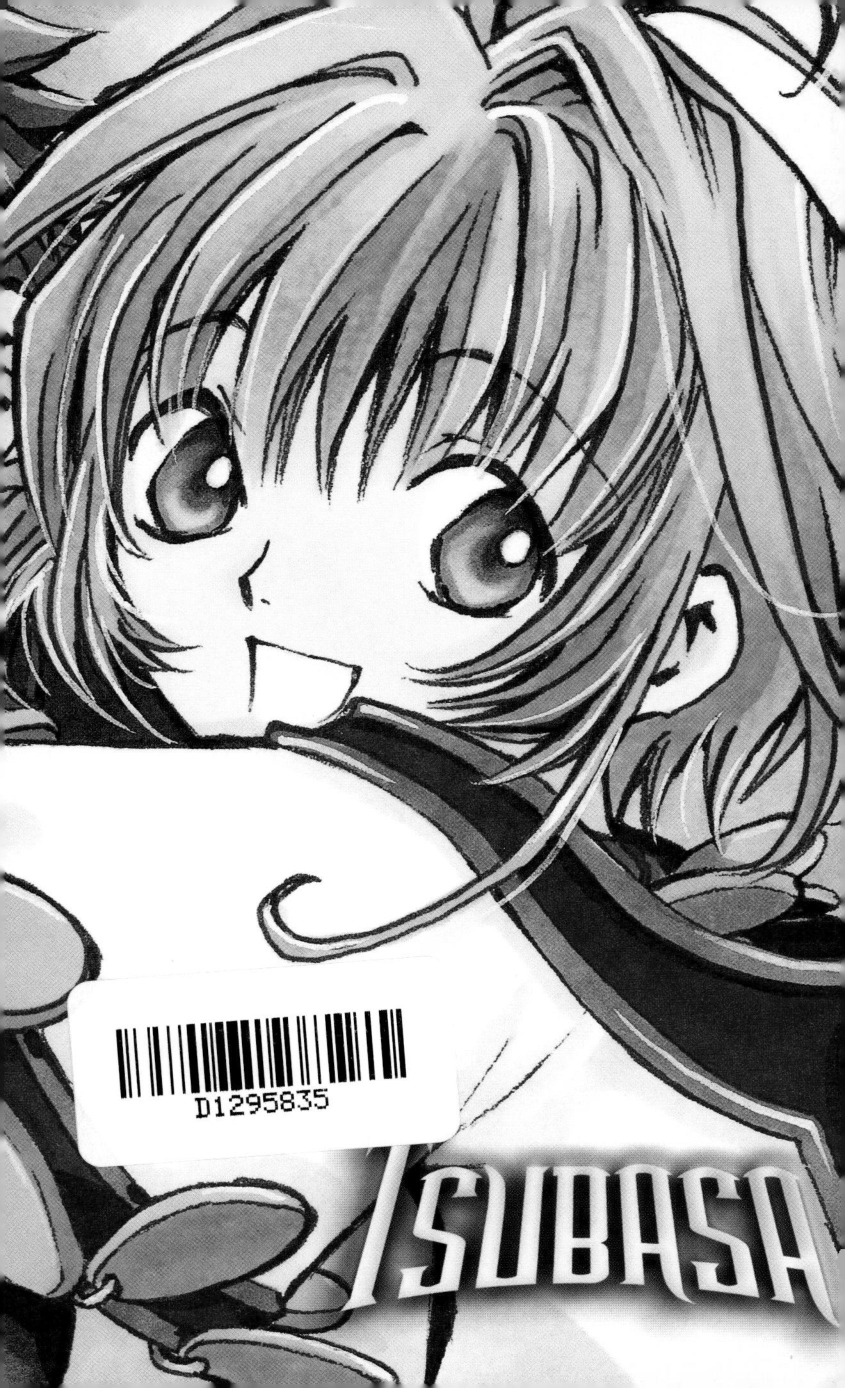
TSUBASA

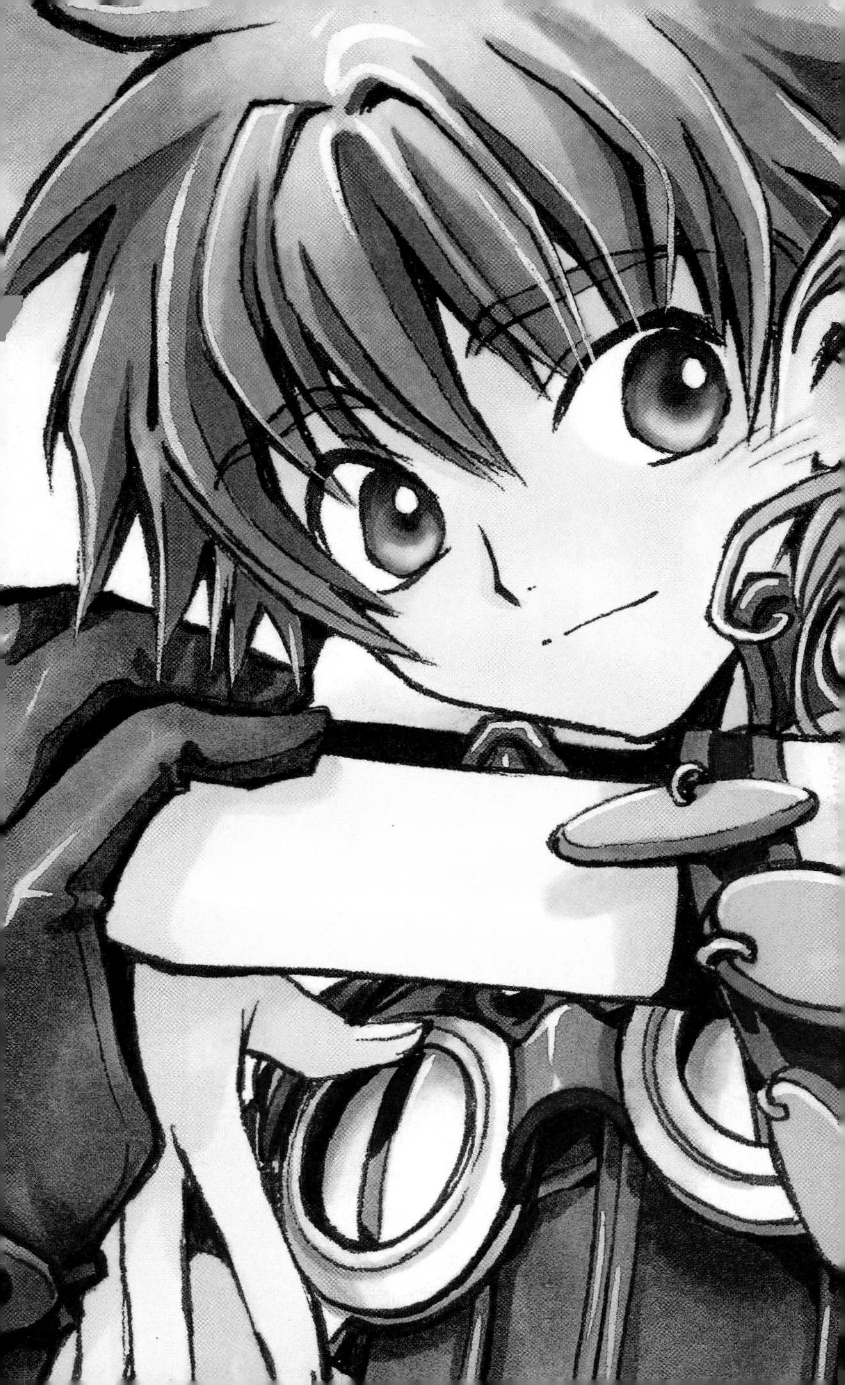

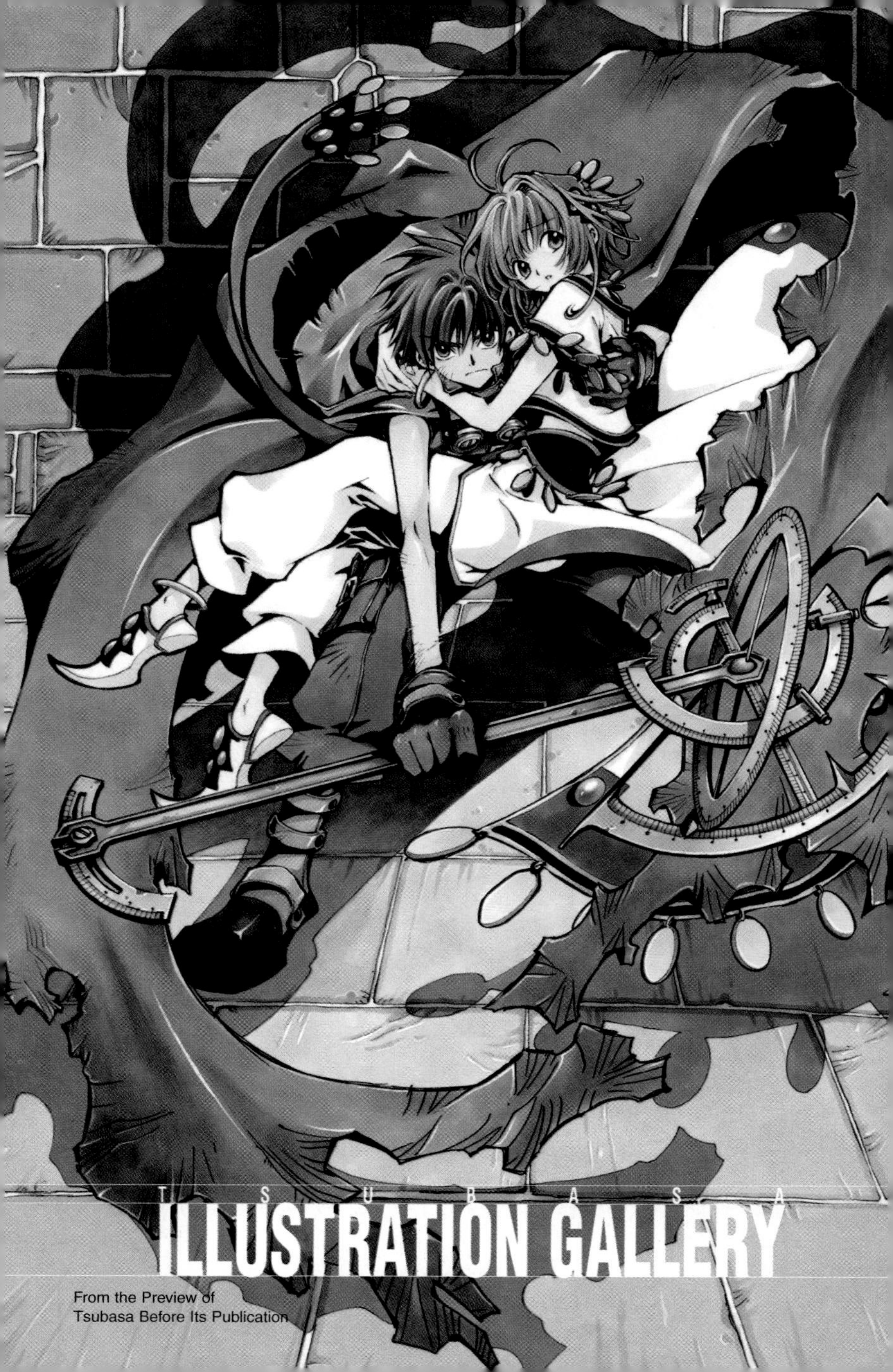

T S U B A S A ILLUSTRATION GALLERY

From the Preview of
Tsubasa Before Its Publication

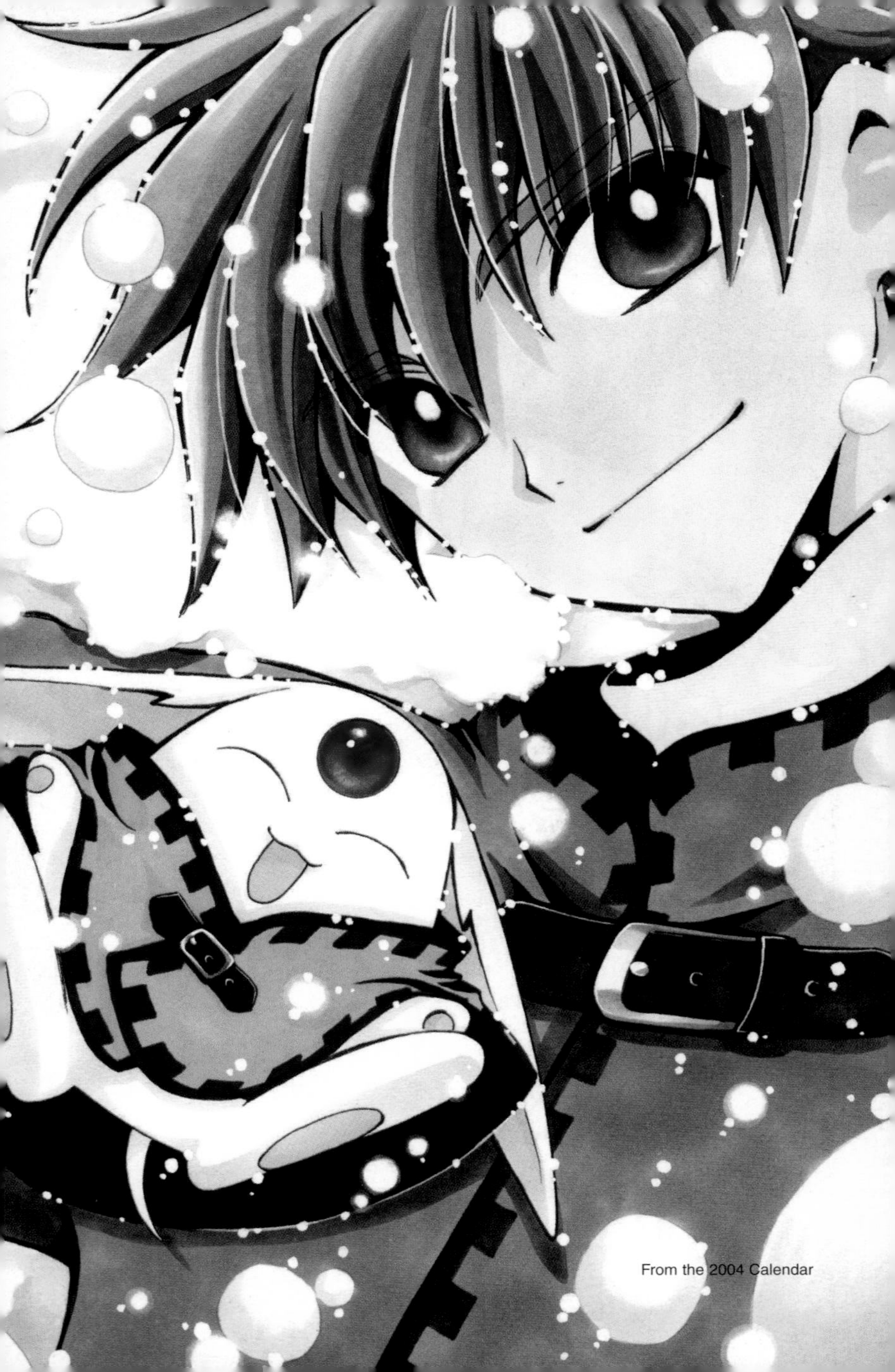

From the 2004 Calendar

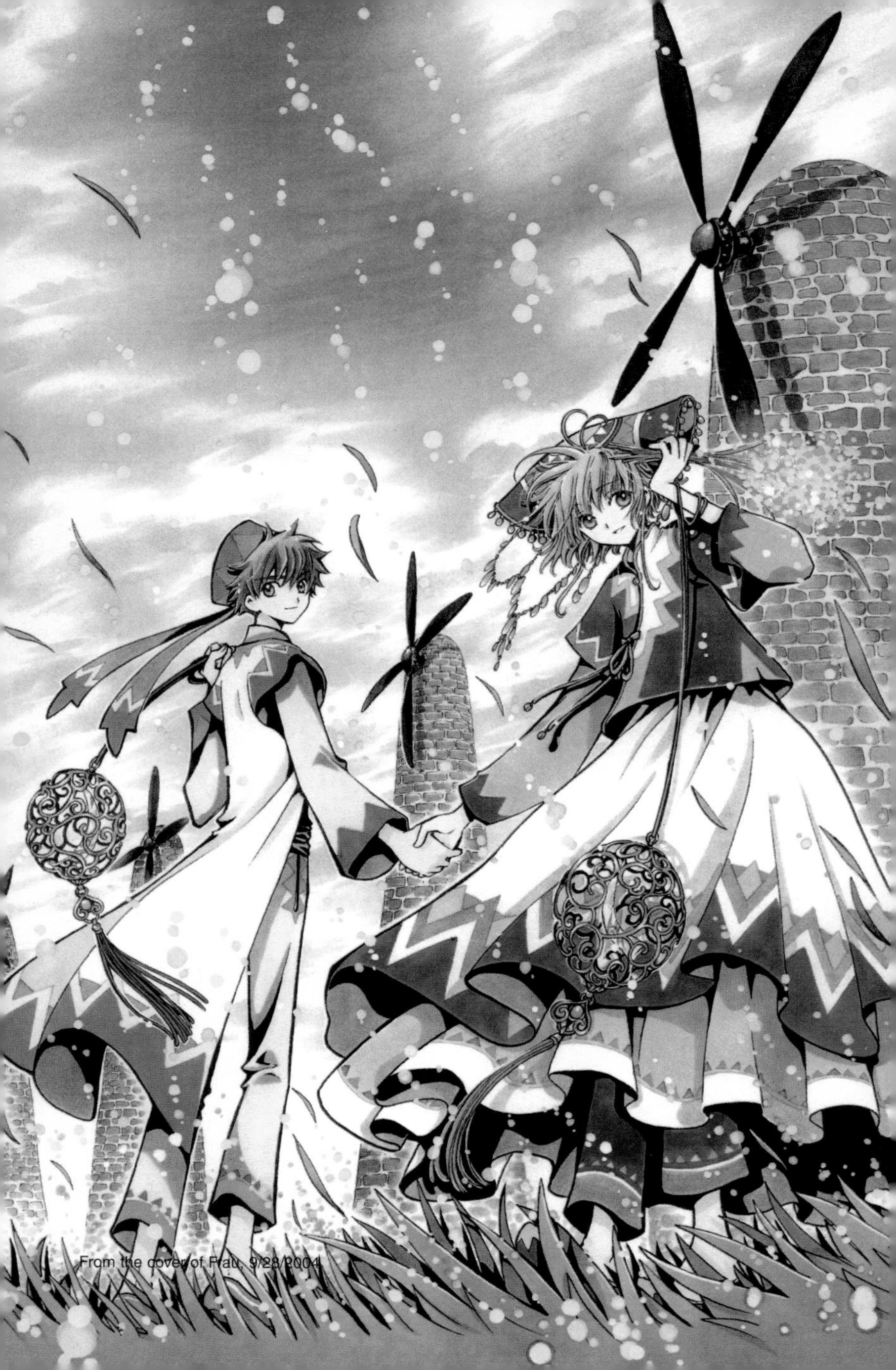

From the cover of Frau, 9/28/2004

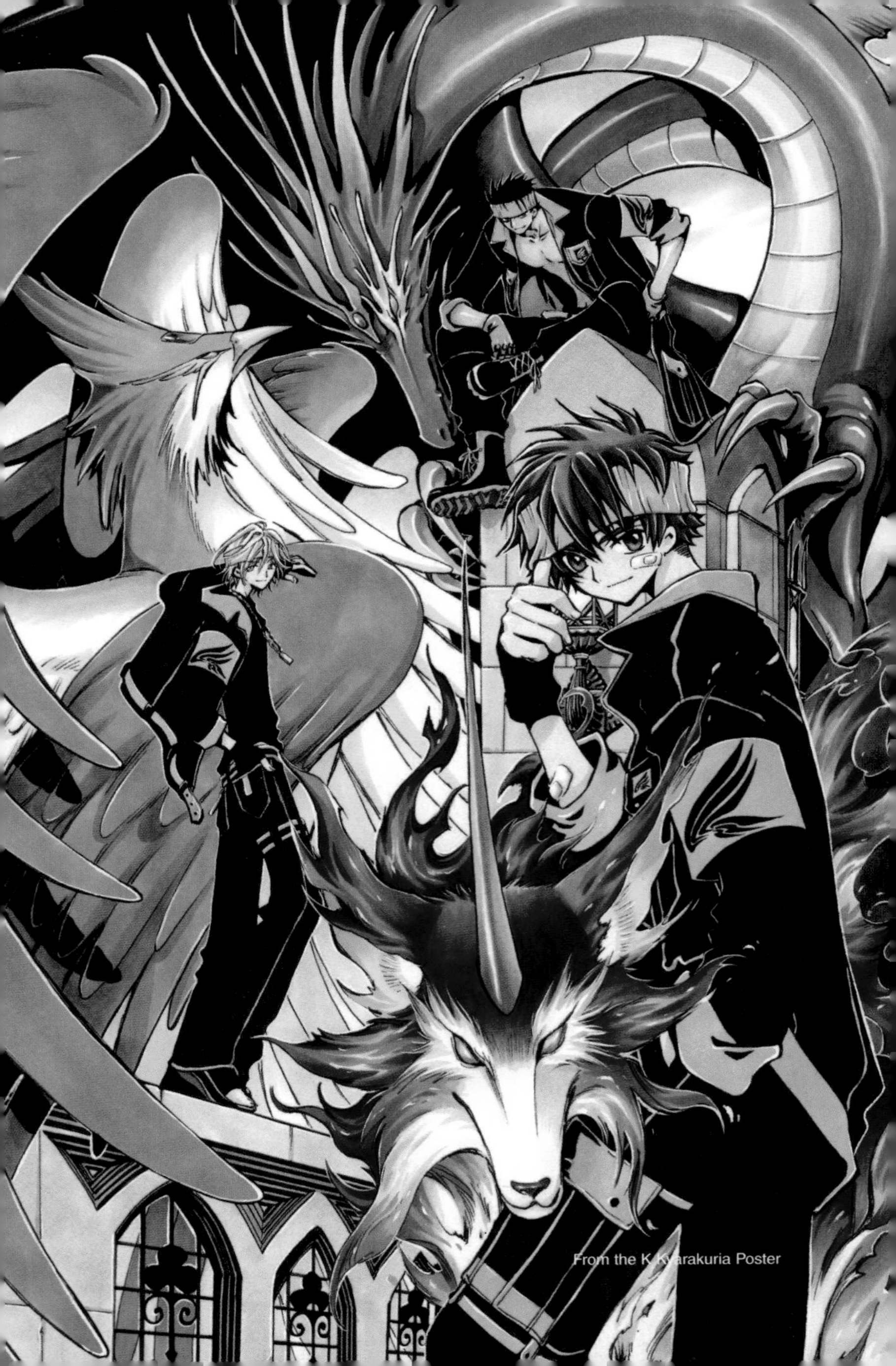

From the K Kyarakuria Poster

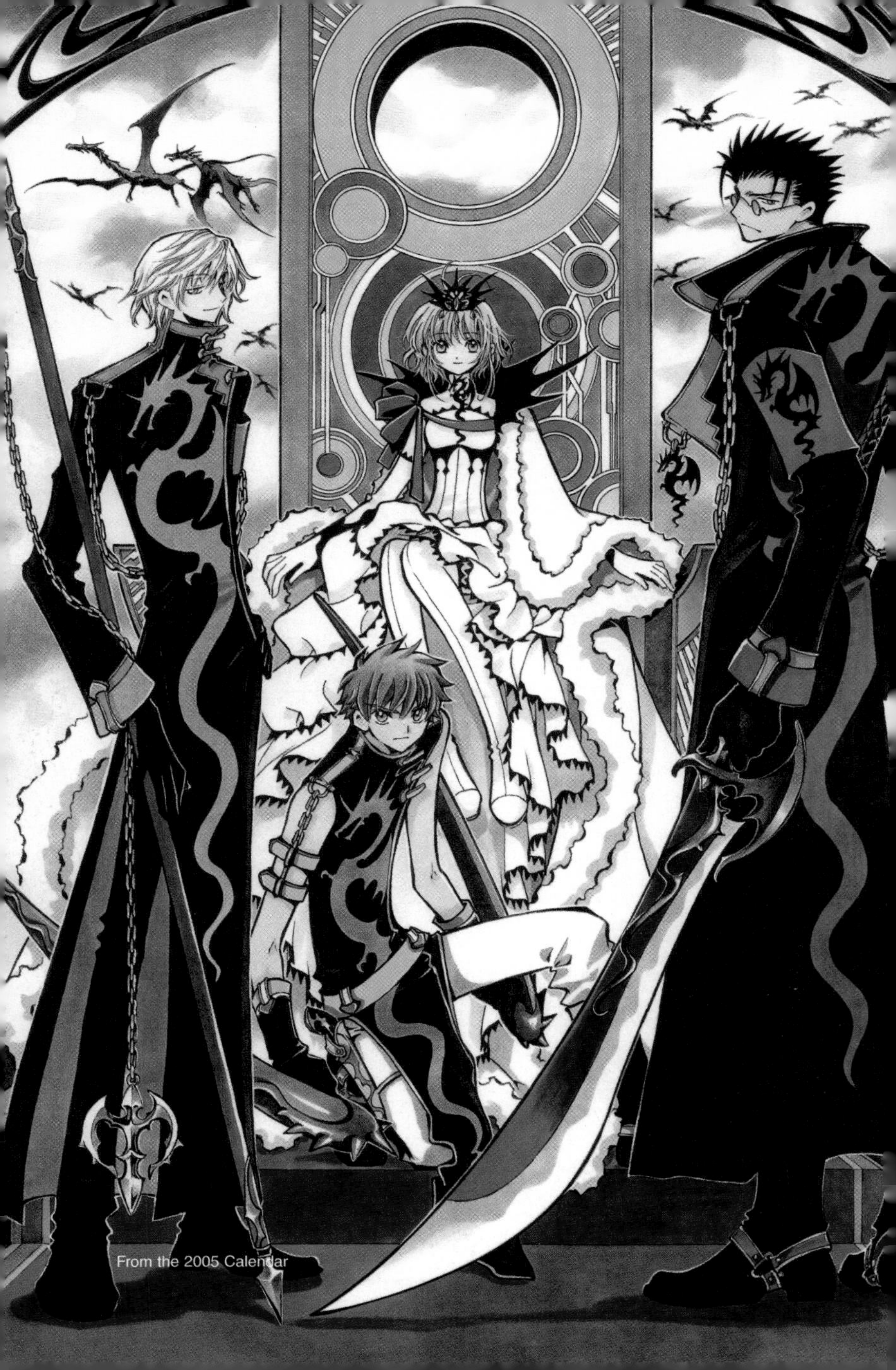

From the 2005 Calendar

From stuffed animals to stationery, in Japan you can find all kinds of licensed Tsubasa goods. Here is an introduction to just a few of the many items available. This merchandise, however, is only available for sale in Japan!

FASTENER MASCOT

Tsubasa and xxxHOLiC Fastener Mascots

These were sold in secret boxes, so open the package to discover what delightful character is inside!

STUFFED TOY

Real Size Mokona Modoki plush toy set.

Not only the same white Mokona that's in Tsubasa, but also the black Mokona that prances around in xxxHOLiC! Take good care of them, okay?

T-SHIRT

Mokona Modoki T-Shirts White and Black

In both white and black, and in sizes S and M. The pretty Mokona are jumping for joy!

UMBRELLA

CLAMP BRAND
Mokona Modoki Folding Umbrella

The Mokona folding umbrella. The handle has a white Mokona, and the black Mokona hangs as a mascot.

MUG CUP

A Mug/Cup set with Mokona Modoki mascots attached.

A set of two ceramic mugs in both black and white. The best points are the white and black Mokona on the handles.

MASCOT

Mokona Modoki Mascot Set

A white and black Mokona set with chains attached. They're as big as the palm of your hand, so attach them to your bag or something similar.

SHOPPER

Tsubasa and xxxHOLiC Shopping Bag

Standing nearly 36 cm tall, measuring around 53 cm long and 15 cm wide, this is one large Shopper. There's an xxxHOLiC illustration on the opposite side.

DESK PAD

Writing Boards

There are loads of writing boards with all kinds of illustrations. You're sure to find one that will delight you.

NOTEBOOK

Twin Ring Notebooks

The cover features a fantastical image of Sakura, and the inside pages hold cute pictures of Mokona Modoki.

LETTER PAPER

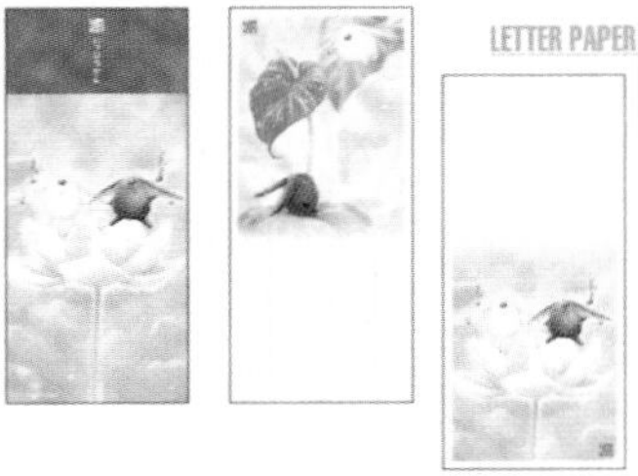

Mokona Modoki Lined Paper

Not just for letter writing, but you can send any message to your family and friends with this easy-to-use lined paper.

LETTER SET

Mokona Modoki Stationery Set

12 sheets of writing paper, 4 envelopes, plus a FAX pad and a clear case make up this set. Let Mokona deliver the feelings expressed in your letter.

PREMIUM ITEM

The following items were special, one-time giveaways and gifts to readers. Treasures that can't be had at any price!

CD-ROM

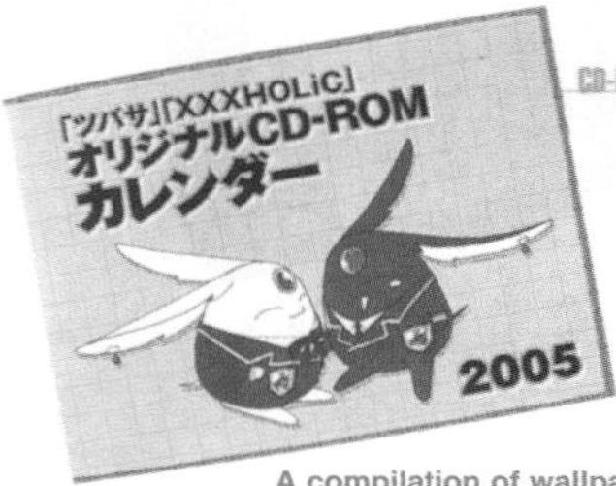
「ツバサ」「XXXHOLiC」
オリジナルCD-ROM
カレンダー
2005

A compilation of wallpaper Images on CD-ROM for your PC

Released along with the Kodansha Comics edition of Volume 8 (11/17/2004), card-style calendars were given out. And a lucky few hit the jackpot and received this CD-ROM along with the calendar.

POSTER

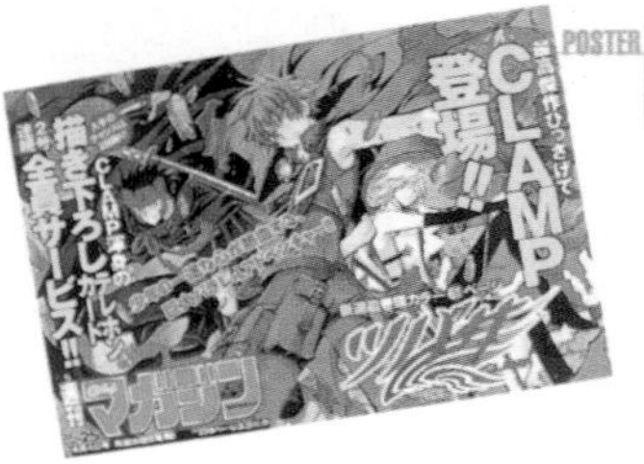
CLAMP
登場!!
マガジン

Commuter Train Advertising Poster

These appeared in trains at the same time that the Tsubasa series started its serialization (*Weekly Shonen Magazine* 2003, Volume 23). With this poster up, many, many people must have known that Tsubasa was starting.

QUO-CARDS

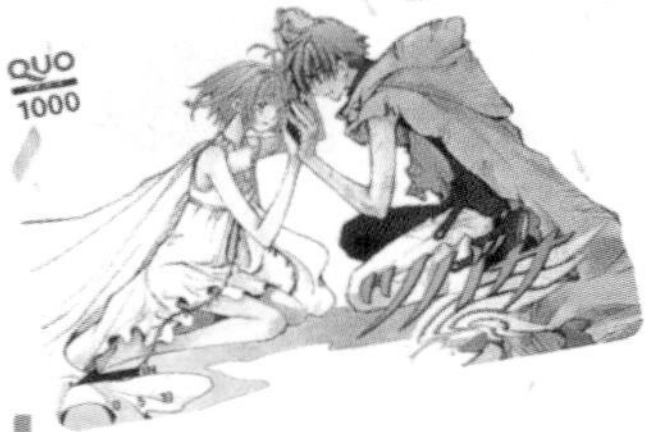
QUO
1000

QUO Cards

This is one of a set of QUO prepaid gift cards that were given out as gifts to readers of *Shonen Magazine*. But aren't they too good to use?

POSTCARD

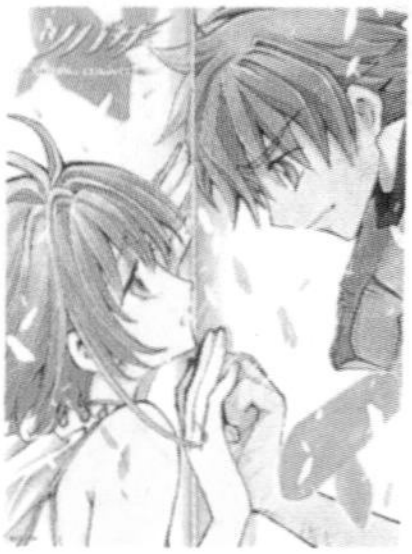

Postcards

This is one of a set of postcards that were attached to *Shonen Magazine* as presents to the readers.

STUFFED TOY

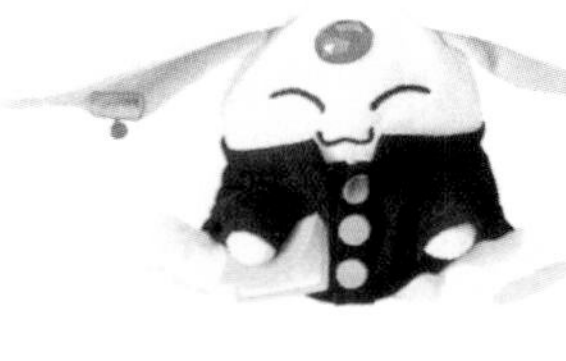

Biker Gang Mokona

Given away in *Shonen Magazine* (2004, Volume 45) as a present to readers. Doesn't Mokona look cute in the Bôsôzoku biker gang–style long coat?

POP

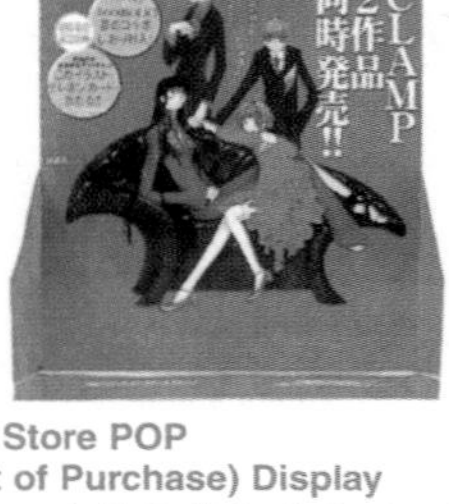
CLAMP
2作品
同時発売!!

Book Store POP (Point of Purchase) Display

This came out with the Kodansha Comics edition of Volume 2 (10/17/2003), and was used in collaboration with xxxHOLiC.

TSUBASA

CHARACTer GuiDE

CLAMP

Weekly Shonen Magazine
Editorial Department

TRANSLATED AND ADAPTED BY

William Flanagan

LETTERED BY

Dana Hayward

BALLANTINE BOOKS · NEW YORK

A Del Rey Trade Paperback Original

Tsubasa Character Guide copyright © 2005 by CLAMP
English translation copyright © 2006 by CLAMP

Published in the United States by Del Rey Books, an imprint of The
Random House Publishing Group, a division of Random House, Inc.,
New York.

DEL REY is a registered trademark and the Del Rey colophon is a
trademark of Random House, Inc.

Publication rights arranged through Kodansha Ltd.

First published in Japan in 2005 by Kodansha Ltd., Tokyo.

ISBN 0-345-49484-9

Printed in the United States of America

www.delreymanga.com

9 8 7 6 5 4 3 2

Translator and adaptor—William Flanagan
Text design—Dana Hayward

Honorifics Explained

Throughout the Del Rey Manga books, you will find Japanese honorifics left intact in the translations. For those not familiar with how the Japanese use honorifics and, more important, how they differ from American honorifics, we present this brief overview.

Politeness has always been a critical facet of Japanese culture. Ever since the feudal era, when Japan was a highly stratified society, use of honorifics—which can be defined as polite speech that indicates relationship or status—has played an essential role in the Japanese language. When addressing someone in Japanese, an honorific usually takes the form of a suffix attached to one's name (example: "Asuna-san"), or as a title at the end of one's name or in place of the name itself (example: "Negi-sensei," or simply "Sensei!").

Honorifics can be expressions of respect or endearment. In the context of manga and anime, honorifics give insight into the nature of the relationship between characters. Many translations into English leave out these important honorifics, and therefore distort the "feel" of the original Japanese. Because Japanese honorifics contain nuances that English honorifics lack, it is our policy at Del Rey not to translate them. Here, instead, is a guide to some of the honorifics you may encounter in Del Rey Manga.

-san: This is the most common honorific, and is equivalent to Mr., Miss, Ms., Mrs. It is the all-purpose honorific and can be used in any situation where politeness is required.

-sama: This is one level higher than "-san" and it is used to confer great respect.

-dono: This comes from the word "tono," which means "lord." It is an even higher level than "-sama" and confers utmost respect.

-kun: This suffix is used at the end of boys' names to express familiarity or endearment. It is also sometimes used by men amongst friends, or when addressing someone younger or of a lower station.

-chan: This is used to express endearment, mostly toward girls. It is also used for little boys, pets, and even among lovers. It gives a sense of childish cuteness.

Bozu: This is an informal way to refer to a boy, similar to the English terms "kid" or "squirt."

Sempai/senpai: This title suggests that the addressee is one's senior in a group or organization. It is most often used in a school setting, where underclassmen refer to their upperclassmen as "sempai." It can also be used in the workplace, such as when a newer employee addresses an employee who has seniority in the company.

Kohai: This is the opposite of "-sempai," and is used toward underclassmen in school or newcomers in the workplace. It connotes that the addressee is of a lower station.

Sensei: Literally meaning "one who has come before," this title is used for teachers, doctors, or masters of any profession or art.

-[blank]: This is usually forgotten in these lists, but it is perhaps the most significant difference between Japanese and English. The lack of honorific means that the speaker has permission to address the person in a very intimate way. Usually, only family, spouses, or very close friends have this kind of permission. Known as *yobisute*, it can be gratifying when someone who has earned the intimacy starts to call one by one's name without an honorific. But when that intimacy hasn't been earned, it can be very insulting.

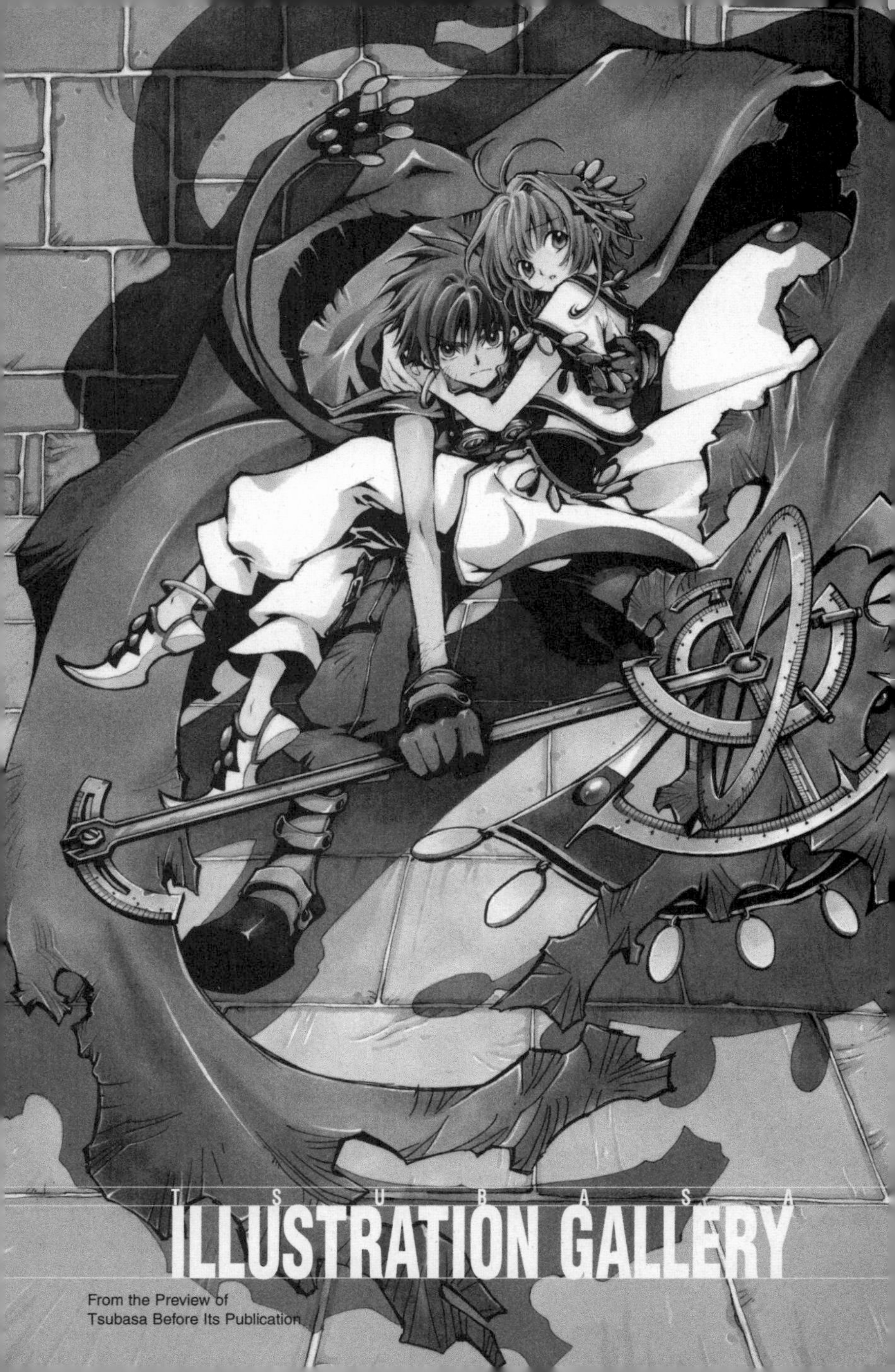

T S U B A S A ILLUSTRATION GALLERY

From the Preview of
Tsubasa Before Its Publication

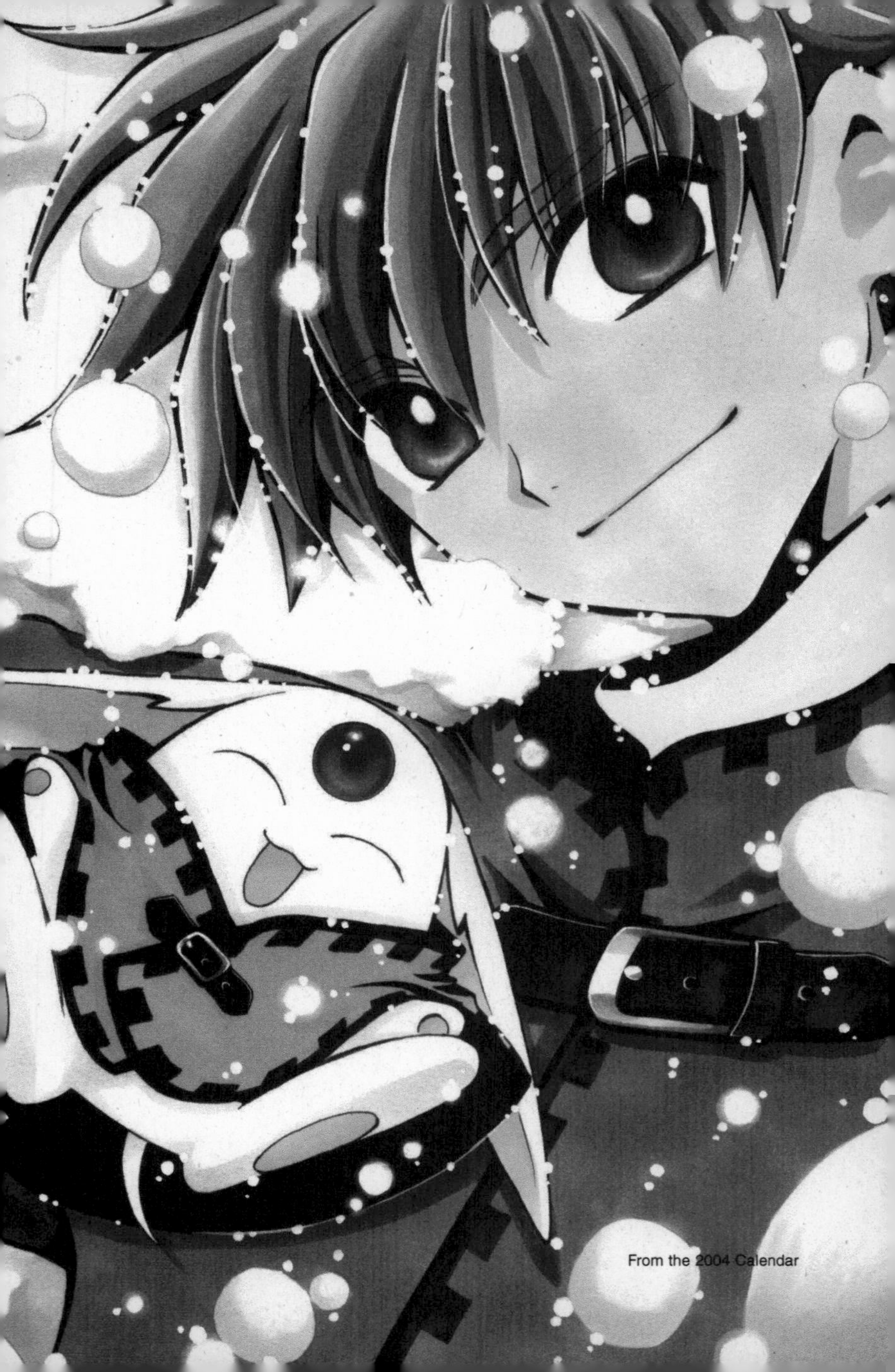

From the 2004 Calendar

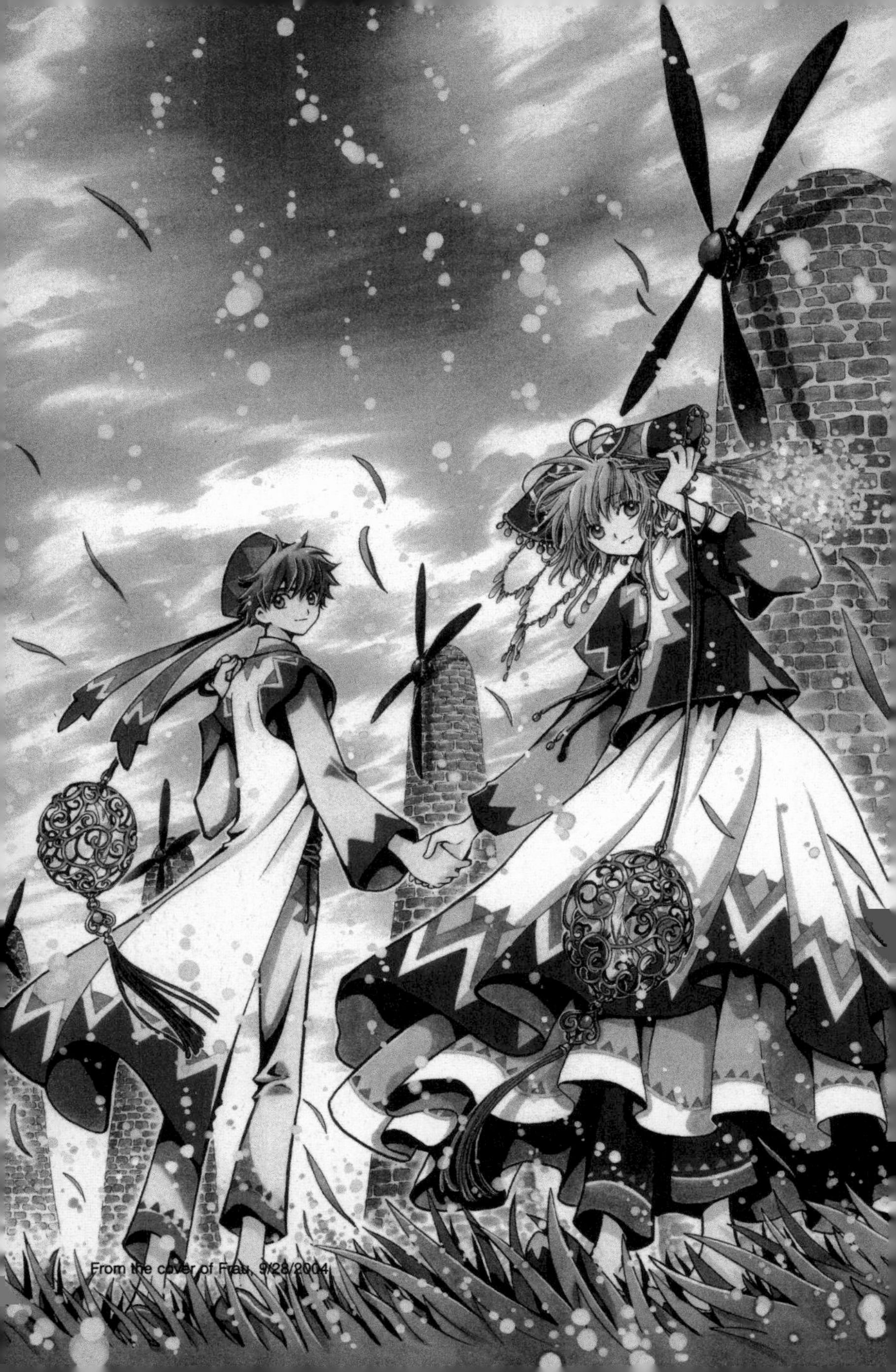

From the cover of Frau, 9/28/2004

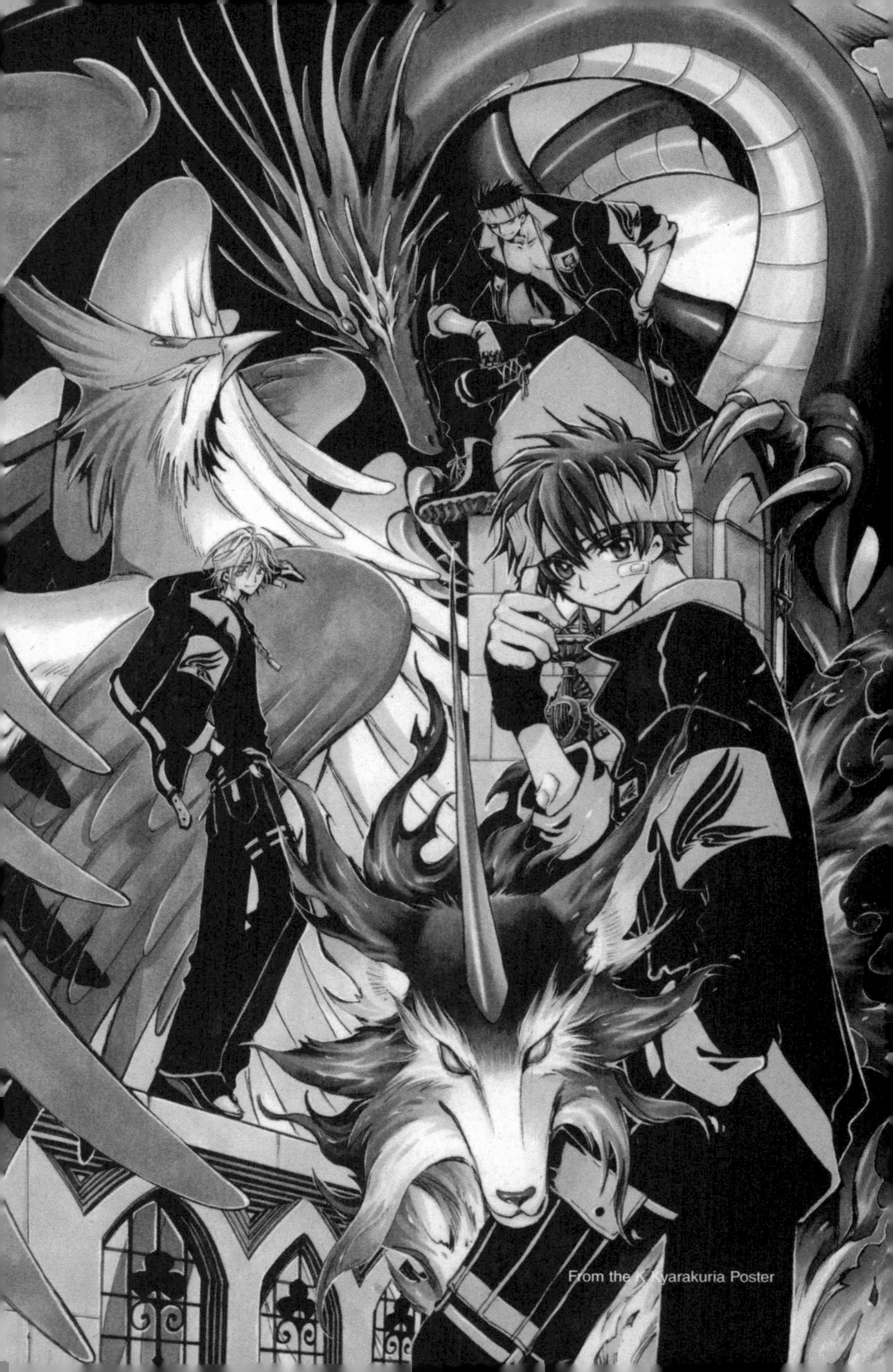

From the K. Kyarakuria Poster

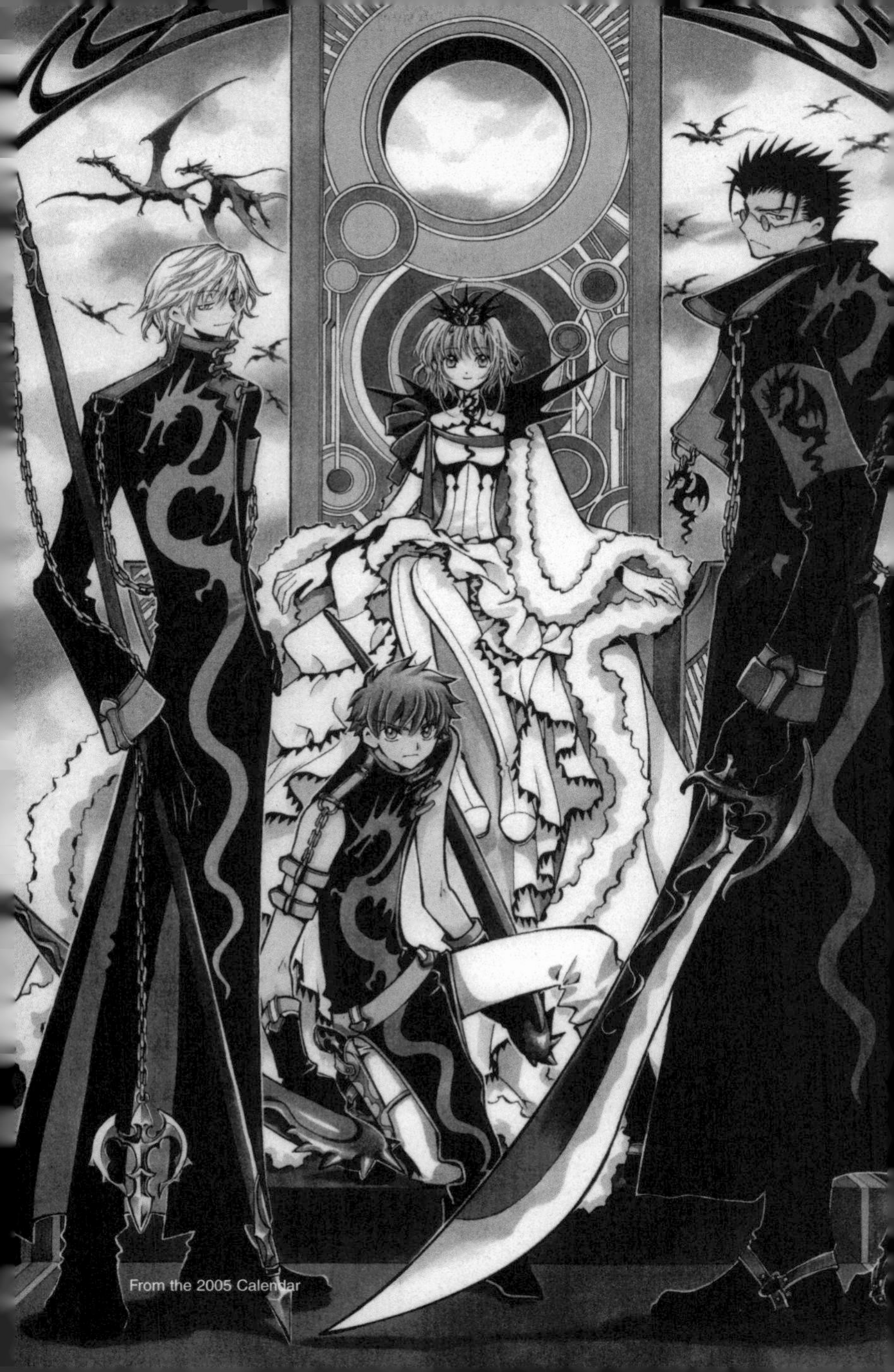

From the 2005 Calendar

GOODS SELECTION

Goods Selection

From stuffed animals to stationery, in Japan you can find all kinds of licensed Tsubasa goods. Here is an introduction to just a few of the many items available. This merchandise, however, is only available for sale in Japan!

FASTENER MASCOT

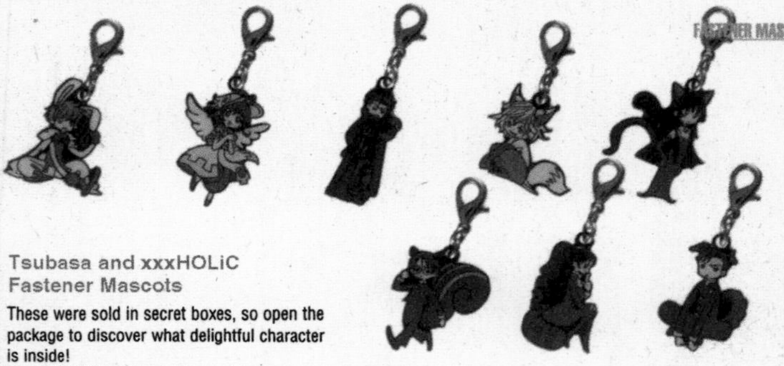

Tsubasa and xxxHOLiC Fastener Mascots

These were sold in secret boxes, so open the package to discover what delightful character is inside!

STUFFED TOY

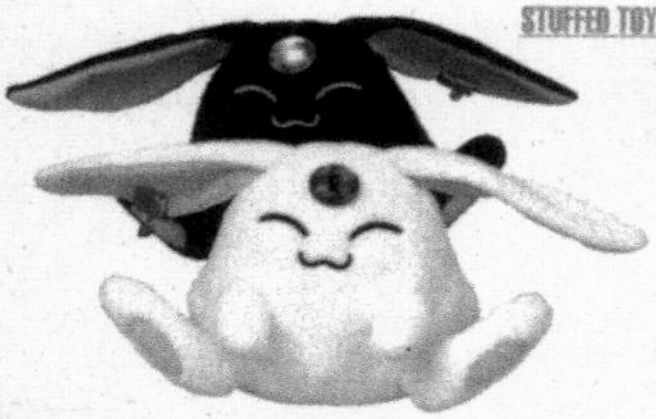

Real Size Mokona Modoki plush toy set.

Not only the same white Mokona that's in Tsubasa, but also the black Mokona that prances around in xxxHOLiC! Take good care of them, okay?

T-SHIRT

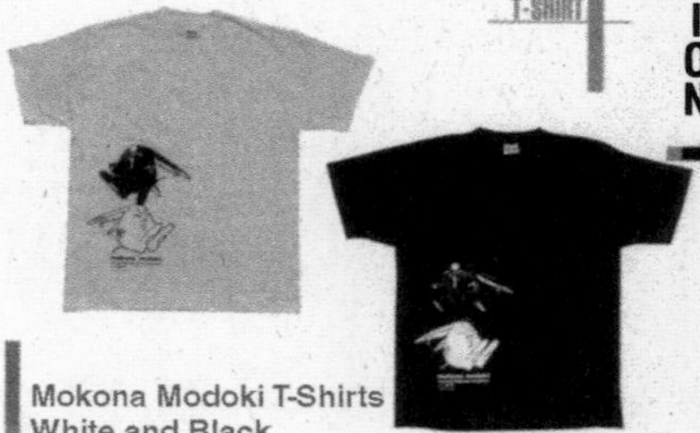

Mokona Modoki T-Shirts White and Black

In both white and black, and in sizes S and M. The pretty Mokona are jumping for joy!

UMBRELLA

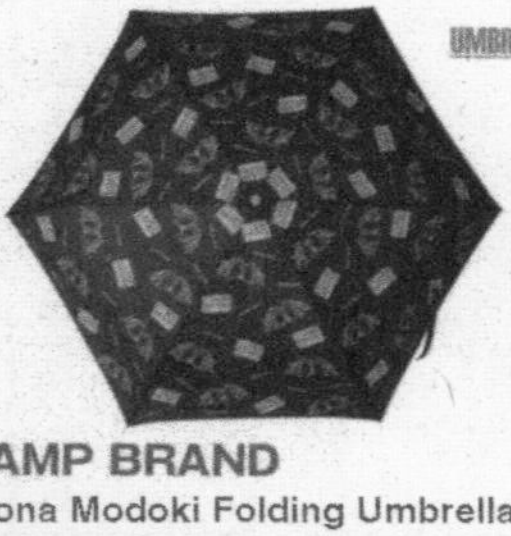

CLAMP BRAND

Mokona Modoki Folding Umbrella

The Mokona folding umbrella. The handle has a white Mokona, and the black Mokona hangs as a mascot.

MUG CUP

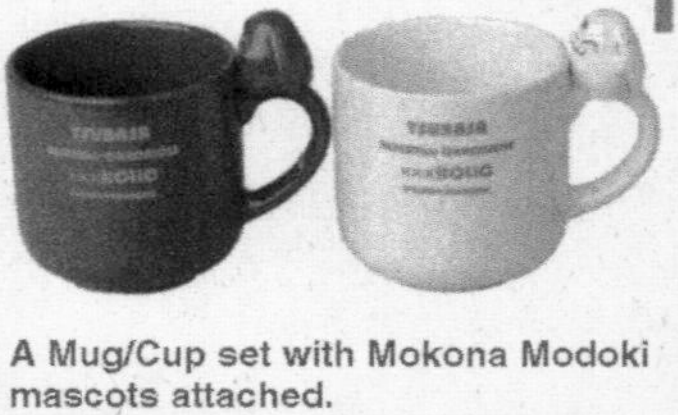

A Mug/Cup set with Mokona Modoki mascots attached.

A set of two ceramic mugs in both black and white. The best points are the white and black Mokona on the handles.

MASCOT

Mokona Modoki Mascot Set

A white and black Mokona set with chains attached. They're as big as the palm of your hand, so attach them to your bag or something similar.

SHOPPER

Tsubasa and xxxHOLiC Shopping Bag

Standing nearly 36 cm tall, measuring around 53 cm long and 15 cm wide, this is one large Shopper. There's an xxxHOLiC illustration on the opposite side.

DESK PAD

Writing Boards

There are loads of writing boards with all kinds of illustrations. You're sure to find one that will delight you.

NOTEBOOK

表
裏

Twin Ring Notebooks

The cover features a fantastical image of Sakura, and the inside pages hold cute pictures of Mokona Modoki.

LETTER PAPER

Mokona Modoki Lined Paper

Not just for letter writing, but you can send any message to your family and friends with this easy-to-use lined paper.

LETTER SET

Mokona Modoki Stationery Set

12 sheets of writing paper, 4 envelopes, plus a FAX pad and a clear case make up this set. Let Mokona deliver the feelings expressed in your letter.

PREMIUM ITEM

Prize Items

The following items were special, one-time giveaways and gifts to readers. Treasures that can't be had at any price!

CD-ROM

「ツバサ」「XXXHOLiC」
オリジナルCD-ROM
カレンダー
2005

A compilation of wallpaper Images on CD-ROM for your PC

Released along with the Kodansha Comics edition of Volume 8 (11/17/2004), card-style calendars were given out. And a lucky few hit the jackpot and received this CD-ROM along with the calendar.

POSTER

CLAMP
登場!!

Commuter Train Advertising Poster

These appeared in trains at the same time that the Tsubasa series started its serialization (*Weekly Shonen Magazine* 2003, Volume 23). With this poster up, many, many people must have known that Tsubasa was starting.

QUO-CARDS

QUO
1000

QUO Cards

This is one of a set of QUO prepaid gift cards that were given out as gifts to readers of *Shonen Magazine*. But aren't they too good to use?

POSTCARD

Postcards

This is one of a set of postcards that were attached to *Shonen Magazine* as presents to the readers.

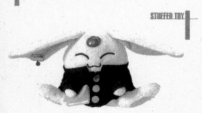

STUFFED TOY

Biker Gang Mokona

Given away in *Shonen Magazine* (2004, Volume 45) as a present to readers. Doesn't Mokona look cute in the Bôsôzoku biker gang–style long coat?

POP

CLAMP
2作品
同時発売!!

Book Store POP (Point of Purchase) Display

This came out with the Kodansha Comics edition of Volume 2 (10/17/2003), and was used in collaboration with xxxHOLiC.

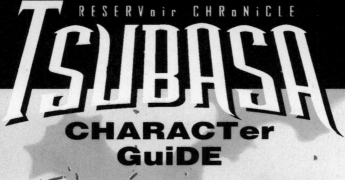

RESERVoir CHRoNiCLE
TSUBASA

CHARACTer GuiDE

TSUBASA

ツバサ

CHARACTer GuiDE

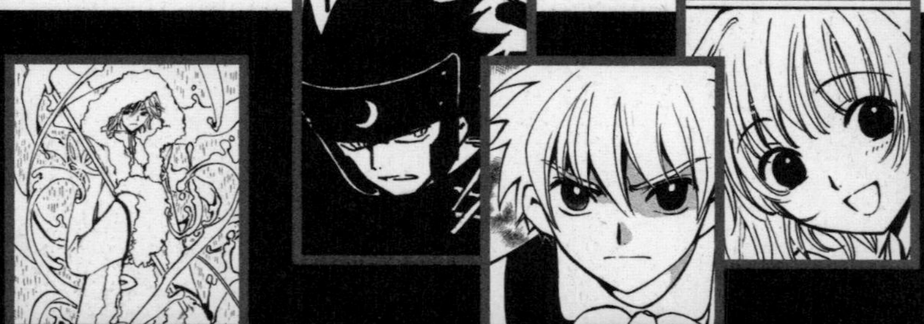

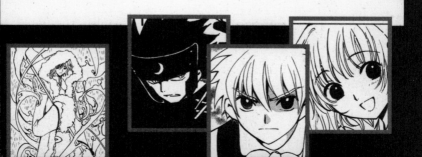

CONTENTS

Country of Japan's greatest Ninja, Kurogane's
CHARACTER BATTLE-STRENGTH REPORT 118

AUTHOR INTRODUCTION 123

CLAMP Guide / Special Interview / Comic Drawn Especially for this Guide
"Tsubasa: World of the Untold Story #2" / Special Contribution: Oh!great /
Special Contribution: Kazuki Yamamoto

CONTENTS

STORY DIGEST

In order to find the feathers of Sakura's memory . . .

In order to return to a home world . . .

In order to wander the worlds and never return . . .

The travelers each have their own reasons to wander from world to world.

Let's follow in their footsteps.

I WISH YOU ALL THE BEST FORTUNE ON YOUR JOURNEY.

Find the Girl's Lost Memories!

One fateful day a boy from foreign lands, Syaoran, met the princess of a desert kingdom, Sakura. As their relationship deepened, the tragedy drew closer. A mysterious foe appeared from ruins buried in the desert sands, and they attacked the kingdom. In the midst of the confusion, Sakura lost consciousness and had her memories ripped from her. Syaoran's journey began in earnest!

But to Sakura, Syaoran is such an important person that she doesn't care about social stations.

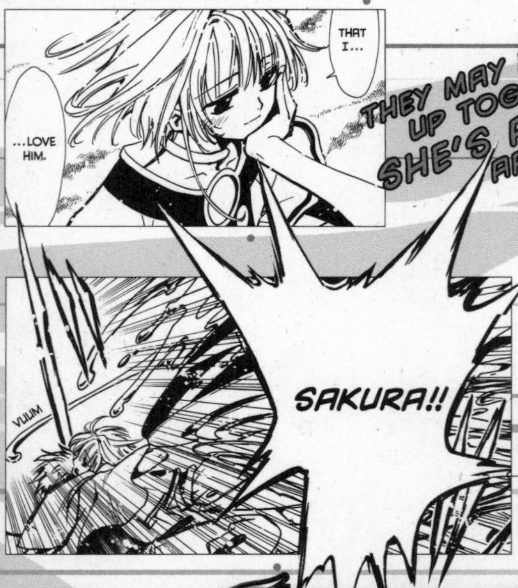

THAT I...
...LOVE HIM.
THEY MAY HAVE GROWN UP TOGETHER, BUT SHE'S A PRINCESS AFTER ALL.
SAKURA!!
VUUM

◄ Almost as if Fate wanted to test their bonds, Syaoran and Sakura are torn from each other.

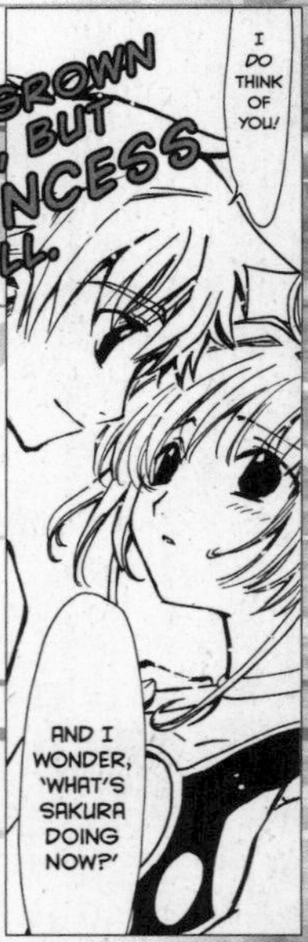

I DO THINK OF YOU!
AND I WONDER, 'WHAT'S SAKURA DOING NOW?'

Even though the two grew up together, Syaoran never forgets the difference in their stations.

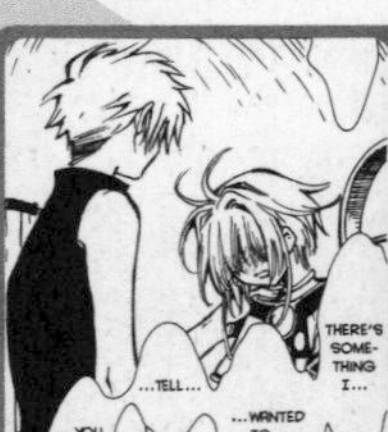

THERE'S SOME-THING I...
...WANTED TO...
...TELL...
...YOU.

According to Yukito, Syaoran holds a special place in Sakura's heart.

KEY WORD **ONE FATE**

One can only say that fate itself brought the two young people together. Sakura and Syaoran were drawn together from the start. It was Yukito, a man who can read the future, who said that Syaoran is the one Princess Sakura is destined for. He also forecast that the two of them have adversity awaiting them. Adversity like no one has ever seen. And now, just as Yukito predicted, their bond has been mercilessly torn apart. If Syaoran is to truly be Sakura's one fate, then the question remains as to whether he can collect all of Sakura's memories and bring back the bonds they once shared. But is that possible . . . ?

SCENE 1 The Boy Starts His Journe

KINGDOM OF CLOW

◀ Fai of the country of Seresu travels to see the Time-Space Witch in order to be far away from a certain being.

▼ A ninja of the Country of Japan, Kurogane is also sent to the Witch by his Princess Tomoyo.

CHI?
I HAVE TO BE ON MY WAY.

LOOK, I WANT TO BE BETTER THAN I AM!
I WANT TO BE THE BEST!!
THAT'S WHY I FIGHT!
AND IF MY ENEMY LIVES OR DIES IN THE PROCESS, IT'S NOT MY WORRY!

I WILL NEVER ALLOW SAKURA TO DIE!

WOULD YOU PLEASE...
I NEED YOU TO SAVE SAKURA!!

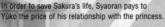

In order to save Sakura's life, Syaoran pays to Yûko the price of his relationship with the princess.

THERE IS A PRICE.
ARE YOU STILL WILLING?

▲ The Time-Space Witch is also called Yûko. Syaoran, Kurogane and Fai agree to terms with her that allow them to embark on a long journey through dimensions.

SAKURA!!

These fragments of memory aren't simply impressions of the past, but at the same time they are a part of Sakura's very life force.

KEY WORD: FRAGMENTS OF MEMORY

These are the feathers of Sakura's memory that have been scattered throughout many different worlds. But these aren't simply pieces of her memory, they are also feathers of great magic that give those who hold them enormous power. There are those who use the powers for evil purposes and those who do evil in order to get their hands on a feather. During the travels through the worlds, Syaoran and his friends encounter all kinds of enemies. Syaoran's group of travelers have managed to weave their way through the plots of evil people in search of the feathers, but the near future seems to hold even more dangers for the group.

A Kudan-vs.-Kudan Free for All!

The first world the group of travelers go to is the Hanshin Republic. In this country everyone has a strange power that comes in the form of creatures called Kudan. Syaoran and his group, in search of clues to the whereabouts of the feather, find out about gangs of young men who battle using their Kudan for territory in the city. As Syaoran faces battle with one of these young men, Shôgo Asagi, Mokona exclaims that the feather is very close by!

YOU SEEM TO HAVE A SPECIAL KUDAN, DON'T YOU?

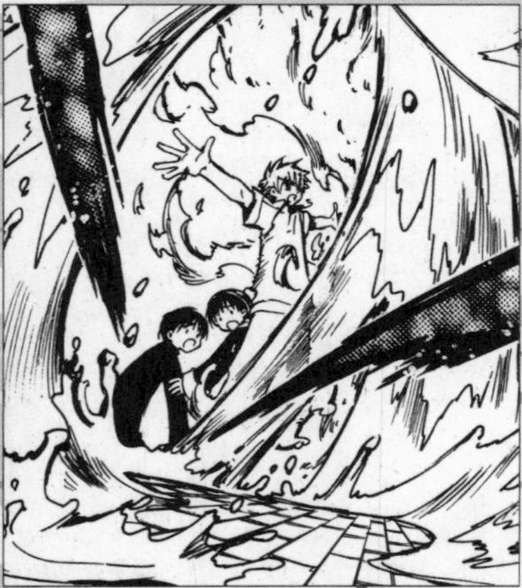

Without thinking, Syaoran involves himself in the young men's battle by bringing out a Fire Kudan and standing up to the young leader Shôgo.

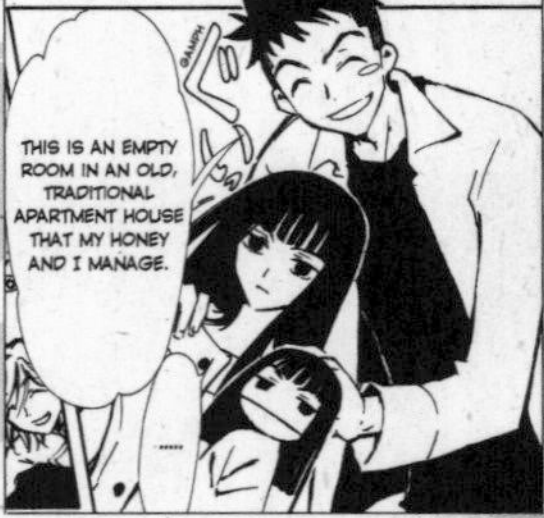
THIS IS AN EMPTY ROOM IN AN OLD, TRADITIONAL APARTMENT HOUSE THAT MY HONEY AND I MANAGE.
.....

The first people to meet the dumbfounded group of travelers are two people who know Yûko.

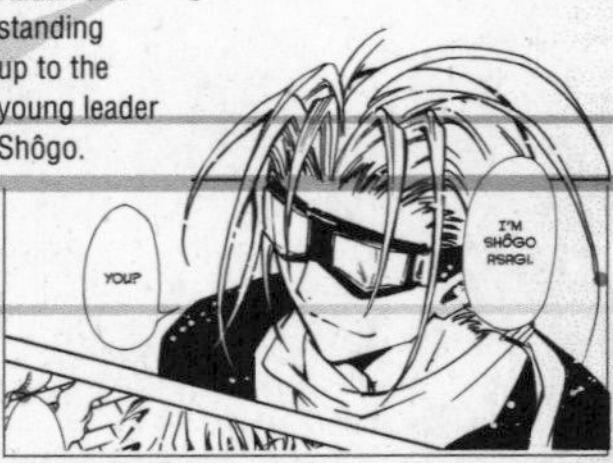
I'M SHÔGO ASAGI.
YOU?

➤ Shôgo Asada, the leader of one of the gangs, has his own special-level Kudan, and he recognizes that Syaoran's is also special level.

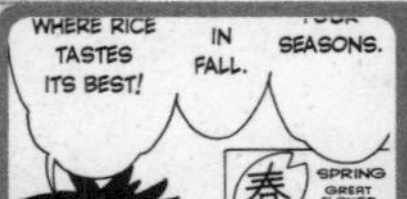
SEASONS.
IN FALL.
WHERE RICE TASTES ITS BEST!
春 SPRING GREAT FLOWER VIEWING!
夏 SUMMER SEASON FOR BEER!
秋 FALL RICE TASTES ITS BEST!
WINTER

In each different world, the culture and technologies are completely different.

KEY WORD

OTHER WORLD

Where Syaoran and his companions travel, they pass between the infinite other worlds that exist parallel to ours. On these different worlds, of course, the climate, culture, and languages are different, but even the flow of time can vary. Also two people, each on different worlds, may look the same, but they could have developed entirely different personalities. To travel between worlds is painful and dangerous in many ways, but it also leads to new discoveries and encounters with many good people. Even in the very first world, the Hanshin Republic, Syaoran and his group learn this fact very well.

SCENE 2

Where Is Sakura's Feather?!

HANSHIN REPUBLIC

SAKURA'S FEATHER IS VERY CLOSE!

YOU'RE DOING THIS FOR A TOTAL STRANGER?

When she finally awakens, all of Sakura's memories of Syaoran have vanished.

KWOOO
WHO...
...ARE YOU?

▲ Finally, Syaoran gets his hand on one of the feathers of Sakura's memory.

YOU'RE ASKING ME TO WIELD YOU?
SHINGG

▲ Responding to the challenge of the leader of a different gang, Kurogane's Kudan becomes a weapon as Kurogane responds with a finishing blow.

▲ Syaoran suddenly understands the reality that seems to be crashing around him.

THAT WAS A SURPRISE.

➤ Fai's Kudan is an enormous bird, and through its power, Fai can move through the sky.

EVEN IF YOU RETRIEVE ALL OF HER MEMORIES ...
... THE ONE MEMORY THAT YOU WILL NEVER RETRIEVE WILL

A relationship. The price that Yûko requires of Syaoran is the most cruel of all.

KEY WORD **RELATIONSHIP**

Syaoran's price for traveling worlds was his relationship with Sakura. No matter what memories Sakura may gain back, she will never recover any memories that relate to Syaoran. In other words, Sakura and Syaoran will never return to the feelings that they used to have for each other. That is what it means to sacrifice a relationship. But despite that, Syaoran is willing to continue his journey, all for Sakura's sake. When all of the feathers are gathered, the question remains: What will become of Syaoran's emotions?

f the Ryanban father and son!

In the country of Koryo, the people of the town of Ryonfi are suffering under a tyrannical Ryanban. According to Chu'nyan, a girl the travelers met there, one year ago the Ryanban suddenly became very powerful and chased off the original Ryanban. Figuring that Sakura's feather has something to do with the matter, and in order to help save the town, Syaoran and his group head toward the castle.

EVEN IF SHE GETS ALL OF HER FEATHERS BACK, SHE'LL NEVER BE ABLE TO REMEMBER SYAORAN-KUN.

...NO MATTER HOW PAINFUL IT WILL BE FOR HIM IN THE END.

Kurogane and Fai discuss Syaoran's difficult fate.

IF YOU DON'T WANT TO BE KICKED, DON'T GO ATTACKING PEOPLE AT RANDOM!
YOU STUPID LITTLE BOY!!

Chu'nyan's mother was a Shinban (magician), and Chu'nyan inherited her power. She stands against the Ryanban who had her mother killed.

Seeing the tyrannical nature of the Ryanban's son, Syaoran explodes in an enraged kick.

MY OMONI (MOTHER) FOUGHT THEM... AND THE RYANBAN MURDERED HER!

THIS IS THE POWER OF THE RYANBAN!

▲Although the townspeople would like to fight, they can't stand up to the Ryanban's enormous powers.

I'LL HAND OVER SOME-THING THAT WILL HELP BREAK THE MAGIC ARTS SURROUNDING THE CASTLE.
BUT I'LL EXPECT PAYMENT IN RETURN.

◄ Syaoran and his group bargain with Yûko to get something to break through the Ryanban's magics.

SCENE 3

Defeat the feather enhanced magic power

COUNTRY OF KORYO

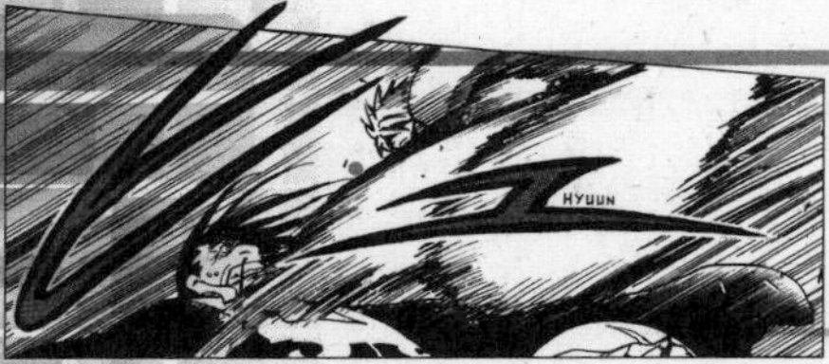
HYUUN

Syaoran goes on ahead to face the Ryanban. His goal is to recover the memory feather and to free Chu'nyan and the townspeople.

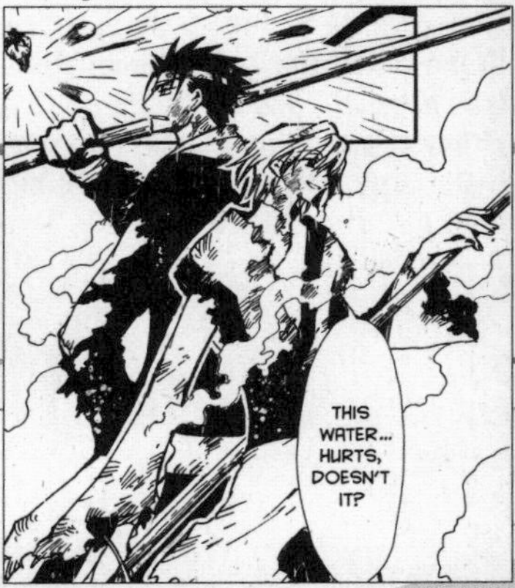
THIS WATER... HURTS, DOESN'T IT?

➤ After our group of heroes enter the castle, a battle is waiting for them against the Kiishim under the control of the Ryanban.

I'LL MAKE SURE YOU NEVER USE THE TOWNSPEOPLE AGAIN!

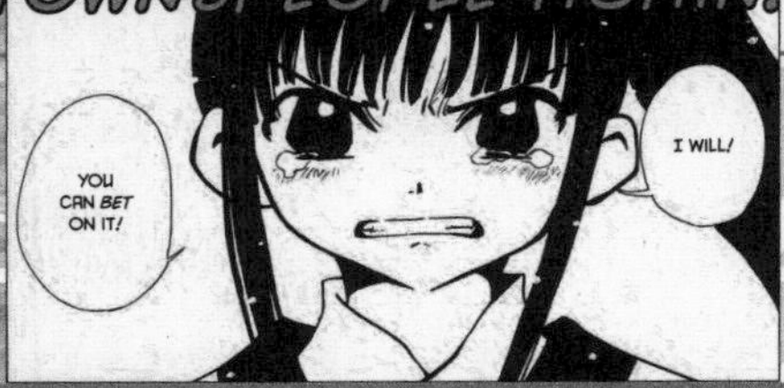
I WILL!
YOU CAN *BET* ON IT!

Someday Chu'nyan will follow her mother and become a Shinban! The young girl matures in her battle with the Ryanban.

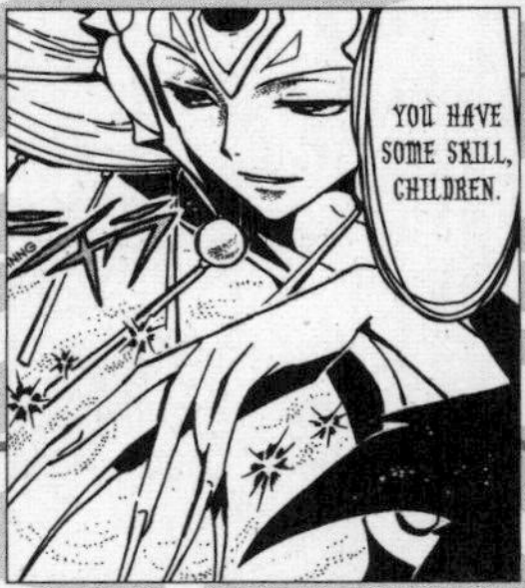
YOU HAVE SOME SKILL, CHILDREN.

➤ The most powerful Kiishim in the Country of Koryo is the obstacle that Kurogane and Fai must face.

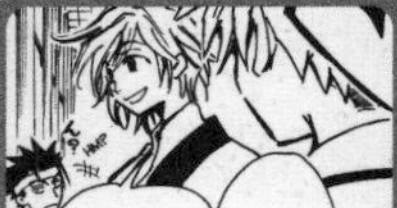
FOR THIS KIND OF MAGIC...
...THE PLACE WHERE THE MAGIC IS STRONGEST IS THE SOURCE OF THE POWER.

Fai can use magic power, but he's forbidden himself from using it.

KEY WORD **MAGIC**

Just as demonstrated in the Country of Koryo with the magics of Chu'nyan and the Ryanban, there are many worlds where the inhabitants can wield magic-like powers. Fai's country of Seresu was one, and in Kurogane's world, the woman he served, Princess Tomoyo, held strong magic powers. In the country of Jade, it seems that there were no practitioners of magic operating openly; however, whether they really exist or not is in question. There are many different types of power and many different sources, but if one thinks of the similarities in the quality of power, it's possible that a great power of something like magic runs through all of the worlds.

What's the Truth Behind this Ominous Legend . . . ?!

After passing through a world with a town at the bottom of a lake, Syaoran and his group next arrive at the Country of Jade. There, in a town called Spirit, a mystery was brewing. Just as in a legend of a golden-haired princess who took the children away three hundred years before, children have disappeared now as well. Is this really the curse of the golden-haired princess, Princess Emerald?

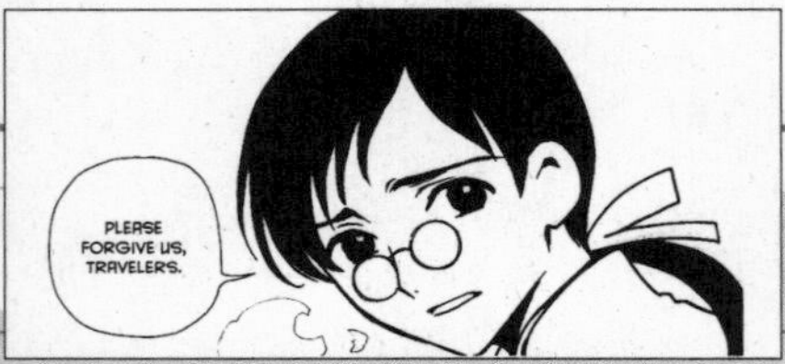
PLEASE FORGIVE US, TRAVELERS.

Dr. Kyle is a man who shows great worry over the vanishing children. He seems to see the goodness in Syaoran and his friends, and he aids them in their research.

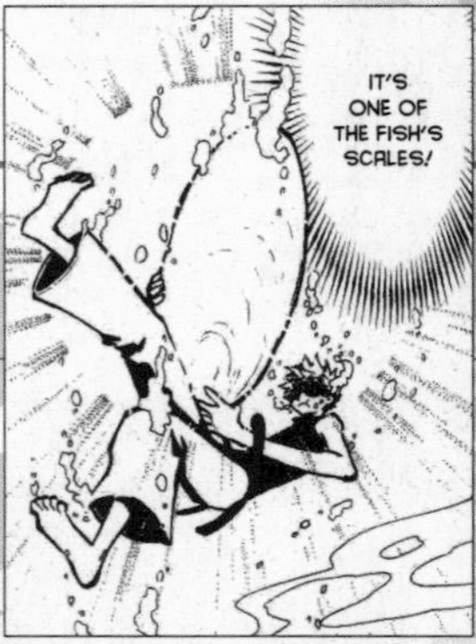
IT'S ONE OF THE FISH'S SCALES!

There's a tiny town at the bottom of a lake, brightened by a light-emitting fish. But this world does not hold any of Sakura's feathers.

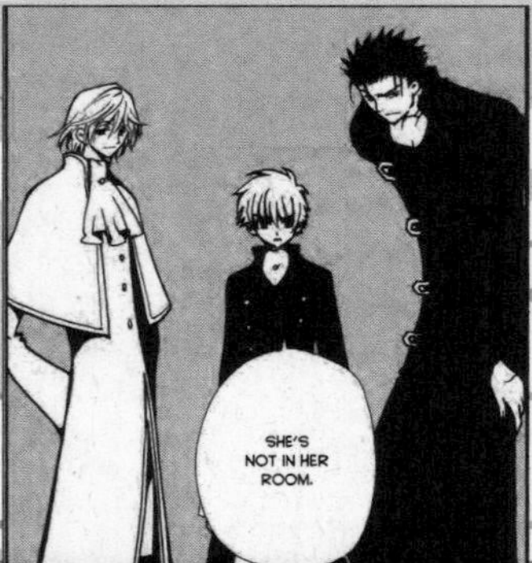
SHE'S NOT IN HER ROOM.

Sakura has disappeared!! Could she have been captured by the golden-haired princess?! Or could it be. . . ?

THE GOLDEN HAIRED PRINCESS...?!

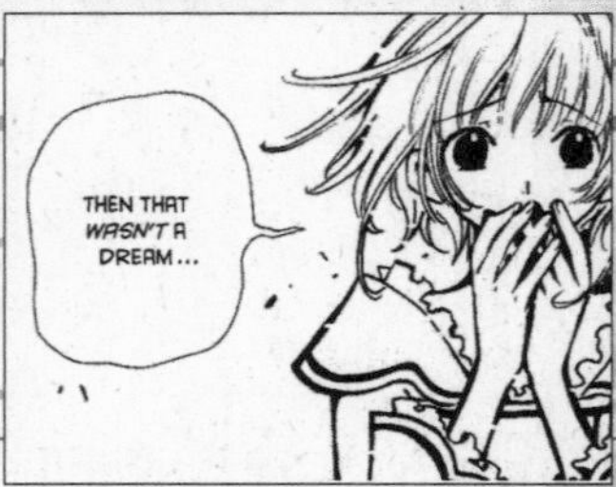
THEN THAT *WASN'T* A DREAM...

In the town of Spirit, Sakura witnesses a blonde princess leading children away.

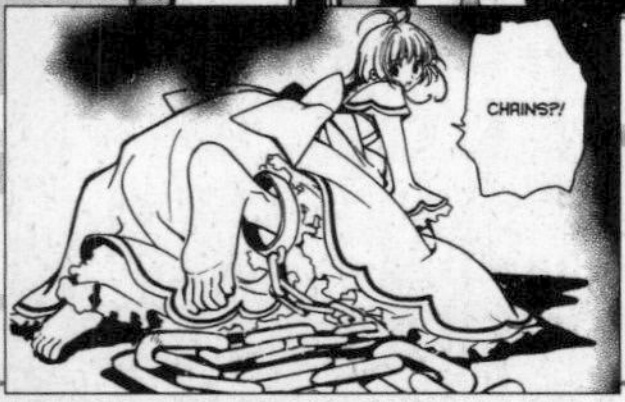
CHAINS?!

Sakura lost consciousness while trying to follow the golden-haired princess. She wakes up within the castle in the north . . .

SAKURA IS GONE!!

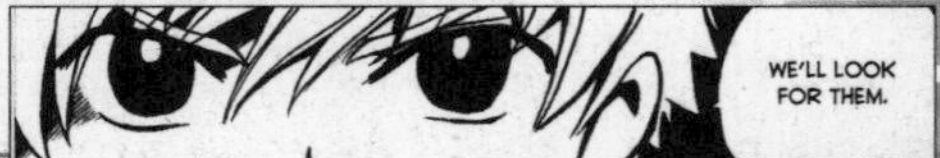
WE'LL LOOK FOR THEM.

There is no fear when it comes to finding Sakura. Syaoran's eyes show the light of his determination.

SCENE 4

The Vanishing Children and the Golden-Haired Princess.

COUNTRY OF JADE

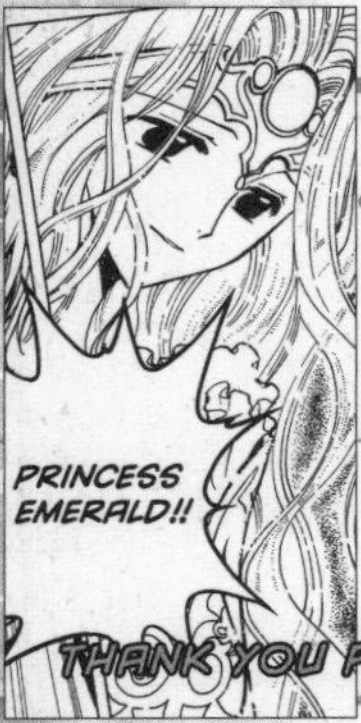
PRINCESS EMERALD!!
THANK YOU FOR SAVING THE CHILDREN!

Princess Emerald long ago used the power of Sakura's feather to save the children, now she tries to return the feather.

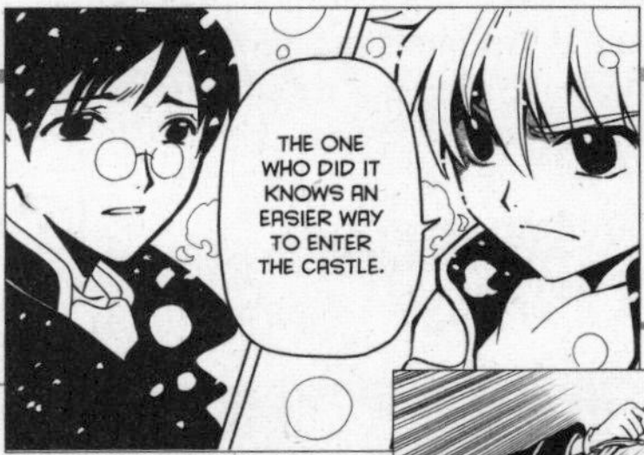
THE ONE WHO DID IT KNOWS AN EASIER WAY TO ENTER THE CASTLE.

The one who most cared for the children, Dr. Kyle, was in fact the one who kidnapped them!!

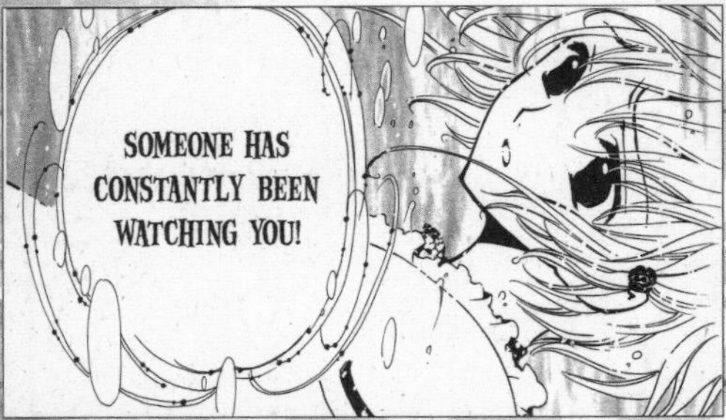
SOMEONE HAS CONSTANTLY BEEN WATCHING YOU!

When returning the feather to Sakura, Princess Emerald warns that someone has been watching her and her friends from afar.

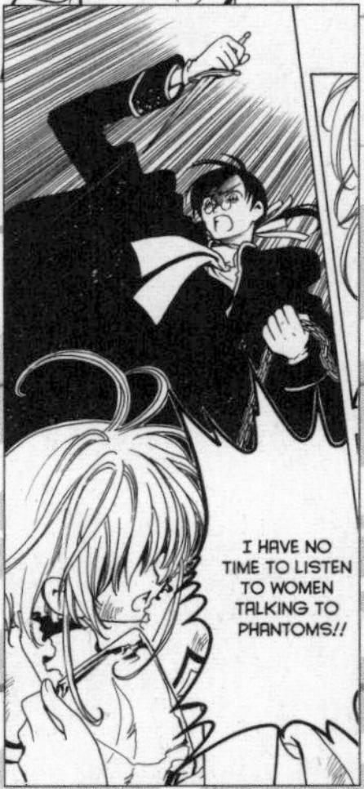
I HAVE NO TIME TO LISTEN TO WOMEN TALKING TO PHANTOMS!!

Trying to get the power of the feather, Kyle attacks Sakura. Syaoran arrives an instant before it's too late, but...

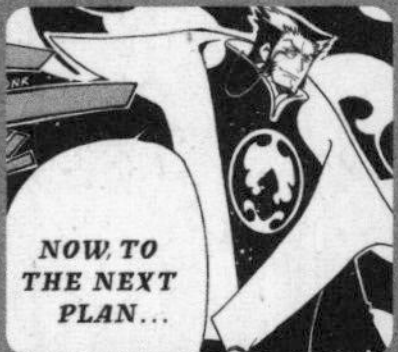
NOW, TO THE NEXT PLAN...

This is the man who is interfering in the journey of Syaoran and his friends. What is his purpose for wanting the power to traverse dimensions?

KEY WORD

THE ONE WHO WATCHES THE JOURNEY

As Syaoran and his group are preparing to leave the Country of Jade, they realize that "someone" is watching their journey. And it's true that at the time that the feathers of Sakura's memory were scattered, and when Syaoran and the group went to other worlds or whenever the power to move between worlds was exercised, the shadow of some mysterious man flickered. When a spy says, "The doctor (Kyle) failed," the mysterious man responds, "I am irritated at how little I am able to affect events." But those very words make clear that he does have the ability to somehow affect the events of other worlds. So who is this man . . . ?

yaoran Must Renew His Determination!

While Syaoran and his friends were still looking around in amazement, they were rushed off to be registered at the city hall in the country of Ôto and given a place to stay. Since they were required to do some sort of work, Sakura and Fai ran a coffee shop while Syaoran and Kurogane became "Oni Hunters," people who hunt down monsters called Oni and exterminate them. But even as newcomers, they can see, the world is undergoing a change.

YOU ARE BLIND IN YOUR RIGHT EYE.

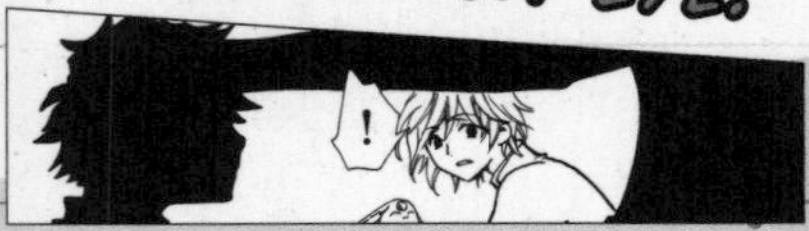
!

Gradually, Kurogane became aware of the fact that Syaoran has lost the use of his right eye.

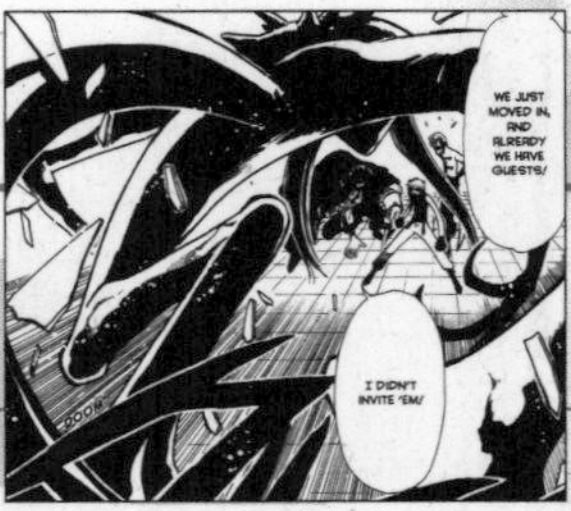
WE JUST MOVED IN, AND ALREADY WE HAVE GUESTS!
I DIDN'T INVITE 'EM!

The country of Ôto was opened wide to the travelers, but it is also a town made for the warriors who fight the Oni.

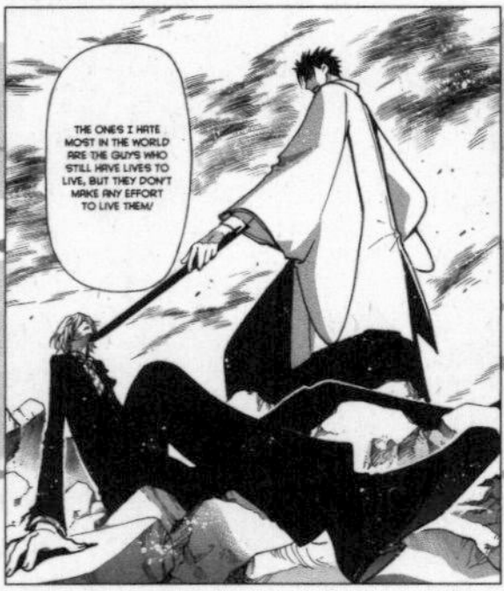
THE ONES I HATE MOST IN THE WORLD ARE THE GUYS WHO STILL HAVE LIVES TO LIVE, BUT THEY DON'T MAKE ANY EFFORT TO LIVE THEM!

Kurogane becomes enraged at the lack of regard to which Fai is willing to throw his life away. What happened in Fai's past?

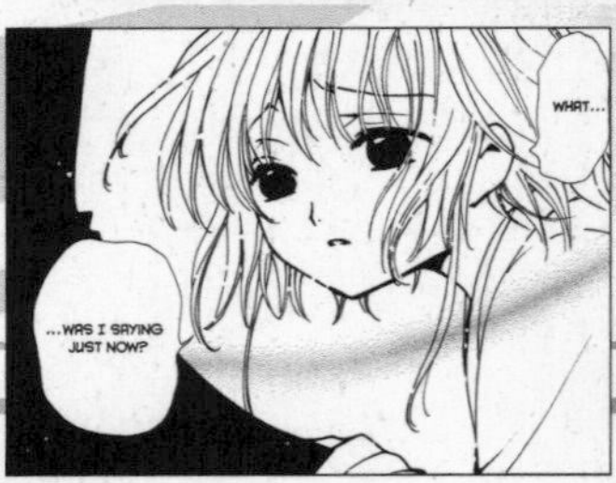
WHAT...
...WAS I SAYING JUST NOW?

Sakura had her relationship with Syaoran bargained away, and just as she was on the verge of remembering Syaoran, her memory is lost again.

THIS PLACE IS WEIRD. THIS COUNTRY...

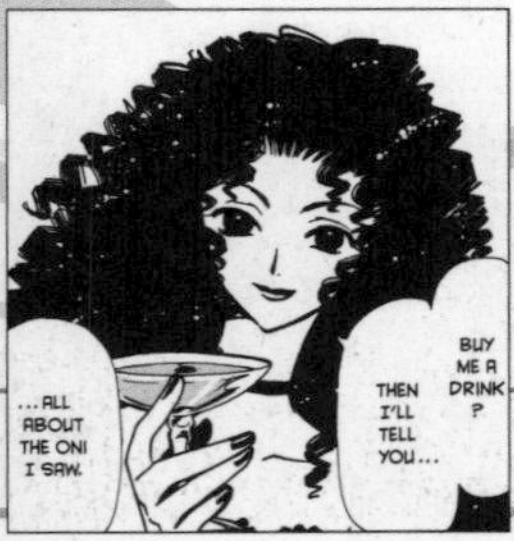
BUY ME A DRINK?
THEN I'LL TELL YOU...
...ALL ABOUT THE ONI I SAW.

As the movements of Oni change more and more, Fai and Kurogane go to find out more about the mysterious man who can control Oni.

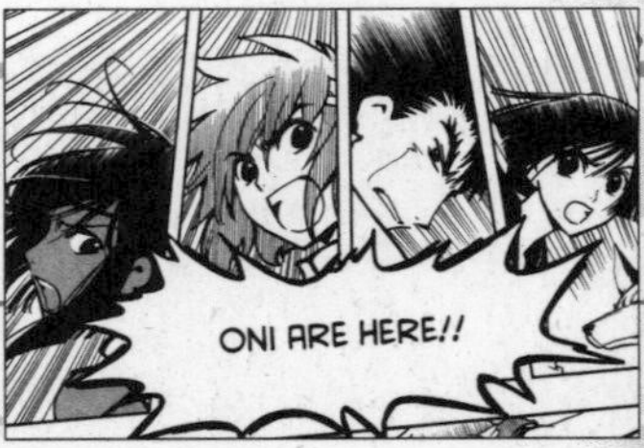
ONI ARE HERE!!

If they defeat the Oni, they get bounty money for it. The Oni Hunters are warriors that fight monsters for money and glory.

SCENE 5

In Order to Become Stronger Than He Is Now

COUNTRY OF ÔTO, PT. I

COULD YOU TEACH ME HOW TO USE A SWORD?

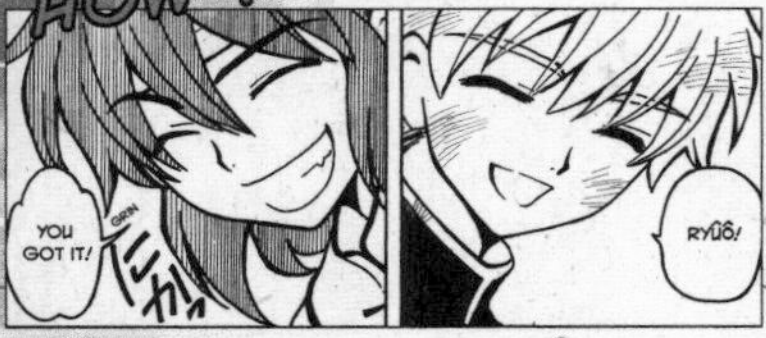
RYÛÔ!
GRIN
YOU GOT IT!

The bonds of friendship between warriors are strengthened in battle. Syaoran and Ryûô have become fast friends as fellow warriors and as rivals.

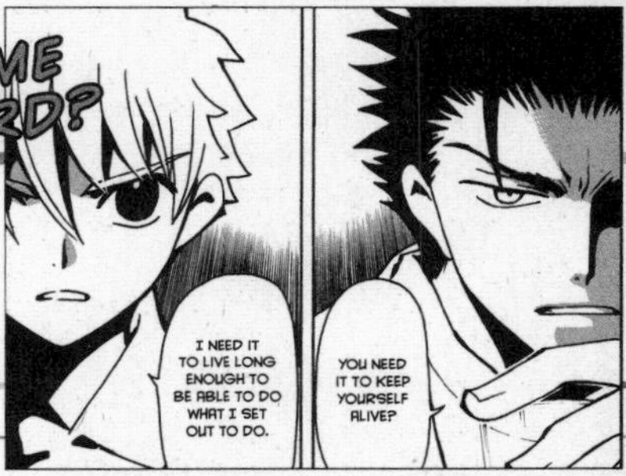
YOU NEED IT TO KEEP YOURSELF ALIVE?
I NEED IT TO LIVE LONG ENOUGH TO BE ABLE TO DO WHAT I SET OUT TO DO.

The upper-level Oni aren't affected by martial arts techniques. So to survive, Syaoran must learn swordsmanship from Kurogane.

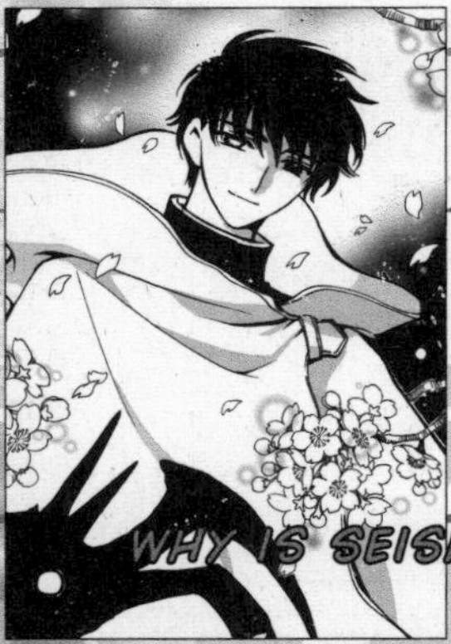
WHY IS SEISHIRÔ-SAN ...?!

The one controlling the Oni is someone Syaoran never expected!!

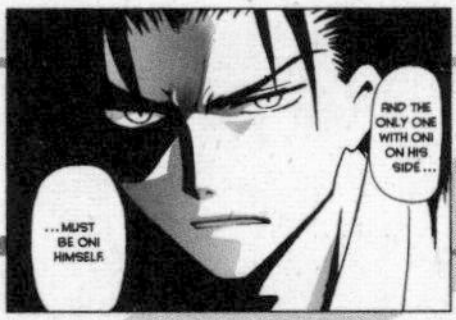
AND THE ONLY ONE WITH ONI ON HIS SIDE...
...MUST BE ONI HIMSELF.

What can this new Oni be? Kurogane has his doubts as well.

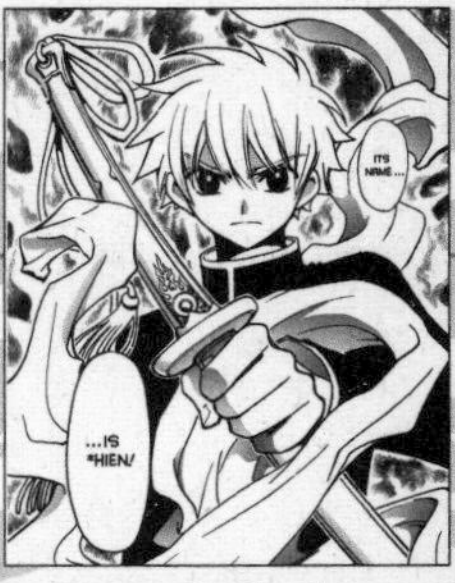
ITS NAME...
...IS *HIEN!

Finally, Syaoran receives his own sword. And with sword in hand, the young man grows up a little more.

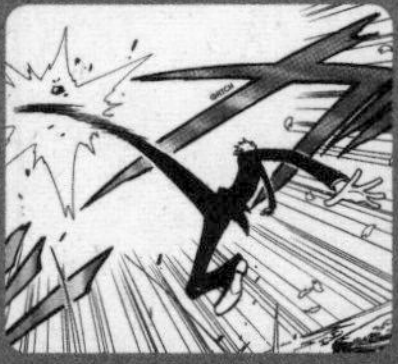

Syaoran was taught to fight by Seishirô. His method of fighting through kicks was learned under Seishirô's tutelage.

KEY WORD: LEARNING HOW TO FIGHT

Hand-to-hand martial arts, sword fighting, marksmanship, darts—there's more than just one way to fight. The strength of martial arts in close combat is unmatched. Gun marksmanship is best for long-range warfare. Each weapon and style has its advantages and demerits. For missile-type weapons, once the missiles have been shot, the only thing left for a target would be to run away. However, even though hand-to-hand martial arts doesn't have that problem, one has to get within arm's length or one cannot show one's skills. Right now, Syaoran is adding sword fighting to his present martial arts skill set. We have a young man handicapped with the loss of sight in his right eye, but the question is, how much stronger can he get?

nd the Reunion Between Syaoran nd Seishirô.

Seishirô, the man who long ago taught Syaoran how to fight, stands amid a wave of Oni whose attacks have become totally unpredictable. With a cold bearing, he eliminates anyone who stands between him and his ambition to defeat the I-1 Oni! Before Seishirô does battle with Syaoran, the secret of the Country of Ôto is uncovered.

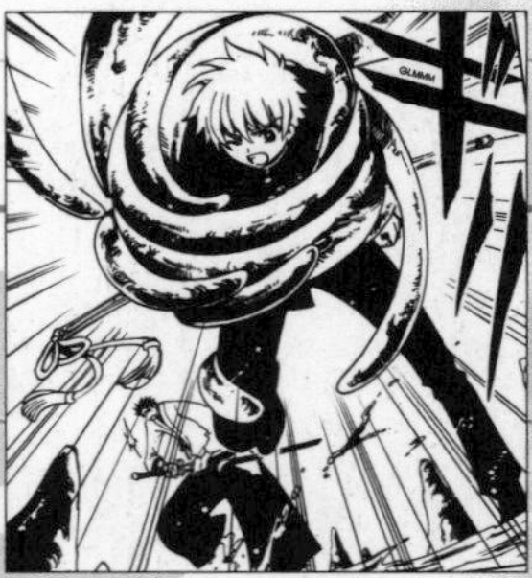

In search of information about something that can control Oni, Syaoran and Kurogane enter the very dangerous building, The Tower of the Little People.

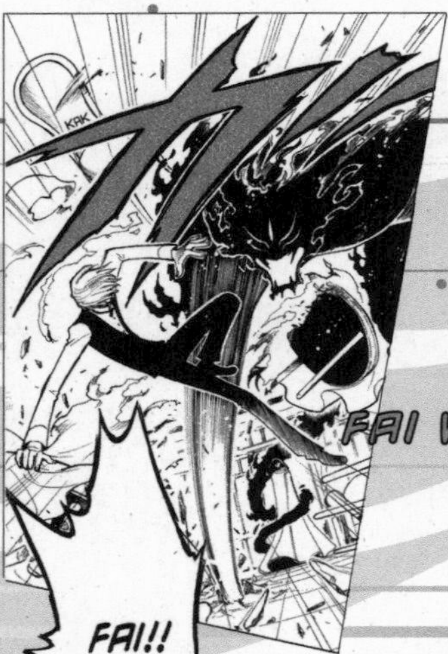
KAK
FAI!!

Seishirô proves by force that he is a man who wields a great power. Fai is the target of his attack...

FAI WAS KILLED BY AN ONI!!

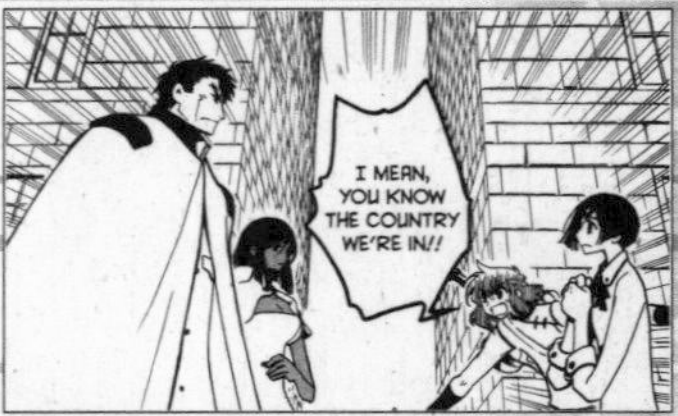
I MEAN, YOU KNOW THE COUNTRY WE'RE IN!!

The Oni Hunters predict the severity of the changes occurring within the Country of Ôto, and they're nervous.

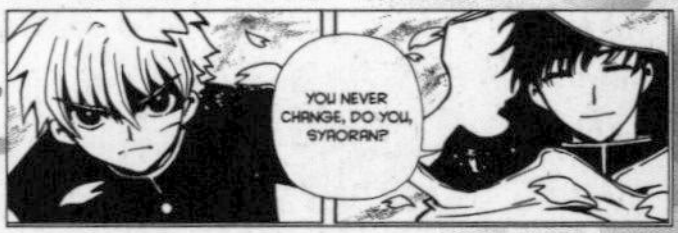
YOU NEVER CHANGE, DO YOU, SYAORAN?

Wanting to ask why Fai was attacked, Syaoran confronts Seishirô, and enters into a battle to the death with his master.

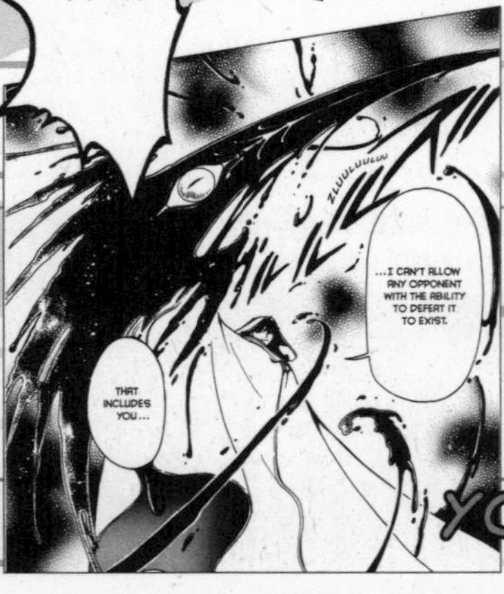
...I CAN'T ALLOW ANY OPPONENT WITH THE ABILITY TO DEFEAT IT TO EXIST.
THAT INCLUDES YOU...

Seishirô's power is incredible. Syaoran, with no way to effectively fight him, is pierced through the chest.

YOU MUST DIE!!

SCENE 6

The Collapse of the Dream of a Country

COUNTRY OF ÔTO, PT. II

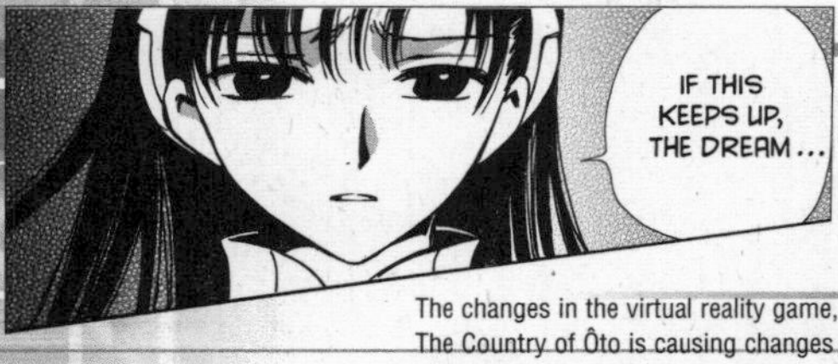
IF THIS KEEPS UP, THE DREAM...

The changes in the virtual reality game, The Country of Ôto is causing changes in the Country of Edonis in reality.

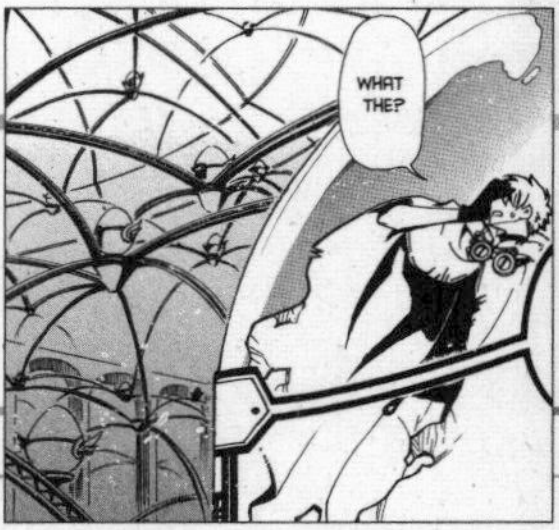
WHAT THE?

Syaoran awakens in a place he has no memory of. The Country of Ôto and everything in it was a game. All of their experiences were in virtual reality.

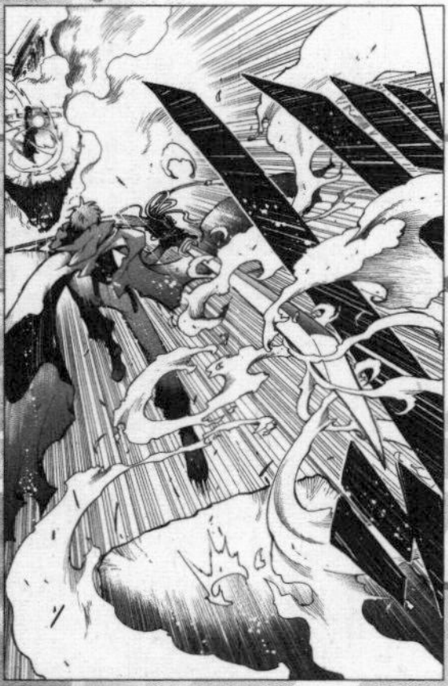

Seishirô is about to leave the world while in possession of one of Sakura's feathers. So Syaoran unsheathes his sword and attacks!

MY CHANCE MAY BE NEAR ZERO, BUT I'LL TAKE THAT CHANCE!!

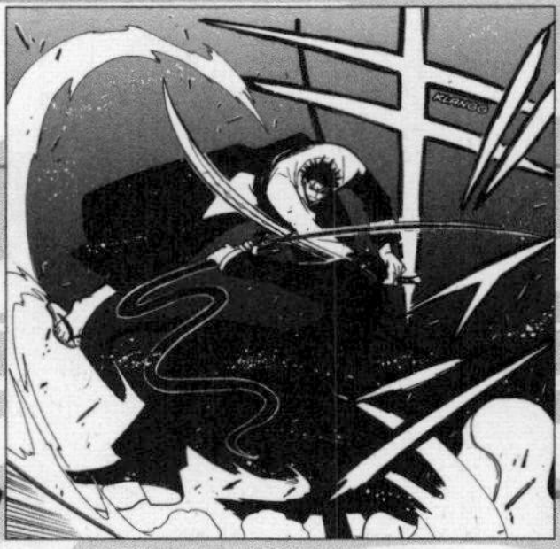
KLANGG

In an attempt to avenge his companions, Kurogane starts a sword-to-sword battle with the nearly all-powerful Seishirô.

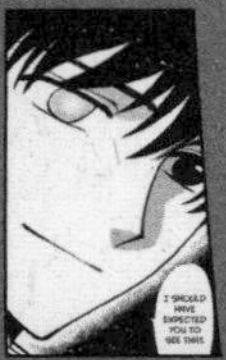
I SHOULD HAVE EXPECTED YOU TO SEE THIS

Seishirô's power to wander the universes is limited, but he is able to choose the world to which he wishes to go.

KEY WORD

THE POWER TO TRAVEL THE WORLDS

Starting with the Time-Space Witch, only those with the greatest magic have the power to traverse dimensions. Because Syaoran and his group paid the price, they've been able to travel the worlds with the help of Mokona, but it seems that Seishirô wasn't able to strike the same bargain. He exchanged his right eye for the power to journey between worlds, but only for a limited number of times. So we have the example of Syaoran's group who travel between worlds in search of Sakura's feathers without first seeing what they are getting into, and Seishirô who is able to determine if the two vampires he must kill seem like they are in a world before going there. It leads one to question whether these people are fated to meet again.

Your Personality and Your Recommended Country!

Traveller's Fortune

You don't want to just read Tsubasa, you want to share the adventure with Syaoran and his group! But which character do you resemble most, and in what country are you most suited to have adventure? Follow the paths and see!

◁ =YES

◀ =NO

I'LL DO IT!

Are you extremely determined?

Are you one who has someone you love, but your loved-one's family is opposed to the match?

ME? I ALWAYS HAVE FUN!
EH HEH HEH HEH

Are you a consummate optimist?

AND YOU'RE GOOD WITH THE JOKES, TOO!
あははは
AH HA HA HA
IT WASN'T A JOKE, ACTUALLY...

Do you love jokes?

Are you good at housework?

Is your motto, "I will eliminate anyone who comes after me!"

Can you get home from a park blindfolded?

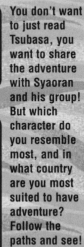

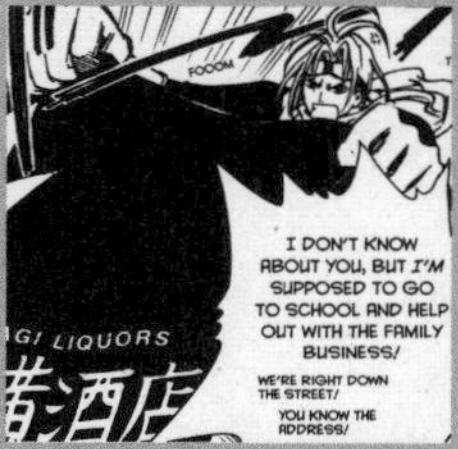
FOOOM
I DON'T KNOW ABOUT YOU, BUT I'M SUPPOSED TO GO TO SCHOOL AND HELP OUT WITH THE FAMILY BUSINESS!
WE'RE RIGHT DOWN THE STREET!
YOU KNOW THE ADDRESS!

Do you usually help out your family?

Do you have problems getting along with those who laugh, saying "Eh heh heh…"?

Turn to the next page.

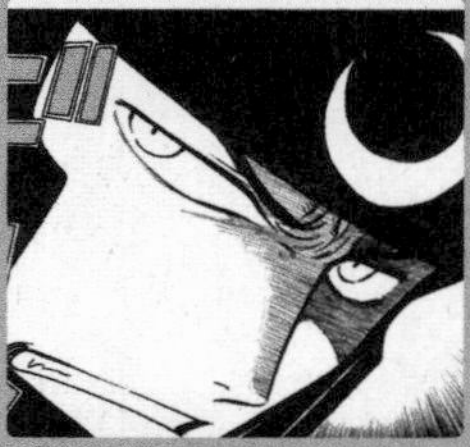

Do people often tell you that you have an evil stare?

Turn to the next page.

Are you undefeatable when wielding a sword?

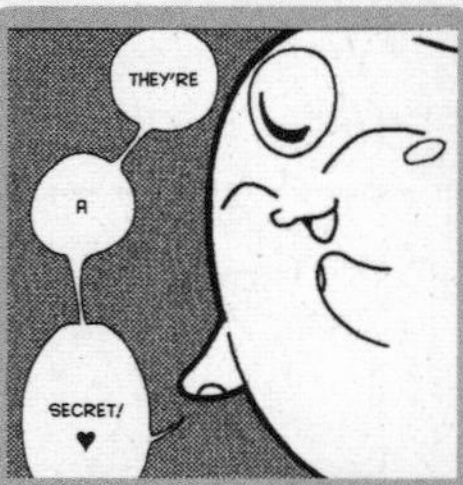
THEY'RE
A
SECRET! ♥

Do you have secrets that you never tell anyone?

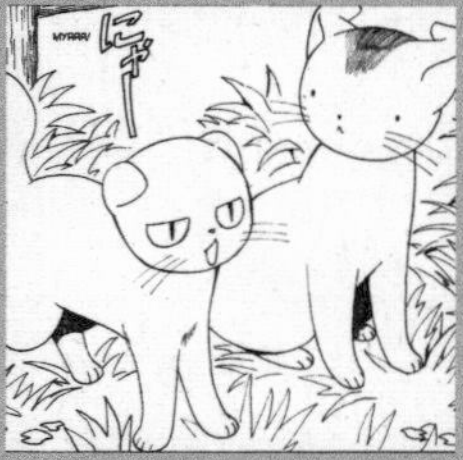

Between puppies and kitties, do you like kitties better?

Turn to the next page.

Turn to the next page.

Would you rather learn magic from Fai than swordsmanship from Kurogane?

Are you so popular with the opposite sex that everyone turns when you walk by on the street?

Turn to the next page.

FOLLOWED FROM THE PREVIOUS PAGE.

You may like Shonen Magazine, but do you really want to read Shonen Maganyan?

FOLLOWED FROM THE PREVIOUS PAGE.

Do you really want to sing?

FOLLOWED FROM THE PREVIOUS PAGE.

Between Princess Sakura and Princess Tomoyo, do you like Princess Sakura better?

FOLLOWED FROM THE PREVIOUS PAGE.

WHEET-WHOO!
THAT WAS ONE OF THE STONES OF THE GAME THAT FAI AND KUROGANE WERE PLAYING AT CHU'NYAN'S HOUSE!
SYAORAN-KUN, YOU'RE GOOD.

Are you a person who can't whistle?

FOLLOWED FROM THE PREVIOUS PAGE.

Do you like sweet things?

I WOULDN'T SO MUCH CALL IT MAGIC.
IT'S MORE LIKE INTUITION.

Do you have good intuition?

If you had a Kudan, are you sure it'd be a special-level Kudan?

If you find what you're looking for, do you go, "!!"?

Remember your alphabet letter. It will tell you your personality later.

This fortune will take this personality profile as a base and then determine your most appropriate world.

If you sense you are in danger, do you reflexively kick out?

Do you have something precious that you will protect?

Once asleep, is it difficult for anyone to wake you?

Are you as lucky as Sakura?

Do you have a large number of special attacks?

AH! AND IT MAKES KURO-PIN HAPPY, TOO!

Do you excel at giving others nicknames?

Are you a good swimmer?

"I'm not a white manju bun!"

A

B

C

D

E

A

A STARTS HERE.

SWEAT
あわ
SWEAT
あわ
Д8чю

Do you speak languages other than Japanese? [English?]

Should a different dimension version of yourself be king?

Do you hold a lot of respect for your mother?

B

B STARTS HERE.

If you went to the country of Ôto, would you be an Oni Hunter?

Do you want to take down a bad Ryanban with your own hands?

C

C STARTS HERE.

Between a doctor or landowner, is the bad guy the doctor?

Do you become friends quickly with just about anyone?

D

D STARTS HERE.

Have you ever ridden a horse?

E

E STARTS HERE.

Do you think that's about what a City Hall is like?

Are you the type to forgive easily if a great-looking popular idol were to destroy a cultural treasure?

The number represents the country that best suits you as determined by your answers. Don't forget the number!

The answers for your personality and recommended country.

1

2

3

4

5

Do you know the kanji for Amen'osa?

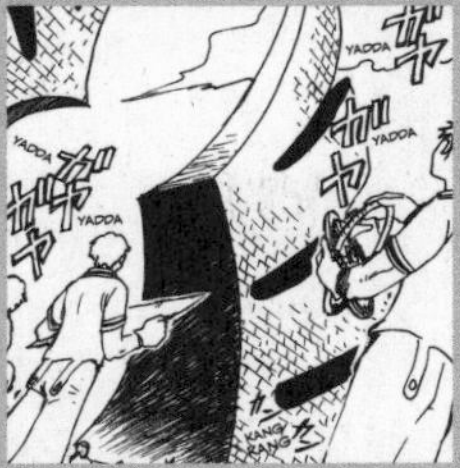
YADDA
YADDA
YADDA
YADDA
YADDA
KANG KANG

Do you think that ancient ruins are romantic?

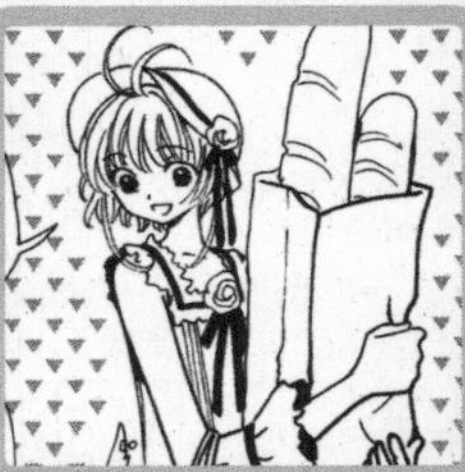

Do you love shopping?

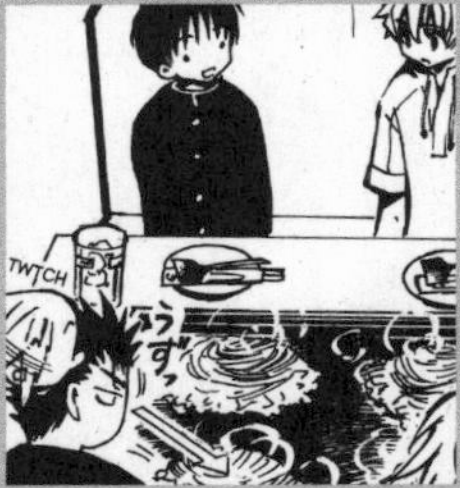
TWITCH

Do you love Okonomiyaki?

Are you a big fan of the Hanshin Tigers baseball team?

Do have a great interest in stories with princesses and old legends?

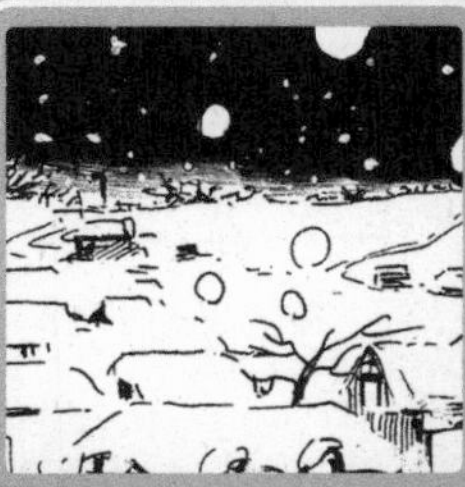

Do you like snowy lands better than southern lands?

If you were to open a cafe, would its name be Cat's Eye?

PERSONALITY

FIND THE RESULTS HERE

What's your personality?

What character are you most like? Here are the results! You may resemble someone you never expected.

C

KUROGANE

Social Misfit but a Heart of Fire

Do you ever get the feeling that you have few friends because of your blunt speech? But the truth is everyone relies on your tough skills.

A

SYAORAN

A Protector of What's Most Important

You are a person of conviction with a strong will. Once you have decided on a course, you will see it through. You are a wonderful person who will find that precious person with your strong heart.

D

FAI

The Popular One Who Seems to Have Everything

You're upbeat, and you seem to be able to do everything better than the average person. Everybody around you likes you. But when pressed, people think you're a little capricious.

B

SAKURA

A Gentle Smile is a Tonic for the Heart

Because of your energetic and kind personality, friends should naturally come and surround you. So smile and make friends, and everyone will be happier with you around.

E

MOKONA

One With Hidden Talents No One Would Expect

Yes, you have many talents, but the timing of when you display those talents is very important. Choose the time with determination, and everyone will enjoy it.

COUNTRY

FIND THE RESULTS HERE

What's your recommended country?

If you were to have an adventure, where would it be? We started with your personality, and this is the description of the country we recommend for you.

1

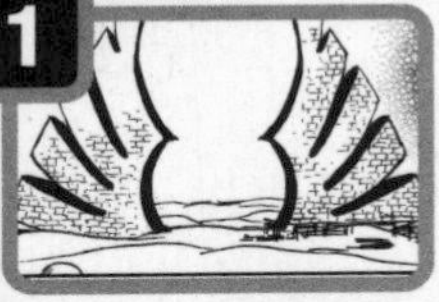

KINGDOM OF CLOW

A Mysterious Kingdom of Sand and Ruins

More than the fashionable tourist locations, you prefer places with legendary status, and so this is the place we recommend for you. If you wander around the ruins, there's a chance you may discover something of historic significance.

2

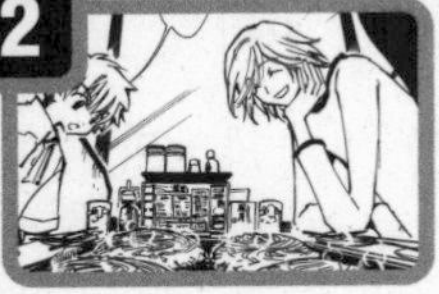

HANSHIN REPUBLIC

A Glutton's Paradise Overflowing With Energy

Busy shopping districts with delicious food! This place is perfect for having a fun time with your friends. So, what kind of Kudan will attach itself to you?

3

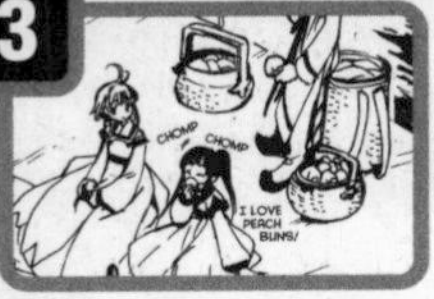
CHOMP
CHOMP
I LOVE PEACH BUNS!

COUNTRY OF KORYO

A Town With Magic and an Old-World Feel

This has a distinctive Asian ambiance of lined houses. It's a place where you'll meet people you've never seen before such as Amen'osa and Shinban.

4

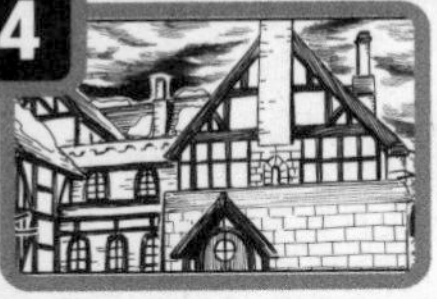

COUNTRY OF JADE

A Country of an Old Castle and Forest Where Legends Sleep

You want to travel to a world steeped in legends and old tales, and this is the location for you. But there's also plenty of books and literature, so be sure to enjoy a good mystery.

5

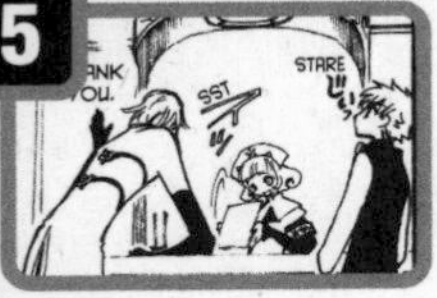
SST
STARE

COUNTRY OF ÔTO

A Town Full of Outsiders

This world contains the recent-past romanticism and town-views of the Taisho Era (1912–1925). There are a lot of people from outside the country, so if you make friends with them, you'll hear many interesting stories.

TSUBASA MINI REPORT ①

MINI REPORT

That Girl in the Sailor-suit School Uniform
Who Is She?

There's a young girl wearing the sailor-style school-girl's uniform in every country that Syaoran's group travels to. Considering the number of countries she's been seen in, could it be that she travels the worlds as well?

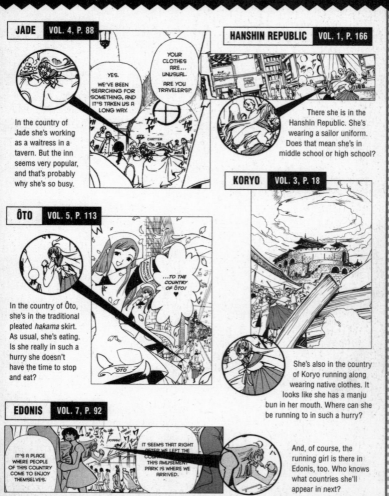

JADE **VOL. 4, P. 88**

YOUR CLOTHES ARE... UNUSUAL.
ARE YOU TRAVELERS?
YES.
WE'VE BEEN SEARCHING FOR SOMETHING, AND IT'S TAKEN US A LONG WAY.
CHATTER
CHATTER

In the country of Jade she's working as a waitress in a tavern. But the inn seems very popular, and that's probably why she's so busy.

HANSHIN REPUBLIC **VOL. 1, P. 166**

There she is in the Hanshin Republic. She's wearing a sailor uniform. Does that mean she's in middle school or high school?

KORYO **VOL. 3, P. 18**

She's also in the country of Koryo running along wearing native clothes. It looks like she has a manju bun in her mouth. Where can she be running to in such a hurry?

ÔTO **VOL. 5, P. 113**

WELCOMING COMMITTEE
...TO THE COUNTRY OF ÔTO! ♥
ÔTO

In the country of Ôto, she's in the traditional pleated *hakama* skirt. As usual, she's eating. Is she really in such a hurry she doesn't have the time to stop and eat?

EDONIS **VOL. 7, P. 92**

IT SEEMS THAT RIGHT
THIS AMUSEMENT PARK IS WHERE WE ARRIVED.
IT'S A PLACE WHERE PEOPLE OF THIS COUNTRY COME TO ENJOY THEMSELVES.

And, of course, the running girl is there in Edonis, too. Who knows what countries she'll appear in next?

CHARACTERS FILE

The five travelers, Syaoran, Sakura, Kurogane, Fai, and Mokona, have different mother worlds and different reasons for traveling. If we take a good look at their personalities and actions, we may be able to see new sides to each of them.

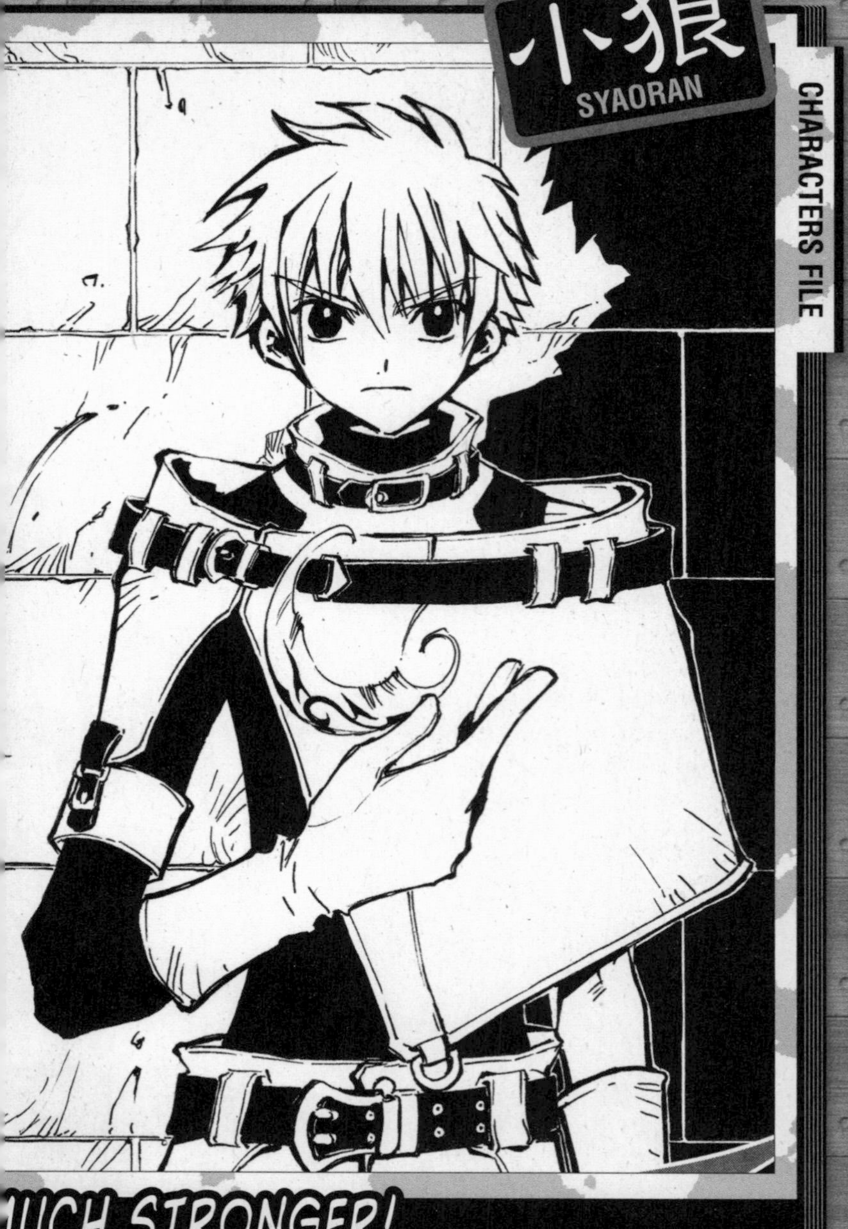
小狼
SYAORAN
CHARACTERS FILE
IUCH STRONGER!

SYAORAN

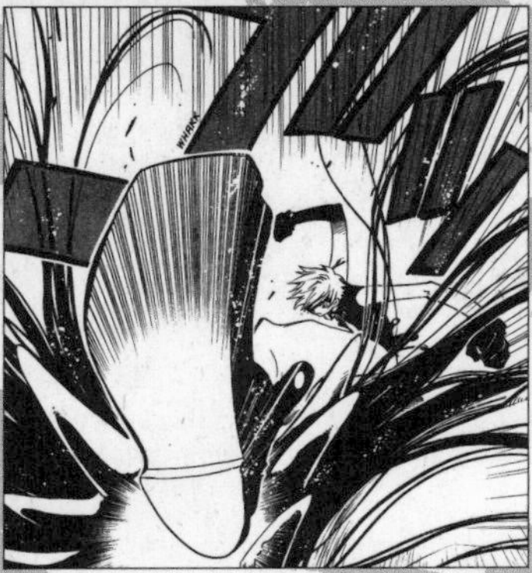
WHAK

When you think of Syaoran, you think of kicks. He can defeat strong Oni with a single kick. And as he continues his journey, perhaps he'll become even more powerful.

PARAMETER

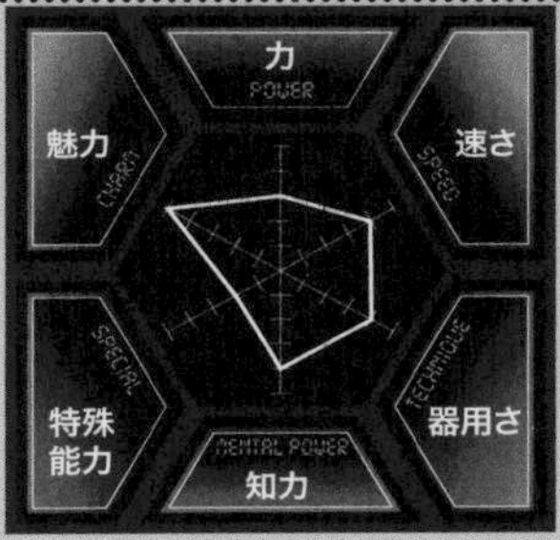
力
POWER
速さ
SPEED
器用さ
TECHNIQUE
知力
MENTAL POWER
特殊能力
SPECIAL
魅力
CHARA

Syaoran has no special abilities such as magical powers, but he has shown wisdom and academic prowess during his travels. He can grapple and has kicking skills, but the one place where he knows no equal is in the strength of his heart.

The "memories" of Syaoran's childhood friend, Princess Sakura of the Kingdom of Clow, were scattered into many different worlds. Since Sakura is the most important person in the world to Syaoran, the young man has gone off on a journey with the likes of Kurogane and Fai to retrieve her memories. His personality shows that he is a serious person with a strong sense of justice, and he possesses an indomitable will that will see any course of action to its conclusion once he has made his decision. It may have something to do with the fact that he was raised by his archaeologist stepfather, Fujitaka, but he seems enraptured every time he comes across history, ruins, or odd things in the other worlds that he visits. He is presently learning swordsmanship from Kurogane so that he will have the strength necessary to gather all of Sakura's memory feathers.

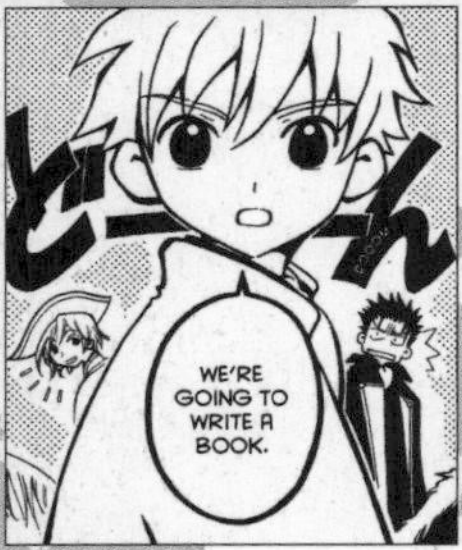
WE'RE GOING TO WRITE A BOOK.

There are quite a few areas where he has useful knowledge he received while traveling from country to country with his stepfather Fujitaka. Even when there's trouble, Syaoran can take care of it without ever panicking.

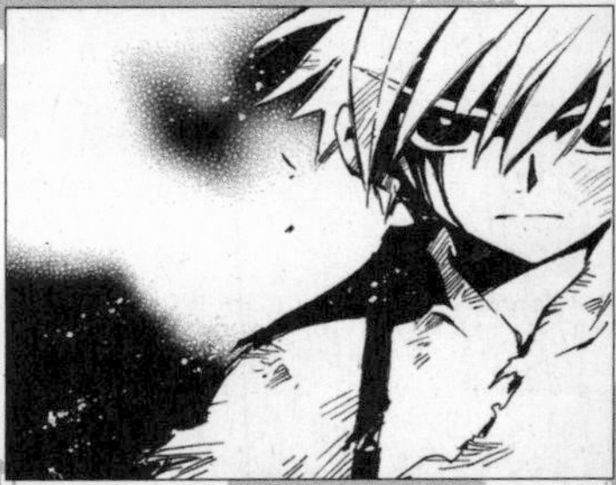

Syaoran's main advantage is that he has the strength of heart to never give up no matter what. Part of that strength comes from his strong feelings toward Sakura.

NEVER GIVE UP! GET STRONGER

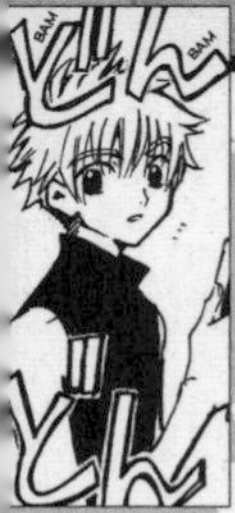
BAM
BAM

yaoran was busy very day with the xcavations in the ingdom of Clow. ecause of that, e has been bsent from his ome for long eriods of time.

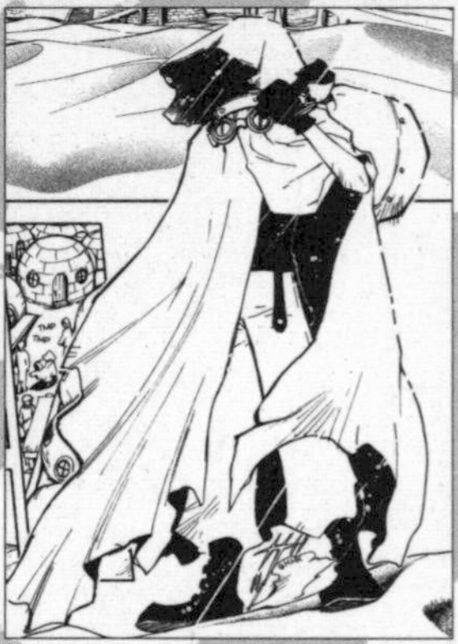

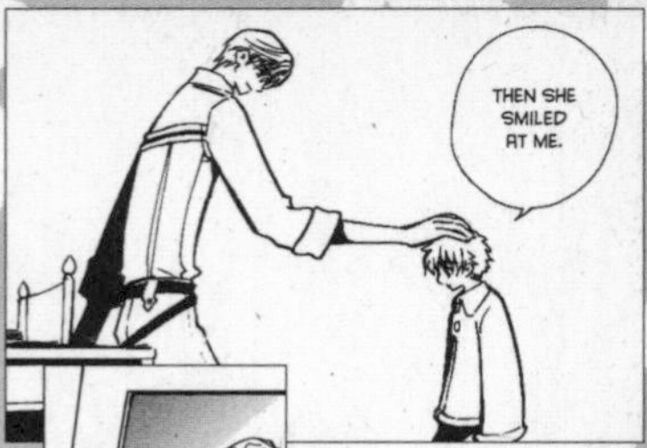
THEN SHE SMILED AT ME.

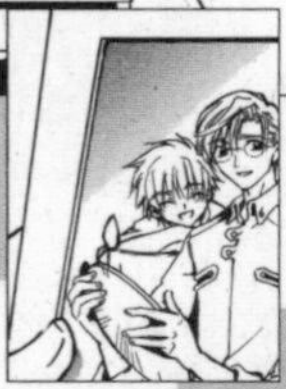

Archaeologist Fujitaka took the very young Syaoran on as his adopted son, and rather than giving him pity, Fujitaka gave him love.

CHARACTERS FILE

Syaoran's Journey Chronicle

THE PAST

- Met Fujitaka. Soon after, became his adopted son and has lived with him since.

KINGDOM OF CLOW

- Arrived at the Kingdom of Clow with Fujitaka. Met Sakura, and since has shared a close relationship.
- Met Seishirô. Began training under Seishirô in kicking attacks and other hand-to-hand martial arts.
- Fujitaka died due to an accident during the excavations of ruins.
- Sakura's memories were scattered. Paid the price of his relationship with Sakura in order to travel through dimensions with Kurogane, Fai, and Mokona and collect her memory feathers.

ANSHIN REPUBLIC

- Visited the Hanshin Republic. Found the first of Sakura's feathers. Took shelter with the married couple Sorata and Arashi Arisugawa.
- Recovered the second of Sakura's feathers from within Masayoshi's Kudan. Sakura returned to consciousness.

OUNTRY OF KORYO

- Visited the town of Ryonfi in the country of Koryo. Met Chu'nyan and took shelter in her house.
- Battled the Ryanban and his son. Recovered the third of Sakura's feathers.

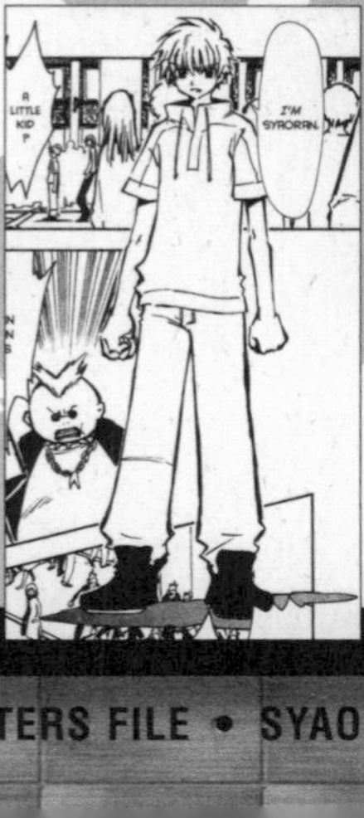

He had a special-level Kudan, but because of it, he becomes an object of interest for gangs of Kudan users.

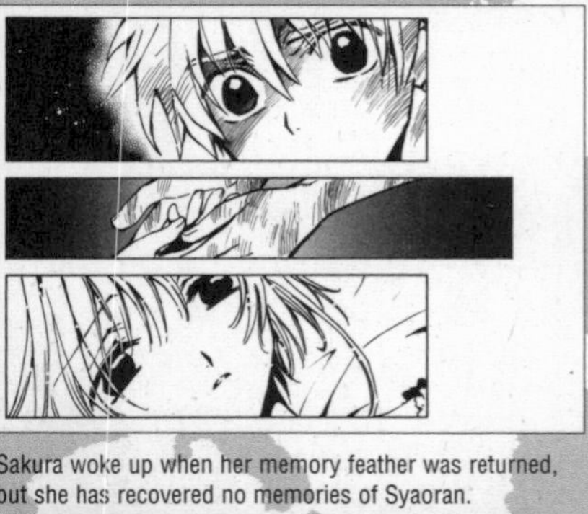

Sakura woke up when her memory feather was returned, but she has recovered no memories of Syaoran.

SYAORAN

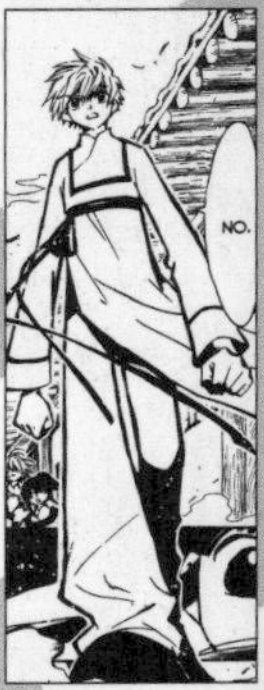
NO.

➤ Syaoran heads out to the Ryanban's castle along with Kurogane and Fai. Even though his enemy has powerful magics, Syaoran shows no fear.

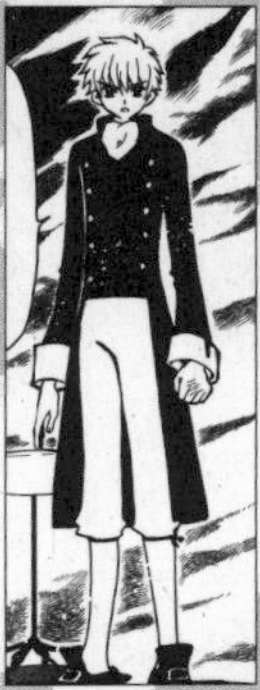

▲ In the Country of Jade, they were mistaken for the ones who kidnapped the children, but Syaoran's deductions led them to the true culprit.

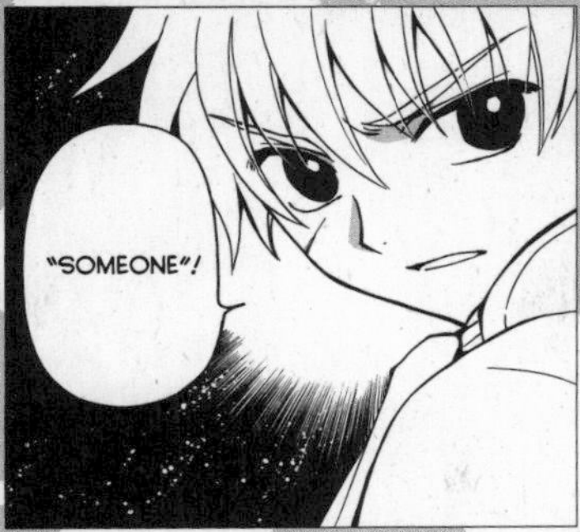
"SOMEONE"!

Syaoran becomes aware that someone is interfering in his journey. What is that someone's purpose?

- Requested to learn swordsmanship from Kurogane.
- Received the fire sword, Hien.
- Battled Seishirô. Lost the battle. Was drawn out of the Country of Ôto. Became aware that the Country of Ôto was actually a virtual reality game for the amusement of residents of the country of Edonis.
- Through the power of the feather that Seishirô was holding, the game world merged with reality.
- Did battle again with Seishirô, but failed in his attempt to recover Sakura's feather. Seishirô exited to enter a different world.
- Left along with Sakura, Kurogane, Fai, and Mokona for a new world.

COUNTRY OF FOG

- Visited the country of fog.

COUNTRY OF JADE

- Visited the town of Spirit in the Country of Jade. Took shelter with the town's doctor, Kyle Rondart.
- Sakura went missing.
- Received the fourth of Sakura's memory feathers from Princess Emerald.

COUNTRY OF ÔTO/EDONIS

- Visited the Country of Ôto. Paired with Kurogane as Oni Hunters.
- Met Oni Hunters Yuzuriha Nekoi, Shiyû Kusanagi, Ryûô, and Sôma.

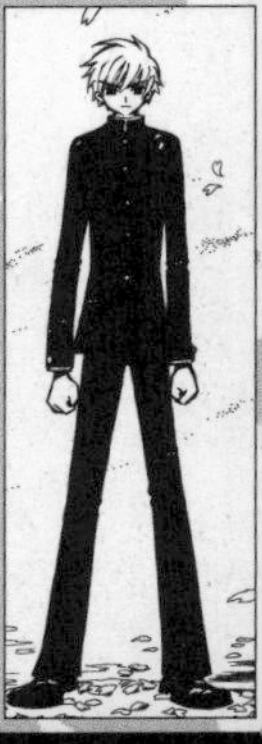

➤ Syaoran begins a training journey to learn the sword under the tutelage of Kurogane. It is more intense than he imagined.

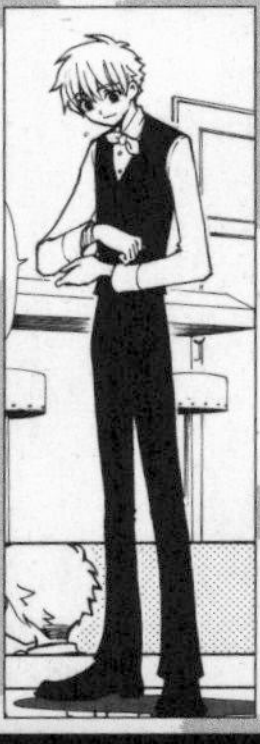

◄ Even when helping at the café Cat's Eye, the smart waiter uniform looks good on him.

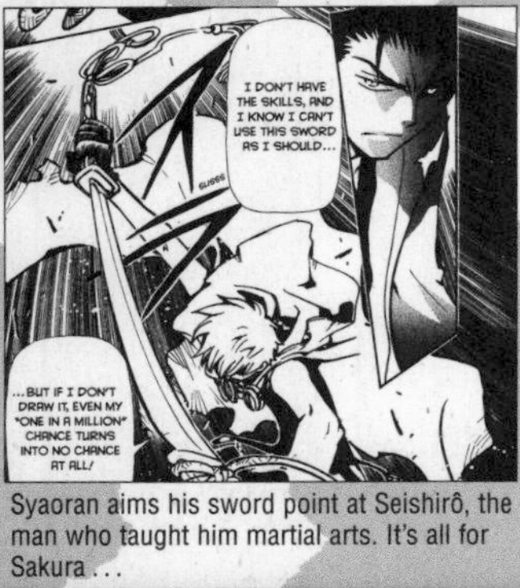
I DON'T HAVE THE SKILLS, AND I KNOW I CAN'T USE THIS SWORD AS I SHOULD...
...BUT IF I DON'T DRAW IT, EVEN MY "ONE IN A MILLION" CHANCE TURNS INTO NO CHANCE AT ALL!

Syaoran aims his sword point at Seishirô, the man who taught him martial arts. It's all for Sakura . . .

FROM BEFORE THE TIME HE WAS FOUND BY HIS ADOPTIVE FATHER, HE REMEMBERS NOTHING.

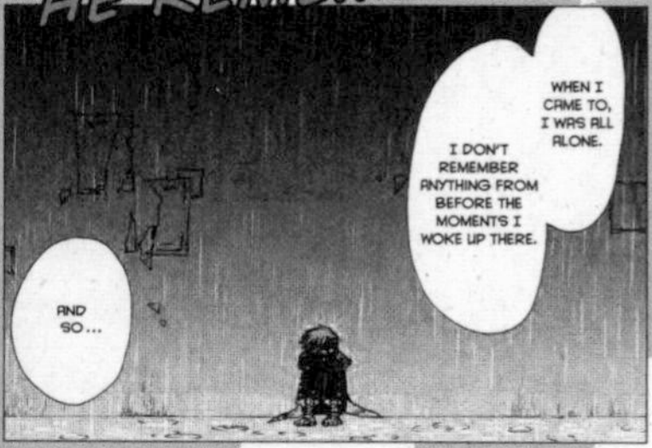
WHEN I CAME TO, I WAS ALL ALONE.
I DON'T REMEMBER ANYTHING FROM BEFORE THE MOMENTS I WOKE UP THERE.
AND SO...

If he had never met Fujitaka, Syaoran might have spent his entire life alone.

No one seems to know what happened to Syaoran in his early childhood, and Syaoran doesn't remember it himself. The events that shaped his early life remain a mystery.

THE SMILE HER HIGHNESS GAVE ME... ...WAS SO WARM!!

The thing that eventually thawed Syaoran's frozen heart was Sakura with a smile as warm as the sun. Syaoran will never forget her smile from that moment.

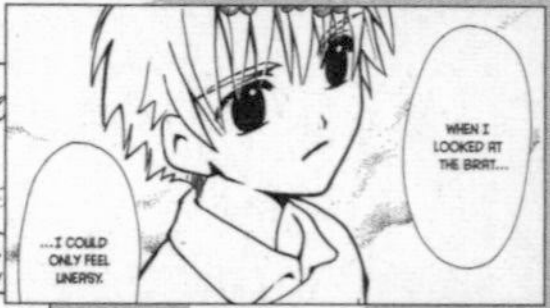
WHEN I LOOKED AT THE BRAT...
...I COULD ONLY FEEL UNEASY.

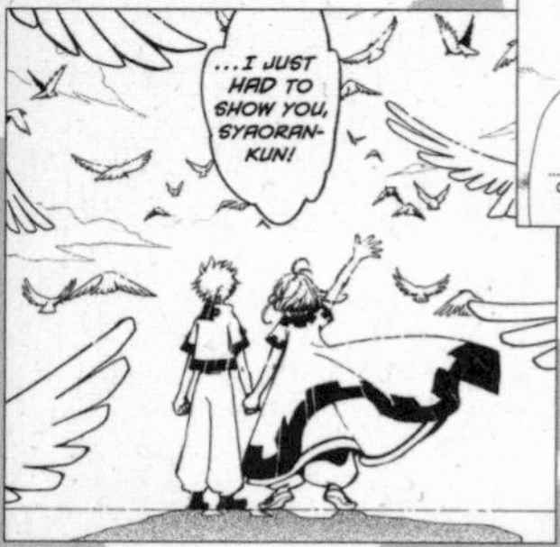
...I JUST HAD TO SHOW YOU, SYAORAN-KUN!

Until Syaoran had met Sakura, he had never shown very much emotion.

TEACH ME HOW TO FIGHT!

Syaoran has lost the sight in his right eye. The one who taught him how to fight was Seishirô, a vampire hunter who shares the same disability.

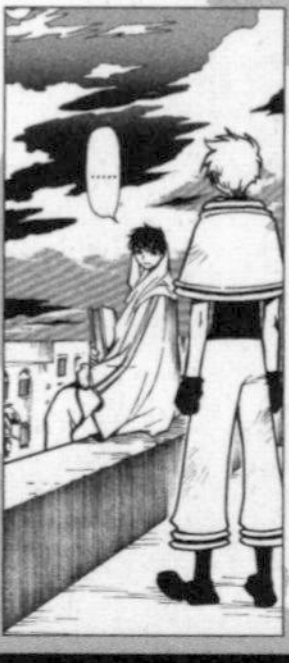
......

➤ From this point Syaoran decided to get stronger.

TOPIC 1

Memories of the Past

Syaoran sets out on a journey to find Sakura's memories. Among them are her lost memories of him. Why did Syaoran lose his early memories and the sight in his right eye?

WHEN I DECIDE TO DO SOMETHING, I DO IT! AND THAT'S ALL!

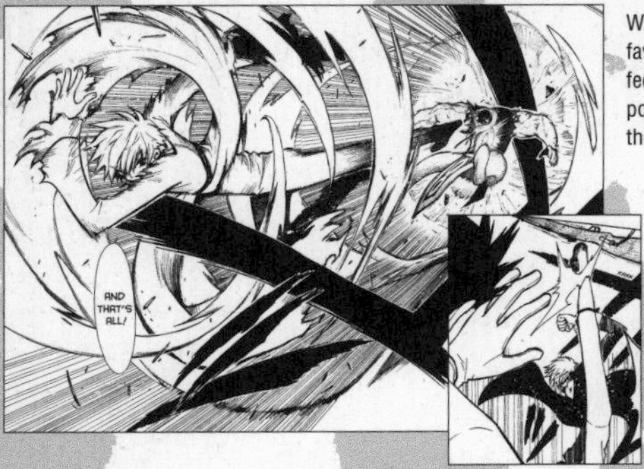
AND THAT'S ALL!

Without trying to favor his wounded feet, he aims a powerful kick at the Ryanban's son.

He aims his kick only at the gun. He never uses more power than is necessary, even for the sake of protection.

He is determined to return Sakura's memories, and to that end, he's willing to ignore wounds he may suffer. There are no half-measures to what he's prepared to do.

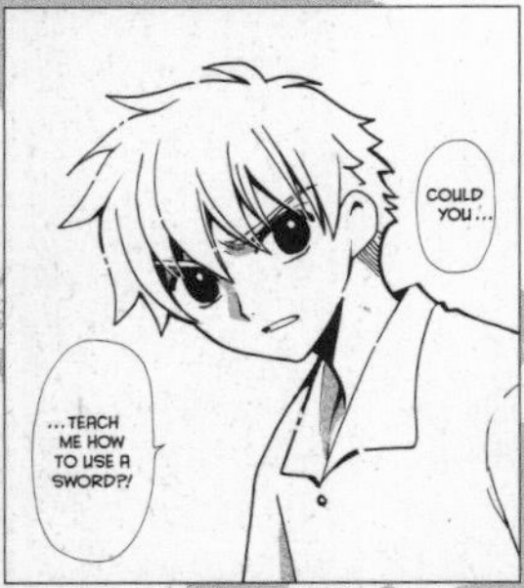
COULD YOU...
...TEACH ME HOW TO USE A SWORD?!

Syaoran asks Kurogane to teach him swordsmanship. One of the reasons is to effectively retrieve Sakura's memories.

I WANT TO PROTECT SOMEONE WHO IS PRECIOUS TO ME.

The way he was at that moment, he wasn't able to protect anyone precious to him, and that's why Syaoran wanted a new skill, the skill of "the sword."

I WANT TO BECOME STRONGER!

Strength is not simply flailing out with power. To protect that which needs protection, one must use power correctly. That's when power becomes strength.

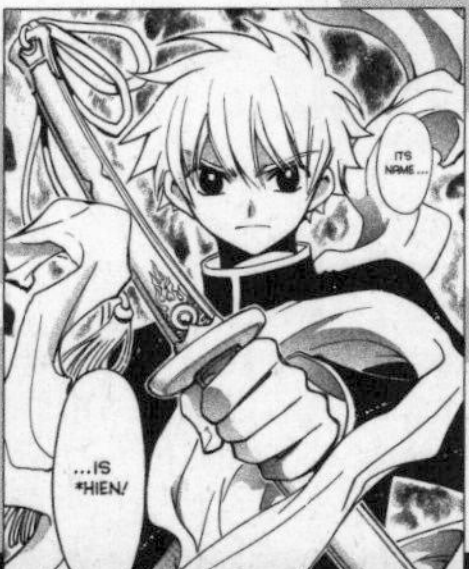
ITS NAME...
...IS *HIEN!

The sword of flame, Hien, displays the fire in Syaoran's heart.

TOPIC 2

The Strength to Protect

Sometimes it is necessary to be able to fight in order to protect that which is precious. That is why Syaoran seeks to become stronger. In order to protect precious Sakura.

SO IF IT BURNS ME, LET IT BURN!!

STRENGTH AND WEAKNESS AREN'T ONLY MEASURED IN BATTLE.

In response to Masayoshi's courage, Syaoran retrieves the feather from the fires of Masayoshi's Kudan.

Strength is more than the power to do battle. One form of strength is the courage to endure pain for the sake of a friend.

STAY HERE AND WAIT WITH PRINCESS SAKURA.

Syaoran refuses to take Chu'nyan with him. Part of the reason is for her own safety:

I'M GOING TO GO AND TAKE DOWN THAT RYANBAN!
I HAVE TO AVENGE MY OMONI!

Because Syaoran knows the extreme danger he faces in his battle with the powerful magics of the Ryanban and his son, he didn't allow Chu'nyan to come along. Even in his blunt attitude, one can feel his compassion.

RYÛÔ, YOU'RE A SWORD MASTER TOO...

Perhaps their personalities just meshed, but the two young men were fast friends almost from the moment they met.

RYÛÔ!
YOU GOT IT!
GRIN

Even if they are traveling different paths, their goals are the same, and that small fact leads to a certain joy. Someone else understands! It's wonderful to have a friend like that.

TOPIC 3

Emphasis on Friendship

There isn't much time spent in each world Syaoran's group visits, but if personalities connect, then even with that short time, lasting friendships can emerge.

CHARACTERS FILE

TOPIC 4

Feelings Toward Sakura

Syaoran can do anything so long as it is in an effort to keep Sakura's warm smile shining. Even if it means that Sakura will never remember him . . .

SAKURA IS THE ONE MOST PRECIOUS TO ME!

In order to save Sakura's life, Syaoran never hesitates, even when the price is his precious relationship with her.

I WILL NOT LET SAKURA DIE!

Syaoran wants most to restore Sakura to her former happy state, even if it means she will forget all about him. One can only describe feelings that ask for nothing in return as pure.

SAKURA DOESN'T CHANGE EVEN WITHOUT HER MEMORIES.

Even though she has no memories, her personality at it's heart is no different. Even now, Sakura acts as if she holds some degree of love in her heart for Syaoran.

...IS A WARM HUMAN BEING!

Sakura's smile doesn't change. It's as warm as finding a place in the sun, even without her memories.

I WILL RETURN HER MEMORIES TO HER!

The memories of Syaoran will never return to Sakura, even if all other memories are returned. But still, Syaoran is determined to gather all of her memories. It's all for Sakura's sake.

Sakura can't remember even when she tries to do so herself. A "price paid" is just that serious.

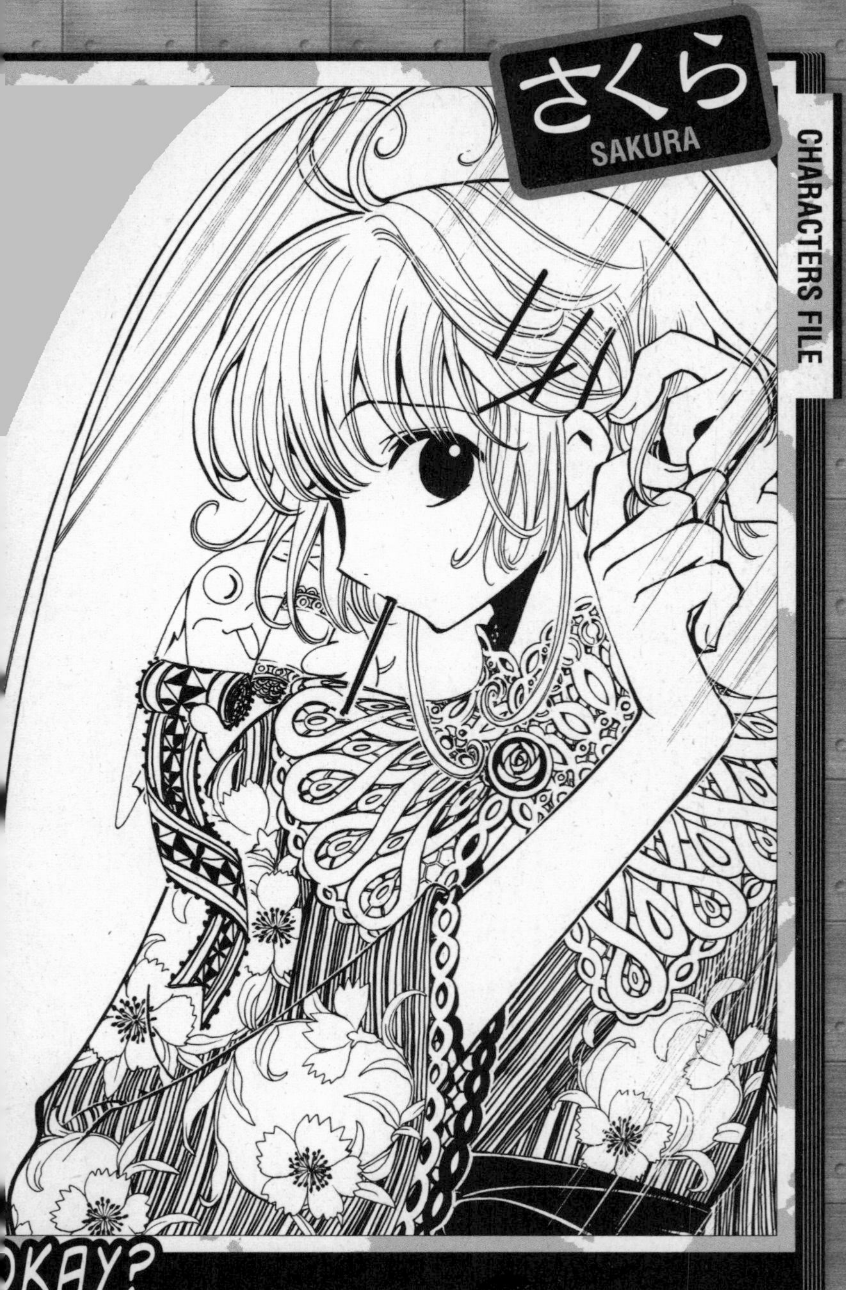
さくら
SAKURA
CHARACTERS FILE
OKAY?

SAKURA

YES...
THAT'D MAKE ME VERY HAPPY!

Sakura has many charms, but the most noticeable is her warm smile. No matter how painful the task, if one sees that smile, one can find the will to persevere.

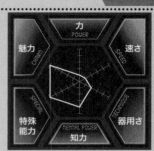

PARAMETER

力
POWER
速さ
SPEED
器用さ
TECHNIQUE
知力
MENTAL POWER
特殊能力
SPECIAL
魅力
CHARM

Sakura's greatest charm is her smile. She doesn't have much ability in battles, but she has luck that seems given by the gods, and she has some ability to see spirits and ghosts.

With a natural innocence and a carefree smile, Kingdom of Clow's princess Sakura is loved by all of the citizens. She and Syaoran were childhood friends, but recently her emotions have developed into something stronger than just friendship, and she was determined to tell him how she feels. She headed to the underground sections of the excavated ruins in the desert, but before she could tell him, her memories were scattered throughout the worlds, and she lost consciousness. To retrieve them, she starts on a journey with Syaoran and the rest of the group. As she retrieves feather after feather, she regains more of her memories. But a deal was made with the Time-Space Witch that prevents Sakura from remembering Syaoran. Still, her kind, gentle smile has never changed.

YOU SAVED THE CHILDREN!
THANK YOU SO MUCH!

Ever since she was a child, she has always had an odd power. She's been able to see and talk to certain people and other living beings who should be dead.

ズラーッ
ZURARA
UM...
THEY CAME OUT LOOKING LIKE THIS.

Because of her miraculous luck, she is undefeatable in games of chance. Due to that, the group has no want for money even when they travel to other worlds.

NEVER LEAVE ME ALONE

Sakura gives Syaoran a big hug after he returns from a long excavation of the ruins. Syaoran's heart races from her head-on approach.

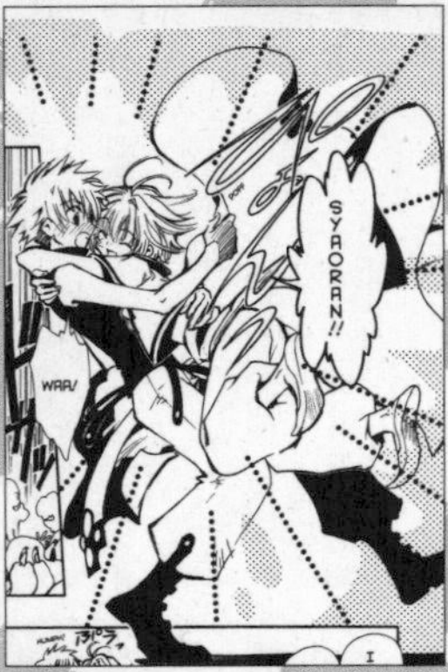
SYAORAN!!
WAA!

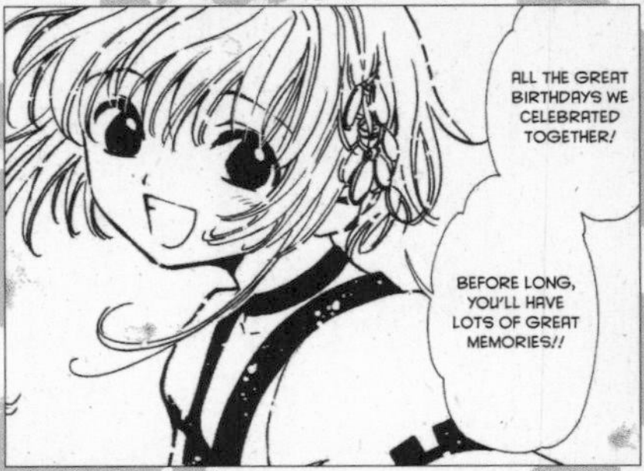
ALL THE GREAT BIRTHDAYS WE CELEBRATED TOGETHER!
BEFORE LONG, YOU'LL HAVE LOTS OF GREAT MEMORIES!!

Young Sakura seems to like Syaoran at first sight, and soon they're close friends.

Sakura's Journey Chronicle

COUNTRY OF KORYO

- Visited the town of Ryonfi in the country of Koryo. Met Chu'nyan and took shelter in her house.
- Played dice with townsmen. Won everything.
- Syaoran, Kurogane, Fai and Mokona battled the Ryanban and his son to recover the third feather. Through it, recovered the memory of a birthday party. However Syaoran's name and face remain unremembered.

COUNTRY OF FOG

- Remembered the first meeting of Syaoran, but did not realize the person remembered is Syaoran.

THE PAST

- Met Syaoran who came to the Kingdom of Clow with Fujitaka. Helps Syaoran to rediscover his lost emotions.

KINGDOM OF CLOW

- Lost memories to the different dimensions at the ruins. Lost consciousness.

HANSHIN REPUBLIC

- Took shelter with the married couple Sorata and Arashi Arisugawa.
- Life was taken out of danger through a memory feather discovered on Syaoran's clothes.
- Received second feather from Masayoshi's Kudan. However memory of Syaoran is not recovered.

Chu'nyan cries in frustration as Sakura holds her so gently she could almost be Chu'nyan's mother.

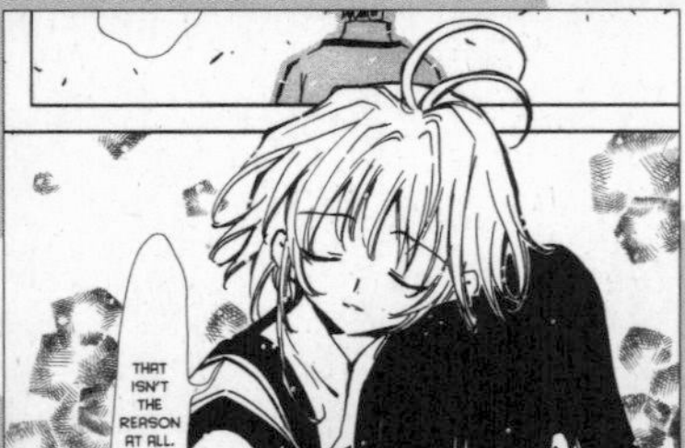
THAT ISN'T THE REASON AT ALL.

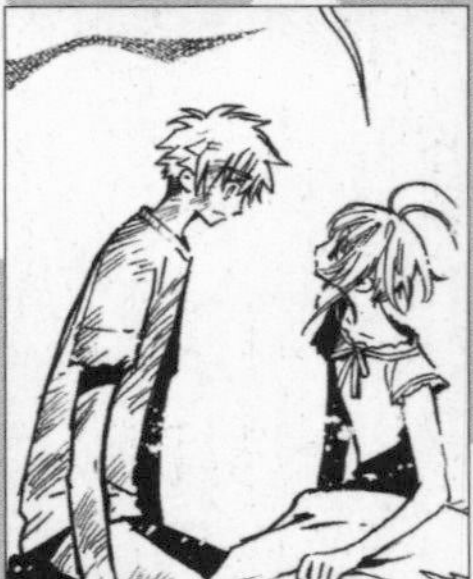

Even though she recovered a feather, her memory of Syaoran didn't return, and her careless first words to him strike him like a knife.

SAKURA

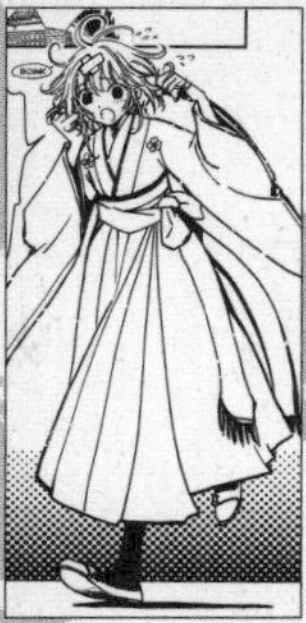

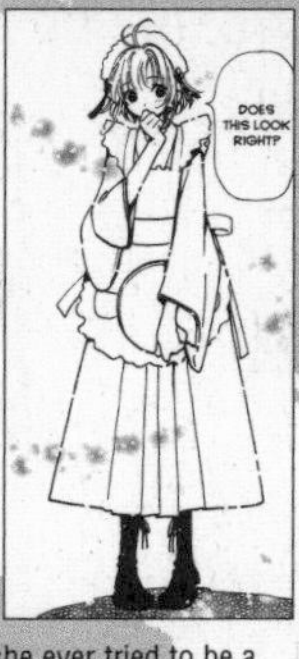
DOES THIS LOOK RIGHT?

▲ This being the first time she ever tried to be a waitress, she had difficulties, such as clumsily dropping trays full of cups and plates.

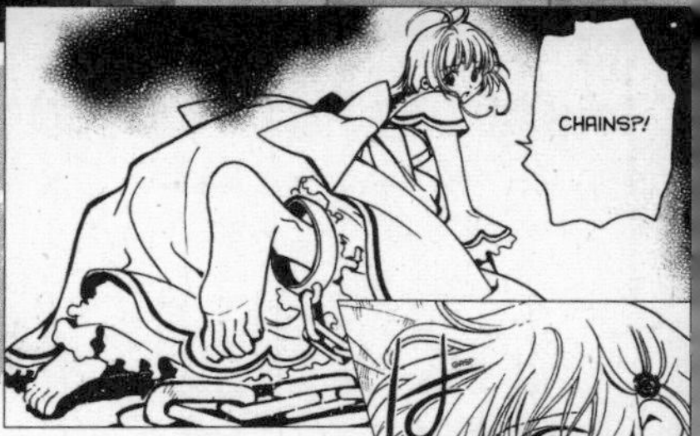
CHAINS?!

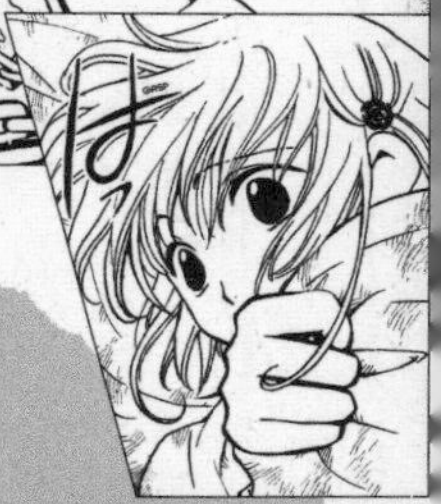

▲ Sakura was imprisoned by some unknown force in the Northern Castle. The shackles attached to her ankle look like they hurt.

Emerald. At the same time, received a warning from Princess Emerald about someone watching the group.

COUNTRY OF ÔTO/EDONIS

- Visited the Country of Ôto. Together with Fai, opened the Cat's Eye café and began work.
- Asked Syaoran about their relationship. However, due to the contract with the Time-Space Witch, the conversation itself was forgotten.
- Met Oni Hunters Yuzuriha Nekoi, Shiyû Kusanagi, Ryûô, and Sôma.
- Left along with Syaoran, Kurogane, Fai, and Mokona for a new world.

COUNTRY OF JADE

- Joined in a card game in a tavern, and once again, won every pot in the game.
- Visited the town of Spirit in the country of Jade. Took shelter with the town's doctor, Kyle Rondart.
- Followed after the golden-haired princess and went missing.
- Woke up in a cell in the Northern Castle. Found out that the children were being put to work with the goal of digging out a memory feather that was encased in an ice-like substance.
- Spoke to Princess Emerald. Learned the truth of the legend about her.
- Received the fourth memory feather from Princess

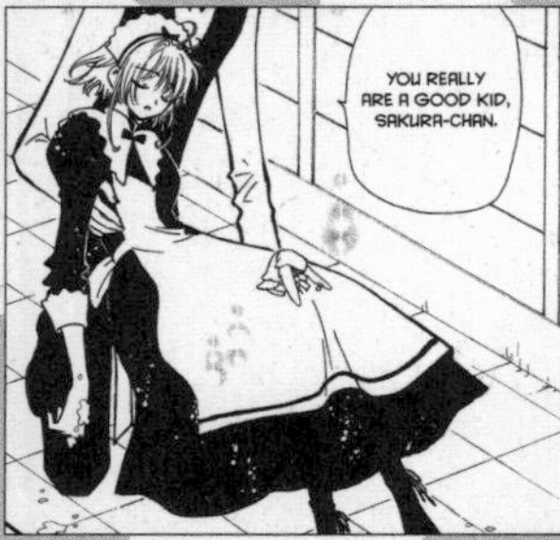
YOU REALLY ARE A GOOD KID, SAKURA-CHAN.

▲ Sakura falls victim to one of her sudden sleep attacks. It seems that it will still be a long time before she recovers all of her memories.

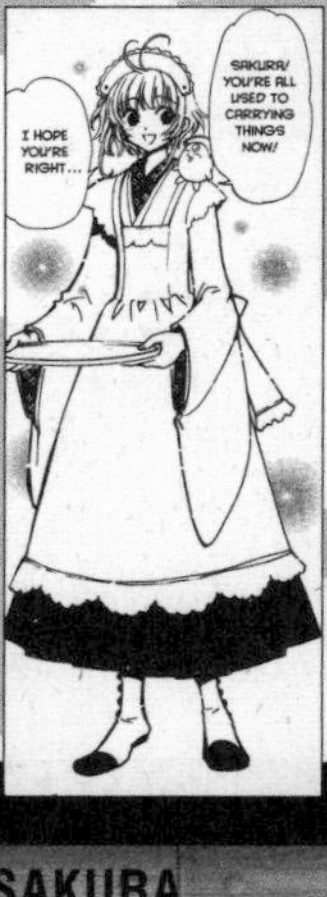
SAKURA! YOU'RE ALL USED TO CARRYING THINGS NOW!
I HOPE YOU'RE RIGHT...

➤ Sakura goes out shopping with Fai. It seems that she's become very comfortable living life in the Country of Ôto.

◀ As the Cat's Eye café becomes more and more popular, Sakura becomes much busier. But can she become a good waitress soon enough?

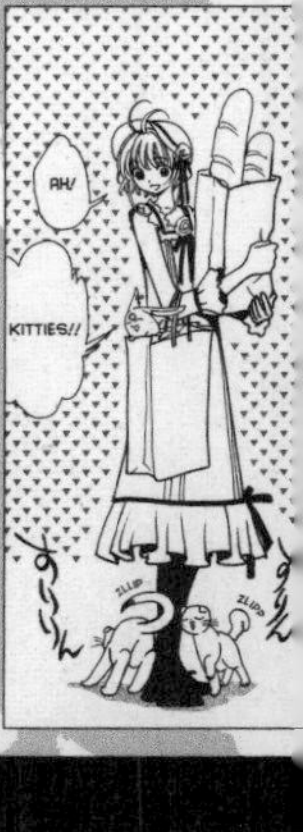
AH!
KITTIES!!

TOPIC 1

Lost Memories

Sakura had emotions that she kept safe within her heart, emotions that were the most important in the world to her. But now, she can't even remember that she had feelings she treasured.

TOMORROW...I'LL TELL HIM! TELL SYAORAN...THAT I LOVE HIM!

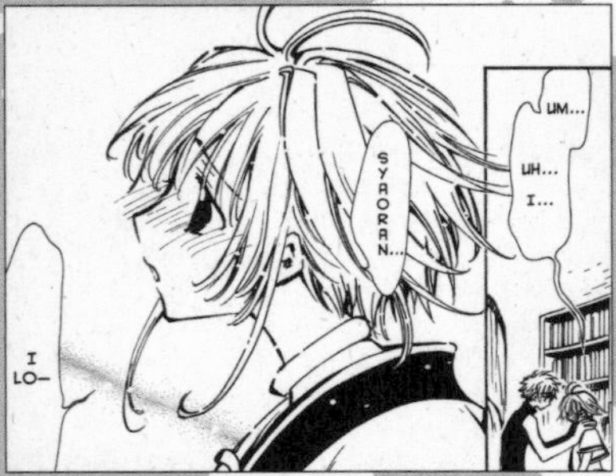
UM...
UH... I...
SYAORAN...
I LO—

Sakura promised herself that next time she'd be sure to tell Syaoran about her feelings for him. But before she can, her memory feathers get scattered throughout the worlds.

Now the question is when will the next time that Sakura can say, "I love you," to Syaoran actually be?

COULD IT BE THAT EVER SINCE SHE WAS A LITTLE GIRL, SHE FELT THAT HE WAS A VERY IMPORTANT PERSON TO HER...?

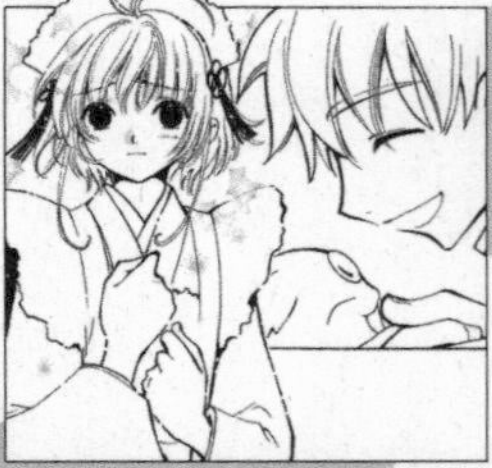

She tries to remember her relationship with Syaoran, but she always quickly forgets it.

Just the sight of Syaoran, who risks his life for her, makes Sakura's heart tremble. But her memories of her past with him will never return.

THERE WAS NOBODY THERE, BUT I WAS SO HAPPY...!

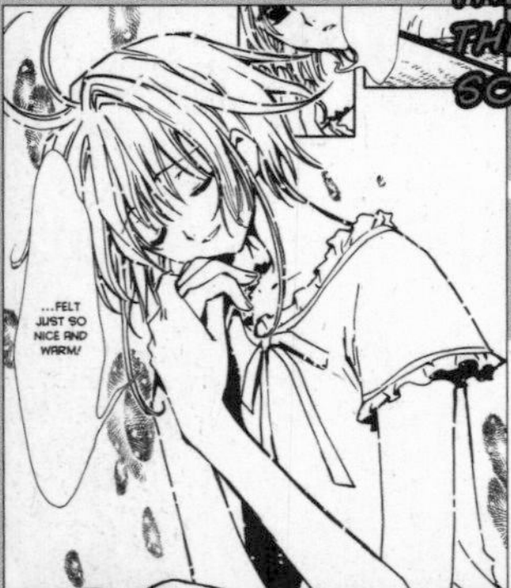
...FELT JUST SO NICE AND WARM!

Although the memories in her head and heart have been lost, there are things that her body remembers. Her body will never forget when she was sick as a child, and Syaoran stayed by her holding her hand.

◀ The warmth of Syaoran remains on her hand, and it lends her peace of mind.

TOPIC 2

Unchanging Warmth

Even though she has lost her memories, her heart remains the same. Sakura still has a smile as warm as the sun and a kindness as strong as ever.

ANYTHING I CAN DO TO HELP, EVEN IF IT'S JUST A LITTLE, I WANT TO GIVE IT MY BEST!

AND SOME-DAY...
...IF ONLY JUST A LITTLE...
...I'D LIKE TO BEAR MY SHARE OF EVERYONE'S BURDEN AND...

Hoping that it will help everyone even a little, she washes dishes with gusto. Sakura tries to do her best at everything.

Sakura doesn't want to be saved all of the time. She wants to help any way she can. That straightforward heart of hers is the same one the citizens of the Kingdom of Clow fell in love with.

SYAORAN-KUN, SOMETIMES YOU REALLY...LOOK LIKE YOU'RE ALL ALONE.

Sakura can't just ignore people who are suffering from loneliness. That's the warmth of Sakura that years ago melted Syaoran's frozen heart, but even now, Sakura is trying to save Syaoran's heart from hardening.

DON'T BE LONELY, OKAY?

➤ Sakura worries because she can sense Syaoran's loneliness. Her eyes always turn to Syaoran.

A SMALL CHILD CAN TAKE SMALL STEPS. AND THOSE STEPS ARE BOUND UP IN DESTINY TO COME.

She has a straightforward attitude that trusts in the future. That's the basis of Sakura's kindness, and perhaps part of her strength.

Even after losing her memory, Sakura is always bright and optimistic. She may not be much in a battle, but her heart has strength to win against anyone.

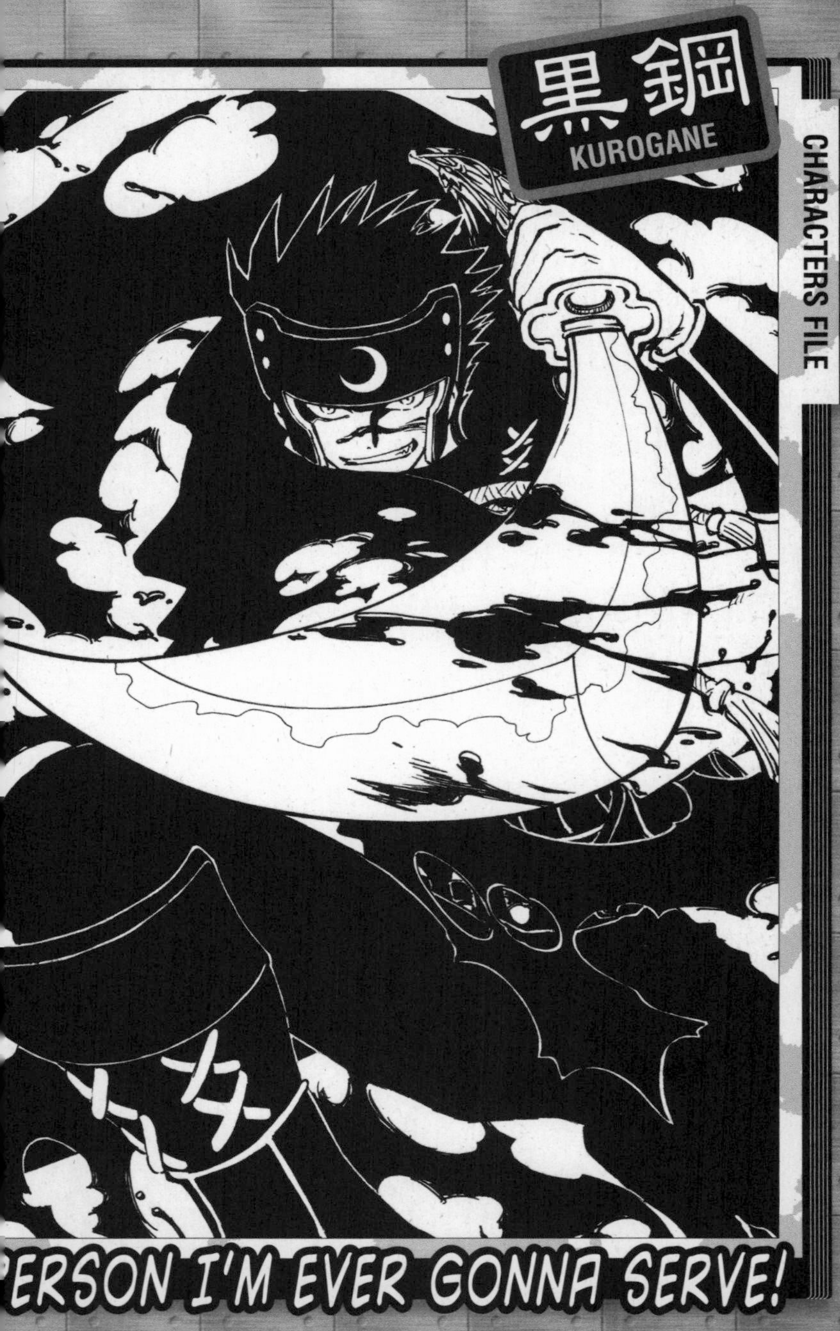
黒鋼
KUROGANE
CHARACTERS FILE
ERSON I'M EVER GONNA SERVE!

KUROGANE

> I GOTTA ADMIT IT. THIS AIN'T A BAD SWORD.

Kurogane is very strong in hand-to-hand combat, but the time he shows his greatest skills is when there is a sword in his hand. There is no enemy so strong they can't be defeated by Kurogane's sword.

PARAMETER

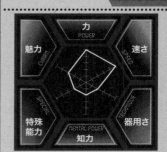

力 POWER
魅力 CHARM
速さ SPEED
特殊能力 SPECIAL
器用さ TECHNIQUE
知力 MENTAL POWER

Kurogane is originally a ninja, and because of that, he's the one among the party with the most battle experience. His senses are so peaked that he can determine his enemy's presence and abilities by sight alone.

Kurogane is the most accomplished ninja of the country, named Japan, that is ruled by Princess Tomoyo. And Kurogane has determined that Tomoyo is the only person he will ever serve under. He has a nearly unlimited number of special attacks such as Hama Ryū-Ō-Jin (Magic Wave: Dragon King Sword) among others, that make use of his sword. His one wish is to become stronger than anyone else, and that is why he never showed mercy or pity on the battle field. But the waste of life sickens Princess Tomoyo, and to chastise him for it, she sends him off to a different world. At the same time, she places a curse on him that with each person he kills, his strength will lessen. He's so blunt and tactless that he should probably stay away from human interaction, but when faced with a depressed Syaoran, his strict ways were able to offer encouragement in his own rough way, and there were other times when he allowed himself to show kindness.

> KANI-NABE SENKAI!*

*CRAB-POT REVOLUTION

As a ninja with incredible speed and agility, no normal attack can even touch him.

A little wall isn't much to Kurogane as a single punch turns it to rubble. There may be no one who can defeat Kurogane in a battle of strength.

IN MY LIFE, THERE'S ONLY ON

When
e met
yaoran
nd the
thers, all
e could
iink about
as getting
ack to his
ountry of
apan as
oon as
ossible.

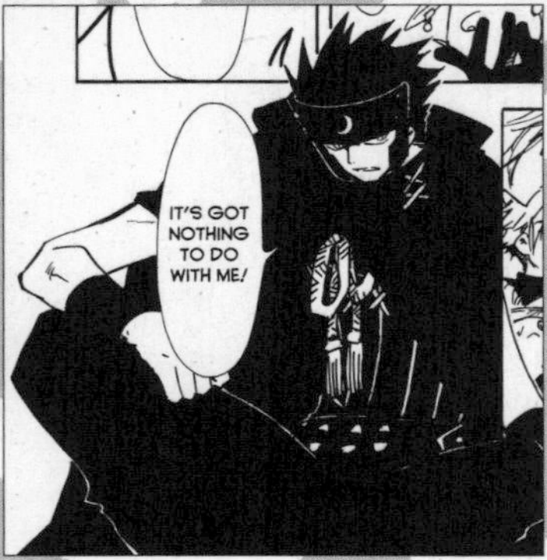
IT'S GOT NOTHING TO DO WITH ME!

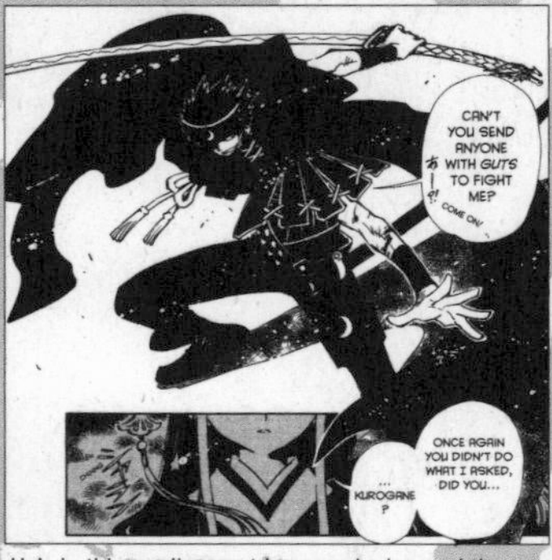
CAN'T YOU SEND ANYONE WITH GUTS TO FIGHT ME?
COME ON!
ONCE AGAIN YOU DIDN'T DO WHAT I ASKED, DID YOU...
... KUROGANE?

He's in this predicament because he ignored the princess's wishes and killed people one after another.

Kurogane's Journey Chronicle

THE COUNTRY OF JAPAN

- Was sent by Princess Tomoyo to the Time-Space Witch. At the same time, he was cursed such that if a person is killed, his skills will lessen.
- As part of the price for traveling worlds, handed over magic sword Ginryû to the witch. Began to travel with Syaoran, Sakura, Fai and Mokona on their quest to recover Sakura's memories.

HANSHIN REPUBLIC

- Visited Hanshin Republic. Took shelter with the married couple Sorata and Arashi Arisugawa.
- Was chosen by a level-one Kudan. Defeated enemy's Kudan using Hama: Ryû-Ô-Ken attack.

OUNTRY OF KORYO

- Visited the town of Ryonfi in the country of Koryo. Met Chu'nyan and took shelter in her house.
- Fought along with Fai against the Kiishim. Managed to overcome the magic illusions to triumph.

OUNTRY OF FOG

- Visited Country of Fog.

OUNTRY OF JADE

- Visited the town of Spirit in the Country of Jade. Took shelter with the town's doctor, Kyle Rondart.
- Sakura went missing.
- Participated in rescue of Sakura.

His Kudan turns into a large magic sword. It only takes one attack with the level-one Kudan to defeat his enemy.

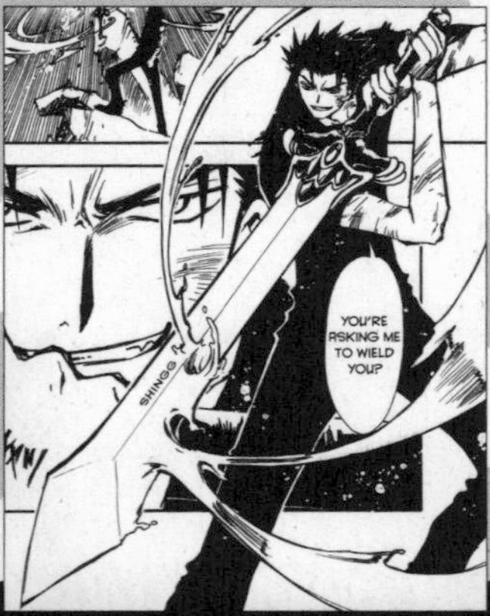
YOU'RE ASKING ME TO WIELD YOU?
SHINGG

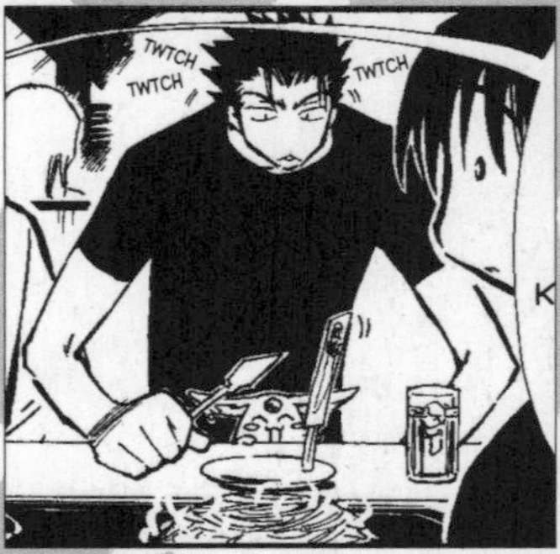
TWTCH
TWTCH
TWTCH

▲ Staring at the Okonomiyaki, Kurogane twitches with excitement. He has some unexpectedly childlike qualities.

KUROGANE

THE PEOPLE OF THE TOWN CERTAINLY THOUGHT THE STORY WAS REAL.
GRIN
DRIBBL DRIBBL

➤ In the Country of Jade, Fai's lie gives Kurogane the role of the hired help. But doesn't he seem to have too much dignity for hired help?

➤ Having grown up in a country that only uses chopsticks, Kurogane has great difficulty trying to eat with knife, fork and spoon.

I'M GLAD WE'RE IN, BUT...
HOW FAR IS THIS HALLWAY SUPPOSED TO GO?
WE'RE GONNA BE WALKING FOR A LONG TIME!

In the Country of Koryo, Kurogane was wounded by the Ryanban's magic. It's possible that magic and illusion are two of his very few weak points.

- Went to Tower of the Little People with Syaoran. Learned of the strongest Oni there.
- Learned that the Country of Ôto was a game in Fairy Park amusement park in the country of Edonis.
- Defeated Oni that attacked Cat's Eye using Tenma Shô-Ryû-Sen attack.
- Faced off in battle with Seishirô. The evenly matched battle becomes fierce.
- Left along with Syaoran, Sakura, Fai and Mokona for a new world.

COUNTRY OF ÔTO/EDONIS

- Visited Country of Ôto. Received cute nickname of "Big Puppy" from Fai. Understood that Syaoran had lost the use of his right eye. Began Oni-hunting with Syaoran.
- Was attacked by a swarm of Oni, but defeated them using Chi-ryû Chi-en-bu attack.
- Met Caldina and Oruha in the bar Clover. Learned information on the new kind of Oni.
- Began to teach Syaoran swordsmanship.
- Obtained sword Sôhi from swordmaker Chanan.

A LONG SWORD.
I SEE YOU ARE USED TO THEM.
IT IS NAMED SÔHI.
I DON'T SEE A NAME. HOW DO YOU KNOW?

Kurogane is able to get his hands on the long sword Sôhi. It seems to be a pretty famous sword.

➤ When Kurogane is faced with Oni in the Country of Ôto, he defeats them without hesitation.

➤ Neither Fai nor Syaoran know how to wear hakama, but people wear them in Kurogane's home country of Japan.

BUT KURO-RUN, I HAVE NO IDEA HOW YOU WEAR WHAT YOU'RE WEARING.
I'M AMAZED AT HOW FAST YOU WERE ABLE TO PUT IT ON.
THIS? IT'S A HAKAMA.

I JUST WANT TO GET STRONGER! STRONGER THAN ANYONE ELSE!

Kurogane thinks of a strong enemy only as a chance to make himself even stronger. And so the stronger the enemy, the happier Kurogane is.

With his sure-fire attack, Hama Ryū-Ō-Jin, he cracks the hard shell of his enemy's Kudan and sends it down to defeat. Nothing can defeat Kurogane's sword.

A man like Kurogane who lives to battle knows that a weapon is a tool for killing. And so anyone who carries one must be prepared for the consequences.

In battle even an instant's hesitation can mean life or death. So if anyone points a weapon at him, he will take out the threat without a second's pause.

IF YOU'RE GONNA CARRY A WEAPON, THEN YOU CAN'T COMPLAIN IF YOU DIE.

The people Kurogane hates most are people who don't try to live by their own power.

> THE ONES I HATE MOST IN THE WORLD ARE THE GUYS WHO STILL HAVE LIVES TO LIVE, BUT THEY DON'T MAKE ANY EFFORT TO LIVE THEM!

IF THERE'S SOMEPLACE YOU WANT TO GO, YOU SHOULD JUST GO THERE.

People have to decide for themselves what path they have to go down. That's what Kurogane has always done. Kurogane's strength is the power of a man who has freely decided what life he wants to live.

TOPIC 1

An Unwavering Strength

Kurogane was a man with the single-minded purpose of getting stronger. Relying solely on his own power, he never knew the meaning of the word doubt.

KUROGANE

One can wallow in one's sadness, but that won't change anything. Become strong enough to carve your own way through fate. That is Kurogane's advice for Syaoran.

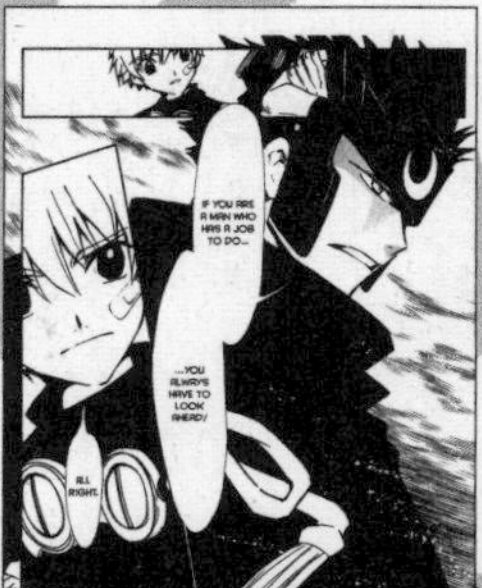
IF YOU ARE A MAN WHO HAS A JOB TO DO...
...YOU ALWAYS HAVE TO LOOK AHEAD!
ALL RIGHT.

Syaoran was depressed when Sakura didn't recognize him. But he received new determination through Kurogane's words.

IF YOU DON'T WANT TO CRY THEN MAKE YOURSELF STRONGER!

Kurogane isn't one to become anyone's best buddy, but he certainly isn't made of ice. He may say, "It's got nothing to do with me," but he'd never allow his fellow travelers to be harmed if he can help it.

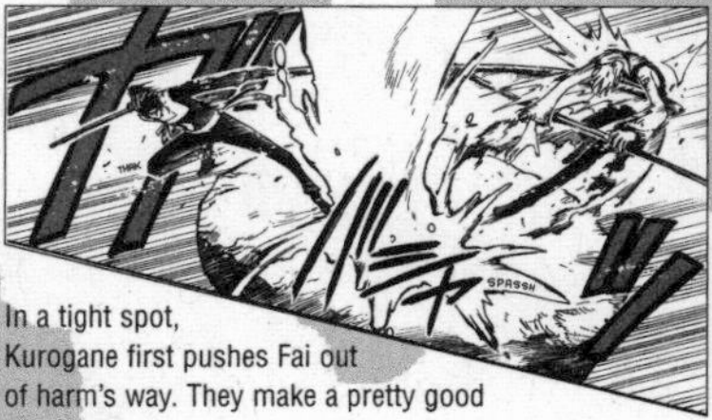
THNK
SPASSH

In a tight spot, Kurogane first pushes Fai out of harm's way. They make a pretty good combination.

IF I DIDN'T PUSH YOU, YOU'D BE MELTED BY NOW!

YOU'LL FEEL MY SWORD!!

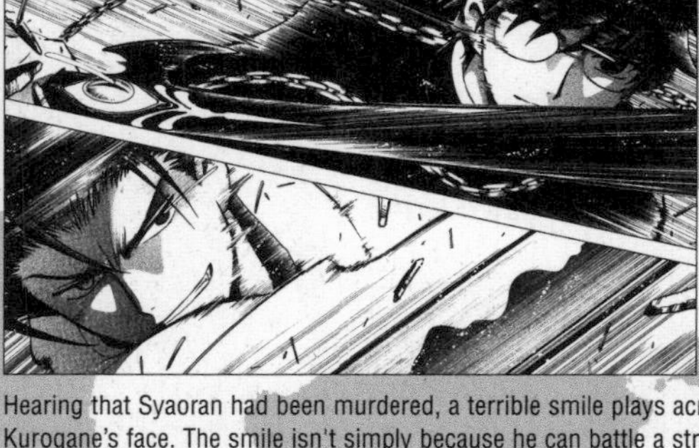

Thinking that Seishirô killed Syaoran and Fai, Kurogane unleashes his sword on him.

Hearing that Syaoran had been murdered, a terrible smile plays across Kurogane's face. The smile isn't simply because he can battle a strong enemy, but more because he feels "something" more fierce and more sublime.

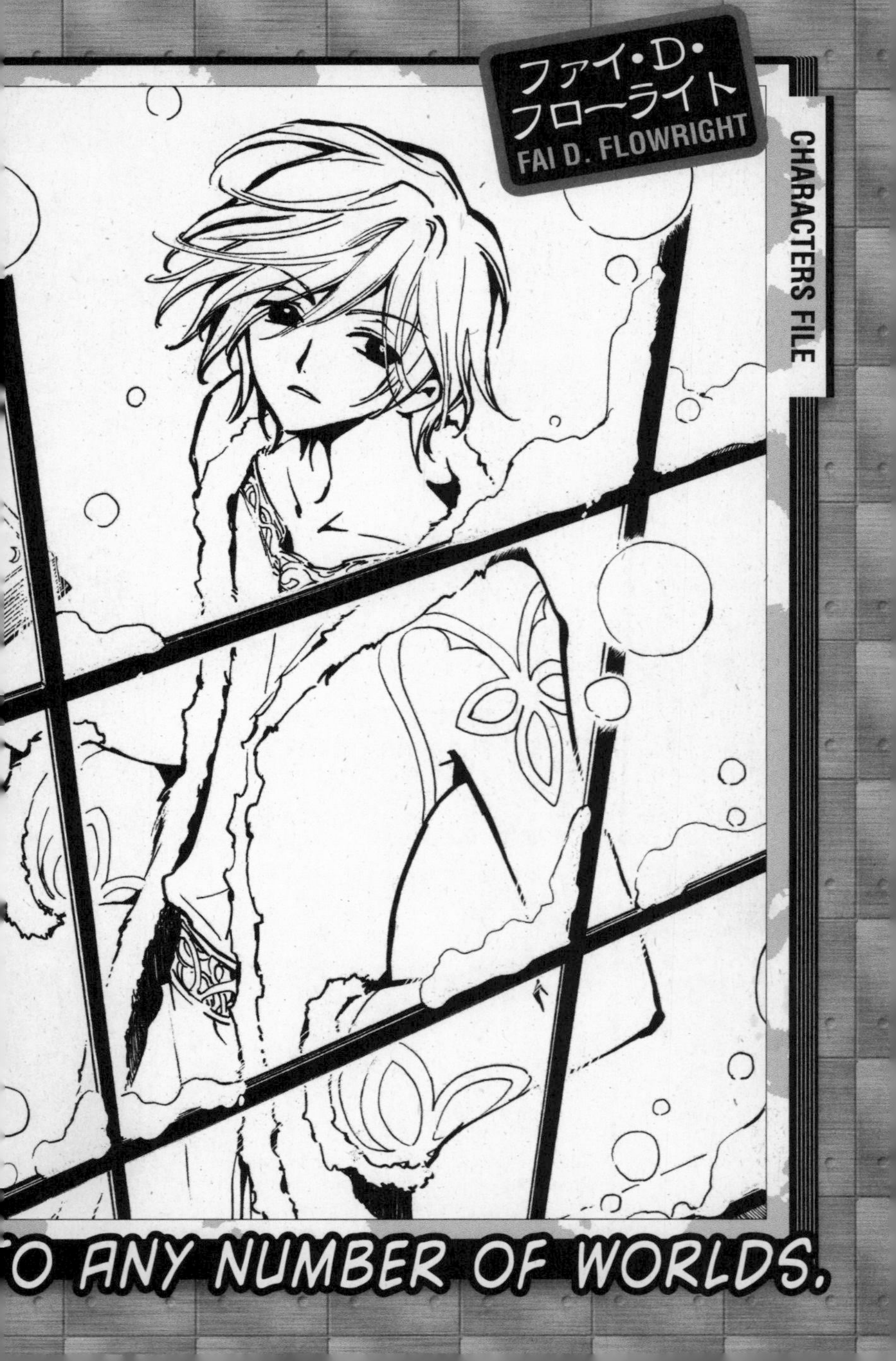
ファイ・D・
フローライト
FAI D. FLOWRIGHT
CHARACTERS FILE
TO ANY NUMBER OF WORLDS.

FAI D. FLOWRIGHT

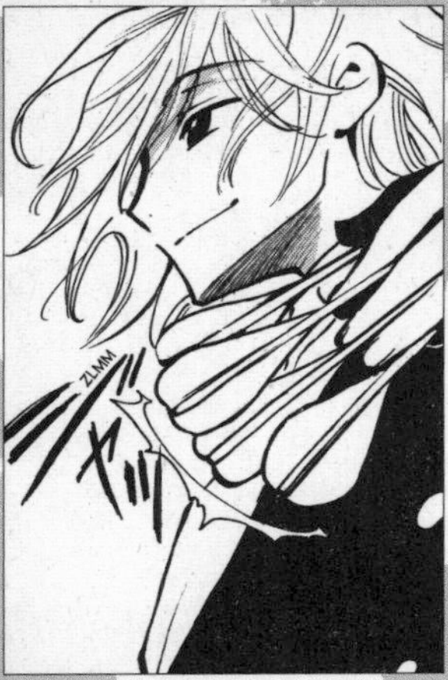
ZLMM

He never seems to show his true power, but even so, he has the skill in battle to drive back the average enemy.

PARAMETER

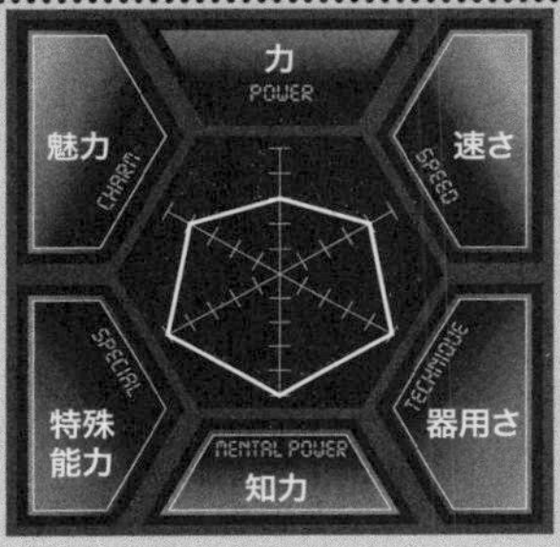
力
POWER
速さ
SPEED
器用さ
TECHNIQUE
知力
MENTAL POWER
特殊能力
SPECIAL
魅力
CHARM

Fai does not display any powers, but he can handle himself in many situations. He has all of the knowledge of a wizard, and he has another side that's good at cooking and art.

Fai is the wizard of the snowy land, the Country of Seresu. The facts are sketchy, but something put King Ashura into a deep sleep, and he felt the need to escape to the world of the Time-Space Witch. In order to run from King Ashura, he joined Syaoran's group to travel from world to world. He includes himself easily in plans, and he has a casual, talkative style, but under his quick smile his true heart sometime peeks out from where it is hidden. He has made a vow not to use magic when he gave away his markings as his price to travel worlds. Even in deep trouble, he keeps his vow. But whether the reason for that has to do with King Ashura remains shrouded in mystery.

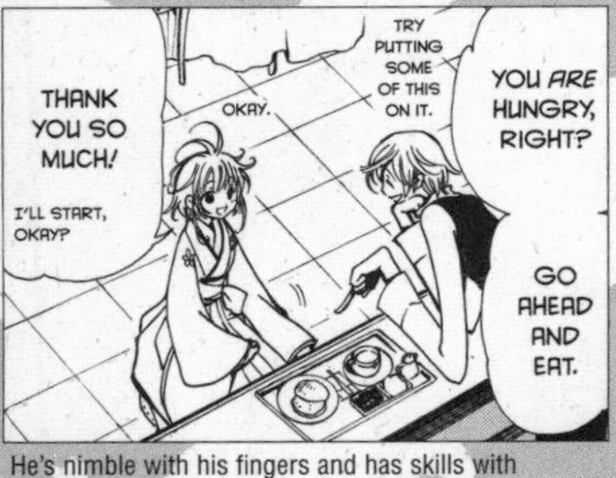
YOU ARE HUNGRY, RIGHT?
TRY PUTTING SOME OF THIS ON IT.
OKAY.
THANK YOU SO MUCH!
I'LL START, OKAY?
GO AHEAD AND EAT.

He's nimble with his fingers and has skills with cooking and art. He has a special reputation with chocolate cake.

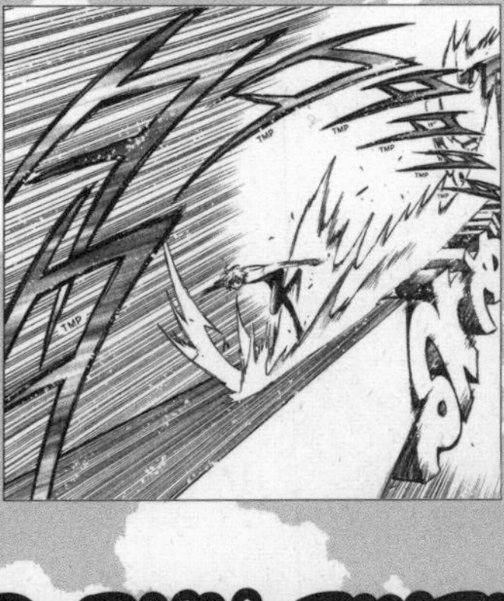
TMP
TMP
TMP
TMP

He seems very used to battle, so he's handy in a fight. He even avoids the attacks of Primela's special-leve Kudan's attacks with ease.

I HAVE TO RUN AWAY..

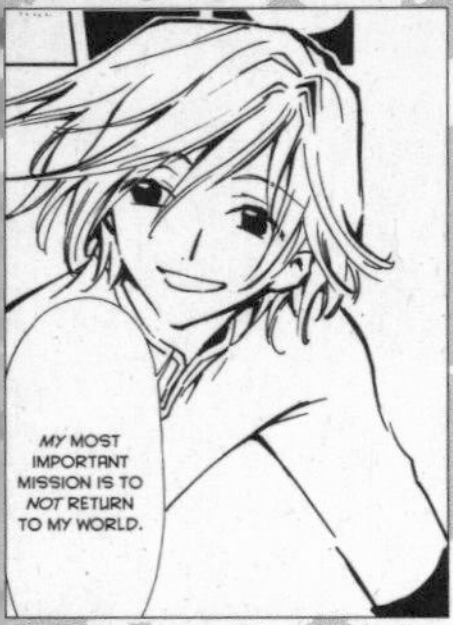
MY MOST IMPORTANT MISSION IS TO *NOT* RETURN TO MY WORLD.

Aside from never returning to the Country of Seresu, there doesn't seem to be anything special he wants to do.

He is able to travel to another world under his own power, and using that ability, he travels to the world of the Time-Space Witch. One can only assume that it takes a lot of power to do that.

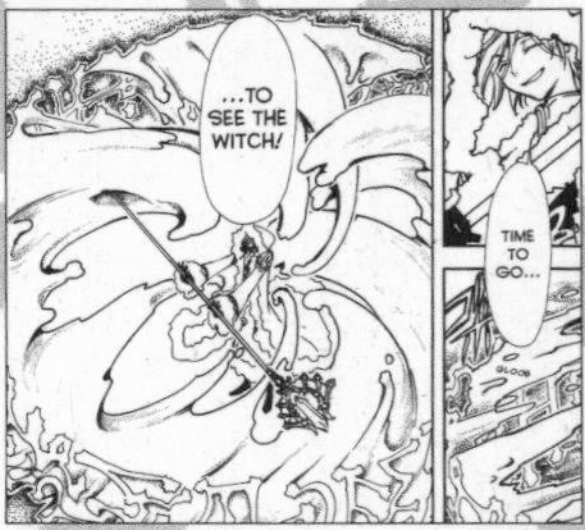
TIME TO GO...
...TO SEE THE WITCH!

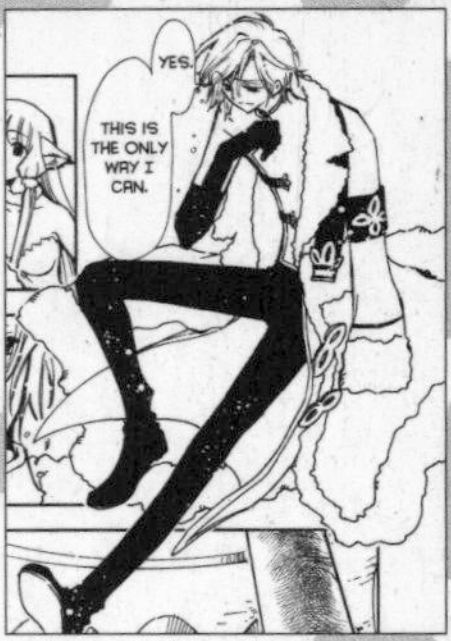
YES.
THIS IS THE ONLY WAY I CAN.

Fai deep in thought. The question is, what was he thinking when he went to visit the witch?

Fai's Journey Chronicle

THE COUNTRY OF SERESU

- Went to the Time-Space Witch by own power in order to go to worlds where King Ashura does not exist.
- As part of the price for traveling worlds, handed over his markings to the witch. Began to travel with Syaoran, Kurogane, Sakura, and Mokona on their quest to recover Sakura's memories.

HANSHIN REPUBLIC

- Visited Hanshin Republic. Discovered the first memory feather on Syaoran's clothes. Took shelter with the married couple Sorata and Arashi Arisugawa. Began giving Kurogane unusual nicknames.
- Battled Primela.

OUNTRY OF KORYO

- Visited the town of Ryonfi in the country of Koryo. Met Chu'nyan and took shelter in her house.
- In order to combat the magic of the Ryanban, paid to the Time-Space Witch the price of his magical staff.
- Fought along with Kurogane against the Kiishim. Although in life-threatening situation, refused to use magic. Assisted Kurogane in overcoming the magic illusions to triumph.

OUNTRY OF FOG

- Visited Country of Fog.

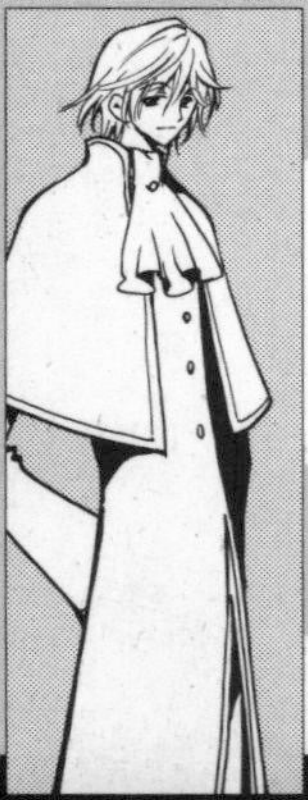

➤ Wearing his new clothes in the Country of Jade, if one didn't know better one would say he's some kind of aristocrat.

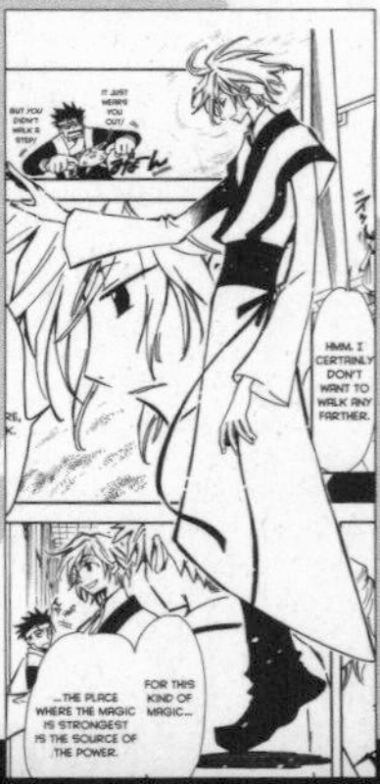
HMM, I CERTAINLY DON'T WANT TO WALK ANY FARTHER.
FOR THIS KIND OF MAGIC...
...THE PLACE WHERE THE MAGIC IS STRONGEST IS THE SOURCE OF THE POWER.

➤ In the Country of Koryo, Fai quickly saw through the magical trap that the Ryanban set. The group can count on his abilities.

➤ Fai wanders through their first world the group visits, the Hanshin Republic, and he blends easily into the scenery.

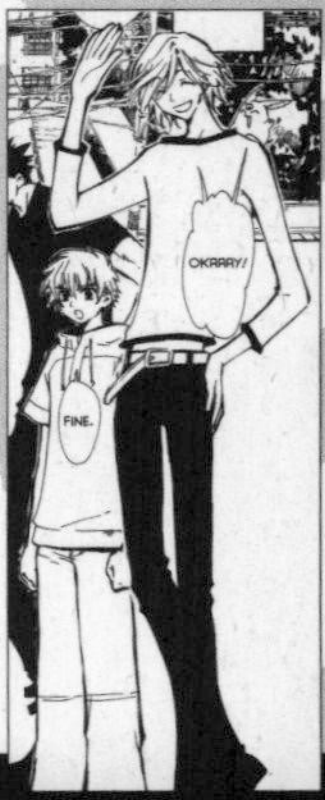
OKAAAY!
FINE.

FAI D. FLOWRIGHT

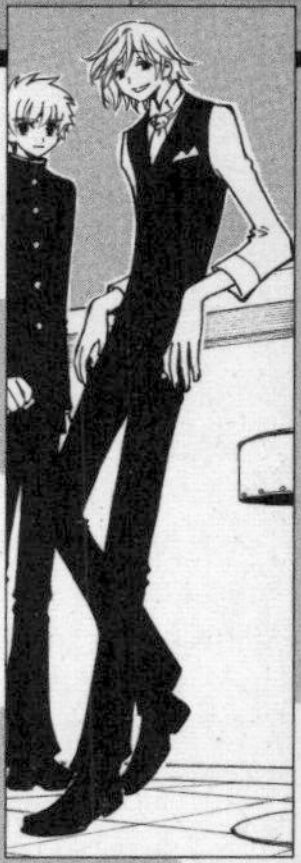

➤ Since he is a skilled cook and good with people, Fai makes the perfect owner of a café.

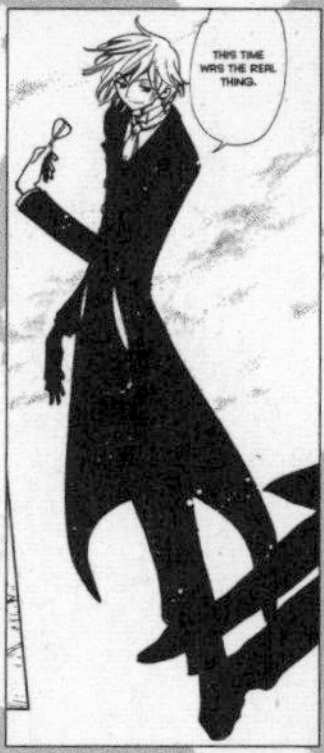
THIS TIME WAS THE REAL THING.

⮜ He can take down an enemy with an elegant toss of a dart. It isn't just magic—he also has great skills in battle.

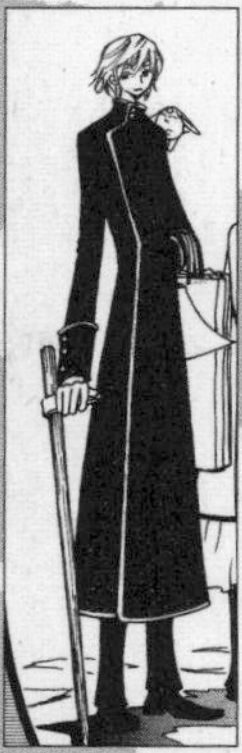

Fai's left leg is injured in a fight with the Oni. It is that wound that cost him his life in the battle with Seishirô.

- Battled Seishirô. Despite battling a very dangerous opponent, did not use magic and thus was defeated. Was drawn out of the Country of Ôto.
- Met Syaoran and Chitose in Edonis. Learned that someone is interfering.
- Due to the power of the memory feather, Seishirô mixes the game world with reality.
- Left along with Syaoran, Sakura, Kurogane and Mokona for a new world.

COUNTRY OF JADE

- Visited the town of Spirit in the Country of Jade. Took shelter with the town's doctor, Kyle Rondart.
- Sakura went missing.
- Helped rescue Sakura

COUNTRY OF ÔTO/EDONIS

- Visited the Country of Ôto. Separated group into puppies and kitties and named them. Together with Sakura, opened the Cat's Eye café and began work.
- Battled group of Oni. Injured left leg.
- Met Caldina and Oruha in the bar Clover. Learned information on the new kind of Oni.

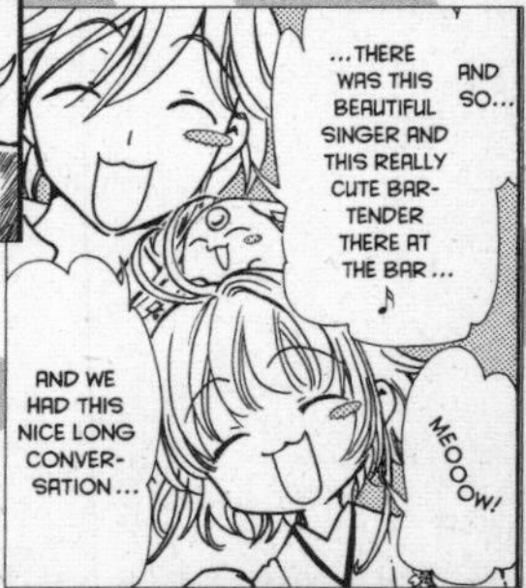
AND SO...
...THERE WAS THIS BEAUTIFUL SINGER AND THIS REALLY CUTE BAR-TENDER THERE AT THE BAR... ♪
MEOOOW!
AND WE HAD THIS NICE LONG CONVER-SATION...

➤ Fai drinks the hard stuff with Sakura and Mokona. Could it be that Fai gets drunk easily?

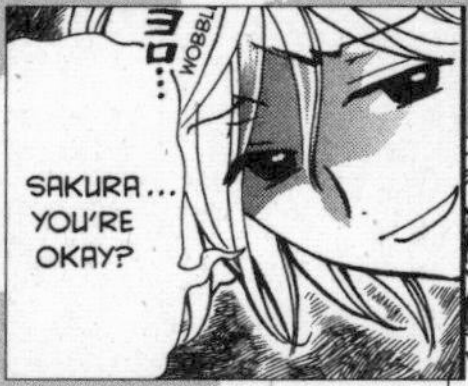
WOBBL...
SAKURA... YOU'RE OKAY?

⮝ Fai suffering from a hangover. It's odd to see him looking so under the weather.

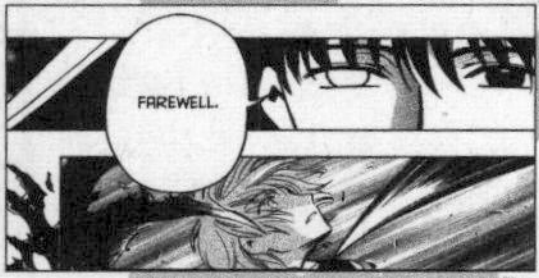
FAREWELL.

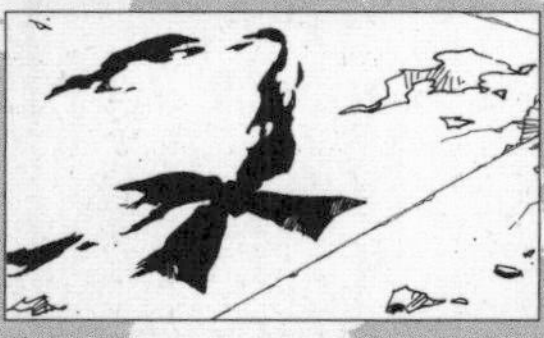

⮝ Fai defeated by Seishirô. Is his vow not to use magic more important than his life?

TOPIC 1

Witty Bearing

Fai is always smiling, but he very rarely shows his true feelings. However, that smile may be a mask that hides a deep sadness in his heart.

WHAT'S THIS "PUPPY PAIR" THING...?!

Fai uses words on Kurogane that grade-schoolers use to make crybabies cry, proving that Fai has no fear for his life. Kurogane loses control around him.

KURO-WOOF-WOOF! PLEASE BRING THE BAG!
QUIT CALLING ME LIKE I'M SOME KIND OF DOG!!
JIKK

Fai gets his fun from giving Kurogane all kinds of nicknames. Kurogane seems annoyed by it, but...

I'D SAY OUR SITUATION IS SERIOUS.

THIS WATER... HURTS, DOESN'T IT?
THAT'S 'CAUSE WHATEVER IT HITS, IT MELTS. CLOTHES... SKIN...

When he says the situation is serious, it's probably life and death.

YOU SEE...
...I DON'T DIE VERY EASILY.

No matter how dire the circumstances, Fai never seems to lose his smile. He'll probably smile even in the moment he loses his life.

ME? I ALWAYS HAVE FUN.

The look that Fai gives to Mokona shows a sadness that normally one couldn't imagine from him. Fai's true feelings appear for just an instant.

YEAH... THAT'D BE NICE.

➤ It'd be nice if Fai lost some of his sadness little by little during the journey, but...

FAI D. FLOWRIGHT

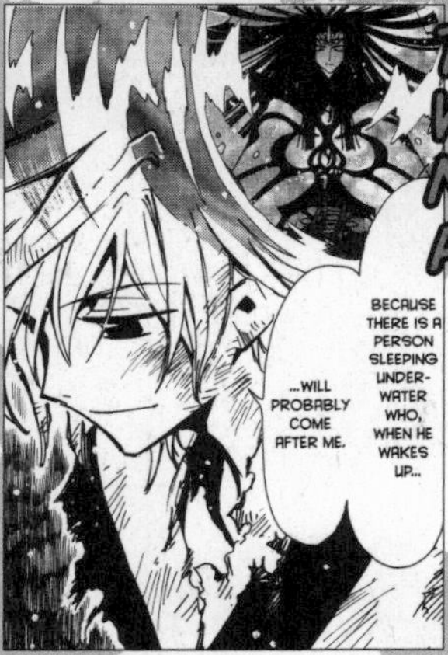
BECAUSE THERE IS A PERSON SLEEPING UNDER-WATER WHO, WHEN HE WAKES UP...
...WILL PROBABLY COME AFTER ME.

TO SOME WORLD WITH NO KING ASHURA.

Unlike Syaoran and Kurogane, Fai travels between worlds by his own choice. Why did he throw everything away to run…? Only he knows for sure.

➤ There seems to be some big secret between Fai and King Ashura.

I DECIDED THAT WITHOUT IT, I WON'T USE MAGIC.

Even when in life-or-death danger, Fai will never use magic. It's there where one senses a strong, unwavering will within Fai.

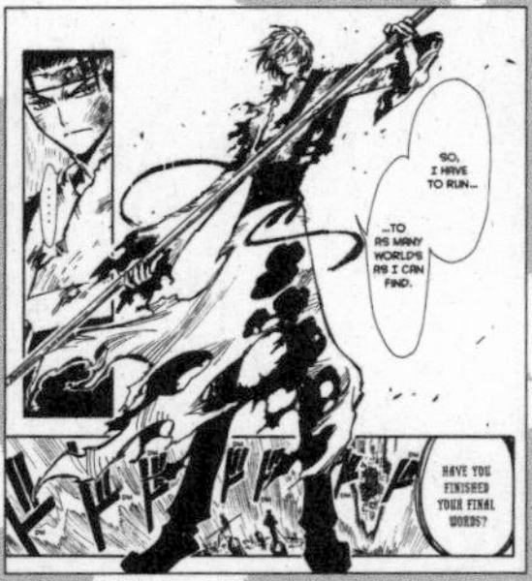
SO, I HAVE TO RUN...
...TO AS MANY WORLDS AS I CAN FIND.
HAVE YOU FINISHED YOUR FINAL WORDS?

His markings were supposed to hold his magic in check. If he were finally to use his magic, how powerful would he be?

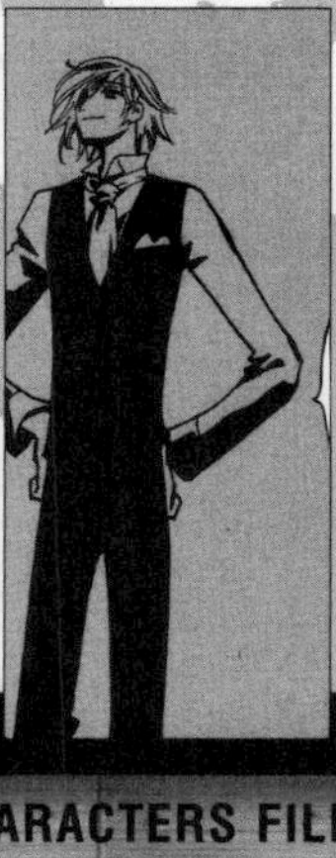

Unlike Kurogane who is always straightforward, a lot of times Fai's words contains some sort of hidden meaning.

I WAS A GUY WHO ALWAYS WAITED FOR THE ONE WHO WOULD TAKE ME ALONG.

Even though he has the power to travel to another world, Fai always waited for someone to go with him. Who was Fai waiting for, and where did he want to go?

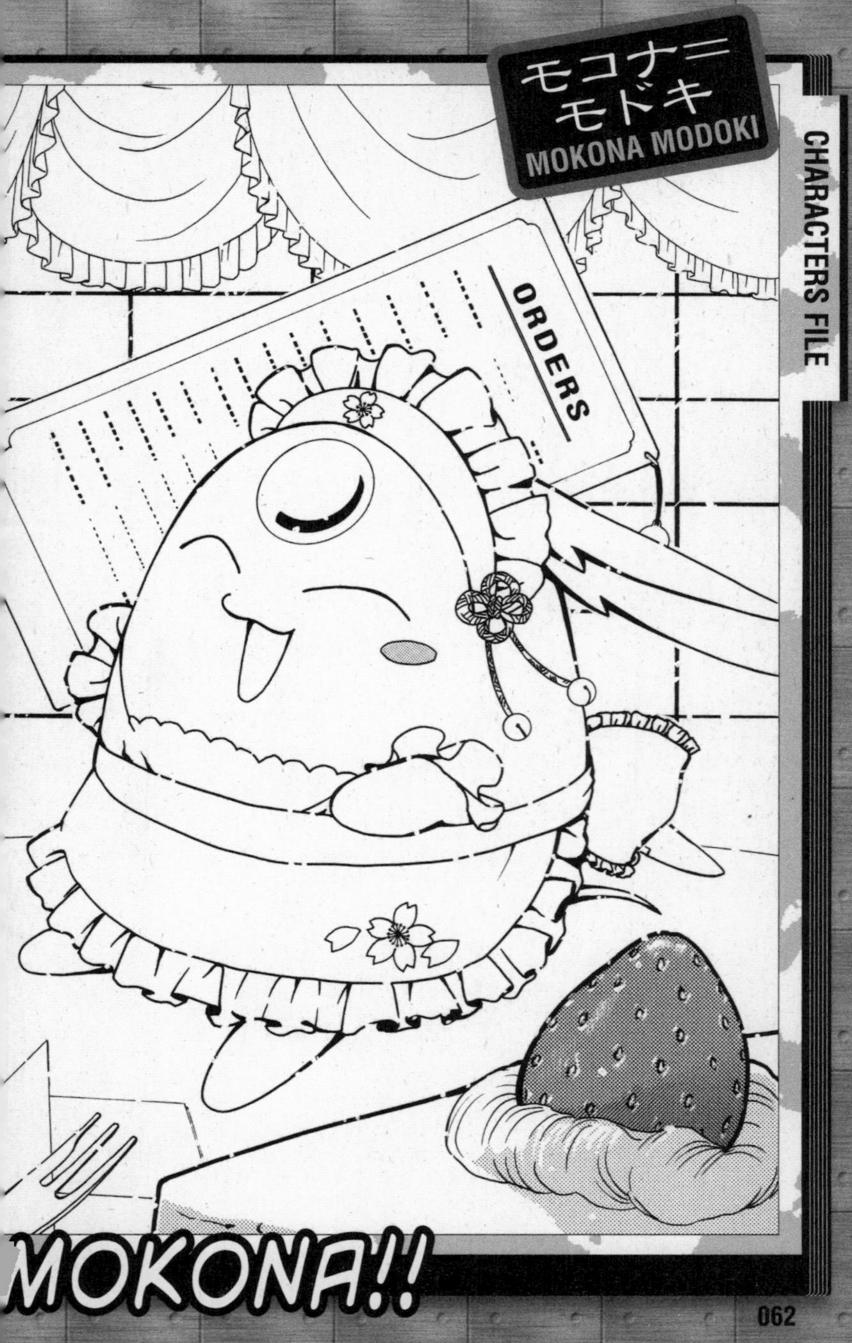
モコナ=モドキ
MOKONA MODOKI
CHARACTERS FILE
ORDERS
MOKONA!!

MOKONA MODOKI

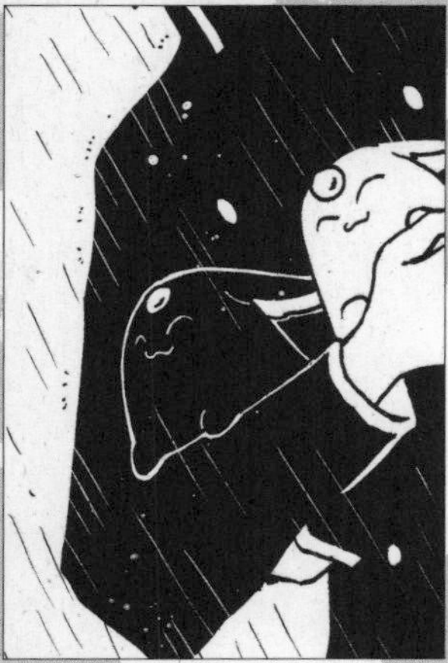

Black Mokona is exactly like White Mokona except for the color. Their personalities as jokers are the same for both Mokona.

PARAMETER

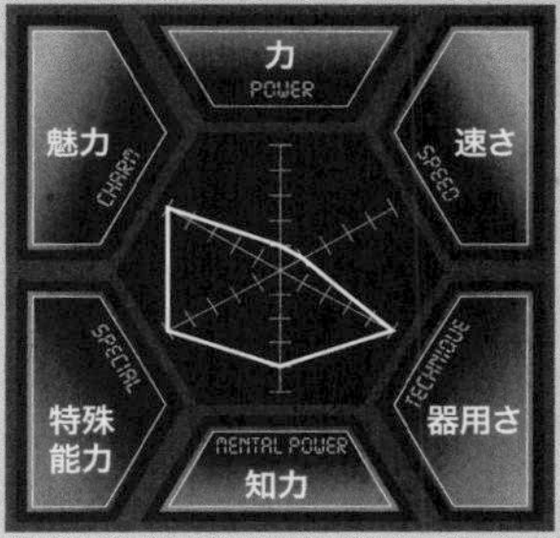

力
POWER
速さ
SPEED
器用さ
TECHNIQUE
知力
MENTAL POWER
特殊能力
SPECIAL
魅力
CHARM

Without Mokona, the journey to different worlds would not be possible. Mokona is the party's mascot character and reflects the party's mood.

In exchange for their "most valuable items" paid by Syaoran, Kurogane and Fai, they received from the Time-Space Witch a strange life form—a glutton who sees very little other than good food. Aside from transporting Syaoran's group from world to world, Mokona can also sense Sakura's feathers; automatically translate languages to something understandable; and perform other odd tasks. With a natural charm and love of fun, Mokona is a "mood maker" that can turn the most painful of worlds into something bright. There is another Mokona with a blue earring and black fur, but that has different powers such as communications and the ability to see spirits.

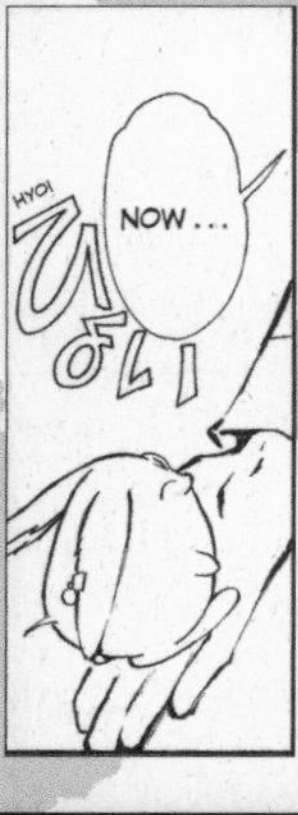

NOW...
HYO!

➤ Cute Mokona is such an attraction to the girls from other worlds! But the people of the country of Koryo had the opposite reaction. They thought Mokona was just odd.

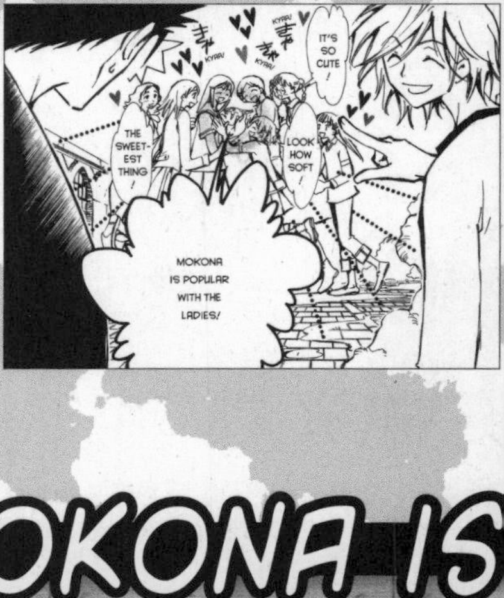

IT'S SO CUTE!
KYAA
KYAA
KYAA
LOOK HOW SOFT!
THE SWEET-EST THING!
MOKONA IS POPULAR WITH THE LADIES!

⮜ Mokona is about the size of the palm of a hand. Its soft-to-the-touch feel and round form is why it is sometimes called the "white pork bun."

MOKONA IS

YOU'RE BOTH LATE!!
ZOOM
AW, SHADDUP!
IT SEEMS THAT QUITE A BIT HAS GONE ON HERE.
SORRY.

◄ It seems to have taken a fancy to Kurogane. It does body attacks and teases him.

Mokona was abducted along with Masayoshi by the fans of Primela and taken to the top floor of Hanshin Castle. Masayoshi was so afraid, he was in tears, but for some reason Mokona was happy. Maybe it likes heights.

ぷらーん
BURUUUUM
きゃっ
KYAA!
きゃっ
KYAA!
うわーん
WAAAAAH!!

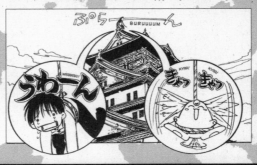

Mokona's Journey Chronicle

OUNTRY OF FOG

- Visited Country of Fog. Used secret techniques of imitating voices and Super Dramatic Power.

OUNTRY OF JADE

- Visited the town of Spirit in the Country of Jade. Took shelter with the town's doctor, Kyle Rondart.
- Used Secret Technique, Super Disguise to uncover Kyle's plot.

OUNTRY OF ÔTO/EDONIS

- Visited the Country of Ôto. Together with Sakura, helped out at the Cat's Eye café.
- Left along with Syaoran, Sakura, Kurogane, and Fai for a new world.

JAPAN

- Began to travel with Syaoran, Kurogane, Sakura and Fai on their quest to recover Sakura's memories.

HANSHIN REPUBLIC

- Visited Hanshin Republic. Took shelter with the married couple Sorata and Arashi Arisugawa. Was petted by a bunch of cute female students.
- Along with Masayoshi, was kidnapped by Primela.

COUNTRY OF KORYO

- Visited the town of Ryonfi in the country of Koryo. Met Chu'nyan and took shelter in her house. Exchanged Fai's staff for an item to combat the magic of the Ryanban.

PAT PAT

Mokona takes care of Syaoran after he was injured in his fight with Oni. Its tender care is so cute to see!

Mokona wears a tiny apron and works alongside Sakura to help out at the café Cat's Eye. Mokona may be small, but it can help with a lot of things.

IT'S CALLED FONDANT AU CHOCOLAT!
THERE'S CHOCOLATE INSIDE!
YOU EAT IT HOT.
REALLY!
HER TIMING IS PERFECT!
LET'S ALL HAVE SOME!
THE TEA IS READY, TOO!
POFF

CHARACTERS FILE

MOKONA MODOKI

MOKONA IS ACTIVELY INVOLVED TOO!

Translation

When Mokona is not in the vicinity, Syaoran's party can no longer talk with each other.

Senses Memory Feathers

AND MOKONA WILL BE LIKE...
GAK!
...THIS!!

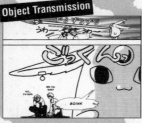

When Mokona senses the waves coming from a memory feather, its eyes go "BOINK," and become very large. It's such an odd look that everyone is startled.

Object Transmission

ARE YOU SURE?
YES... I'M SURE.
BOINK

Dimension Travel

▲ Mokona has the power to travel between worlds. But there's no guarantee that they will find a world where there's a feather.

◄ Mokona can send things to the Time-Space Witch and receive things back from her as well. Even Fai's long staff.

Drama

SAKURA IS... !!

Syaoran was startled by Mokona's Super Dramatic Power. Even a star of a Hollywood movie would be surprised at Mokona's skill.

Voice Imitating

IT'S SCARY. VERY SCARY.
OOH! THAT MAKES KUROGANE SOOO HAPPY!! ♥
DON'T WORRY. I'M HERE TO HOLD YOUR HAND.

Mokona has the ability to imitate anyone's voice. It's used to tease Kurogane.

Understands Sadness

KNOWING WHEN SOMEONE IS SAD.
FAI, KUROGANE, SYAORAN...
...ALL ARE SOMEHOW SAD.

Mokona can tell when people are hiding sadness. Does seeing Mokona soothe people?

Disguise

MOKONA! YOU PLAYED THE CHILD'S PART?
IT'S ONE OF MOKONA'S 108 SECRET TECHNIQUES!
SUPER DISGUISE! ♥
Diagram

This technique fooled Dr. Kyle. Is there a person around who could see through this disguise?

CHARACTER'S ADVICE COLUMN

CAFÉ
Cat's Eye
猫の目
Hello, everyone! How are you all feeling? This is the café Cat's Eye, and I'm its owner. All kinds of customers come in and talk to me, so bring your worries to me, and we'll see if we can do something about them.

Fai's Comment

If you show him your heart, then I'm sure that at some point Kuro-run's heart will open up, too . . .

MOKONA

Kurogane isn't nice to Mokona at all! But Mokona still wants to be friends with Kurogane! What should Mokona do?!

MOKONA: "Mokona tries so hard to make friends with Kurogane, but Kurogane only calls Mokona names like 'that white thing,' or 'white pork bun.' Isn't that just awful?!"

FAI: "I see . . . If you show him your heart, then I'm sure that at some point Kuro-run's heart will open up too . . . I can teach you several methods that will accomplish that."

MOKONA: "Eh? What methods? What methods?"

FAI: "Method 1: When it's lunchtime, give him a present of a boxed lunch with the food arranged into a big heart.
Method 2: Give him a present of a hand-knitted scarf.
Method 3: Go to the baths with him and wash his back.
Method 4: Whisper sweet nothings in his ear while he's sleeping.
Method 5: Wake him up every morning with a big kiss."

MOKONA: "Yaay! Mokona's going to whisper sweet nothings!"

SAKURA: "(I feel sorry for Kurogane-san.)"

SORATA ARISUGAWA

My honey isn't showing how much she loves me.

Fai's Comment

Arashi-san is just shy. Get yourselves to where it's just the two of you.

SORATA: "When I try to show her how much I love her, Honey just puts me off. Could it be she doesn't love me anymore?"

FAI: "Don't worry! Arashi-san is just shy. Get yourself to where it's just the two of you alone, and then give her everything you've got all at once."

SORATA: "That makes sense! Honey! Here I come…!!" (thump, thump, thump.)

SYAORAN: "Fai-san, that advice you just gave…what do you base it on?"

FAI: "Hm? It's based on nothing more than a wild guess. Why do you ask?"

SYAORAN: "I wonder if things will work out okay…"

SAKURA

Why do I keep falling asleep all of the time?

Fai's Comment

Just don't worry about it. If you're sleepy, then just go to bed, right?

SAKURA: "But I'm even sleeping during the times when you all are fighting. I can't help but feeling that I'm a burden to you all."

FAI: "You've lost the feathers that make up your memory, and you fall asleep. What can one do? So Sakura-san, you should do the things that are necessary a little at a time, and you'll be fine!

SAKURA: "…okay…"

FAI: "And…if you try to do too much, Syaoran will start to worry about you."

SAKURA: "I guess that's true . . . (But I'd still like to be of more help to everybody…)"

Fai's Comment

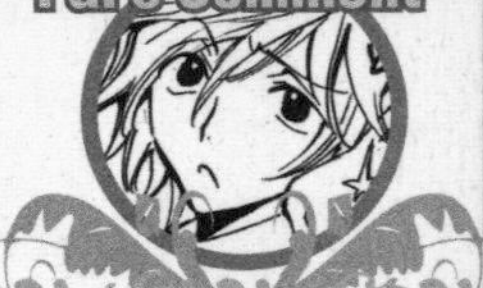

Make it your home and enjoy it. I'd say the best thing for you is to adapt to your situation.

FAI: "This came in as a letter. Kuro-tan? Can you read this?"

KUROGANE: "Let's see . . . This says, 'Scary woman,' and this says, 'lots,' and this one is, 'help me!' And it's from the Ryanban of Koryo."

FAI: "Ah, that man who was dragged into the Kiishim's world. But that Kiishim turned out to be beautiful, so . . . he's got a good deal there."

KUROGANE: "So, you're offering to change places with him?"

FAI: "Not a chance."

KUROGANE: "What kind of answer is that?!"

SYAORAN: "(How did that letter get delivered here…?)"

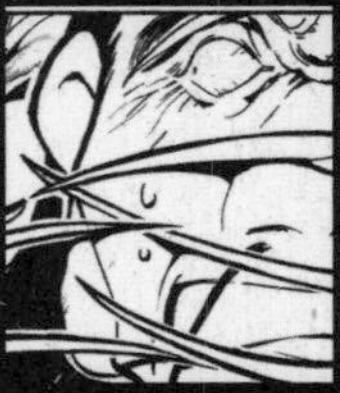

COUNTRY OF KORYO'S RYANBAN

I want to get out of this scary place and go back to my own world!

Fai's Comment

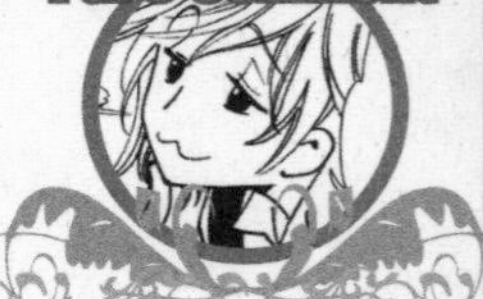

Let's keep the overprotectiveness to a minimum, shall we?

FAI: "So tell me, why is it that you don't like the boy? Is he actually a bad kid?"

TÔYA: "Well…he's sort of a hard worker, kind of serious, and a little considerate…"

FAI: "Those are the qualities of a good kid, right?"

TÔYA: "I wouldn't mind him so much if he'd stay away from my sister."

FAI: "Tôya-san, you really care for your sister quite a bit, huh? But if you do that in the real world, they tend to call it a 'sister complex,' don't they?"

TÔYA: ". . . Just shut up!"

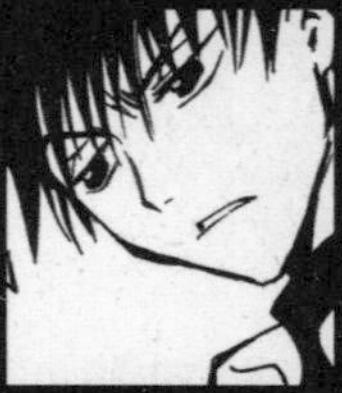

TÔYA

There's this brat who is always hanging around my little sister, and I can't stand him.

Fai's Comment

Perhaps it's time to turn this over to Master Kuro-rin.

SYAORAN: "I'll need to battle strong fighters like Seishirô-san in the future. How do I become strong enough?"

FAI: "Hm…How does a person become stronger? Well, Kuro-rin?"

KUROGANE: "The thing you're gonna have to do is intense practice. The only other thing is find strong opponents, fight them, and gain experience."

FAI: "Isn't there any quicker way to do it?"

KUROGANE: "No! Don't be stupid! If you don't put in your practice and get some experience under your belt, you'll never get any stronger!"

SYAORAN: "I understand. Please teach me as much as possible."

SYAORAN

I want to become much stronger than I am.

Fai's Comment

Those are signs of affection! It's your job to embrace them with all of your heart!

KUROGANE: "There's this guy who went and called me 'Kuro-run!'"

FAI: "The only reason for that is the person is showing you how much he loves you!"

KUROGANE: "I don't need 'love' like that!"

FAI: "You see, that person simply wants to call you a name that is prettier than Kurogane. So from now on, your name will be Kuro-pii!"

KUROGANE: "Listen, creep! Have you heard a word I said?!"

FAI: "Oh, then you'd rather be called Kuro-ron?"

KUROGANE: "Quit calling me names!"

KUROGANE

There's this creep who keeps calling me annoying names all of the time.

TSUBASA MINI REPORT ②

CLAMP Character Appearances

That Character Is Here?!

MINI REPORT

In Tsubasa, CLAMP characters from other series appear here and there in this story. In this section, we'll find some of those characters in unexpected places.

Vol. 6
P. 139

As Syaoran can sense, there are three people near him, but can he sense that they're CLAMP characters?

WHY DID YOU SUDDENLY...
MY HOUSE.
WHERE ARE...
Vol. 3
P. 30

The magazine that Kurogane's reading, Shonen Maganyan, has a CLAMP character on its cover.

EXCUSE ME!
あ
AH!
Vol. 6
P. 153

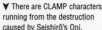

▲ There seems to be quite an age difference between the couple there at Cat's Eye. The girl has a lot more pep than the man.

CHATTER
CHATTER
SORRY TO KEEP YOU WAITING...
TUNK
Vol. 6
P. 152

These two Cat's Eye customers seem to be sisters. Cat's Eye is still a small establishment, but some precocious customers are coming.

▼ There are CLAMP characters running from the destruction caused by Seishirô's Oni.

Vol. 7
P. 116

➤ The character that Chu'nyan summoned in this image is the hero Ryûô from his original universe.

Vol. 7
P. 45

▼ The two who were defeated by Seishirô's Oni are, in fact, also CLAMP characters.

IT'S ONLY A HA-LEVEL ONI!
WHY IS IT SO STRONG?!
Vol. 6
P. 156

WORLD GUIDE

In the worlds that appear in Tsubasa, each has a unique culture and climate such that no two worlds will be alike. Let's look into the worlds that Syaoran's group goes to and the people that they meet.

WHAT COUNTRY HAVE WE COME INTO THIS TIME?

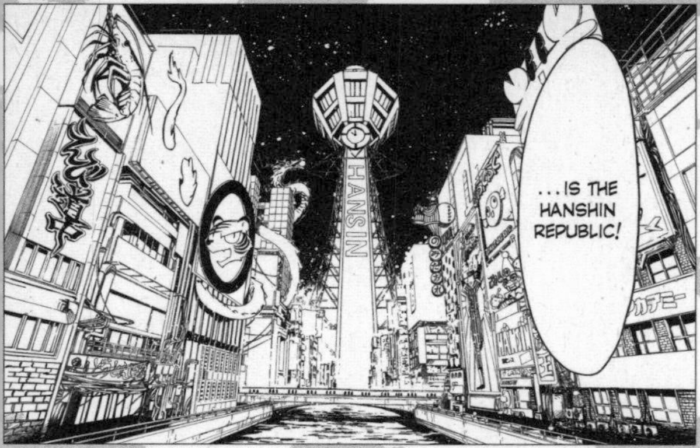
HANSIN
...IS THE HANSHIN REPUBLIC!

Hanshin Republic

For their initial journey, the first country that Syaoran's group visits is a peaceful island nation surrounded by the high seas. The island is vaguely in the shape of a tiger, so it attained the name Country of the Tiger, and it was highly involved in trade with other countries. Many of its people are enthusiastic, passionate, and reluctant to admit defeat. It is very similar to the atmosphere one finds in Osaka of the real-world Japan.

KUDAN

Every person in the world is bestowed with a unique power. It is a thing that is controlled through the strength of one's heart. The person with the stronger heart has a higher level Kudan attached.

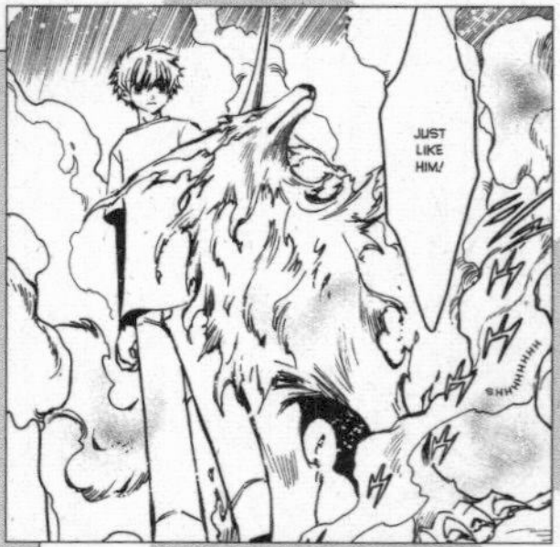
JUST LIKE HIM!

The average person receives anything from fourth level to special level Kudan.

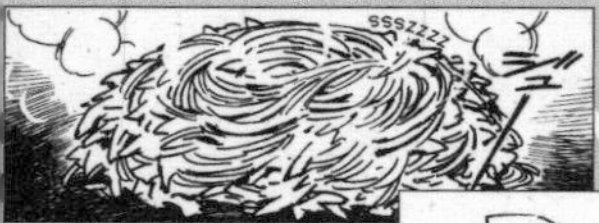
SSSZZZZ

➤ There's Okonomiyaki with lots of cabbage.

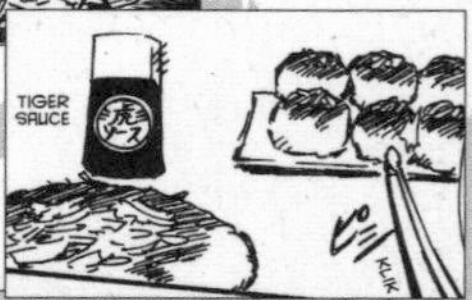
TIGER SAUCE
KLIK

➤ There's also Takoyaki, fried octopus treats eaten with brown sauce.

SPECIALTY FOODS

The most famous product is brown sauce, and the main ingredients of their diet are wheat-based, so the specialty foods are Okonomiyaki and Takoyaki among other foods. In the shopping districts, there are many Okonomiyaki restaurants.

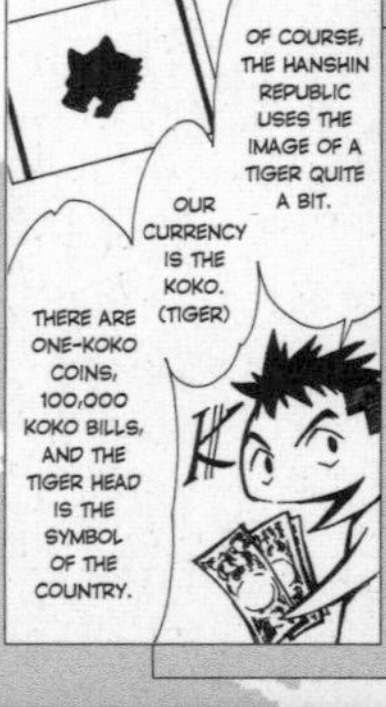
OF COURSE, THE HANSHIN REPUBLIC USES THE IMAGE OF A TIGER QUITE A BIT.
OUR CURRENCY IS THE KOKO. (TIGER)
THERE ARE ONE-KOKO COINS, 100,000 KOKO BILLS, AND THE TIGER HEAD IS THE SYMBOL OF THE COUNTRY.

CULTURE

Like its other name, Country of the Tiger, implies, there are a lot of things in the country that sport the symbol of the tiger. The basic unit of currency is the Koko (Tiger), and the symbol of the country's baseball team is the tiger.

A large street in the middle of the busy shopping district. The roads running between the buildings are well planned and equipped so that it is an easy place to walk.

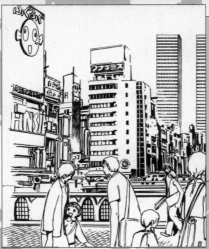

SHOPPING DISTRICT

There are a huge number of tall buildings with bright signs, intermixed with row after row of smaller buildings. There are plenty of people on the walkways that lead to all sorts of stores in the shopping district, but every now and again groups of young people meet in a battle for territory. When day turns to night, the beautiful neon sparkles over the city.

EMPTY ROOM IN SORATA AND ARASHI'S APARTMENT BUILDING

The married couple Sorata and Arashi Arisugawa manage a *gejuku* apartment building. The building itself looks a little old from the outside, but because of Arashi's good management, living there seems like it would be very comfortable. At the time Syaoran and his group arrive, there were several open rooms.

I DOUBT WE'LL FIND ANY MORE IN OUR CLOTHES.
BUT MY QUESTION IS HOW CAN WE FIND THEM NOW...
MUDGE MUDGE
...NEW FEATHERS.

➤ The room Syaoran's party is staying in features Japanese-style *tatami* mats.

➤ The building is situated near the shopping district.

HANSHIN CASTLE

Hanshin Castle is located only a few subway stops down the line from the shopping district, and it is registered as a national treasure and a popular tourist spot. Close by is the Hanshin Dome where the popular sports teams play and where idols hold sold-out concerts.

➤ It's treasured as a historic building... or at least it should be...?

有洙川空汰&有洙川嵐
SORATA ARISUGAWA & ARASHI ARISUGAWA

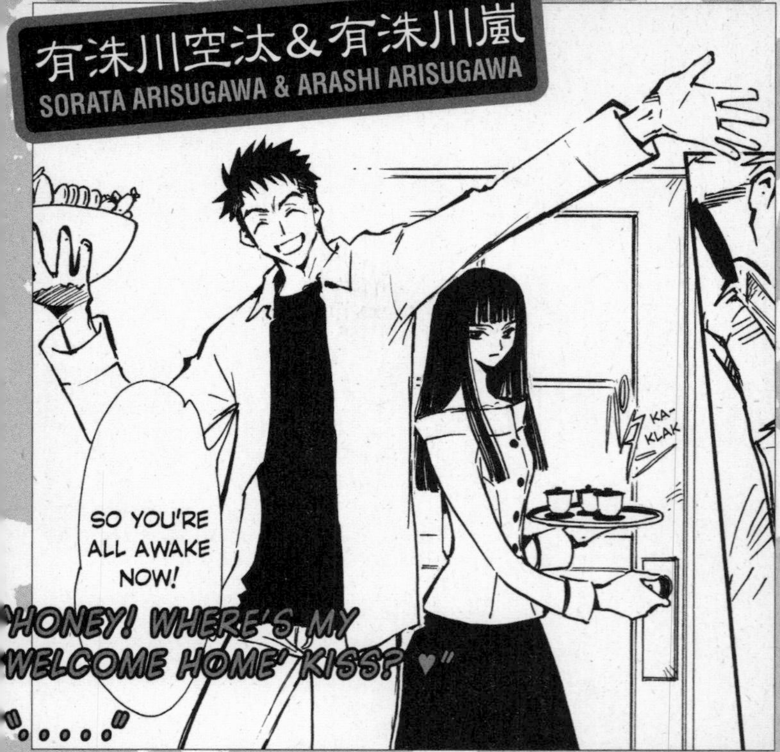
KA-KLAK
SO YOU'RE ALL AWAKE NOW!
"HONEY! WHERE'S MY 'WELCOME HOME' KISS? ♥"
"....."

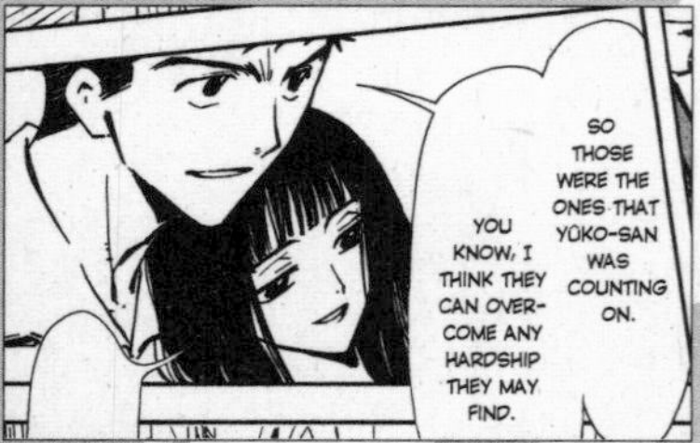
SO THOSE WERE THE ONES THAT YÛKO-SAN WAS COUNTING ON.
YOU KNOW, I THINK THEY CAN OVER-COME ANY HARDSHIP THEY MAY FIND.

▲ Arashi sometimes shows a contented look next to Sorata. Usually she acts cool toward him, but that may just be out of shyness.

A married couple who manage an old "*gejuku*" style apartment building. They're friends of the Time-Space Witch, Yûko, and they try to do their best to help Syaoran's group. Sorata feels very romantic towards Arashi, and even though Arashi is very cool toward him, her actions show that she cares for him too. Actually they're a couple that gets along very well.

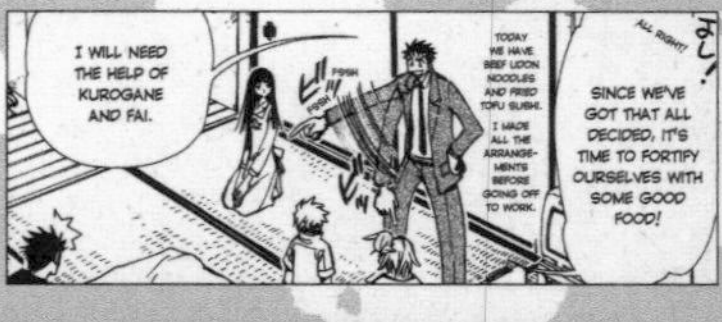
ALL RIGHT!
SINCE WE'VE GOT THAT ALL DECIDED, IT'S TIME TO FORTIFY OURSELVES WITH SOME GOOD FOOD!
TODAY WE HAVE BEEF UDON NOODLES AND FRIED TOFU SUSHI.
I MADE ALL THE ARRANGE-MENTS BEFORE GOING OFF TO WORK.
I WILL NEED THE HELP OF KUROGANE AND FAI.

➤ They split up the housework.

TOPIC 1

Sorata is a history teacher

IT'S MY BELIEF THAT KUDAN ARE AKIN TO GODS IN THIS NATION.

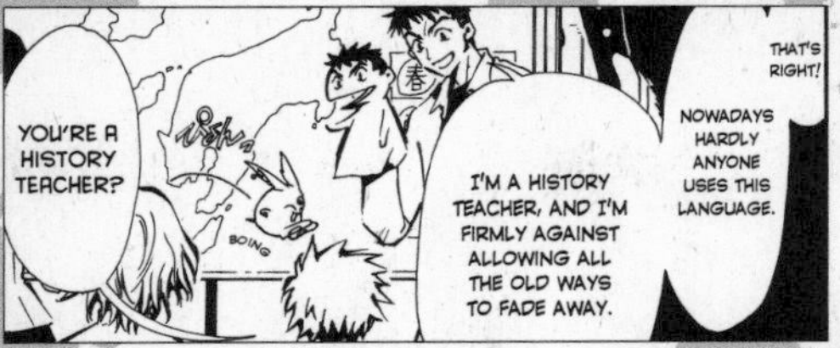
YOU'RE A HISTORY TEACHER?
BOING
I'M A HISTORY TEACHER, AND I'M FIRMLY AGAINST ALLOWING ALL THE OLD WAYS TO FADE AWAY.
NOWADAYS HARDLY ANYONE USES THIS LANGUAGE.
THAT'S RIGHT!

▲ Sorata's accent is an ancient dialect that was spoken in the country long ago. It sounds a lot like the dialect spoken in Osaka today.

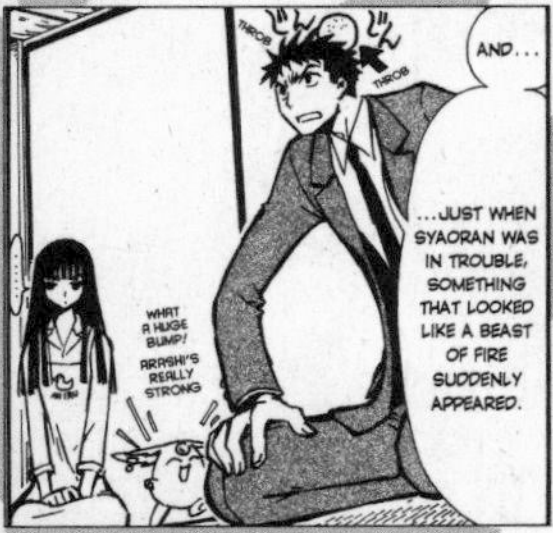
AND...
...JUST WHEN SYAORAN WAS IN TROUBLE, SOMETHING THAT LOOKED LIKE A BEAST OF FIRE SUDDENLY APPEARED.
THROB
THROB
WHAT A HUGE BUMP! ARASHI'S REALLY STRONG

◄ As a teacher, he wears a proper suit and tie on days he commutes to school. But true to his personality, he doesn't necessarily keep it buttoned.

Even though he has a sunny disposition that is a little over the top, Sorata is actually a history teacher. He has knowledge of not only his country's history, but also geography. We see him doing his best to help and take care of Syaoran and his group, but he has another side as a popular teacher with quite a few loyal students.

TOPIC 2

Before marriage Arashi was a Shinto *miko* priestess

I PRAY YOU FIND ONE OF SAKURA'S FEATHERS IN YOUR NEXT WORLD.

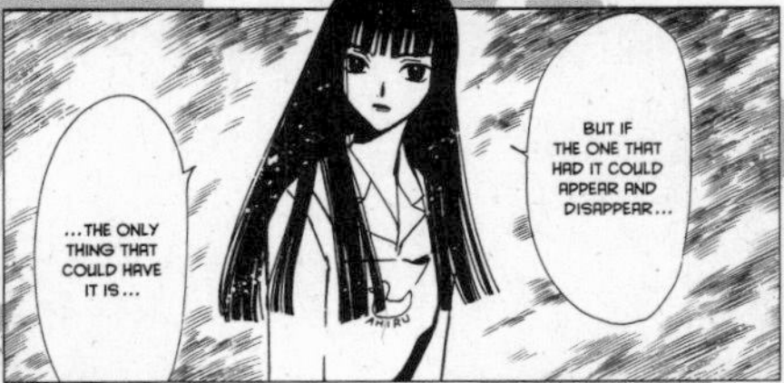
BUT IF THE ONE THAT HAD IT COULD APPEAR AND DISAPPEAR...
...THE ONLY THING THAT COULD HAVE IT IS...

▲ With her penetrating intuition, she becomes aware of something that turns out to be an important clue. Her intuition could stem from her spiritual powers.

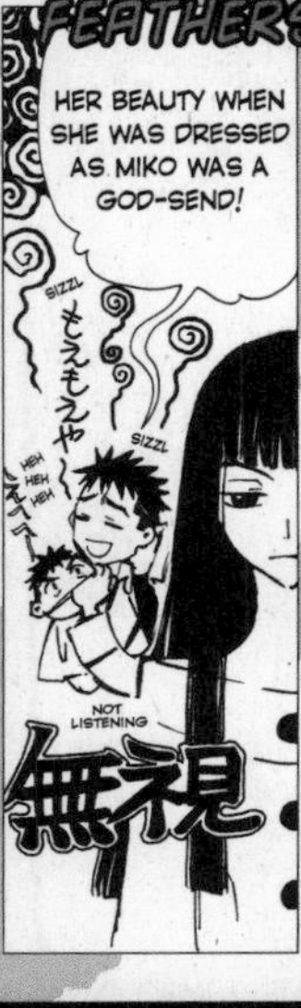
HER BEAUTY WHEN SHE WAS DRESSED AS MIKO WAS A GOD-SEND!
SIZZL
もえもえや
SIZZL
HEH HEH HEH
NOT LISTENING
無視

◄ When Sorata is at his most romantic, Arashi ignores him in splendid fashion. But even in that, Arashi shows her charm.

Arashi is a very beautiful *gejuku* apartment manager. Before marriage, she was a Shinto *miko* priestess, and even now, she still controls quite a lot of spiritual power.

There are many teams of young men fighting for territory in the Hanshin Republic's shopping district. Shôgo is one such team leader. He displayed an interest in Syaoran and the Kudan that attached itself to him saying, "I like your style." But because of those words, Syaoran and his group got themselves involved in a lot of trouble.

浅黄笙悟
SHÔGO ASAGI

I WANTED TO TRY TO TAKE YOU ON IN A BATTLE WITH OUR KUDAN.

PARAMETER

	力 POWER	
魅力 CHARM		速さ SPEED
特殊 能力 SPECIAL	知力 MENTAL POWER	器用さ TECHNIQUE

He doesn't have any abilities that especially stand out, but the balance makes him very strong. His special abilities come from the fact that he has a special-level Kudan attached.

I'D HOPED TO MEET YOU IN OTHER PLACES THAN JUST BATTLE.

I WANTED TO GUIDE YOU AROUND TOWN A BIT.

PRIMELA WAS DISAPPOINTED, TOO.

A pretty good guy who was involved in Syaoran's Kudan battle. If they had spent more time together, they might have become friends.

TOPIC
The Goggle Team Leader

Shôgo is the leader of a team that uses goggles as their trademark, and he has the strength of heart to have a special-level Kudan attached. As such, he is very popular with his members. Although there are many rival teams ready to challenge him, he doesn't take up the challenge all that often since he is kept busy helping out at his family's liquor store.

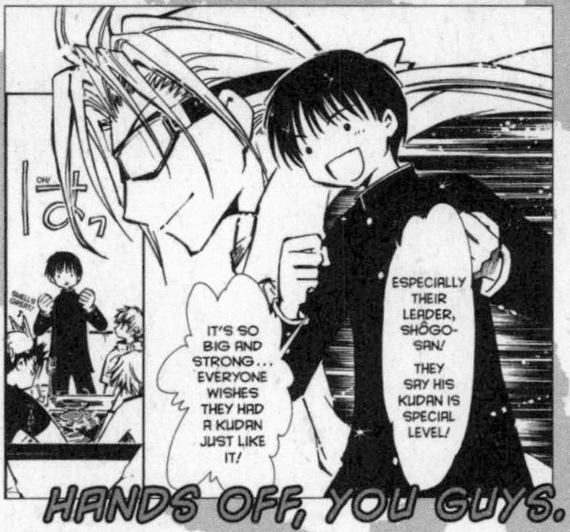
ESPECIALLY THEIR LEADER, SHÔGO-SAN!
THEY SAY HIS KUDAN IS SPECIAL LEVEL!
IT'S SO BIG AND STRONG... EVERYONE WISHES THEY HAD A KUDAN JUST LIKE IT!
HANDS OFF, YOU GUYS.

➤ There are many people who look up to Shôgo because he is strong, cool, and doesn't resort to doing evil things.

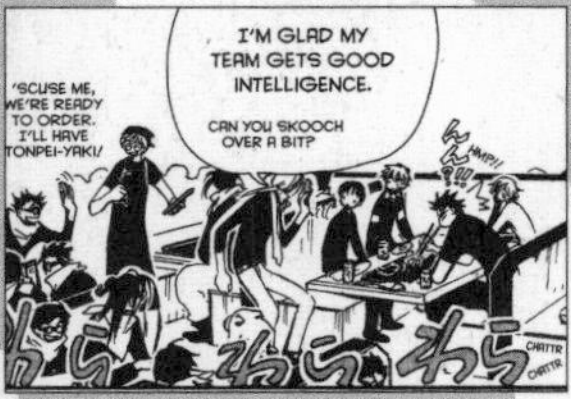
HMP!!
I'M GLAD MY TEAM GETS GOOD INTELLIGENCE.
CAN YOU SKOOCH OVER A BIT?
'SCUSE ME, WE'RE READY TO ORDER. I'LL HAVE TONPEI-YAKI!
CHATTR
CHATTR

➤ There are a lot of strong members on the team that Shôgo leads. He has a wide variety of people on his side, and that's how he gathers information.

TOPIC
A Special-Level Water Kudan

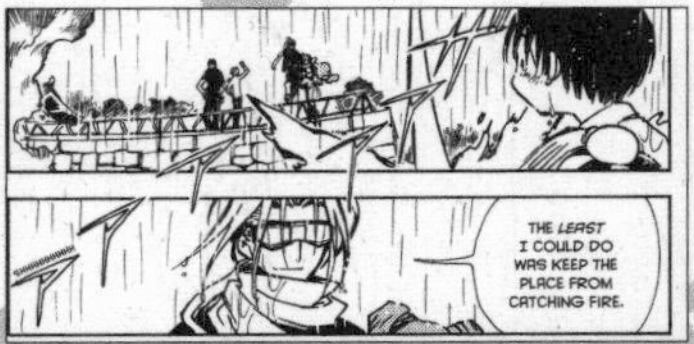
THE LEAST I COULD DO WAS KEEP THE PLACE FROM CATCHING FIRE.

➤ It can make water fall from the sky like rain, and that power keeps the fire caused by Syaoran's Kudan from spreading.

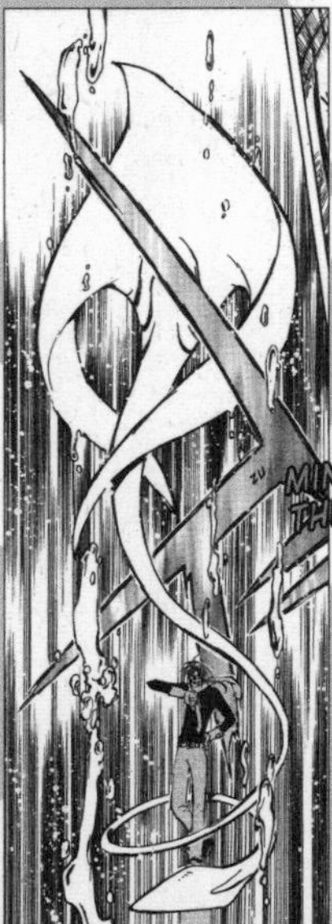
MINE WORKS WATER AND YOURS FIRE. THIS WILL BE INTERESTING.

➤ There seems to be no connection between the strength of a Kudan and its size, but Shôgo's Kudan is pretty big. Especially with its long tail, when it's taken as a whole, it can be counted as being very sizable.

Shôgo's special-level Kudan has a shape like a ray and has the power to control water. It has perfect control to attack with a shot of water akin to a deluge or protect from others' attacks using a wall of water. Maybe it's the strength of his Kudan, but Shôgo seems to love Kudan battles. However with the very limited number of people with special-level Kudan, he seems to want to finally battle someone stronger than himself.

斉藤正義
MASAYOSHI SAITÔ

Masayoshi is a young man whom Syaoran saved from a dangerous situation, and in return he offers to help in the search for Sakura's feather. He's a little preoccupied with the fact that his weak will has attached a weak Kudan to him, and he wishes he were more like Shôgo.

I WANT TO BE STRONGER!

PARAMETER

力
POWER
速さ
SPEED
器用さ
TECHNIQUE
知力
MENTAL POWER
特殊
SPECIAL
魅力
CHARM

He's really a pretty ordinary boy, and so he doesn't have any standout abilities. He has the special ability of having a Kudan attached, but it isn't particularly strong.

GWRRRM

➤ It can't find them if the person is too far away, but it can walk through walls as it leads Masayoshi on its search.

MY KUDAN IS FOURTH LEVEL—THE VERY BOTTOM.

TOPIC

A Kudan that Looks Just Like Him

The level of Masayoshi's Kudan is the very lowest level, a fourth-level Kudan. Its form looks very similar to Masayoshi himself and its size is approximately the same as well. It has no strong attack abilities, but if it meets someone once, it has the special ability to find that person again no matter where the person is.

ALL THE FANS LOVE ME!

プリメーラ
PRIMELA

Primela is a very popular idol and a childhood friend of Shôgo's. She sings, dances, and has a morning talk show. Also she has a special-level Kudan attached. On the other hand, she is willful and selfish, so much so that in order to bring Shôgo to see her, she tried to kidnap Syaoran because Shôgo said that he liked Syaoran's style.

PARAMETER

力
POWER
速さ
SPEED
器用さ
TECHNIQUE
知力
MENTAL POWER
特殊
SPECIAL
魅力
CHARM

Are her charms that bring in the fans the same charms that allowed her image to grace the covers of magazines like *Maganyan*? Or is it her playful personality?

MY KUDAN, COME ON!! ♪

➤ Its normal form is a microphone with an attached speaker, but when it transforms into its mike-stand shape, it can use Primela's voice more effectively.

WHEN MY KUDAN-CHAN BECOMES A MIKE STAND...
...THERE'S NO RUNNING AWAY!

Primela's Kudan is microphone shaped. It's small, but it's rated as a special-level Kudan. And fitting for an idol, it takes her sung words, turns them from sound waves into physical force, and uses them as an attack. When the Kudan transforms into mike stand shape, it increases its abilities many times. It seems it can use this voice-based physical force at will.

TOPIC

An Idol's Voice Is Her Life

桃矢＆雪兎
TÔYA & YUKITO

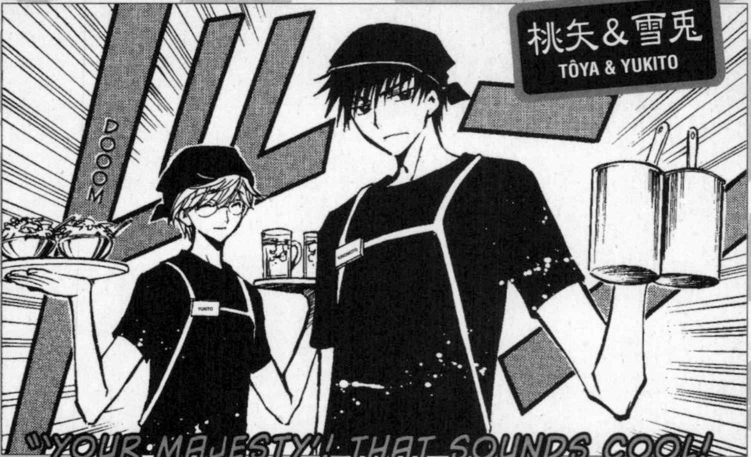
DOOOM
"YOUR MAJESTY"! THAT SOUNDS COOL!
"LEAVE IT, WILL YA?"

In the Hanshin republic, Syaoran came across Tôya and Yukito. In this world, they weren't king and high priest, but rather two normal young men who work at an Okonomiyaki restaurant. But their close friendship was no different.

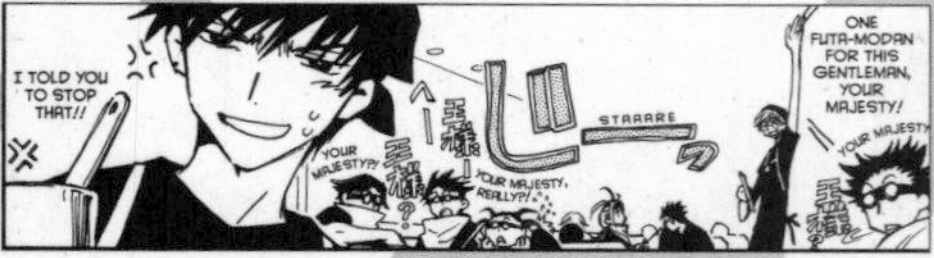
ONE FUTA-MODAN FOR THIS GENTLEMAN, YOUR MAJESTY!
YOUR MAJESTY
STARRRE
YOUR MAJESTY, REALLY?!
YOUR MAJESTY?!
I TOLD YOU TO STOP THAT!!

Because Syaoran called Tôya "Your Majesty," it quickly became his nickname. But Tôya seems to hate the name.

モヒカンチームのリーダー
LEADER WITH THE MOHAWK

This is the leader of a team who wants Shôgo's territory. Under the mistaken impression that Syaoran has been invited into Shôgo's team, the Leader with the Mohawk attacks. He may look like a jolly clown, but his Kudan is first-level.

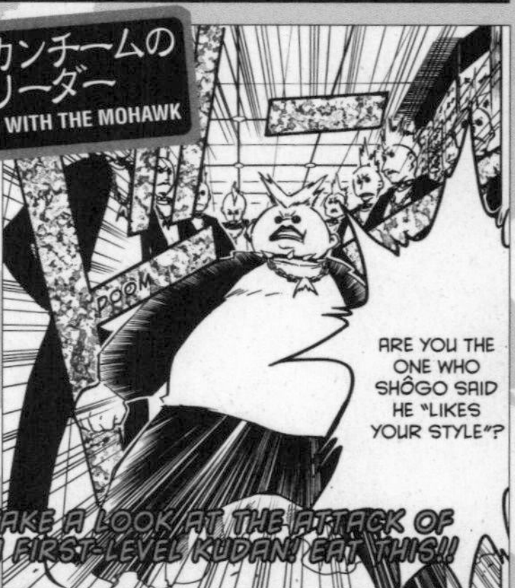
ARE YOU THE ONE WHO SHÔGO SAID HE "LIKES YOUR STYLE"?
DOOM
TAKE A LOOK AT THE ATTACK OF A FIRST-LEVEL KUDAN! EAT THIS!!

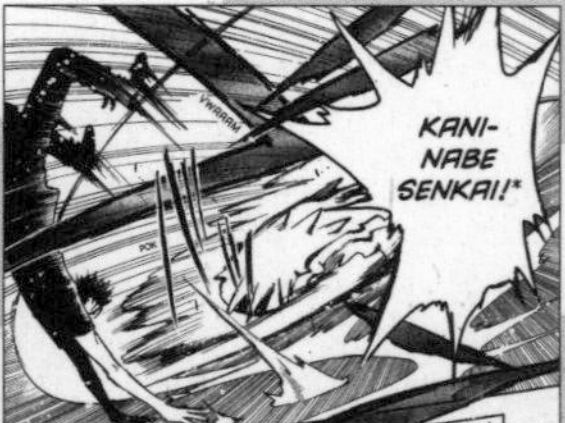
KANI-NABE SENKAI!*

➤ His Kudan is horseshoe crab–type. It has a hard shell and is unusually fast.

➤ Syaoran was soon able to control the Kudan as he wished. Perhaps it's because Syaoran has a very strong heart.

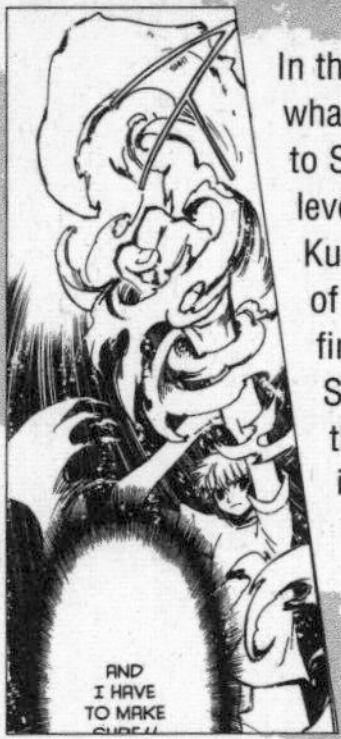
AND I HAVE TO MAKE

In the Hanshin Republic, what attached itself to Syaoran is a special-level fire-controlling Kudan. Its form is that of a beast bathed in fire. While dreaming, Syaoran spoke to the Kudan, and since it was searching for one with a very strong heart, it lent its power to Syaoran.

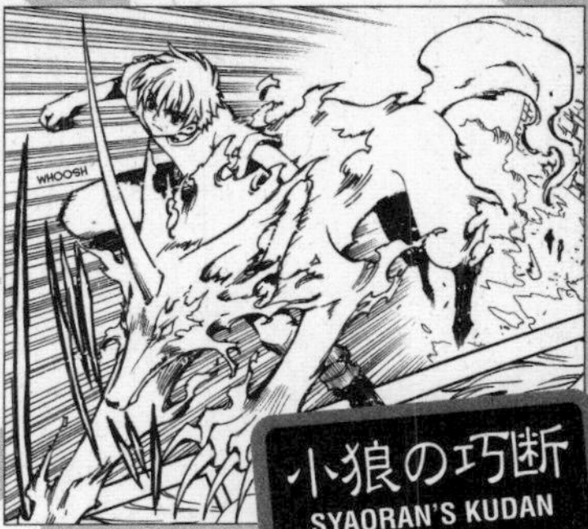
WHOOSH

小狼の巧断
SYAORAN'S KUDAN

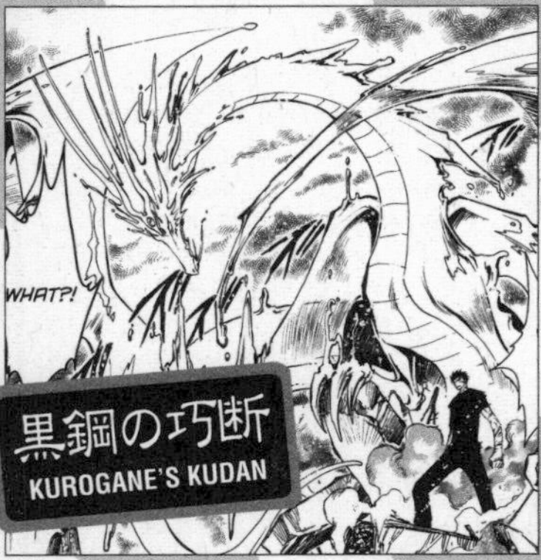
WHAT?!

黒鋼の巧断
KUROGANE'S KUDAN

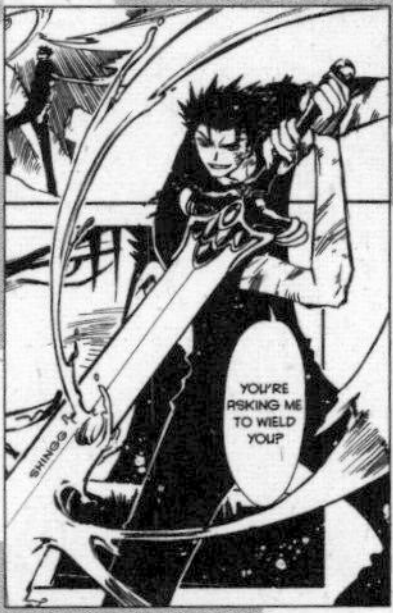
YOU'RE ASKING ME TO WIELD YOU?
SHING

Kurogane holding a Kudan sword. A true double threat.

Just like with Syaoran, Kurogane had a dream where a Kudan appeared. It takes the form of a dragon, and seems to control water, but to match its power with Kurogane's, it transformed into a sword. Seeing how powerful it is, it may be a special-level Kudan.

ファイの巧断
FAI'S KUDAN

The Kudan that attached itself to Fai takes the form of a giant bird. It appears to be able to control wind, and Fai uses this power in order to fly. But since flying doesn't make Fai any stronger, it's Fai himself that does the fighting.

It avoids attacks as if it were the wind itself.

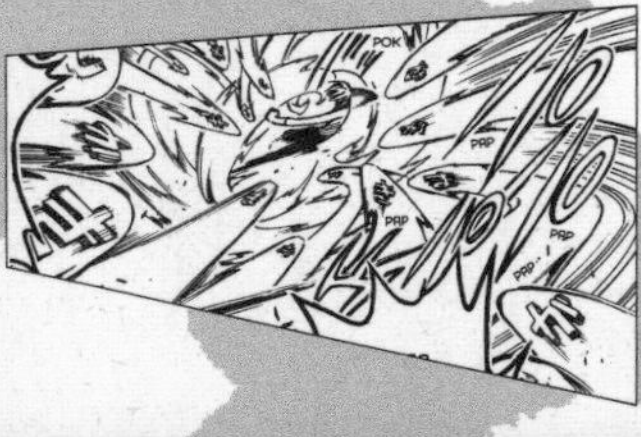
POK
PAP
PAP
PAP

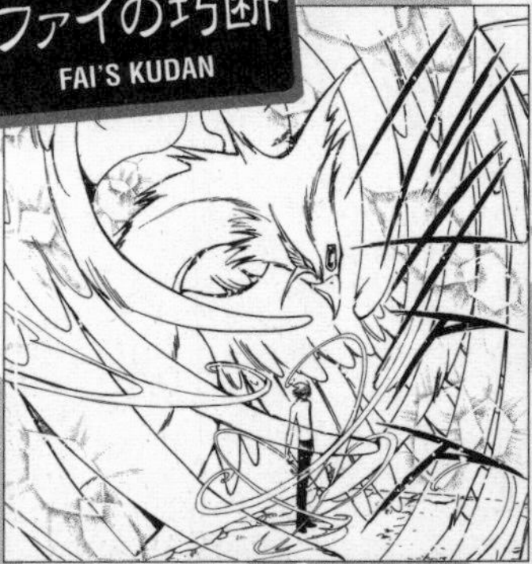

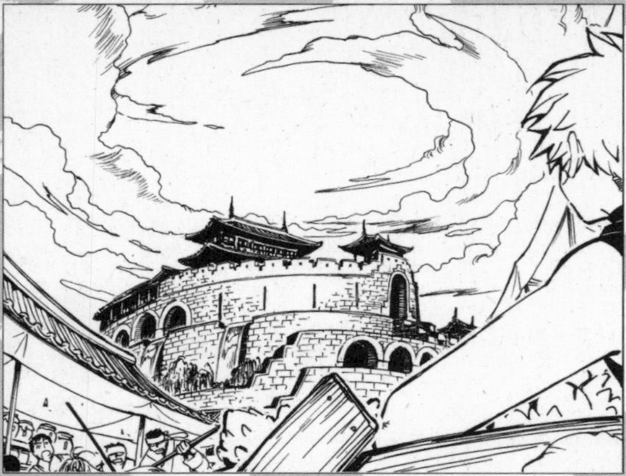

Country of Koryo

The Country of Koryo where rows of buildings made mainly of wood span the wide-reaching land. The town that Syaoran and his group visited amidst this background was named Ryonfi. And in this country, the ruler of each area, the Ryanban, is appointed by the country's central government. However when Syaoran and his group visited, the people of the town of Ryonfi were suffering under the tyranny of a new Ryanban.

MYSTERIOUS POWERS

There appears to be an odd and mysterious power in the Country of Koryo. Those who control the power are called Shinban, and this power can be used to improve the lives of the people.

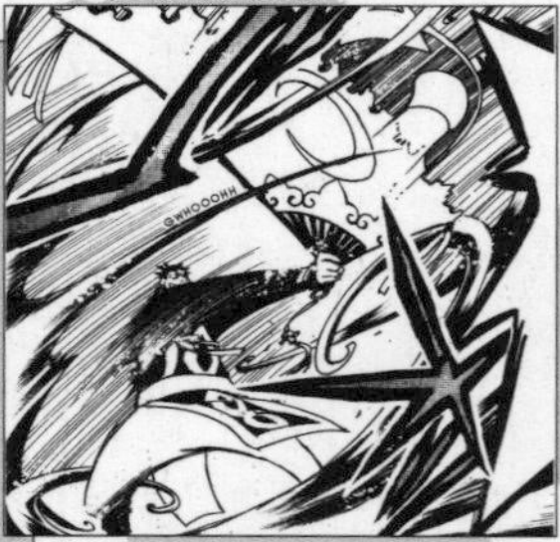

➤ With one wave of his fan, the Ryanban's son raises enough whirlwind to tear down a house. This is part of his mysterious power.

CULTURE

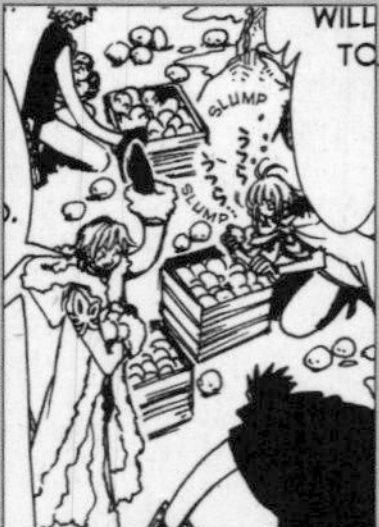
WILL
TO
SLUMP
SLUMP

➤ One can buy most things in stalls along the road.

It becomes obvious that this is one of the cultures that uses kanji for writing names and the like. But they aren't a culture that uses electricity or relies on complex machines.

AMEN'OSA

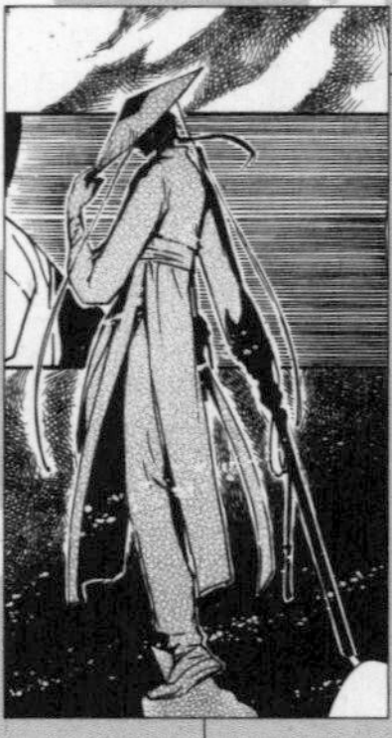

➤ Since their duty is to secretly observe the situation, there are many who have never even heard of them.

Amen'osa are agents of the Koryo central government. They wander the country in disguise to see if the Ryanban are fairly treating the people of the towns under their jurisdiction.

Raised somewhat off the ground, the flooring is made of wooden planks. The mirror, which is one of the items decorating the room, is a magical item passed down to Chu'nyan by her mother.

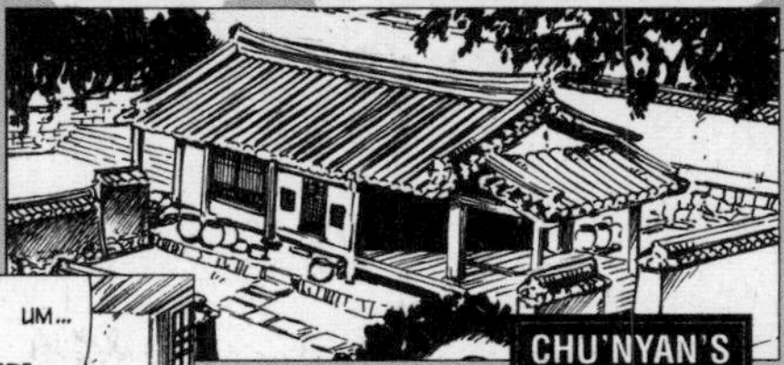

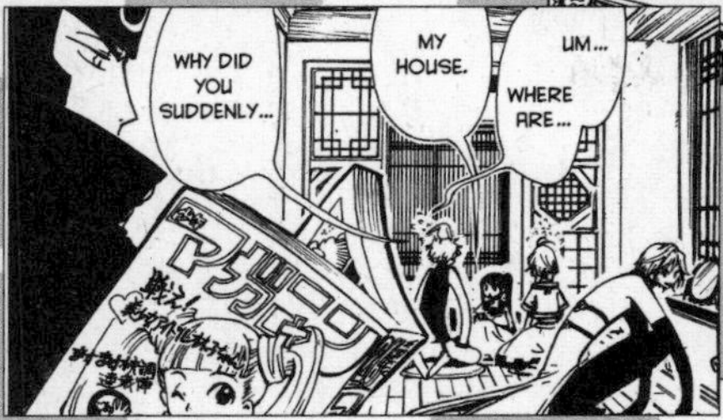
UM... WHERE ARE...
MY HOUSE.
WHY DID YOU SUDDENLY...

CHU'NYAN'S HOUSE

Chu'nyan's lived in her house on her own after her mother was killed. It isn't very large, but it seems a little big and lonely for one young girl living alone. The roof was pulled off by a whirlwind caused by the mysterious power of the Ryanban.

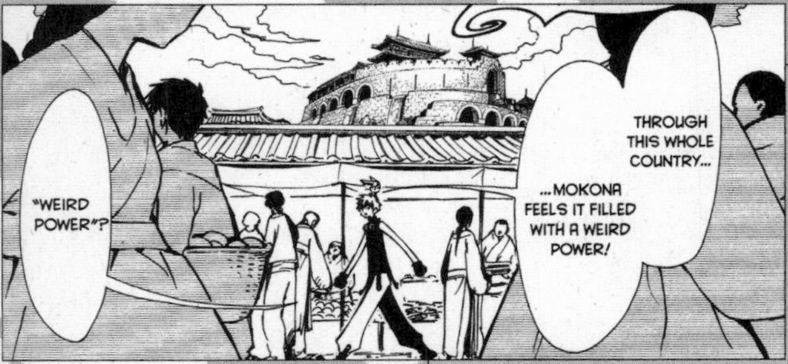
THROUGH THIS WHOLE COUNTRY... ...MOKONA FEELS IT FILLED WITH A WEIRD POWER!
"WEIRD POWER"?

▲ Beyond the wall is the Ryanban's castle. It's a perfect location from which to observe the entire town.

THE TOWN VIEWS OF RYONFI

The town of Ryonfi is separated into sections by a series of low walls next to the roads. People have set up stalls alongside both sides of the road to sell their wares.

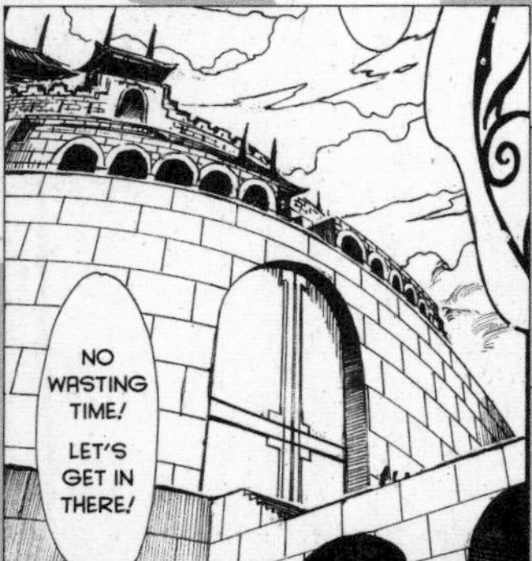
NO WASTING TIME! LET'S GET IN THERE!

KUDAN

Unlike the houses of the people in the town, the castle of the Ryanban is made of sturdy materials such as brick. The castle gate is also heavily guarded. Since this Ryanban came to power, the areas around the castle have been protected by powerful magics so that no one is able to sneak in no matter who they are.

◄ When seen in relation to Syaoran's group, it becomes obvious just how big the castle gate is.

Chu'nyan is a young girl living alone in the town of Ryonfi. Her mother, whom she calls her omoni, specialized in protection wards and medicines, and Chu'nyan is determined to become a skilled Shinban herself. She asked for Amen'osa to come because of her anger over the way the Ryanban is treating the people.

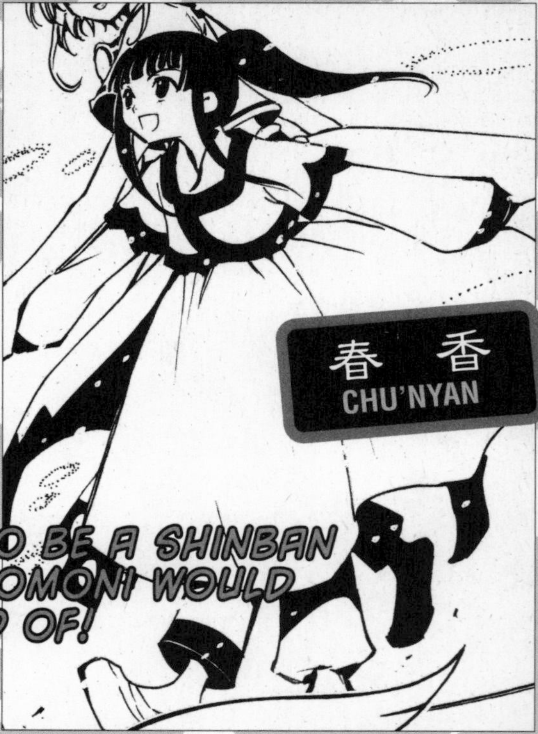

春 香
CHU'NYAN

I WANT TO BE A SHINBAN THAT MY OMONI WOULD BE PROUD OF!

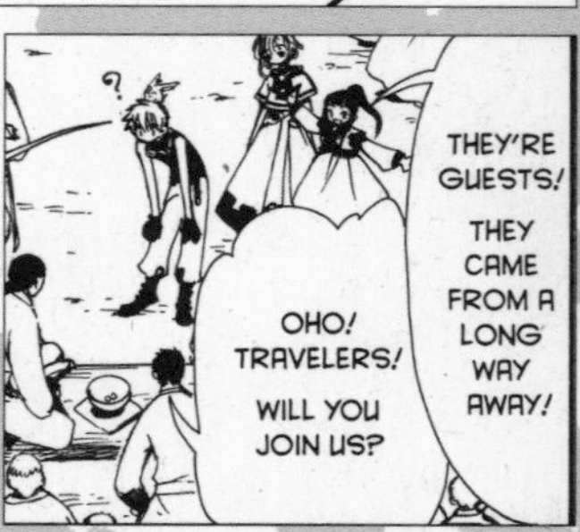
THEY'RE GUESTS! THEY CAME FROM A LONG WAY AWAY!
OHO! TRAVELERS! WILL YOU JOIN US?

Chu'nyan finds it easy to make friends, and she's popular among the people of the town. And thanks to her, the people of the town welcome Sakura and the group.

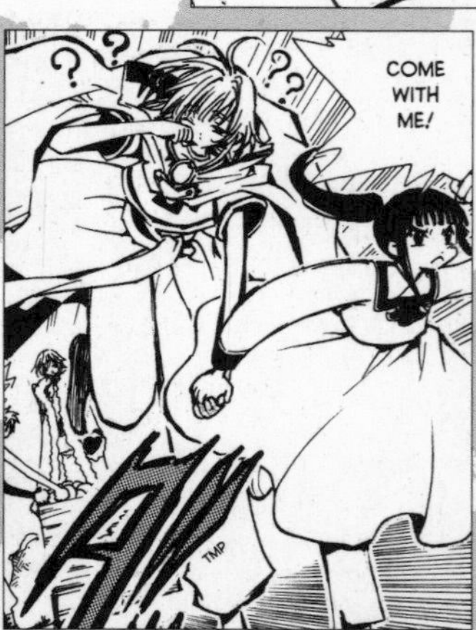
COME WITH ME!
TMP

She's very energetic and strong-willed. But sometimes she goes overboard with her bossiness.

TOPIC 1

Strong Ties to her Mother

NO MATTER HOW MUCH I WANT TO BE WITH HER, I WILL NEVER SEE MY OMONI AGAIN!!

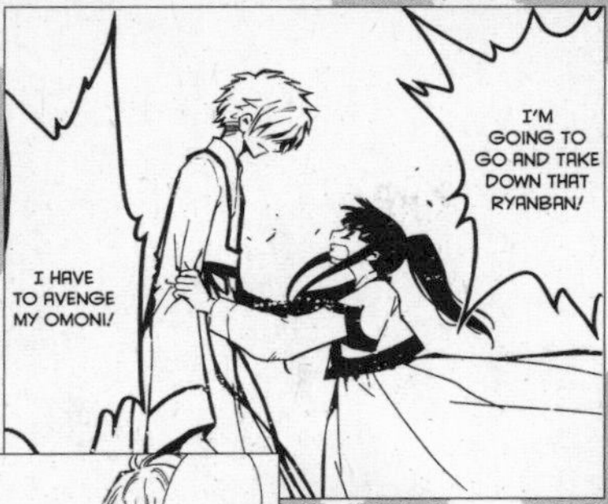
I'M GOING TO GO AND TAKE DOWN THAT RYANBAN!
I HAVE TO AVENGE MY OMONI!

➤ She pleads with Syaoran to join with him and his group in order to take revenge on the Ryanban, but…

Chu'nyan's mother, her only relation, was killed by a creature controlled by the Ryanban. She has great respect for her mother as a Shinban and loved her very much—a feeling that will never fade. The bonds of love with her mother and the happy memories of the time they shared together will stay with her forever.

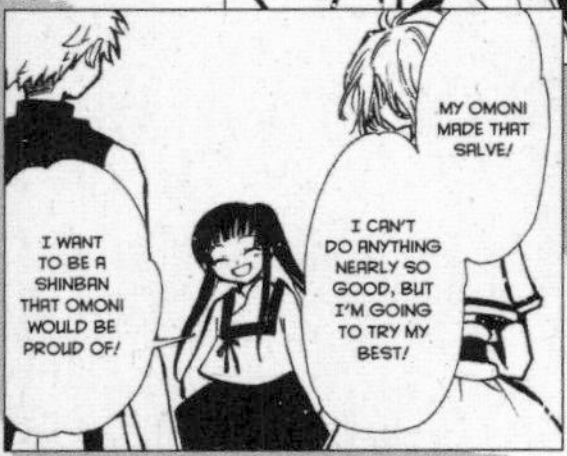
MY OMONI MADE THAT SALVE!
I CAN'T DO ANYTHING NEARLY SO GOOD, BUT I'M GOING TO TRY MY BEST!
I WANT TO BE A SHINBAN THAT OMONI WOULD BE PROUD OF!

Chu'nyan vows to become a Shinban like her mother. And as long as she keeps her beloved mother in mind, she's absolutely sure to see her vow become reality.

TOPIC 2

A Never-Discouraged, Heroic Heart

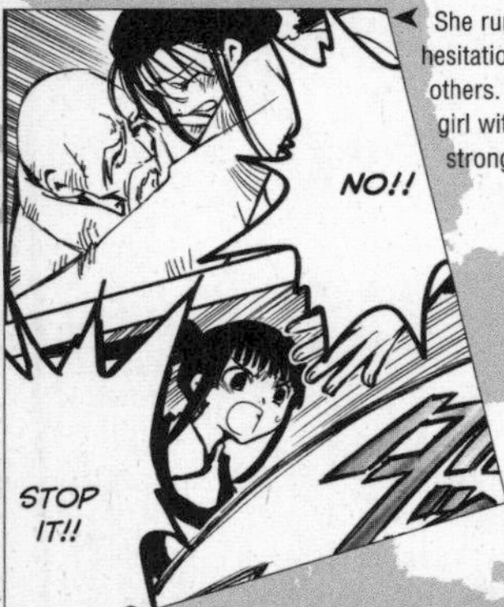
NO!!
STOP IT!!

➤ She runs without hesitation to help others. She's a girl with a very strong heart.

Chu'nyan has a strong sense of justice. Even if she's up against the Ryanban's son, she can't turn away from his unfair dealings despite the danger. And no matter how many times she may suffer from their revenge, she never becomes discouraged.

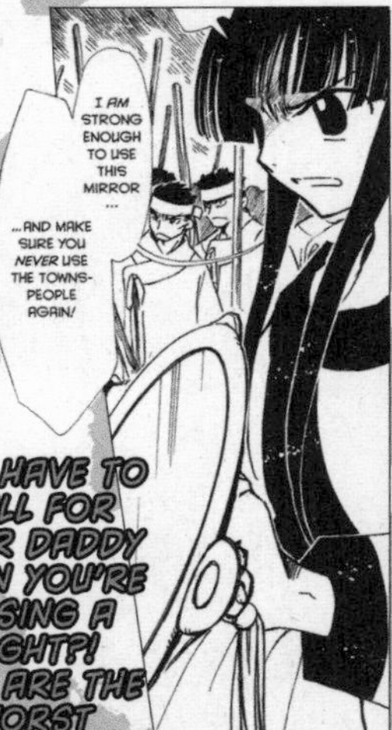
I AM STRONG ENOUGH TO USE THIS MIRROR …
…AND MAKE SURE YOU *NEVER* USE THE TOWNS-PEOPLE AGAIN!

YOU HAVE TO CALL FOR YOUR DADDY WHEN YOU'RE LOSING A FIGHT?! YOU ARE THE WORST EXCUSE FOR A FAMILY I'VE EVER SEEN!

➤ She enters the Ryanban's castle carrying her mother's mirror.

領主 RYANBAN

He was originally a wandering Shinban with no extraordinary powers, but upon getting his hands on one of Sakura's memory feathers, he became a Ryanban with enormous power. Filled with a boundless greed, he subjected the people of Ryonfi to cruel taxes.

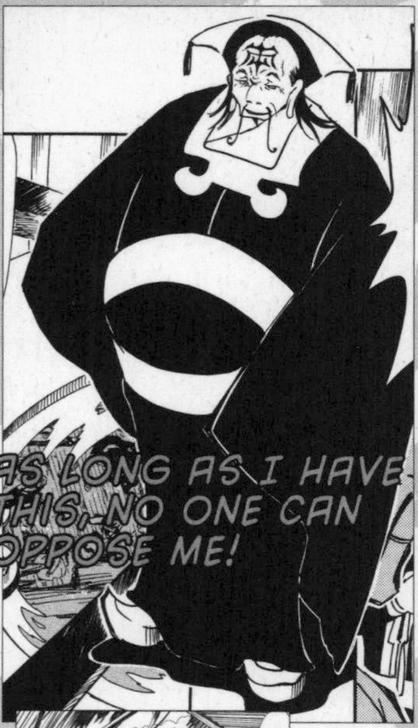

AS LONG AS I HAVE THIS, NO ONE CAN OPPOSE ME!

PARAMETER

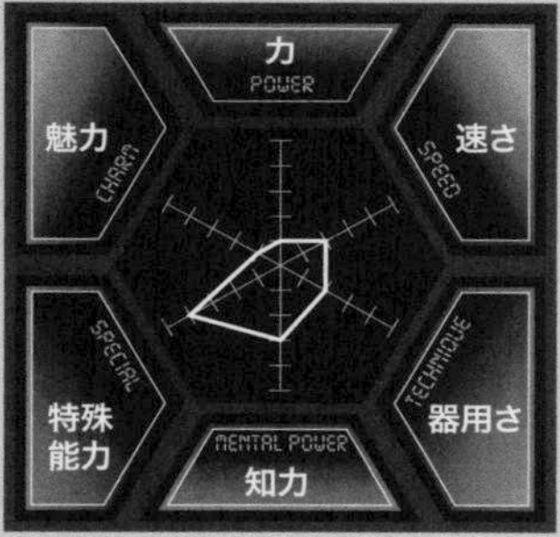

力
POWER
速さ
SPEED
器用さ
TECHNIQUE
知力
MENTAL POWER
特殊能力
SPECIAL
魅力
CHARM

His only attribute that is especially high is his special skills score. His charm, power, and others are very low. Still, even with the high special score, it wasn't originally his special ability.

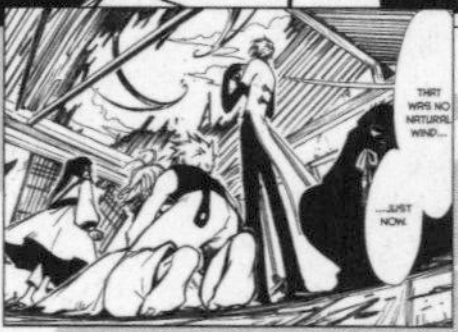

THAT WAS NO NATURAL WIND...
...JUST NOW.

He always gets revenge on those who oppose him. That's how he makes sure his orders are followed.

JUST SET A FINGER ON ME, AND YOU'VE CONDEMNED THEM TO DEATH!!

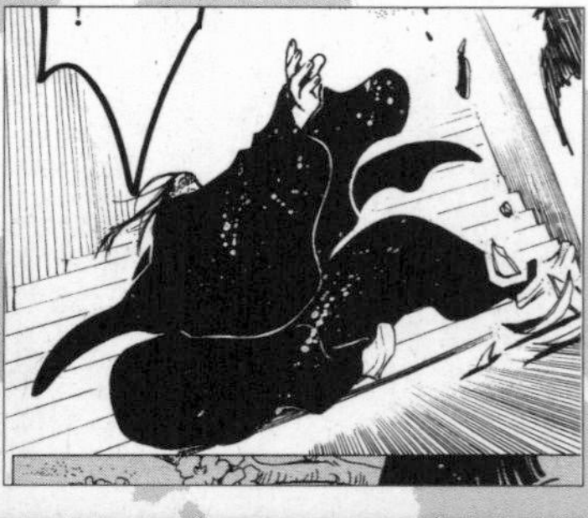

➤ The minute the odds turn against him, he resorts to even worse lies.

TOPIC

A Cowardly Personality

He lays a spell on the townspeople and has them fight for him, and he creates an illusion of Sakura and Chu'nyan and pretends to hold them hostage. The Ryanban's tactics are very cowardly. Only weak-hearted men with no confidence in themselves rely on such tactics to fight.

領主の息子
RYANBAN'S SON

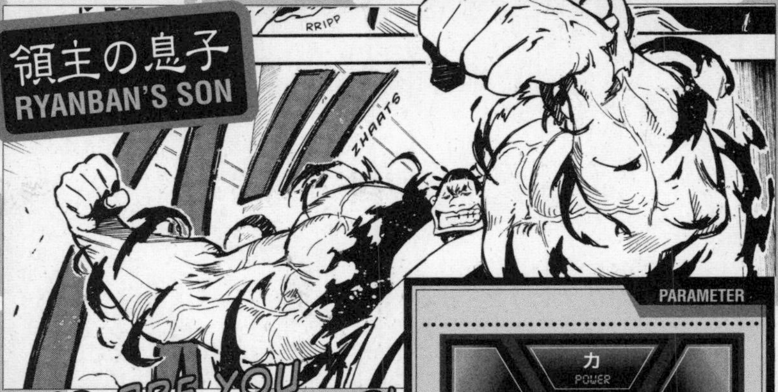
RRIPP
ZHAATS

WHO ARE YOU CALLING STUPID?!

Assuming his father's powers and authority will back him up, the son struts about the town with aristocratic airs, using unreasonable force over and over again. Although he has a powerful physique, his lack of intelligence prevents him from reflecting on his actions.

PARAMETER

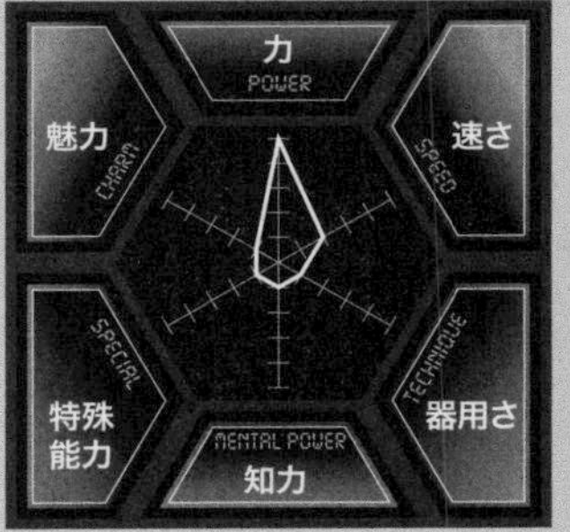
力
POWER
速さ
SPEED
器用さ
TECHNIQUE
MENTAL POWER
知力
特殊能力
SPECIAL
魅力
CHARM

His power score is incredibly high, but that's his only high score. His others are no better than the average person. And now it may be difficult for him to even recover his strength.

YOU AND THE OLD MAN WILL RECEIVE THREE HUNDRED LASHES!

➤ He acts superior even though the power he relies on isn't his own. Who wouldn't hate someone like that?

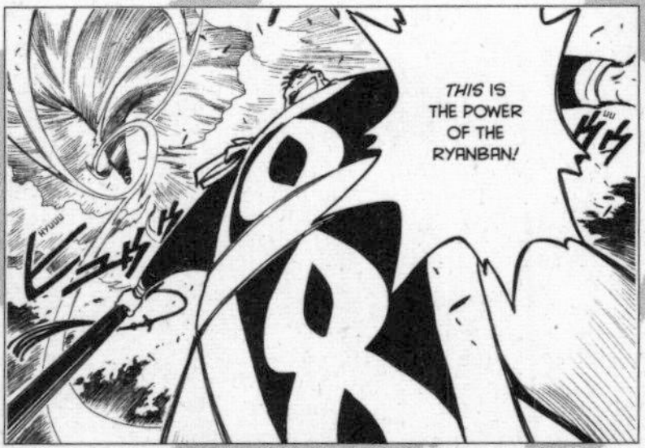
THIS IS THE POWER OF THE RYANBAN!

He tries to dominate others, based only on the fact that he is the Ryanban's son, and of course, that has made the people of the town hate him. But they can do nothing to stop him because of his enormous arm strength and the certain knowledge that the Ryanban will retaliate.

TOPIC

Hated by Everyone in the Town

YOU WILL NOT BE ABLE TO ESCAPE AS THAT PREVIOUS CHILD DID.

▲ When the Kiishim attacks with illusions, she can cause actual wounds to her enemy.

秋妖 KIISHIM

She is the most powerful Kiishim in the country of Koryo, but she was captured by the Ryanban and forced to protect the castle. And when Kurogane broke the stone on her forehead, he set her free to take her former jailor to the country of the Kiishim.

YOU WILL BE RECEIVED WITH THE GREATEST OF WELCOMES!

The incident in the country of Koryo has been taken care of, and Syaoran and his companions left the world. Shortly thereafter, three member group of Amen'osa finally made it to the town of Ryonfi. The reason they were so late was because the Ryanban's power was able to hold them out. At first sight, one may think they were just children, but they quickly pulled out the country's seal proving beyond a doubt that they are the real thing.

暗行御吏 AMEN'OSA

PLEASE ACCEPT OUR APOLOGIES FOR OUR FAR-TOO-LATE ARRIVAL.

COMPARED TO THE PAINS THAT YOUR TOWN HAD TO SUFFER...
...THESE WOUND'S ARE NOTHING!

They had been making every effort to enter the town any way they could. And they finally arrived wearing gentle smiles.

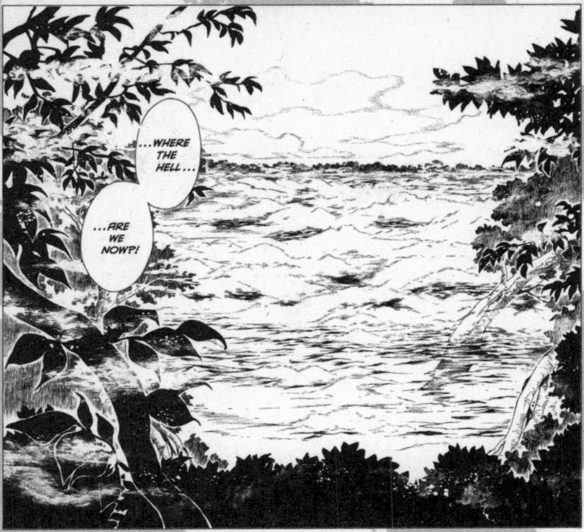
...WHERE THE HELL...
...ARE WE NOW?!

Country of Fog

Syaoran and his party arrived at a land that was covered in fog and stood beside a huge lake. There seemed to be no people there, and they never even learned the name of the country. Although Syaoran discovered a tiny city at the bottom of the lake, there was no way to be certain if it was humans who were living there.

TINY TOWN

At the bottom of the lake was something that looked like a miniature town. There are stone buildings, and from it, Syaoran could hear the bustling of activity.

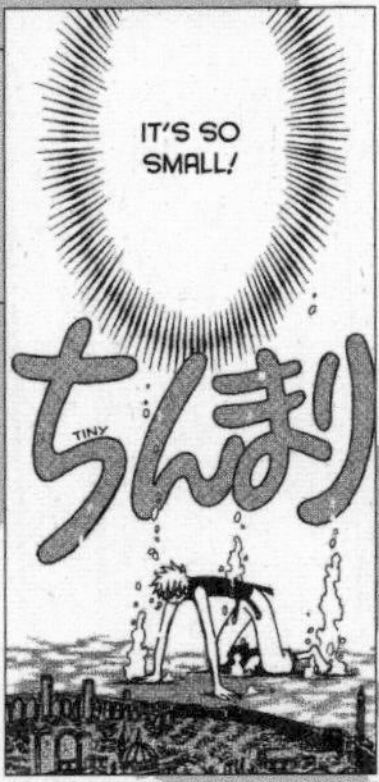
IT'S SO SMALL!
ちんまり
TINY

➤ It was too small to actually see the people who may be living within it. However, Syaoran was sure that something was living there.

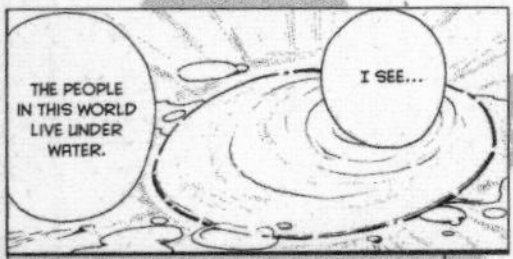
I SEE...
THE PEOPLE IN THIS WORLD LIVE UNDER WATER.

⮜ Mokona was able to sense a great power of some sort from the huge scale.

FISH'S SCALES

This is one scale that the glowing fish dropped. It's so big that Syaoran needed both arms to carry it, and even after he brought it out of the water, it continued to glow from some power within it.

GLOWING FISH

With the light of its body, this enormous fish lights every corner of the town. To those living in the town at the dark lake bed, the fish must seem like the sun coming up.

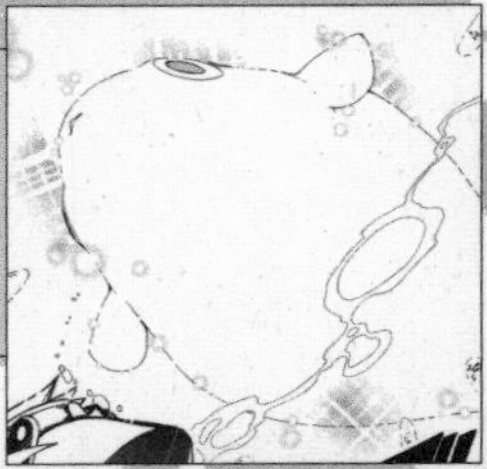

➤ The fish resembles a sunfish, but even sunfish aren't covered in glowing scales.

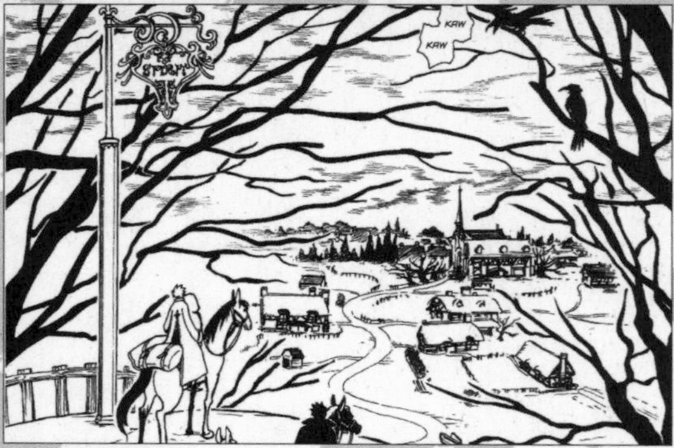
KAW
KAW

Country of Jade

LEGEND

There's a legend in Spirit of a golden-haired princess who took the town's children away. Many of the villagers are convinced that there is some connection with the legend and the present missing children cases.

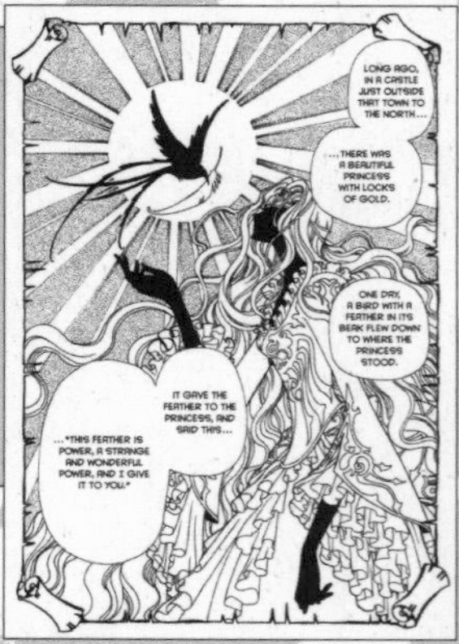
LONG AGO, IN A CASTLE JUST OUTSIDE THAT TOWN TO THE NORTH...
...THERE WAS A BEAUTIFUL PRINCESS WITH LOCKS OF GOLD.
ONE DAY, A BIRD WITH A FEATHER IN ITS BEAK FLEW DOWN TO WHERE THE PRINCESS STOOD.
IT GAVE THE FEATHER TO THE PRINCESS, AND SAID THIS...
..."THIS FEATHER IS POWER, A STRANGE AND WONDERFUL POWER, AND I GIVE IT TO YOU."

➤ The legend of the princess is based on history, and there is even mention of it in the history books.

The country of Jade surrounds one in thick forests with the ground covered in a carpet of snow. Syaoran and the party came to the town of Spirit in this country after hearing rumors that led them to believe that it may contain one of Sakura's feathers. However, because there have been cases of disappearing children happening one after the next, the people are living in an era of terrible unrest.

CULTURE

In a snowy country, it's difficult to grow crops in the best of times, and so the people live frugally. The main method of transportation seems to be the horse.

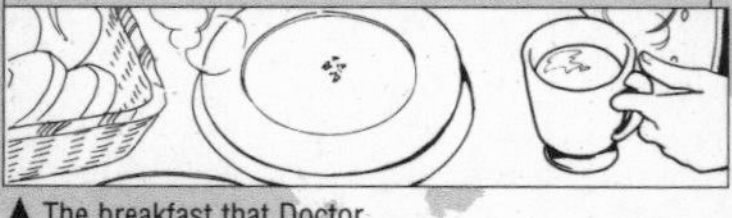

▲ The breakfast that Doctor Kyle presented to Syaoran and his friends consisted of warm soup and bread.

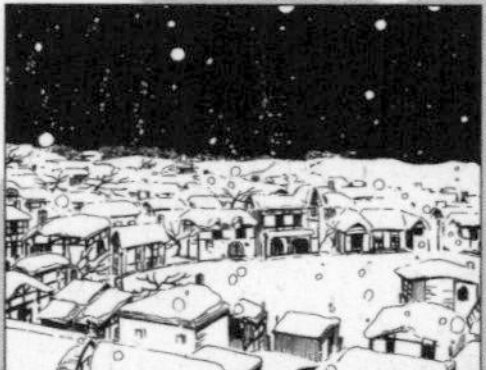

◄ For several years running, the climate has been a problem for the country. Crop failures are still continuing.

CLIMATE

Spirit is located in the cold northern part of the country of Jade. During winter, its cold penetrates right through to the bone.

COUNTRY OF JADE

➤ It's a two-story building with an attic. The entranceway is covered so snow will never block the door.

WELL!

IT LOOKS LIKE WE'RE HERE.

THE GOOD DOCTOR'S INSTRUCTIONS LED US STRAIGHT TO THE MAYOR'S HOUSE.

THE MAYOR'S HOUSE

This is the house where the representative of the town, the mayor, lives. It is far from the palatial mansions of some mayors—this is simply a modest home. Like most houses in cold regions the walls are of thick plaster with small windows. There seems to be a number of maids doing the housework.

➤ With its crumbling walls and leafless trees surrounding it, the castle leaves a chilling impression on any who see it.

NORTHERN CASTLE

This is the castle where they say the golden-haired princess used to live three hundred years ago. Now it's a decayed ruin. Since it's surrounded by a raging river, it's a very difficult place to get access to.

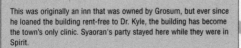

DR. KYLE'S HOUSE

This was originally an inn that was owned by Grosum, but ever since he loaned the building rent-free to Dr. Kyle, the building has become the town's only clinic. Syaoran's party stayed here while they were in Spirit.

▲ It's a very large house, but only Dr. Kyle lives in it. Kyle's room is a few steps from the entranceway.

091   WORLD GUIDE • COUNTRY OF JADE

カイル=ロンダート
KYLE RONDART

Dr. Kyle is a young man who arrived in the town of Spirit two years ago, and seeing that they didn't have a doctor, he set up a clinic. He has a very gentle bedside manner, and he admonished the people of the town for trying to chase off the strangers, welcoming Syaoran and his friends to the town.

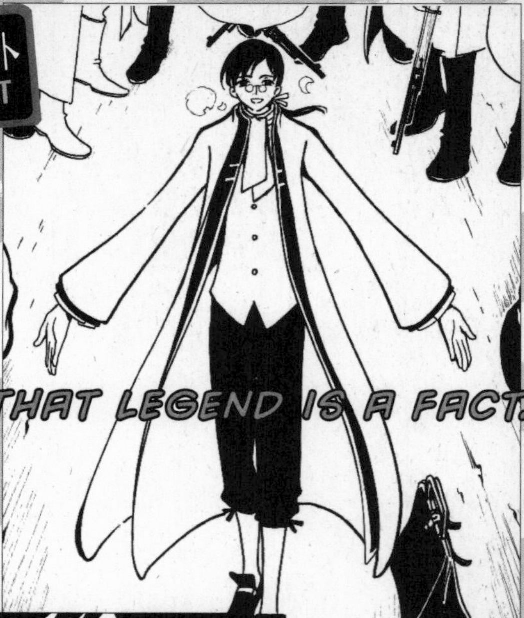
THAT LEGEND IS A FACT.

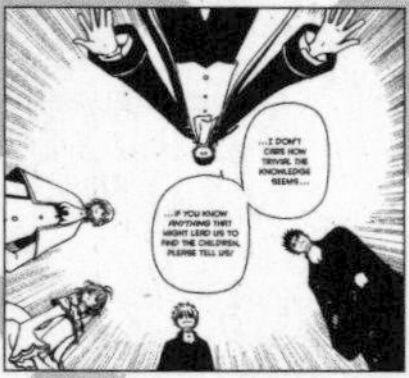
...I DON'T CARE HOW TRIVIAL THE KNOWLEDGE SEEMS...
...IF YOU KNOW ANYTHING THAT MIGHT LEAD US TO FIND THE CHILDREN, PLEASE TELL US!

▲ Kyle seems to be doing everything he can to find the children, but in reality…

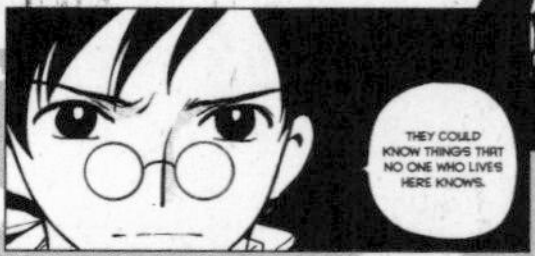
THEY COULD KNOW THINGS THAT NO ONE WHO LIVES HERE KNOWS.

◀ He defends Syaoran's group against the suspicious townspeople.

TOPIC
The Hidden True Face

His gentle smile was just a disguise. In reality, Dr. Kyle was deceiving the people of the town in order to get what he wanted. When Syaoran solved the mystery of the missing children, the truth about the doctor came to light.

THAT FEATHER IS MINE!!

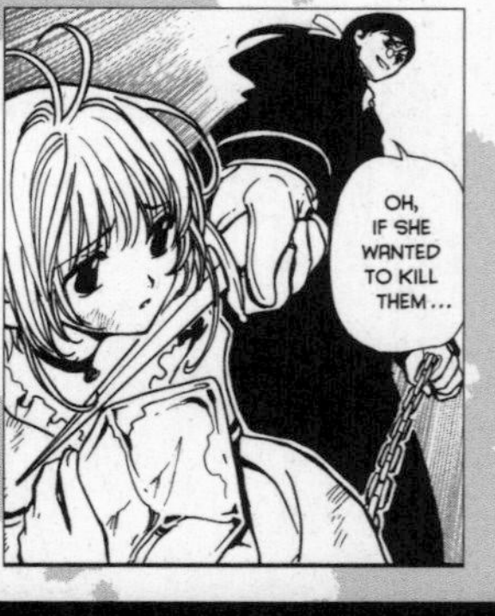
OH, IF SHE WANTED TO KILL THEM...

▶ Dr. Kyle smiles as he holds a knife to Sakura's throat. That's his true face.

エメロード姫
EMERALD

According to the legend, this is the princess who gained a strange power when she received a sparkling feather from a bird three hundred years ago. The legend went on to say that one-by-one the children were drawn to the feather and taken to the castle never to return.

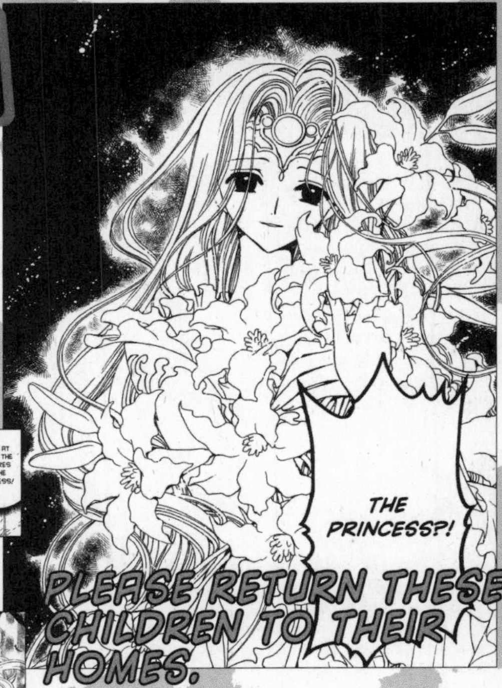
THE PRINCESS?!
PLEASE RETURN THESE CHILDREN TO THEIR HOMES.

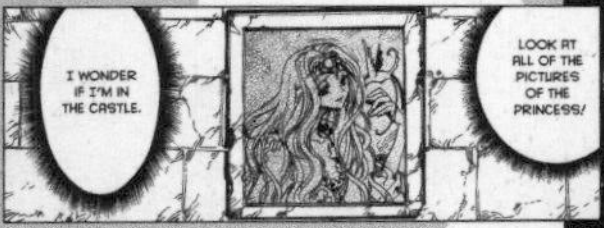
LOOK AT ALL OF THE PICTURES OF THE PRINCESS!
I WONDER IF I'M IN THE CASTLE.

➤ There are still paintings of the princess hanging on the walls of the Northern Castle.

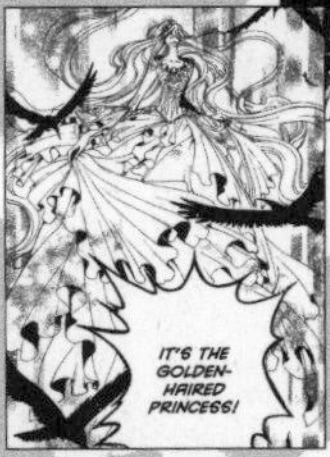
IT'S THE GOLDEN-HAIRED PRINCESS!

➤ The visage of Princess Emerald, who only Sakura can see, seems to be some sort of ghost…

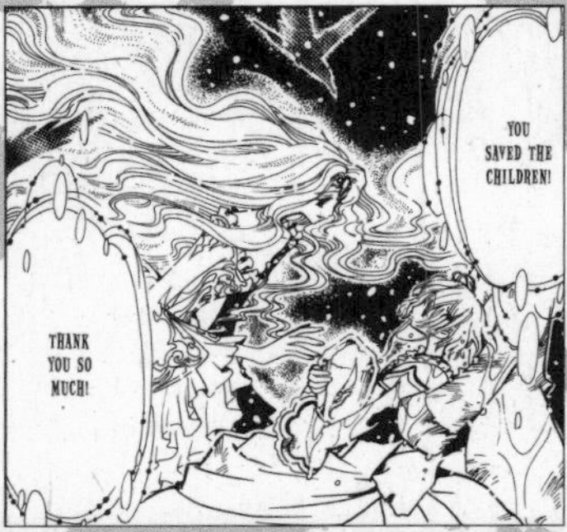
I'M SO GLAD THE FEATHER CAN BE RETURNED TO YOU.
YOU SAVED THE CHILDREN!
THANK YOU SO MUCH!

➤ After the feather was returned to Sakura, the princess never appeared again.

TOPIC

The Truth Behind the Legend

Princess Emerald used the power of the feather to cure the children of the town of a terrible contagious disease. Syaoran and his companions discovered the facts behind the legend, and now, perhaps, the people of the town will pass down the true story.

グロサム
GROSUM

Grosum is a landlord who owns most of the real estate in town. He is very suspicious of Syaoran's group who appeared during a time when children are disappearing, and he only shows a very stern attitude toward them. He seems like a man who is very hard to please, and one almost never sees him smile.

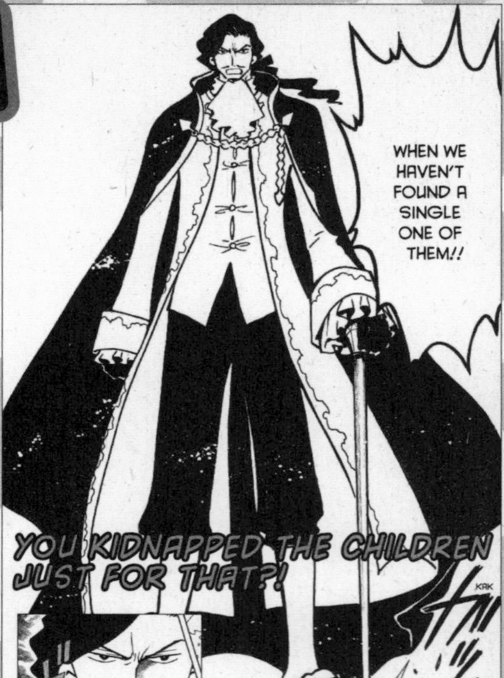
WHEN WE HAVEN'T FOUND A SINGLE ONE OF THEM!!
YOU KIDNAPPED THE CHILDREN JUST FOR THAT?!
KRK

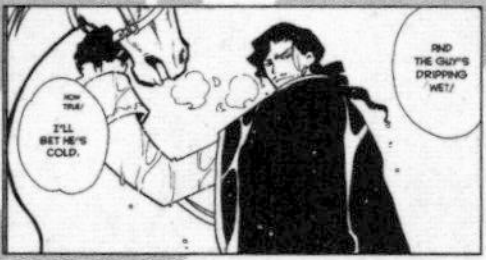
AND THE GUY'S DRIPPING WET!
I'LL BET HE'S COLD.

▲ He wanders around in the middle of the night and is witnessed dripping wet. His actions seem very suspicious, but…

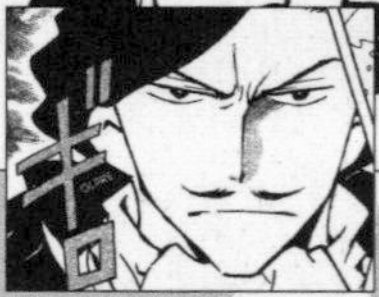

◀ His stare at Syaoran and his friends is sharp as an arrow and cold.

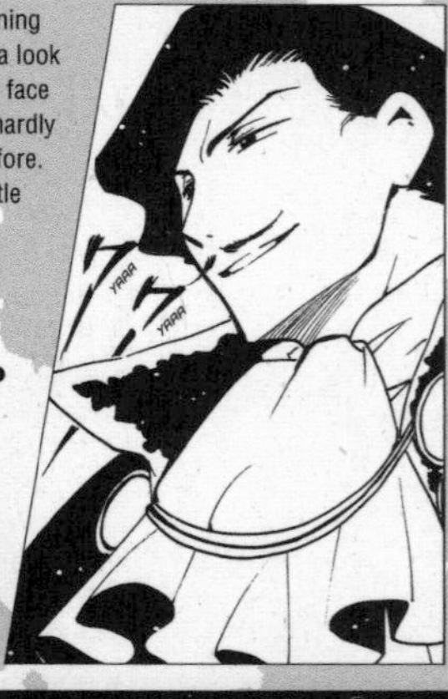
WE SHOULDN'T HAVE TO LEARN IT THROUGH RUMORS!
YAAA
YAAA

➤ The returning children see a look on Grosum's face that they've hardly ever seen before. A warm, gentle smile.

TOPIC

Generous Feeling for the Towns-people

Although Grosum was thought for a while to be the culprit who caused the children's disappearances, the truth is that he was extremely worried for the children's lives. He may have a scary face, but he also has a warm heart.

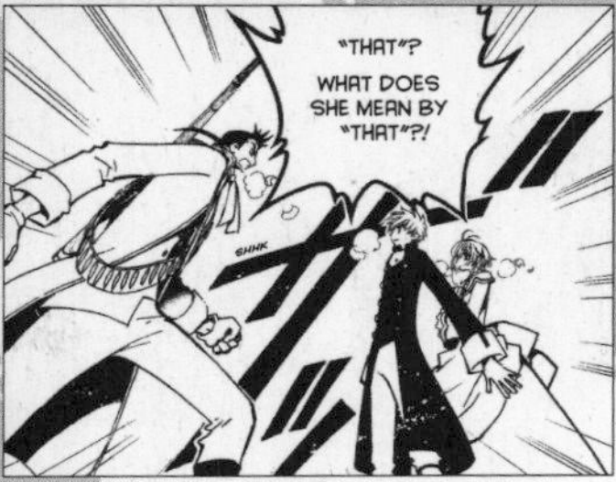
"THAT"?
WHAT DOES SHE MEAN BY "THAT"?!
SHNK

▲ This is his reaction to a short phrase that Sakura muttered under her breath.

CHILDREN HAVE DISAPPEARED AGAIN!

The vigilante leader suits his part to a tee with his sense for justice and his determination to protect the public order of the town. But in his zeal, he has a strong tendency to overdo things.

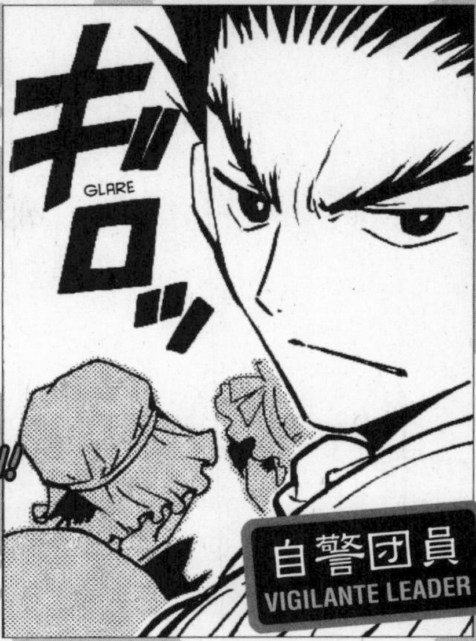
ギロッ
GLARE

自警団員
VIGILANTE LEADER

町　長
MAYOR OF SPIRIT

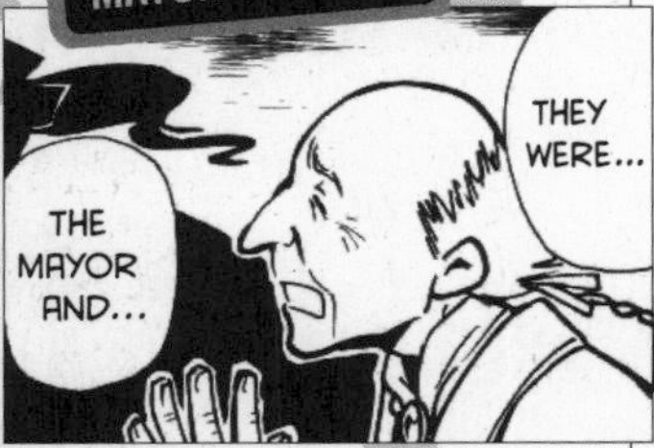
THEY WERE...
THE MAYOR AND...

▲ Instead of a man who leads through his strength of will, the Mayor of Spirit seems more like a man one goes to for advice. Ever since the disappearances started happening, he hasn't been his normal self.

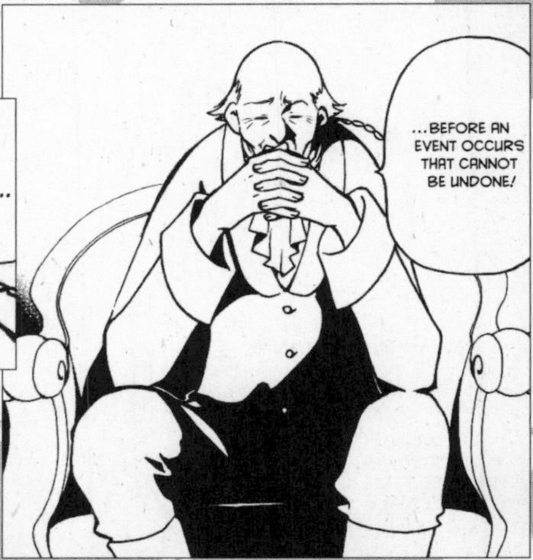
...BEFORE AN EVENT OCCURS THAT CANNOT BE UNDONE!

The town has been afflicted with bad years for their crops, and now the children have been disappearing. The mayor seems to be taking these setbacks to heart. He warns Syaoran's group to leave so they don't get themselves involved in the trouble.

LEAVE THIS TOWN AS SOON AS YOU CAN...

Country of Ôto

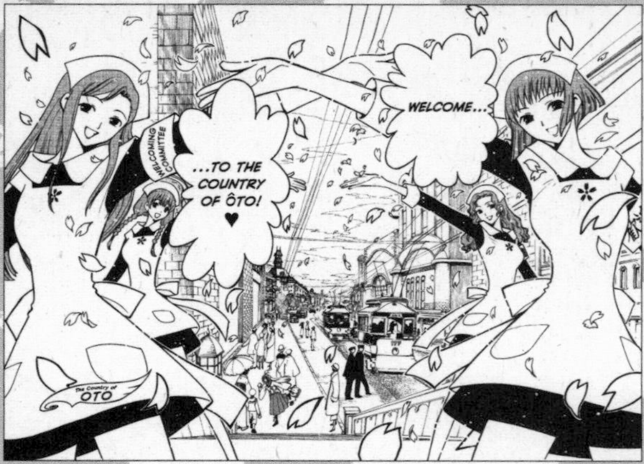
WELCOME...
...TO THE COUNTRY OF ÔTO! ♥
WELCOMING COMMITTEE
The Country of ÔTO

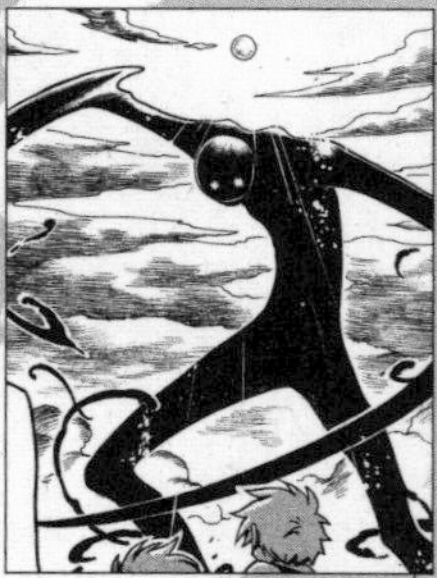

➤ The Oni's abilities change with the level as well. Any Oni above the Ro level cannot be defeated without a special weapon.

ONI

Oni are monsters that appeared in the Country of Ôto. Following the Japanese counting system of I-ro-ha, the strongest is the I-1 Oni and they get weaker as their level goes down to the To-5 Oni.

The Country of Ôto looks as if it were a view straight out of Japan's Taisho Era (1911–1925). But in reality, it's a virtual reality game inside an amusement park, called Fairy Park, in the Country of Edonis. Without knowing this fact, Syaoran and his friends fought monsters called Oni and ran a coffee shop, since they lived there for a while.

Country of Edonis

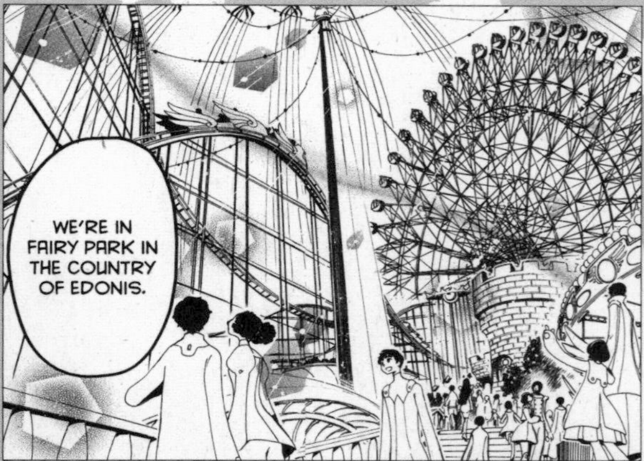
WE'RE IN FAIRY PARK IN THE COUNTRY OF EDONIS.

CLOVER

A place with a nice, relaxing atmosphere. With their popular original mixed drinks and many regular customers, this bar is always bustling. But because Syaoran and Sakura are underage, they can't get in.

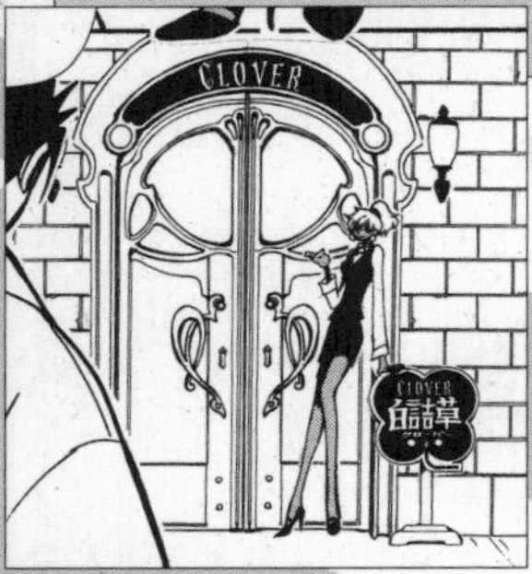
CLOVER

▲ Even the door shows the extravagant decorations. There are a lot of customers who just come to hear Oruha sing.

CITY HALL

City Hall is where the players of the game in the Country of Ôto go to register and receive player support. It's where they register their names and types of employment.

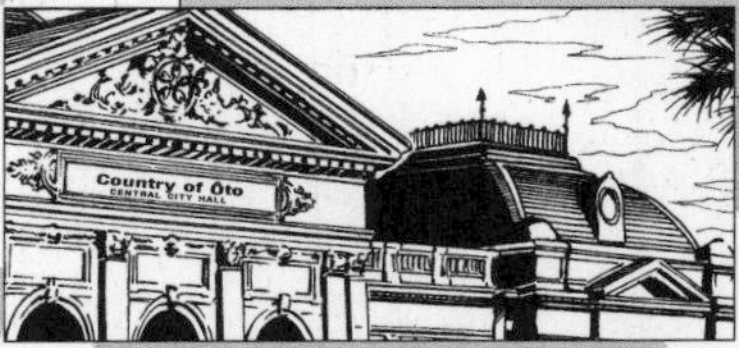
Country of Ôto
CENTRAL CITY HALL

▲ It's built large so that it can accommodate the many players that may come to use it. It might also be a good place to meet up.

CAT'S EYE

This is the coffee shop that Fai opened. Maybe Mokona's gourmand-like tastes played a part, but the café soon got a reputation for cakes and sweets and attracted quite a few customers.

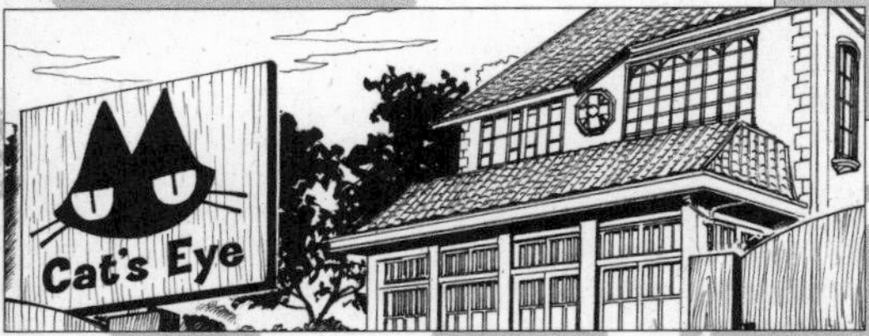
Cat's Eye

◀ It's quite a large building. So big it not only holds a coffee shop but also houses Syaoran and his friends.

TOWER OF THE LITTLE PEOPLE

This tower is supposed to be the location of little people who know information about those who can control Oni. It is such a dangerous place that according to rumor it is difficult for even very skilled Oni hunters to come back alive.

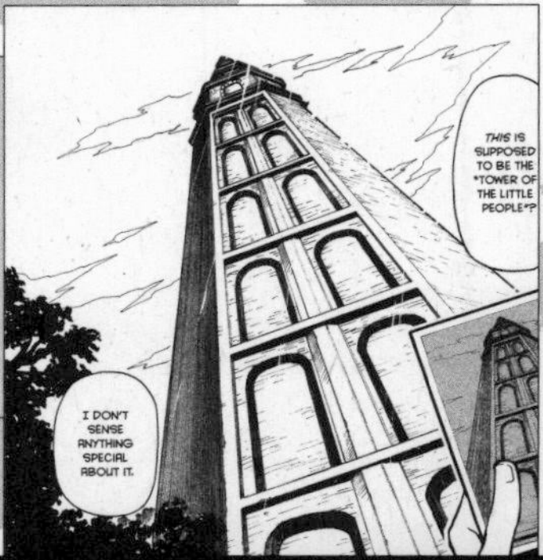
THIS IS SUPPOSED TO BE THE "TOWER OF THE LITTLE PEOPLE"?
I DON'T SENSE ANYTHING SPECIAL ABOUT IT.

➤ It's called the Tower of the Little People, but the building seems to be fine for normal-size humans. There are Oni in there.

星史郎
SEISHIRÔ

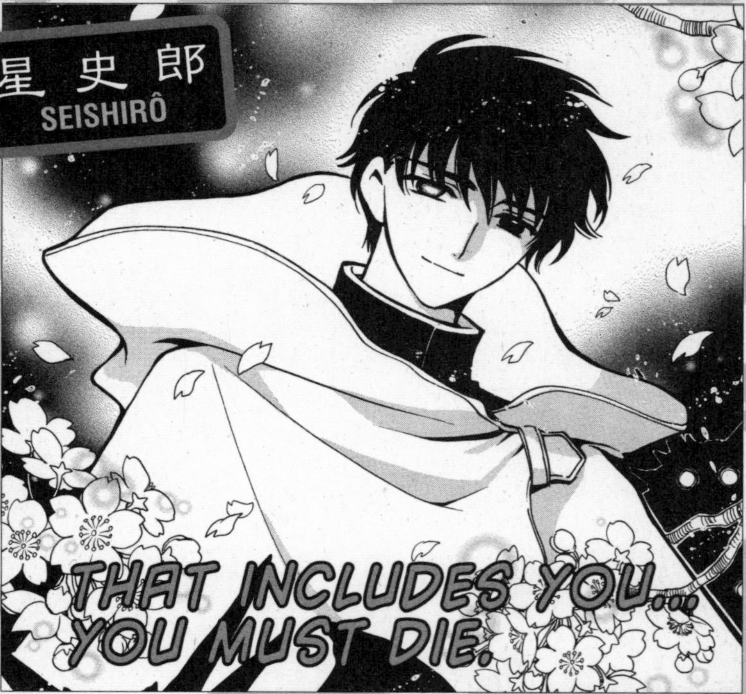
THAT INCLUDES YOU...
YOU MUST DIE.

PARAMETER

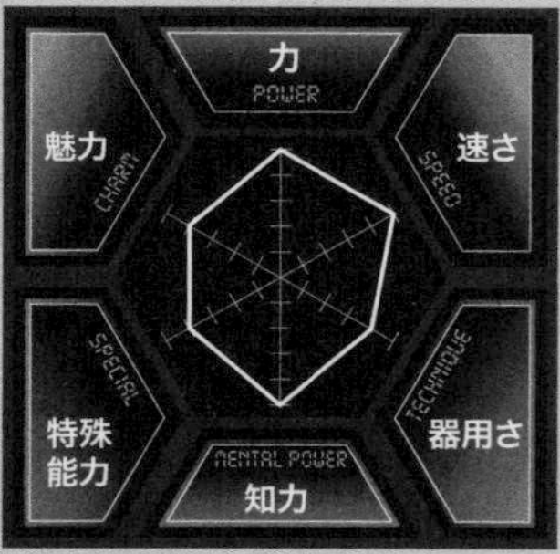
力
POWER
速さ
SPEED
器用さ
TECHNIQUE
知力
MENTAL POWER
特殊能力
SPECIAL
魅力
CHARM

With all of his incredibly strong abilities, he's a man with top-notch skills. Could he have other hidden powers besides the ability to travel between worlds?

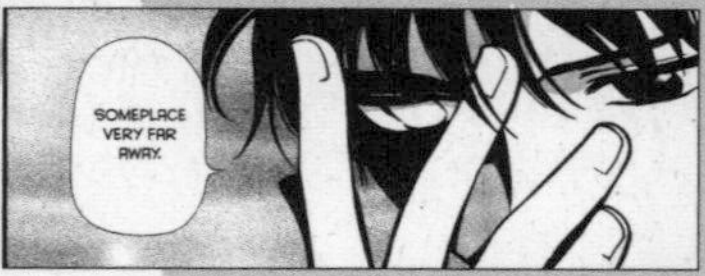
SOMEPLACE VERY FAR AWAY.

▲ Seishirô is on a journey through the worlds. He met Syaoran while in the middle of that journey.

The mysterious man who was controlling the Oni turned out to be Seishirô, the man who taught a very young Syaoran how to fight. He went to the Time-Space Witch for the ability to travel through dimensions, and he used that power to arrive at the country of Ôto. But the man who is there now isn't the same Seishirô that Syaoran knew years ago. Now he will stop at nothing to achieve his goals, including facing off with Syaoran's group as their enemy.

TOPIC 1
Chasing Vampires

VAMPIRES EXIST IN REALITY.

Long ago, Seishirô told Syaoran that his calling was to hunt for vampires. His goal is to search through the worlds until he finds two particular vampires and defeats them. What happened between him and the two vampires? Will the day come when Seishirô tells of his mysterious past?

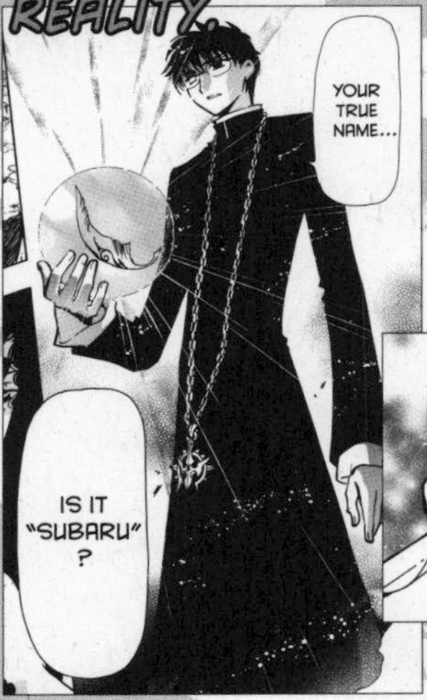
YOUR TRUE NAME...
IS IT "SUBARU" ?

➤ When Seishirô faces the I-1 Oni, Oruha, and uses the name Subaru, is he saying the name of one of the vampires he's hunting?

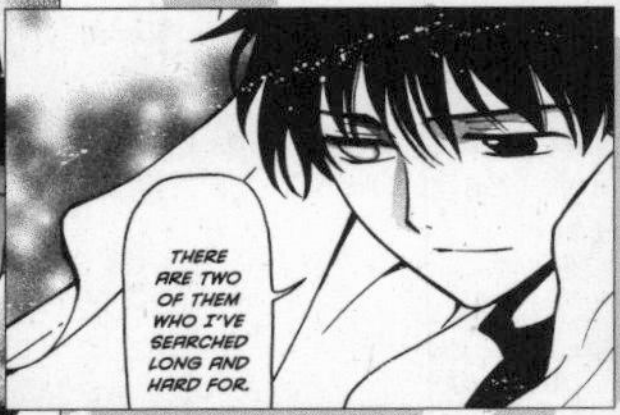
THERE ARE TWO OF THEM WHO I'VE SEARCHED LONG AND HARD FOR.

▲ Even when Syaoran was young, Seishirô was hunting vampires.

TOPIC 2
The Greatest Skill

FOR THE FIRST TIME IN A LONG TIME, I'M IN A MOMENT I MIGHT TRULY ENJOY.

Seishirô's ability to do battle is first rate. He proved his power in a single attack against Syaoran, his one-time disciple in combat techniques, and he fought Kurogane to a draw even though Kurogane was pulling no punches. This master of both the sword and hand-to-hand combat could be the greatest enemy for Syaoran and his group in their search for Sakura's memory feathers.

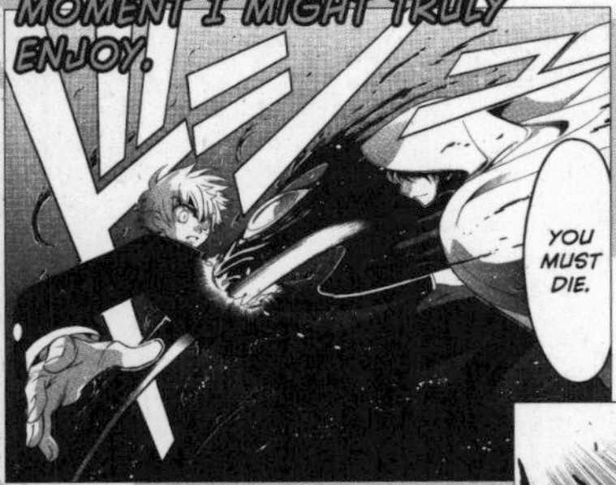
YOU MUST DIE.

▲ He defeated his old disciple without hesitation. Both that and his cold heart can be considered part of his strength.

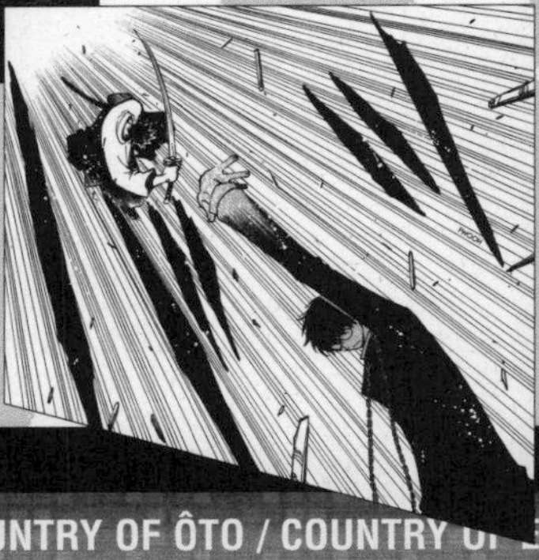

➤ Probably the only one in Syaoran's party who can stand up to an all-out attack by Seishirô would be Kurogane.

PARAMETER

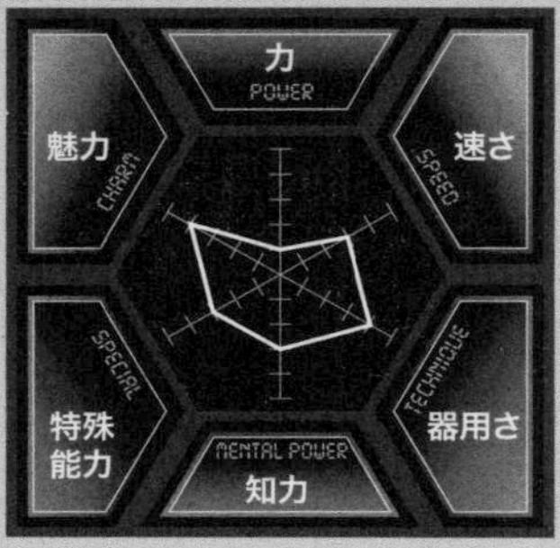
力
POWER
速さ
SPEED
器用さ
TECHNIQUE
知力
MENTAL POWER
特殊能力
SPECIAL
魅力
CHARA

One look will tell you that she's not much for physical strength. But her skill with the gun is more than enough to make up for that one low score.

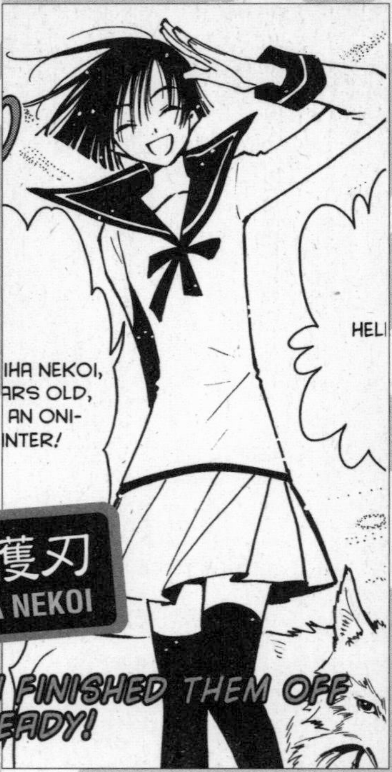
HELI
IHA NEKOI,
ARS OLD,
AN ONI-
NTER!
YOU FINISHED THEM OFF ALREADY!

猫依護刃
YUZURIHA NEKOI

Yuzuriha is an Oni hunter who is paired up with Kusanagi. The young woman is employed as an Oni hunter despite a personality that is bright and very enthusiastic. She sets the mood for the Oni hunters around her.

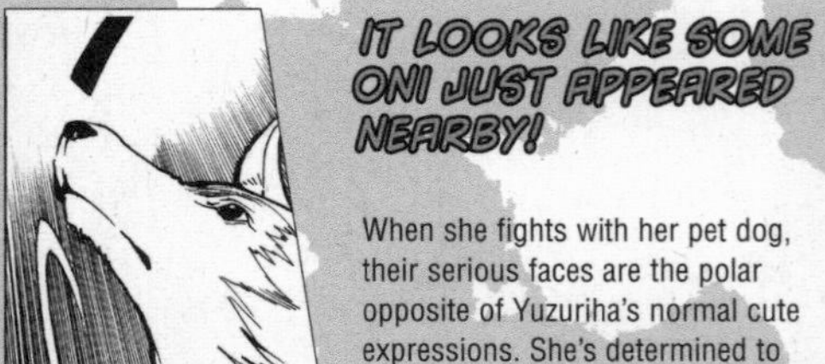
IT LOOKS LIKE SOME ONI JUST APPEARED NEARBY!
KOW
KOW
KOW

When she fights with her pet dog, their serious faces are the polar opposite of Yuzuriha's normal cute expressions. She's determined to get more battle experience in order to defeat the I-1 Oni.

TOPIC

The Cutest Oni Hunter

Yuzuriha cheers up everyone around her with her enthusiastic smile, but cuteness isn't her only attribute. When events make battle necessary, she can take down nearly any Oni with her marksmanship.

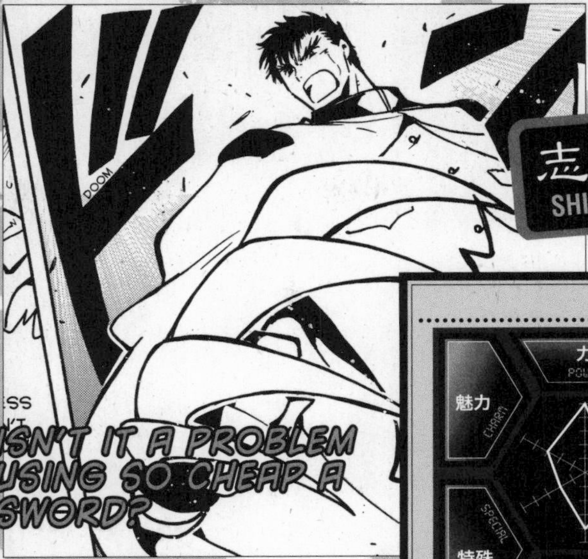
DOOM
ISN'T IT A PROBLEM USING SO CHEAP A SWORD?

志勇草薙
SHIYÛ KUSANAGI

PARAMETER

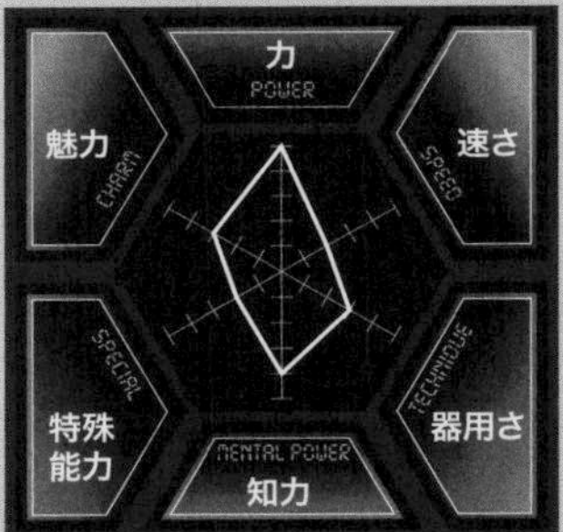
力
POWER
速さ
SPEED
器用さ
TECHNIQUE
知力
MENTAL POWER
特殊能力
SPECIAL
魅力
CHARM

He is able to attract friends to him with his intelligence and arm strength. He isn't as dexterous as some, but when combined with Yuzuriha, their strengths and weaknesses offset each other.

A fighter who may be even tougher than Kurogane, Kusanagi is an Oni hunter who uses a hand-to-hand style of fighting and is armed with metal claws on both hands. He is very observant—he became aware of the gradual changes happening to the country of Ôto before anyone else.

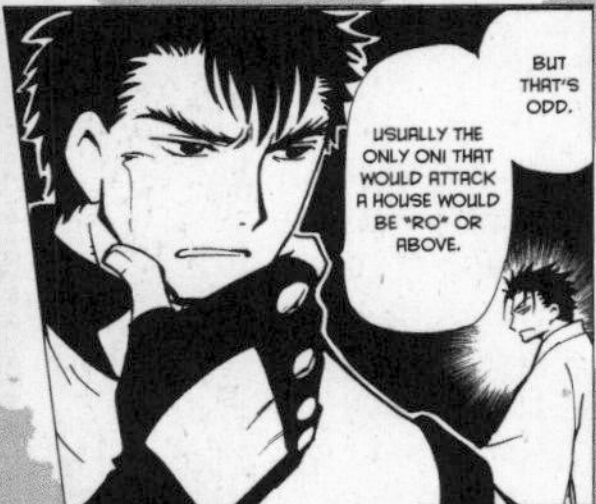
BUT THAT'S ODD.
USUALLY THE ONLY ONI THAT WOULD ATTACK A HOUSE WOULD BE "RO" OR ABOVE.

WAIT! SOMETHING'S NOT RIGHT!

➤ He raises questions regarding the Oni that attacked Syaoran and Kurogane. His insights are on the mark.

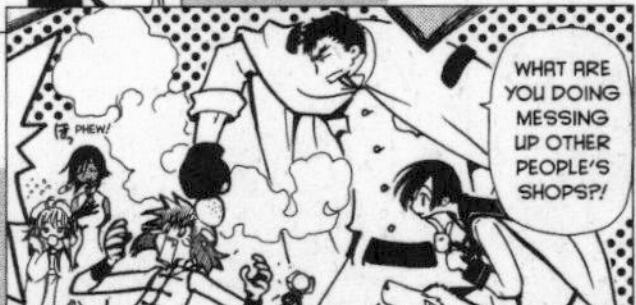
WHAT ARE YOU DOING MESSING UP OTHER PEOPLE'S SHOPS?!
PHEW!

➤ When Ryûô attacks without any consideration for Syaoran, Shiyû stops him with a heavy fist.

TOPIC

Acts as Organizer

Kusanagi is solidly built and normally very calm. He's the one who broke up Ryûô's fight with Syaoran, and he's the one who can guess the level of the Oni. So the other Oni hunters have come to rely on him.

PARAMETER

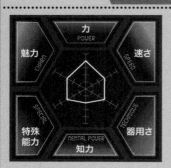

力
POWER

魅力
CHARM

速さ
SPEED

特殊
能力
SPECIAL

器用さ
TECHNIQUE

MENTAL POWER
知力

Although his abilities are well balanced, he still
has room to get much stronger. To get there, he
may have to calm his personality.

龍 王
RYÛÔ

I HEAR YOU GUYS ARE PRETTY STRONG!

Ryûô is a young man who likes
nothing more than to fight a strong
opponent, whether that opponent is
an Oni or human. He has a strong
heart, and one of the signs of it is
that he doesn't flatter himself with
regards to his own battle skills.
He is able to use a large number of
techniques including Kai-ryû-ha and
Kai-ô-jin.

▲ Ryûô is always full of self confidence. Since
both he and Syaoran are trying to improve their
strength, they become fast friends.

I STILL HAVE A LOT OF STRENGTH TO GAIN!

▼ He wants to feel the strength of
his defeated enemy, so Ryûô fights
with a sword.

Ryûô is most
happy when he
sees a strong
enemy. He
loves a good
fight from the
bottom of his
heart, and he
has the sense
to look at a win
as a win and a
loss as a loss.

TOPIC

A
Young
Man
Who
Wants
to get
Stronger

PARAMETER

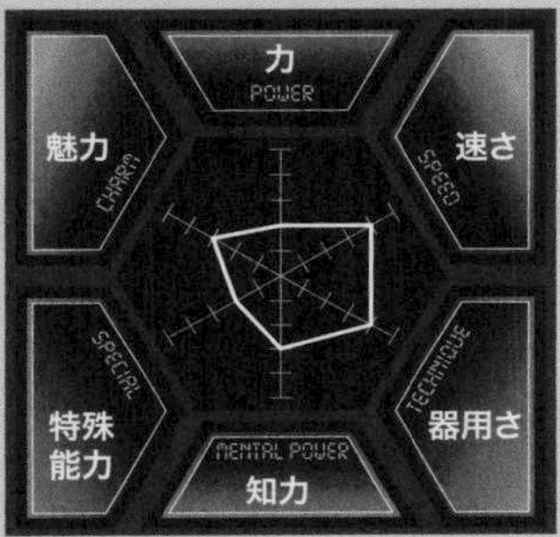
力
POWER
速さ
SPEED
器用さ
TECHNIQUE
知力
MENTAL POWER
特殊
能力
SPECIAL
魅力
CHARM

Sôma's weapon is a boomerang, which may be because her partner is Ryûô who always attacks from the front. She fights so effectively due to her speed and dexterity.

In contrast to her partner Ryûô, Sôma is calm and reserved. She keeps fight-anytime-anywhere-Ryûô's impulses in check, but another side of her can be seen when she is so enraptured by the cakes and treats served at Cat's Eye.

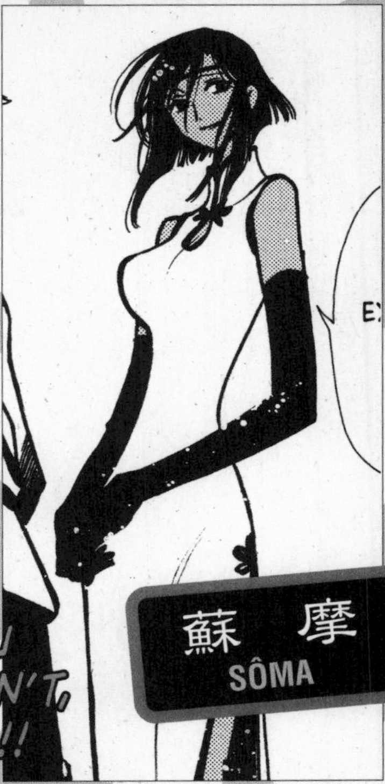
YOU MUSTN'T, RYÛÔ!!

蘇摩
SÔMA

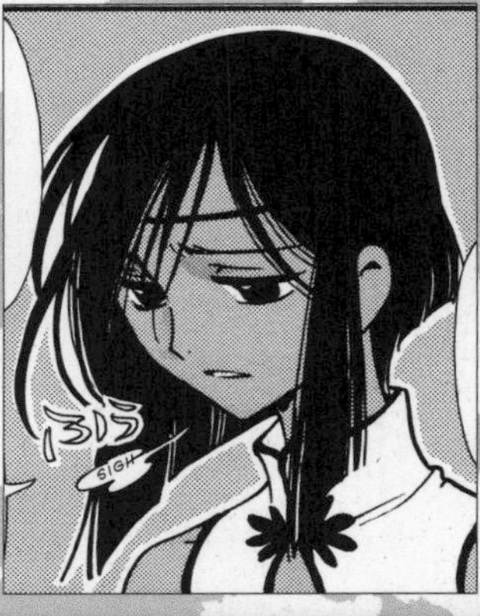
PLEASE ACCEPT MY HUMBLE APOLOGY FOR BEING UNABLE TO STOP RYÛÔ.
SIGH

➤ Sôma's actions are constantly dictated by Ryûô. She has plenty of reasons to sigh.

TOPIC

A Responsible Older Sister

She is always trying to hold Ryûô in check, but that job comes too often to be totally successful. So she apologizes to everyone inconvenienced by him as if she were his older sister. But that doesn't stop her from thinking of him with a smile.

絵里衣&
威&健多朗
ERII, TAKESHI & KENTARÔ

WORLD GUIDE

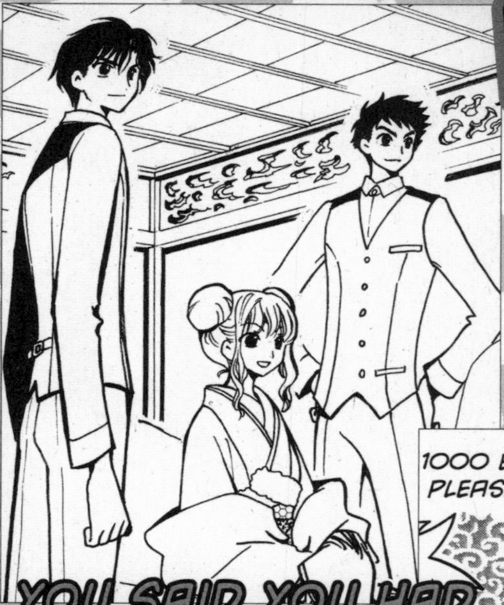

One of the girls in City Hall let Syaoran and Kurogane know about an informant. Erii is that informant. From Erii, they learned that a new kind of Oni seems to have appeared and where to find the one witnessed it. Takeshi and Kentarô are Erii's helpers.

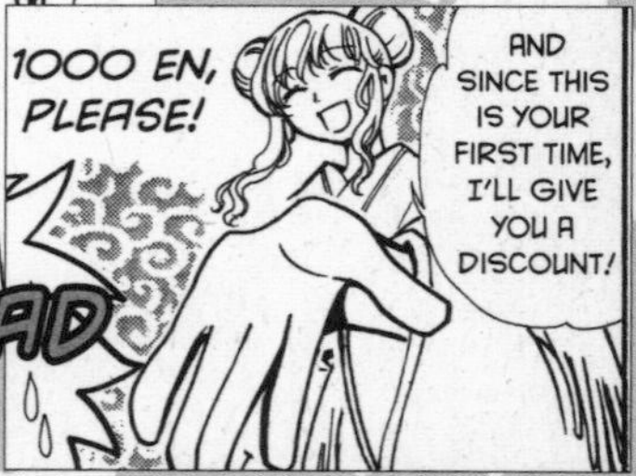
AND SINCE THIS IS YOUR FIRST TIME, I'LL GIVE YOU A DISCOUNT!
1000 EN, PLEASE!

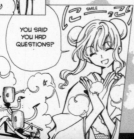

YOU SAID YOU HAD QUESTIONS?

➤ Erii asks for her payment for her information with a smile as wide as her face. She seems greedy, but she was giving them a discount.

YOU PAIR OF DOLTS!!

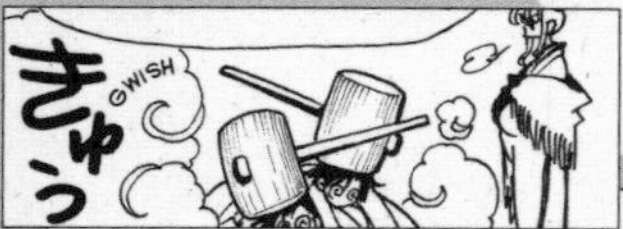
きゅう
GWISH

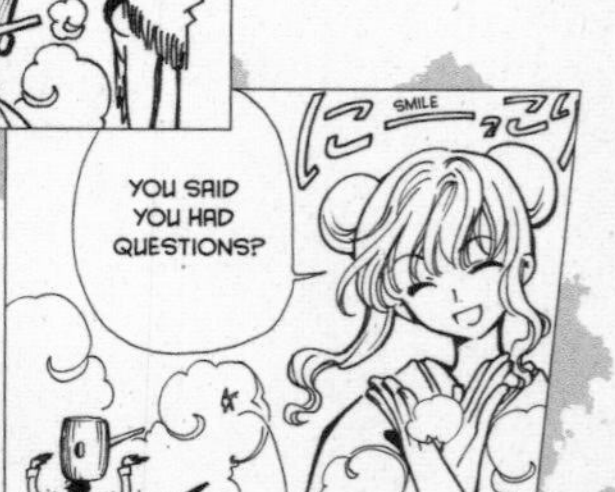
SMILE
YOU SAID YOU HAD QUESTIONS?

➤ Takeshi and Kentarô have defeated Ha-5 Oni, but even with strength like that, they can't avoid Erii's hammer.

Of the three, Erii is the leader of the group. Unfortunately for Takeshi and Kentarô, they can't seem to stand up for themselves.But it's probably not just her personality, Erii may be the stronger fighter as well.

TOPIC

Erii is the Strongest of Them

サンユン
SANYUN

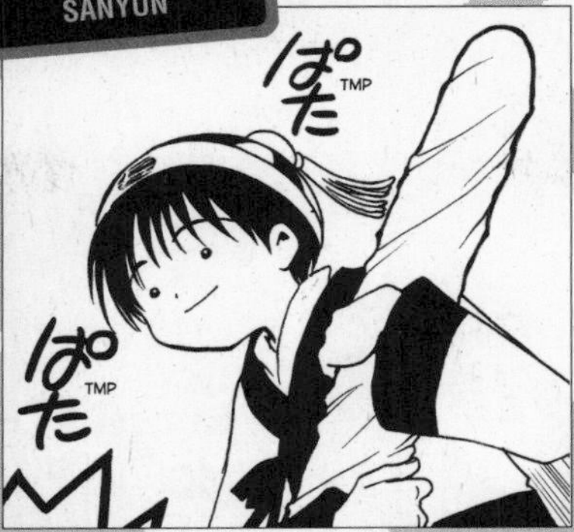
ぽた
TMP
ぽた
TMP

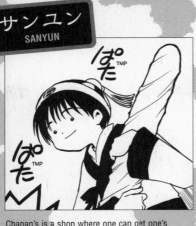

Chanan's is a shop where one can get one's hands on swords and other weapons. The shopkeeper is able to pick suitable swords for Syaoran and Kurogane, and Sanyun helps out.

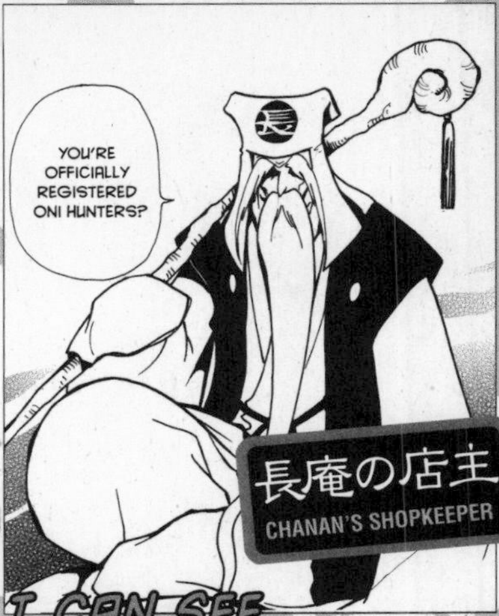
YOU'RE OFFICIALLY REGISTERED ONI HUNTERS?

長庵の店主
CHANAN'S SHOPKEEPER

I CAN SEE A FIRE IN YOUR EYE.

市役所の女の子
GIRLS OF CITY HALL

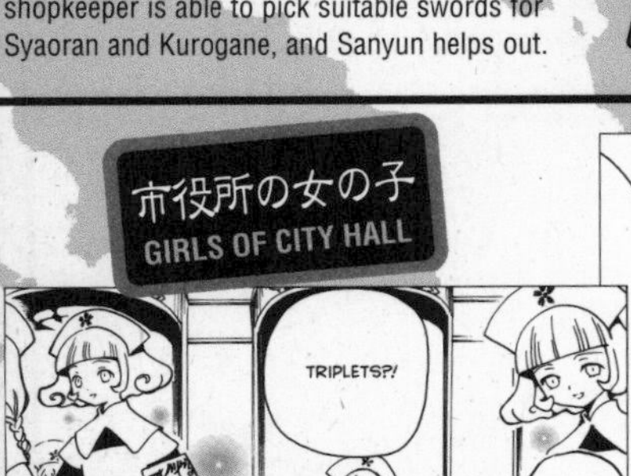
TRIPLETS?!

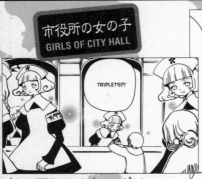

▲It could be because the Country of Ôto is a game world, but all of the girls of City Hall have exactly the same face.

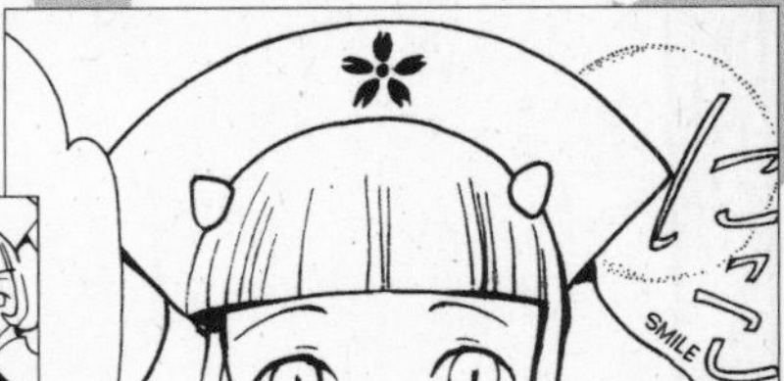
にっこり
SMILE

YOU WERE BUSY LAST NIGHT, HM?

From where to find lodgings to placement with a job, in the Country of Ôto, the first people to talk to for all of the needs in one's life are the girls of City Hall. But you can't rely on them for any extra information outside of their assigned subjects.

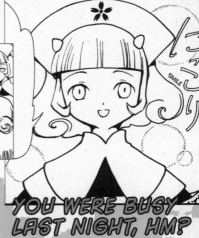

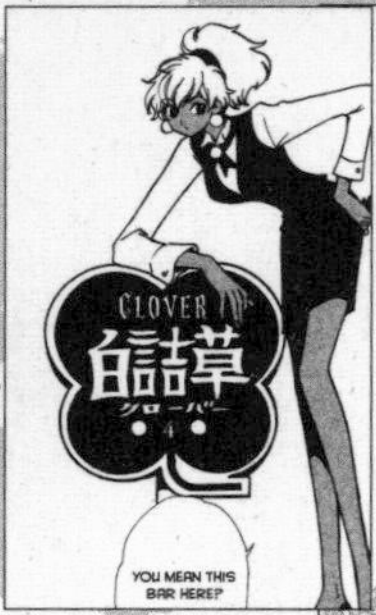
CLOVER 4
臨詰草
クローバー
YOU MEAN THIS BAR HERE?

➤ At first sight, you might think she's a bartender, and you'd be right! A woman with style!

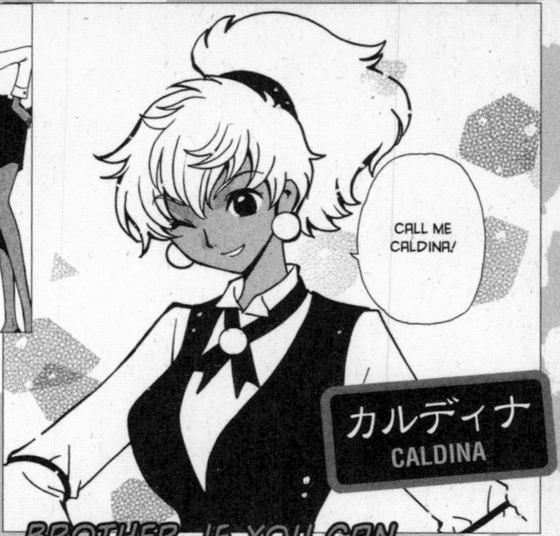
CALL ME CALDINA!
カルディナ
CALDINA

This classy woman is the bartender at a bar named Clover. Her personality is blunt but very friendly, and she talks a lot like Sorata of the Hanshin Republic.

BROTHER, IF YOU CAN TAKE IT, YOU'RE ON!

WELCOME TO THE TOWER OF THE LITTLE PEOPLE!!

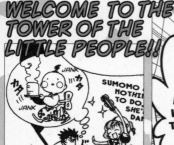

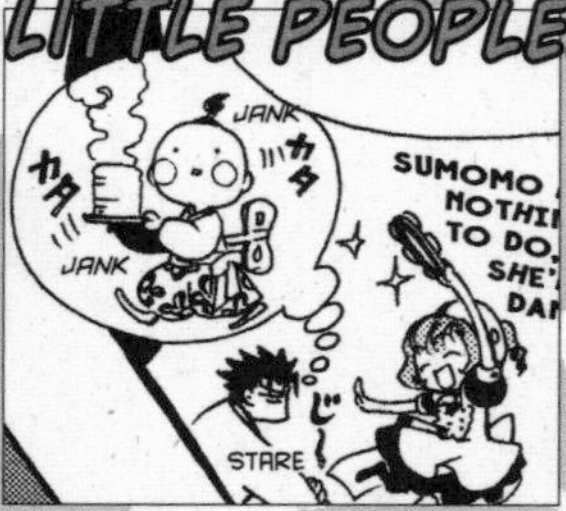
JANK
カタ
カタ
JANK
STARE
じー

➤ Calm, collected Kotoko is the opposite of overly energetic Sumomo.

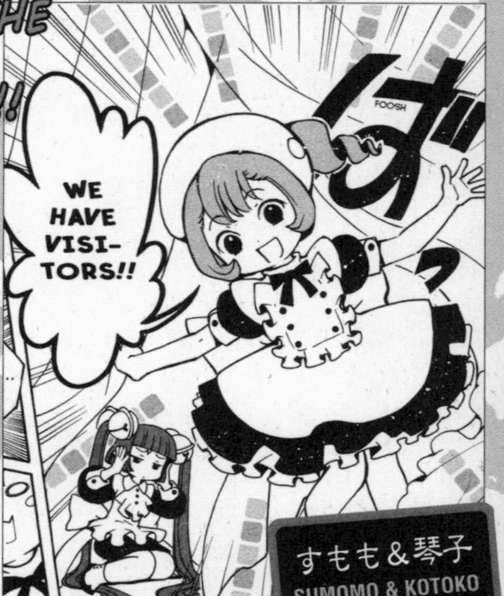
FOOSH
WE HAVE VISI-TORS!!
すもも＆琴子
SUMOMO & KOTOKO

Living in the most inaccessible part of the Tower of the Little People are Sumomo with a single ponytail and Kotoko with a double ponytail look. They are called Little People, but actually they're about the same size as Syaoran.

FOUND YOU!

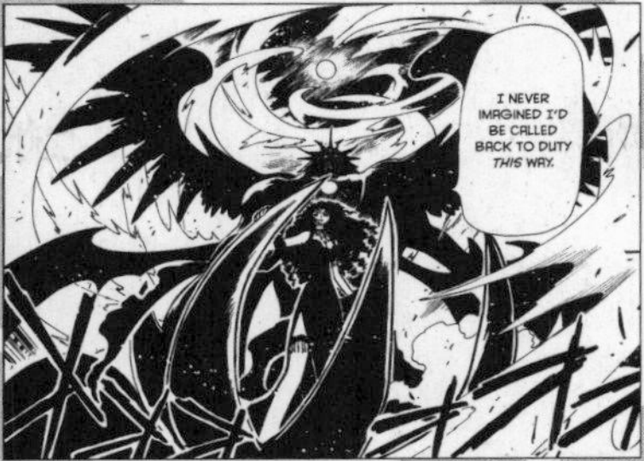
I NEVER IMAGINED I'D BE CALLED BACK TO DUTY *THIS* WAY.

▲ To Oruha, who is a part of the game, Seishirô's appearance was something she never expected.

Oruha has a wide reputation for her singing at the bar Clover. But her true form is that she's the most powerful Oni in the virtual reality world called the Country of Ôto. Seishirô is the one who revealed her identity.

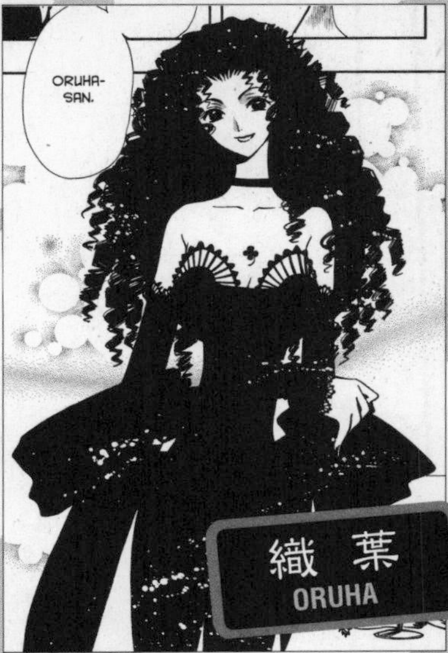
ORUHA-SAN.
織 葉
ORUHA

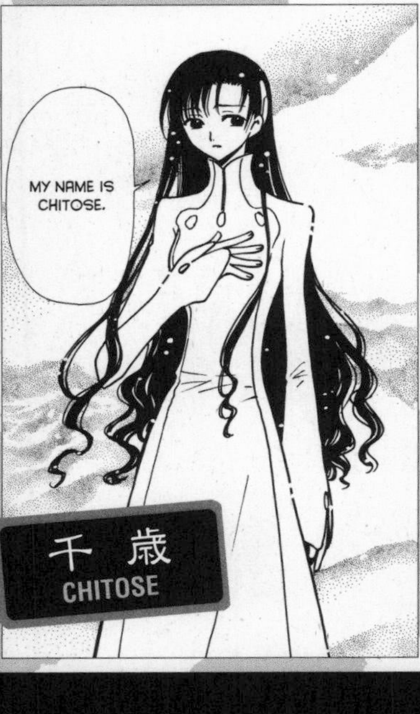
MY NAME IS CHITOSE.
千 歳
CHITOSE

IF THIS KEEPS UP, THE DREAM...

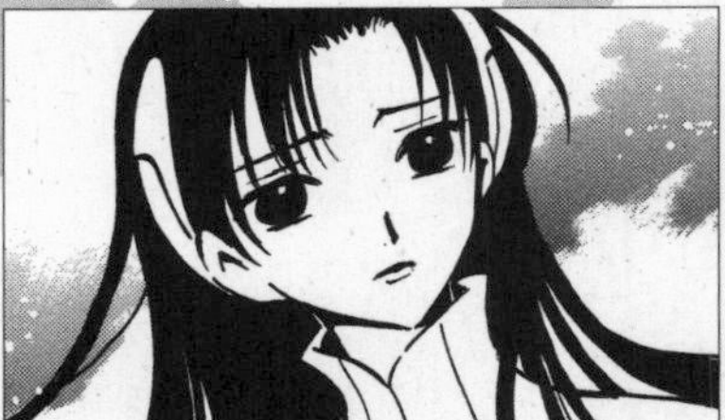

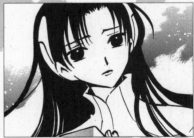

▲ In watching the destruction of the world she spent so much time designing, Chitose shows sadness in her eyes.

Chitose is one of the people who helped to design the theme park, Fairy Land Park. Even as one of the managers of the facility, she wasn't able to stop Seishirô from bringing the virtual reality game into reality.

WORLD GUIDE

Kingdom of Clow

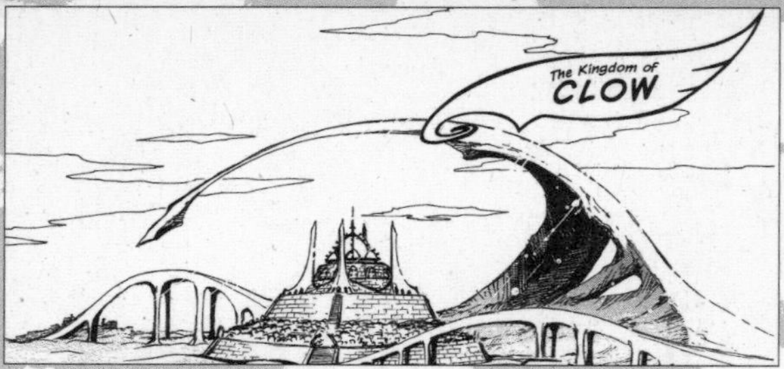
The Kingdom of
CLOW

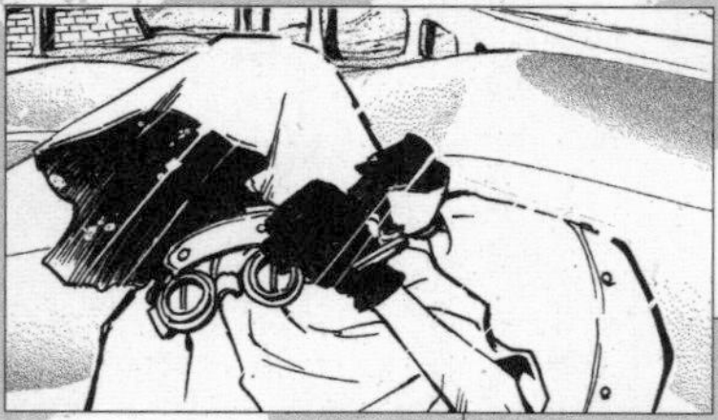

➤ In the desert, a hood to protect one from the sun must be indispensable.

While traveling with his adoptive father Fujitaka, Syaoran arrived at the Kingdom of Clow before he was seven years old. And since Fujitaka stayed in the kingdom to research the local ruins, Syaoran became close to the kingdom's young princess Sakura. Now that Syaoran and Sakura are traveling through the worlds, will they ever come back to the Kingdom of Clow?

CLIMATE

Surrounding the central castle is a town, and beyond that in all directions is desert as far as the eye can see. During the day, the temperatures rise, and the air is very dry.

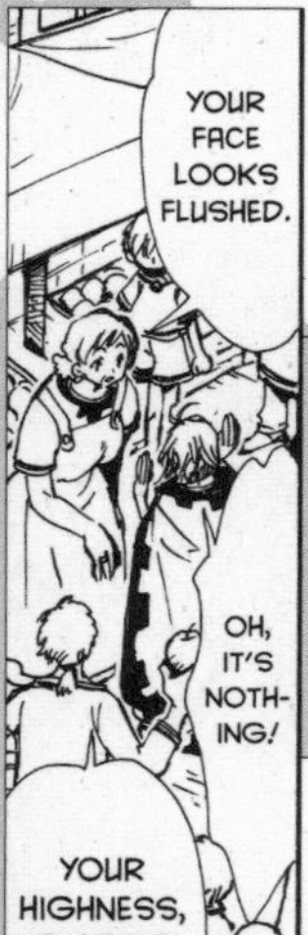
YOUR FACE LOOKS FLUSHED.
OH, IT'S NOTH-ING!
YOUR HIGHNESS, WOULD YOU HAVE AN APPLE?

➤ They treat Sakura as a friend even though she's a member of their royal family.

KINGDOM'S SUBJECTS

Their environment is forbidding, but the character of the people is upbeat. Sakura says that there are only good people in Clow.

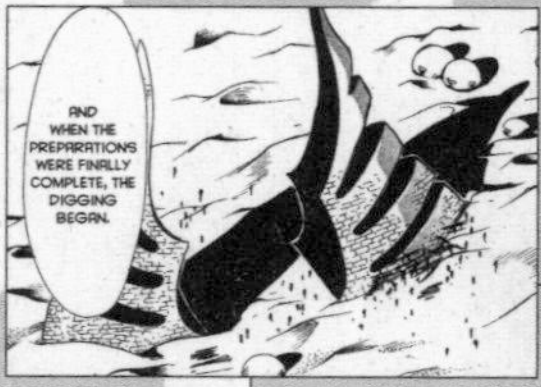
AND WHEN THE PREPARATIONS WERE FINALLY COMPLETE, THE DIGGING BEGAN.

▲ The most distinctive feature of these ruins are the unusual shape of two outstretched wings.

RUINS

The excavations that Fujitaka started still continue. Deep below the surface, there is a room where an odd crest is drawn on a wall.

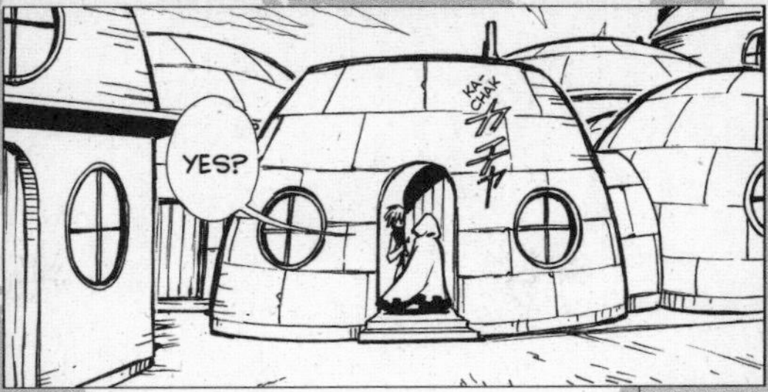
KA-CHAK
YES?

▲ Syaoran keeps pictures of Fujitaka inside. To Syaoran, his home is a place filled with memories of his father.

SYAORAN'S HOUSE

Ever since Fujitaka died in an accident, Syaoran has stayed in his house on his own. But there are a lot of times when he is gone on excavations at the ruins.

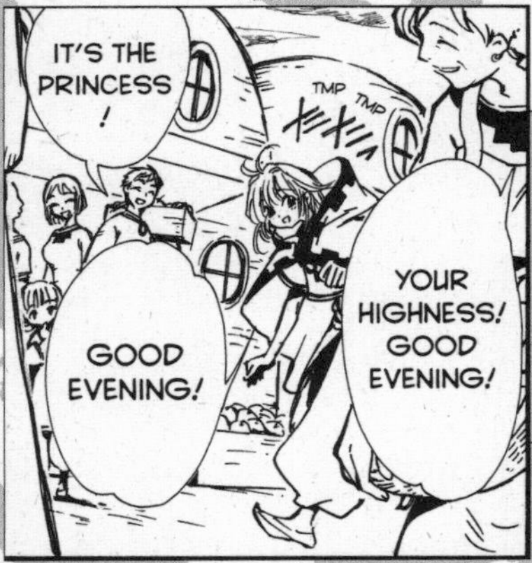
IT'S THE PRINCESS!
TMP TMP
YOUR HIGHNESS! GOOD EVENING!
GOOD EVENING!

TOWN VIEWS

These unusual stone-built domed structures are the standard family dwelling for the Kingdom of Clow. They're built in clusters with the buildings crowding up together.

◄ The wide path running between the buildings is where the people congregate. And the many roadside stalls are very popular with the shopping citizens.

➤ It is similar in shape to the houses of the citizens, but in size and splendor, they just can't compare to the castle. It contains a bell that sounds throughout the entire town informing the citizens of the time.

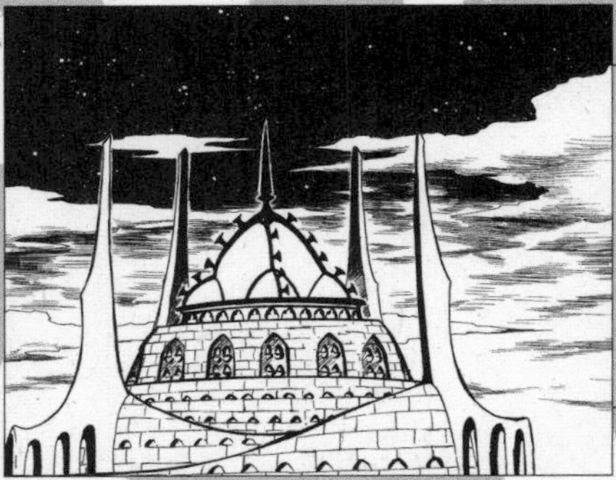

CASTLE

The Kingdom of Clow features an enormous castle with a commanding view of the town. It is there where the royal family members such as Princess Sakura and King Tôya reside, along with those who serve them, such as the high priest.

桃矢
TÔYA

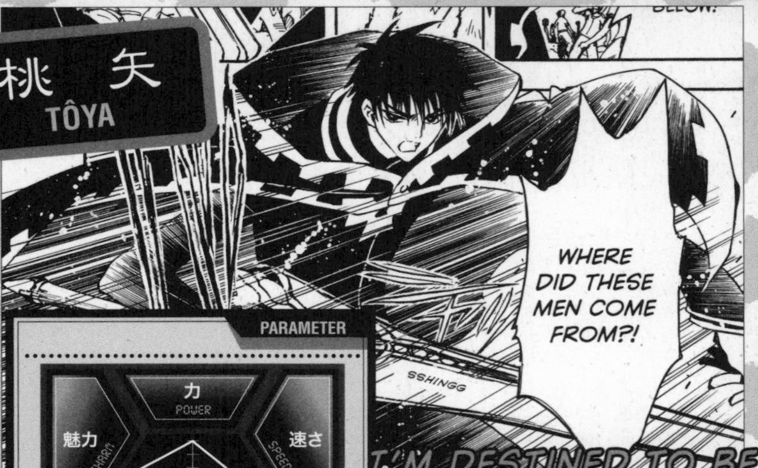
WHERE DID THESE MEN COME FROM?!
SSHINGG

PARAMETER

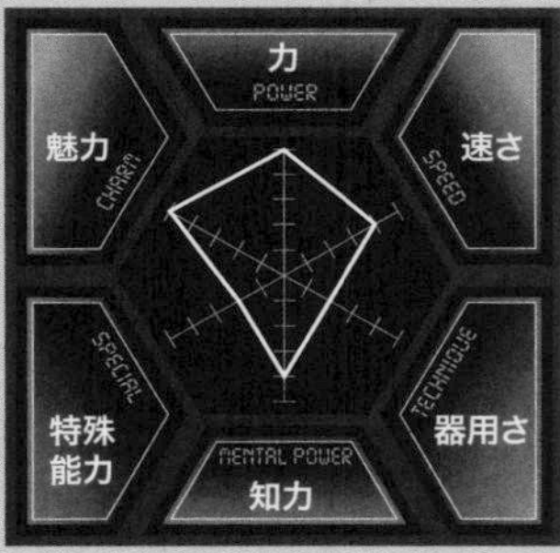
力
POWER
速さ
SPEED
器用さ
TECHNIQUE
知力
MENTAL POWER
特殊能力
SPECIAL
魅力
CHARM

Just as befits the king of Clow, he has striven to become strong. The valiant spirit of the king is what his subjects rely on.

I'M DESTINED TO BE KING AND WARRIOR.

Tôya is the young king who rules the Kingdom of Clow. He's a man with the strength and courage to draw his own sword and personally stand against those who are attacking his country. However, a different side of him is revealed in his attitude toward his sister Sakura and his childhood friend Yukito. An attitude that seems appropriate for his actual young age.

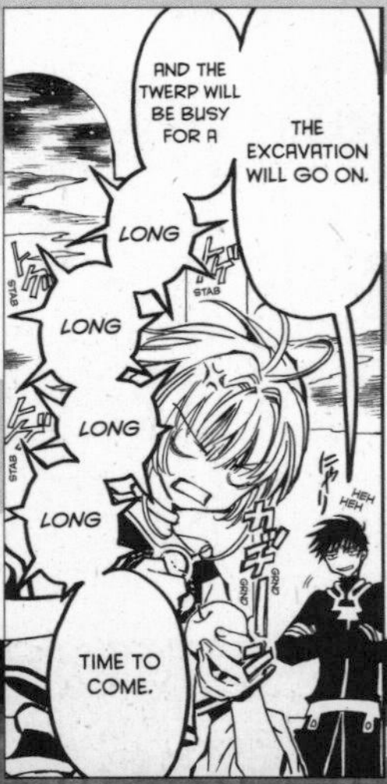
THE EXCAVATION WILL GO ON.
AND THE TWERP WILL BE BUSY FOR A
LONG
LONG
LONG
LONG
TIME TO COME.
STAB
GRIND
HEH HEH

➤ Tôya's goading of Sakura is, according to Yukito, because he thinks she is so cute he can't help himself.

TOPIC

Precious Sister Sakura

YOU'VE BEEN SPOTTED, SAKURA!

He may start arguments with her, but the truth is that no one holds Sakura more dear than Tôya. He doesn't think much of Sakura's relationship with Syaoran, but that may simply be jealousy talking.

Yukito is the high priest serving the Kingdom of Clow. With his calm and gentle manner, he has become Tôya's most trusted advisor. He has the power of premonition, and foresaw that Sakura and Syaoran had great adversity that they must overcome.

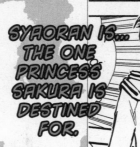

SYAORAN IS... THE ONE PRINCESS SAKURA IS DESTINED FOR.

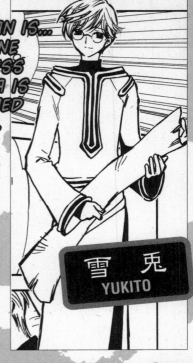

雪兎
YUKITO

PARAMETER

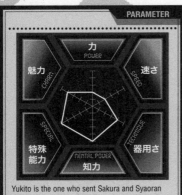

力
POWER
速さ
SPEED
器用さ
TECHNIQUE
知力
MENTAL POWER
特殊能力
SPECIAL
魅力
CHARM

Yukito is the one who sent Sakura and Syaoran across dimensions to the Time-Space Witch. Just that one fact alone proves that he has tremendous magical powers.

TOPIC

When Alone They're Friends

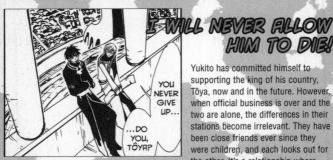

I WILL NEVER ALLOW HIM TO DIE!

YOU NEVER GIVE UP...
...DO YOU, TÔYA?

▲ Their friendship that transcends social position has some of the same feel as Sakura's and Syaoran's relationship.

Yukito has committed himself to supporting the king of his country, Tôya, now and in the future. However, when official business is over and the two are alone, the differences in their stations become irrelevant. They have been close friends ever since they were children, and each looks out for the other. It's a relationship where they never have to watch their words with each other.

FUJITAKA

YOU DON'T HAVE TO APOLOGIZE TO ME, SYAORAN-KUN.

> ...THERE ARE A LOT OF FASCINATING THINGS THAT NO LIVING SOUL HAS EVER SEEN! IN THE WORLD...

▲ It was Fujitaka's influence from which came Syaoran's love of ruins and history.

Fujitaka, Syaoran's adoptive father, raised the boy with deep love. When Fujitaka found Syaoran as a very young boy, Syaoran was expressionless as if he had lost all of his emotions. Syaoran's eventual ability to smile was not the work of Sakura alone. Fujitaka must have played a large part in it. As a man full of curiosity, archaeologist Fujitaka took Syaoran with him as they visited many different countries.

> WOULD YOU LIKE IT IF HE WERE YOUR FRIEND?

▲ The king lets Princess Sakura know that it is all right for her to be friends with Syaoran.

LET'S TRUST IN THE FUTURE, SHALL WE?

PREVIOUS KING

The previous king is the late father of Sakura and Tôya. Upon Fujitaka's request, he gave permission to conduct excavations of the ruins in the Kingdom of Clow. He seemed to be a man with a congenial nature.

 WORLD GUIDE

Country of Japan

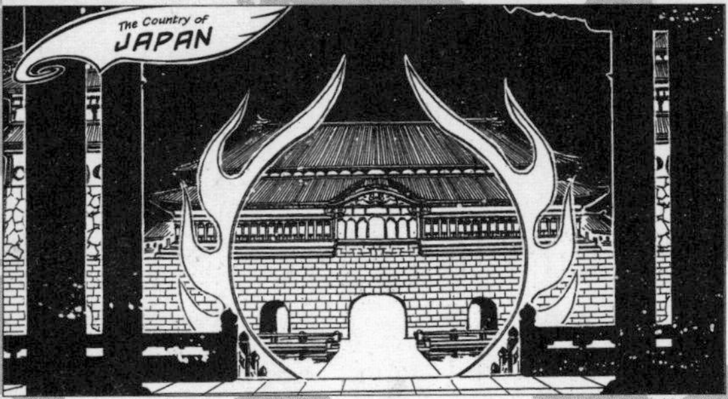
The Country of
JAPAN

The world from which Kurogane came looks similar to Japan in our reality during the Warring States Period (mid-fifteenth to the early seventeenth centuries). In this country, Kurogane served the Shirasaki Castle and Princess Tomoyo. Seeing how the castle was being invaded, it seems that war is not uncommon in this world either.

知世姫 TOMOYO

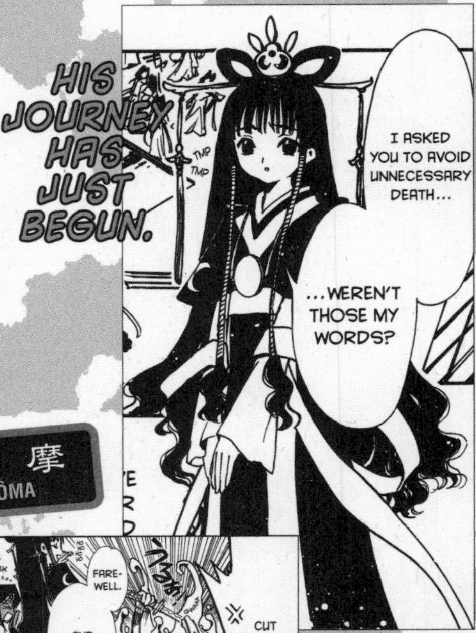
HIS JOURNEY HAS JUST BEGUN.
I ASKED YOU TO AVOID UNNECESSARY DEATH...
...WEREN'T THOSE MY WORDS?

The one who sent Kurogane across universes to the Time-Space Witch is Tomoyo, the princess of Shirasaki Castle. Since she professes a hatred of unnecessary death, Kurogane seemed like something of a thorn in her side. So she placed a curse on him such that his strength will lessen for each person he kills.

蘇摩 SÔMA

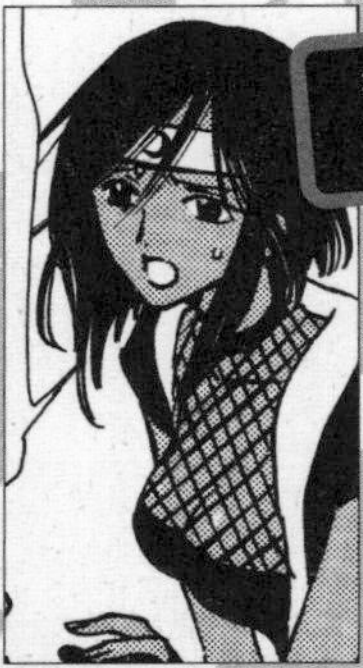

➤ Like Kurogane, Sôma is a ninja who served Princess Tomoyo. She has great loyalty to her princess.

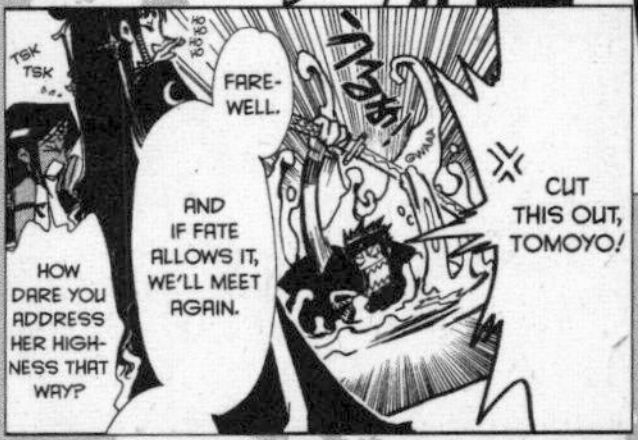
FARE-WELL.
AND IF FATE ALLOWS IT, WE'LL MEET AGAIN.
HOW DARE YOU ADDRESS HER HIGHNESS THAT WAY?
CUT THIS OUT, TOMOYO!

◄ Seeing as how she sent Kurogane off with a laugh, Tomoyo must have a very mischievous personality.

King Ashura sleeps within the castle in the Country of Seresu. Since Fai is intimately related to that fact, he must no longer stay in the world.

Country of Seresu

AFTER ALL, FAI MADE CHII!

チ イ
CHII

I STILL DON'T UNDER- STAND.

Aside from the animal-like ears, Chii looks no different than a normal human girl. As she says, Fai made Chii, so she is willing to do anything that Fai asks of her.

▲ In her new form provided her by Fai, Chii keeps watch on the sleeping King Ashura.

アシュラ王
ASHURA

◄ King Ashura is presently asleep. Fai took up his flight through the worlds in order to escape from him.

COUNTRY OF SERESU?

Fei-Wang Reed is a mysterious man who is plotting to obtain the ability to travel between worlds. It can be assumed that he was behind the scattering of Sakura's memory feathers in the first place. It seems that he and the Time-Space Witch, Yûko, are enemies.

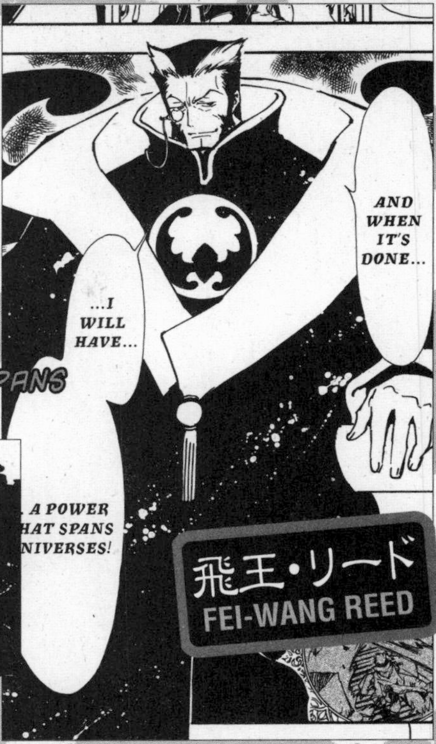
AND WHEN IT'S DONE...
...I WILL HAVE...
A POWER HAT SPANS NIVERSES!

飛王・リード
FEI-WANG REED

I WILL HAVE A POWER THAT SPANS UNIVERSES!

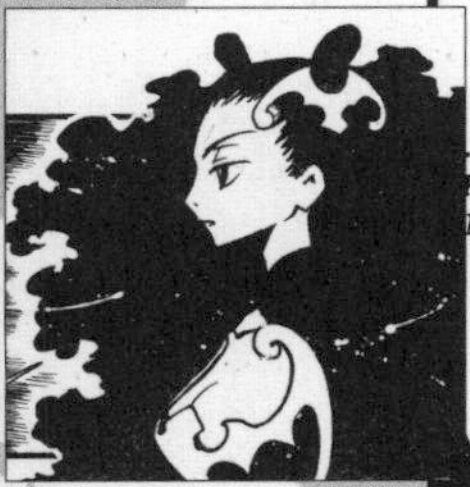

▲ This woman stands by Fei-Wang's side giving him reports and advice.

?

What world can these mysterious people watching Syaoran and his group be from? Perhaps it is only a matter of time before the answer comes.

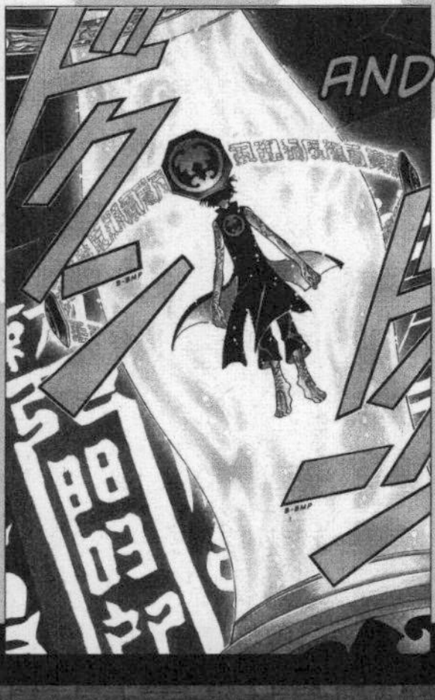

AND I STILL HAVE THAT.

◀ This is another Syaoran that Fei-Wang has gotten his hands on. If one considers Fei-Wang's previous actions, this could have a profound effect on Syaoran.

TOPIC

The Mysterious Trump Card

Fei-Wang has been watching the travels of Syaoran and his friends with the goal of obtaining the power to travel between worlds. He gets annoyed when Yûko interferes with his schemes, but he seems convinced that in the end he will acquire that power. But on what grounds is he basing this conviction?

侑子
YÛKO

The Time-Space Witch and the Far-East Witch are two of the many names for this mysterious woman. And as her names imply, she controls extremely strong magics. The entire reason Syaoran and his party can travel through worlds is because of the creature provided by Yûko, Mokona.

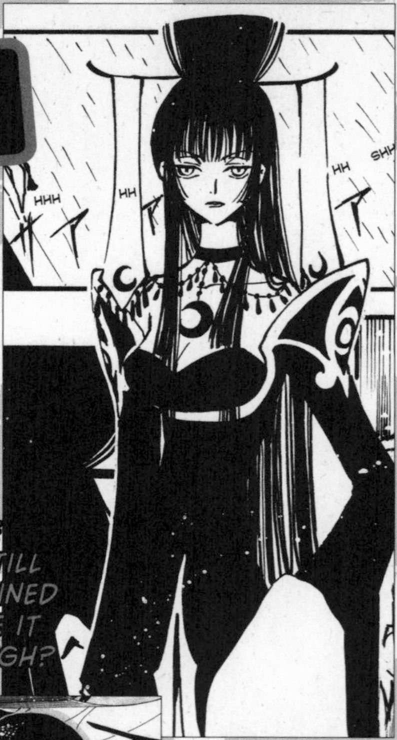
SHH
HH
HH
HHH
ARE YOU STILL DETERMINED TO SEE IT THROUGH?

Japan

This is the world in which we find Yûko's shop. It is the setting for xxxHolic, the series that crosses over with Tsubasa.

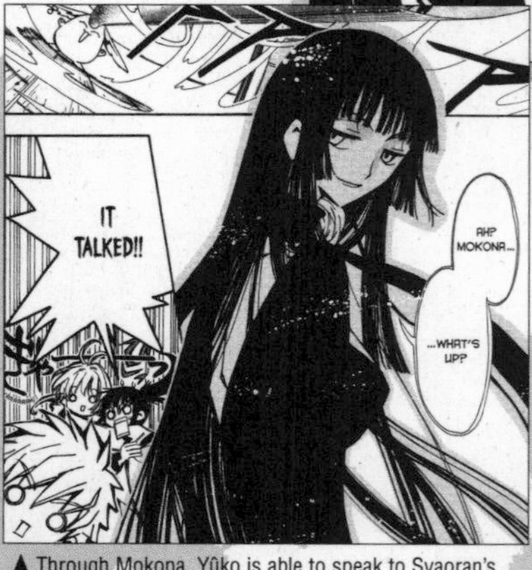
AH! MOKONA...
...WHAT'S UP?
IT TALKED!!

▲ Through Mokona, Yûko is able to speak to Syaoran's group in a different dimension, the Country of Koryo. Even Chu'nyan, who lives in a country with magic, was shocked by the event.

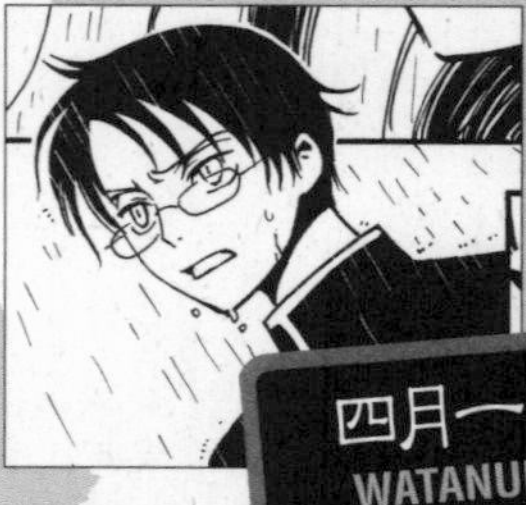

四月一日
WATANUKI

Watanuki is a young man working in Yûko's shop as a part-time job. Under Yûko's orders, he brought the white and black Mokona out of the treasure room.

TOPIC 1
A Price Paid

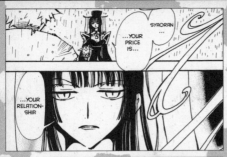

It is said that Yûko will grant any wish for you as long as you pay an appropriate price, and the price she set for Syaoran, Kurogane, and Fai was their most precious possessions. It seems that the power to travel between worlds is so great that the only way to pay for it was to combine their three payments together.

SYAORAN ...
...YOUR PRICE IS...
...YOUR RELATIONSHIP.
I'LL HAND OVER SOMETHING THAT WILL HELP BREAK THE MAGIC ARTS SURROUNDING THE CASTLE.
BUT I'LL EXPECT PAYMENT IN RETURN.

➤ The prices she asks are varied and include Fai's magic staff and intangible items such as Syaoran's relationship with Sakura.

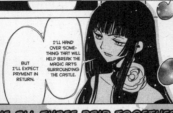

IF ALL THREE PAID TOGETHER, YOU MIGHT JUST BE ABLE TO AFFORD IT.

TOPIC 2
The Witch's Power

THERE IS NO COINCIDENCE IN THE WORLD. WHAT IS THERE IS "HITSUZEN."

Many people from different worlds know Yûko's name and magic including Yukito of the Kingdom of Clow, Tomoyo from the Country of Japan, and Sorata from the Hanshin Republic. It's also thought that Yûko is the only one who can travel between an unlimited number of worlds. No one knows the extent of her power.

IT WOULD TAKE GOING TO A LOT OF WORLDS TO BE ABLE TO COLLECT ALL OF SAKURA-CHAN'S FEATHERS.
AND I THINK THE ONLY ONE WHO CAN SEND SOMEONE TO MANY WORLDS IS THE DIMENSION WITCH.
WHAT THE HELL?!

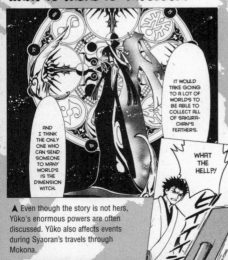

▲ Even though the story is not hers, Yûko's enormous powers are often discussed. Yûko also affects events during Syaoran's travels through Mokona.

Country of Japan's greatest Ninja, Kurogane's

CHARACTER

BATTLE-STRENGTH REPORT

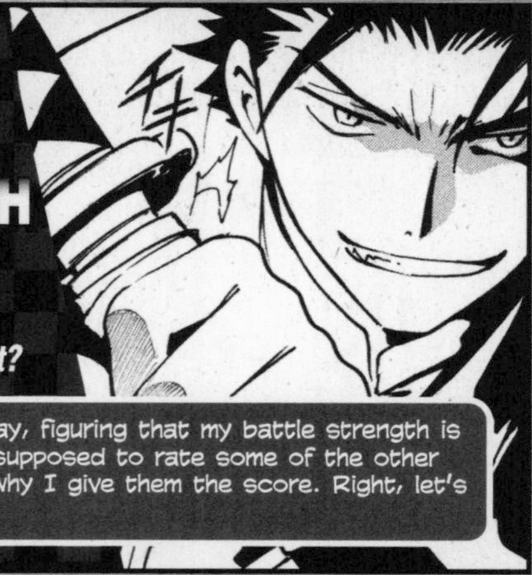

- Syaoran
- Fai D. Flowright
- Shôgo Asagi
- Primela
- Kiishim
- Ryûô
- Seishirô

Who's the strongest?

I'm Kurogane. Okay, figuring that my battle strength is 500 points, I'm supposed to rate some of the other guys and explain why I give them the score. Right, let's get started.

SYAORAN

ATTACK STRENGTH	☆☆☆
MARTIAL ARTS	☆☆☆☆
PHYSICAL STRENGTH	☆☆☆
STRENGTH OF NERVES	☆☆☆☆☆
LATENT ABILITIES	☆☆☆☆

STATS EXPLANATION

Each Stat tops out at five stars. One star is twenty points. Top combined stat score is 500 points.

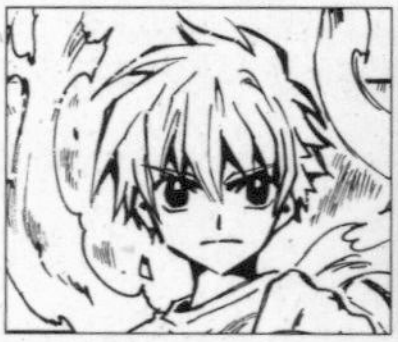

COMBINED STAT SCORE

380 PT

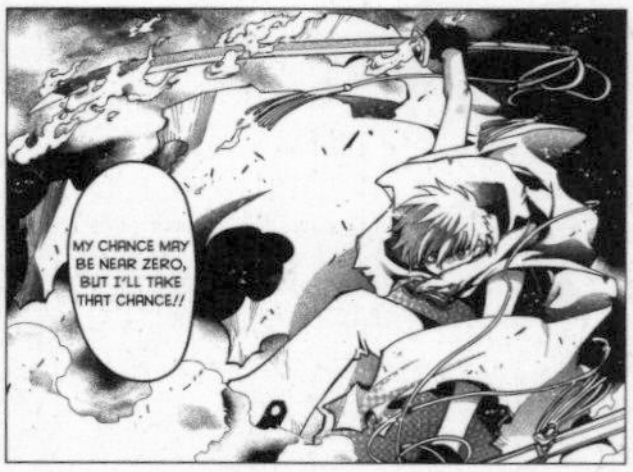
MY CHANCE MAY BE NEAR ZERO, BUT I'LL TAKE THAT CHANCE!!

Kurogane: "The boy has very strong emotions, so the fire sword suits him fine."

COMBINED EVALUATION

Kurogane: "Now this guy's interesting. He can't see out of his right eye, and because of it, he's bound to have problems with distances. So he focuses on his own brand of martial arts that uses kicks as the main attack because of the long reach you get with kicking action. But he wasn't satisfied with leaving it at that, so I started to give him lessons in the sword every now and then. He's got a few muscles, so it isn't all that rough a task. But the biggest thing about him is he's always working to get stronger. That's the sign of a strong will. We'll have to see just how much stronger he can get, but for now, this is about where he's at."

Fai: "You say that, but deep down, you're shivering in your boots that he's going to get stronger than you, aren't you?"

Kurogane: "That ain't one of my worries."

SHÔGO ASAGI

ATTACK STRENGTH	☆☆☆☆
MARTIAL ARTS	☆☆
PHYSICAL STRENGTH	☆☆☆
STRENGTH OF NERVES	☆☆☆☆☆
LATENT ABILITIES	☆☆☆

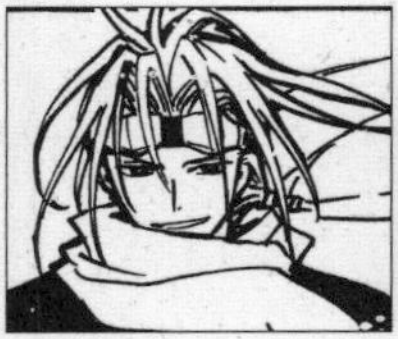

COMBINED STAT SCORE

340 PT

COMBINED EVALUATION

Kurogane: "Anybody who's got a strong Kudan means that he's got strong nerves, so this guy's gotta have nerves of steel. But every attack he made was through his water Kudan, so if he went to a world without Kudan..."

Primela: "Shôgo-kun would be the strongest no matter when or where he goes!!"

Kurogane: "Quit screaming in my ears!"

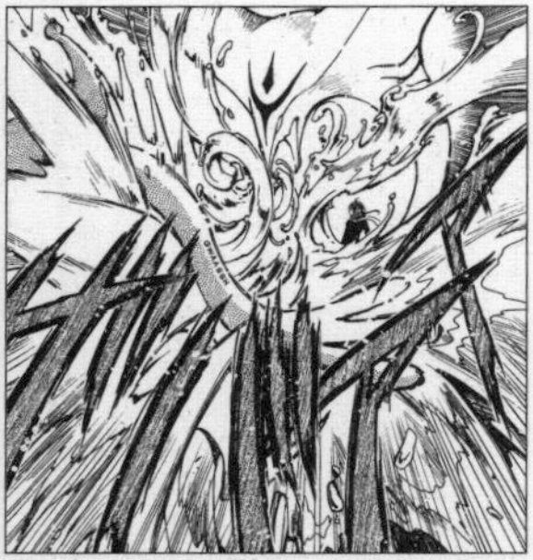

Kurogane: "People think of water as soft, but it can cut and it can bowl people over. It all depends on how you use it."

FAI

ATTACK STRENGTH	☆☆☆
MARTIAL ARTS	☆☆☆☆
PHYSICAL STRENGTH	☆☆☆☆
STRENGTH OF NERVES	☆☆☆☆
LATENT ABILITIES	☆☆☆☆☆

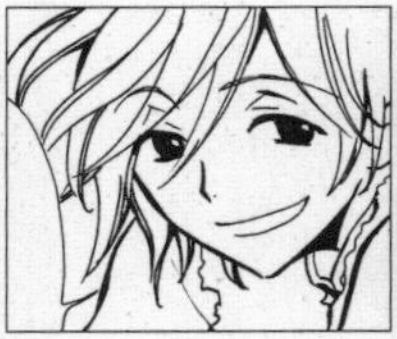

COMBINED STAT SCORE

400 PT

COMBINED EVALUATION

Kurogane: "There's something about this guy I don't like."

Fai: "Oh, I don't know about that."

Kurogane: "Shut up a minute. He's okay with martial arts, but he's supposed to be a wizard, right? He never used his powers so I don't know how powerful he is. But I know he's hiding something..."

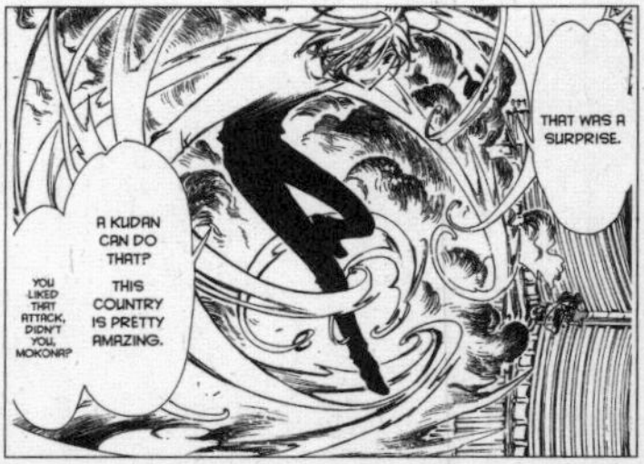
THAT WAS A SURPRISE.
A KUDAN CAN DO THAT? THIS COUNTRY IS PRETTY AMAZING.
YOU LIKED THAT ATTACK, DIDN'T YOU, MOKONA?

Kurogane: "He can use a Kudan to full effect, so he probably has some power he isn't showing me."

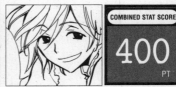

KIISHIM

ATTACK STRENGTH	☆☆☆☆☆
MARTIAL ARTS	☆☆☆☆
PHYSICAL STRENGTH	☆☆☆
STRENGTH OF NERVES	☆☆☆☆
LATENT ABILITIES	☆☆☆☆

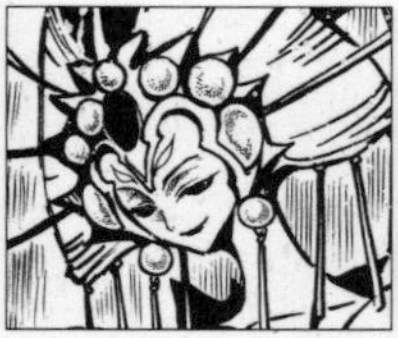

COMBINED STAT SCORE

400 PT

COMBINED EVALUATION

Fai: "Now she was a problem."

Kurogane: "I guess so. She sent orbs of acid or something flying at us as an attack. When we were splashed with it, our clothes started smoldering and our skin was burned."

Fai: "Maybe if the fight had gone on longer, we might have been melted."

Kurogane: "Aw, gimme a break!"

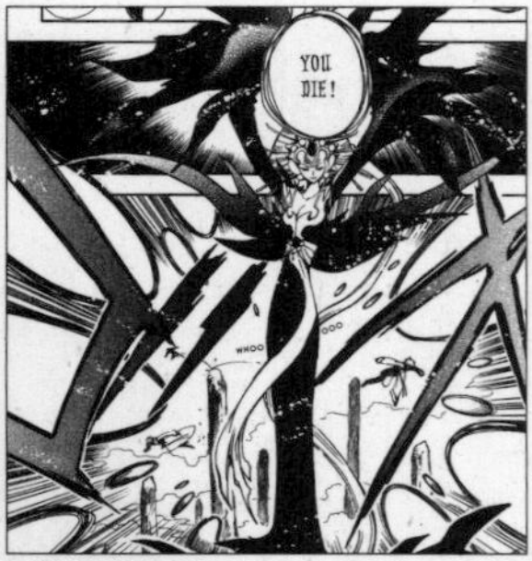
YOU DIE!

Kurogane: "If she had used that melting water of hers from the first time she saw us, we might have had a few extra problems."

PRIMELA

ATTACK STRENGTH	☆☆☆
MARTIAL ARTS	☆
PHYSICAL STRENGTH	☆
STRENGTH OF NERVES	☆☆☆
LATENT ABILITIES	☆☆

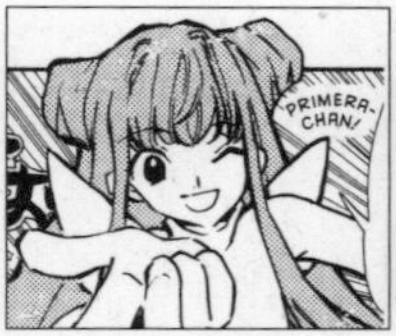
PRIMERA-CHAN!

COMBINED STAT SCORE

200 PT

COMBINED EVALUATION

Kurogane: "This girl uses Kudan, too. She uses it to turn her words into huge letters like you'd find in a manga, and they fly to the attack. But she isn't used to battle, and she overuses her one attack, so if she were fighting me…"

Mokona: "Can Mokona call Kurogane 'Cranky Baby' from now on?"

Kurogane: "Watch it, or I'm gonna boil you on Oden skewers!"

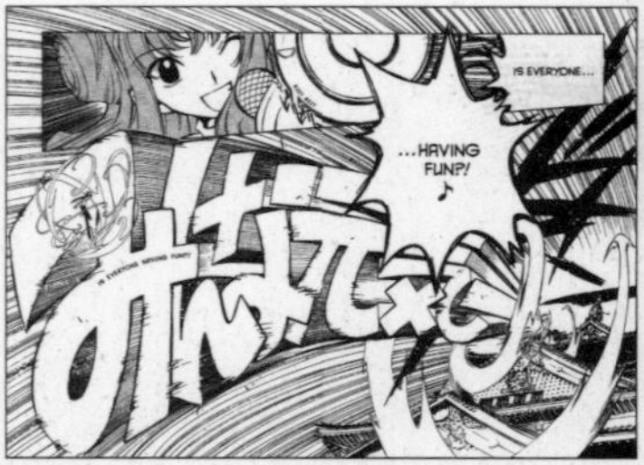
IS EVERYONE...
...HAVING FUN?! ♪

Kurogane: "She doesn't look like she could have one, but her Kudan is special level."

SEISHIRÔ

ATTACK STRENGTH	☆ ☆ ☆ ☆ ☆
MARTIAL ARTS	☆ ☆ ☆ ☆ ☆
PHYSICAL STRENGTH	☆ ☆ ☆ ☆
STRENGTH OF NERVES	☆ ☆ ☆ ☆ ☆
LATENT ABILITIES	☆ ☆ ☆ ☆ ☆

COMBINED STAT SCORE

480
PT

COMBINED EVALUATION

Kurogane: "This guy's tough. He crossed swords with me, and he didn't retreat one step. It also looks like he's got powers, so a dust-up with him would turn into a real battle. I don't know why he killed Fai and the kid, then turned around to try to provoke me, but if he's selling a fight, then I'm buying!"

Syaoran: "Seishirô-san is a very strong fighter. That means that I'm going to have to become much stronger."

RYÛÔ

ATTACK STRENGTH	☆ ☆ ☆ ☆
MARTIAL ARTS	☆ ☆ ☆
PHYSICAL STRENGTH	☆ ☆ ☆
STRENGTH OF NERVES	☆ ☆ ☆
LATENT ABILITIES	☆ ☆ ☆ ☆

COMBINED STAT SCORE

360
PT

COMBINED EVALUATION

Syaoran: "I'd have liked to have tried fighting him all out."

Kurogane: "That'd have been a good match for you at this stage. He's got better skills with a sword than you, but you're better with your attack strength. And you're able to use your body better. But listen, a fight isn't just a place for breaking furniture!"

Syaoran: "I'm sorry…"

Syaoran: "He says he uses a sword because he wants to feel like he's a part of the action."

TSUBASA
MINI REPORT
③

Kurogane's Nickname Selection

MINI REPORT

Kurogane is cool and a great fighter. But the nicknames that Fai gives him are very cute. We've gathered some of the most interesting names from the many that Fai gave him.

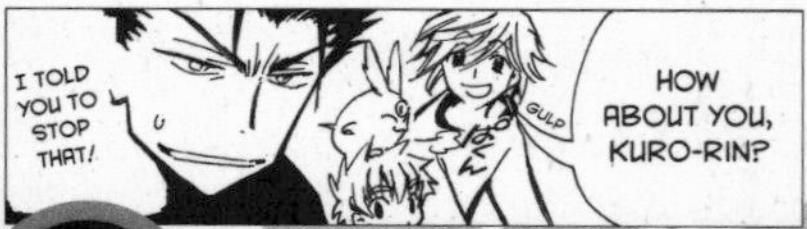
HOW ABOUT YOU, KURO-RIN?
GULP
I TOLD YOU TO STOP THAT!

Kuro-rin
Vol. 1, P. 170
Anger: 70%

This one came directly after Fai called him Kuro-tan. The rapid-fire succession of nicknames seem to put Kurogane off of his game.

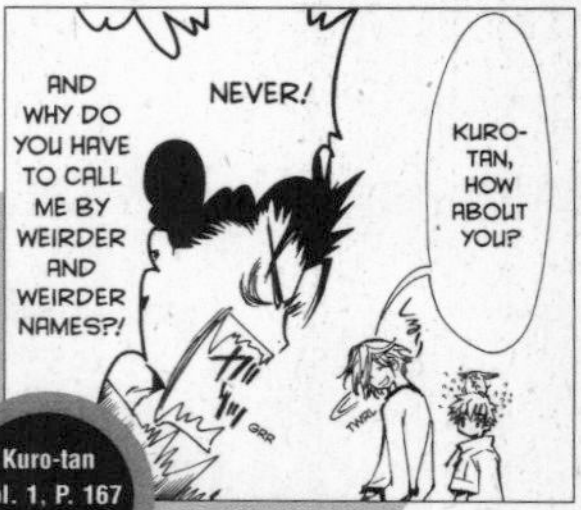
KURO-TAN, HOW ABOUT YOU?
NEVER!
AND WHY DO YOU HAVE TO CALL ME BY WEIRDER AND WEIRDER NAMES?!
GRR
TWIRL

Kuro-tan
Vol. 1, P. 167
Anger: 90%

This is the important inaugural nickname given by Fai. Being given an unexpected, weird (cute?) nickname makes Kurogane explode in anger.

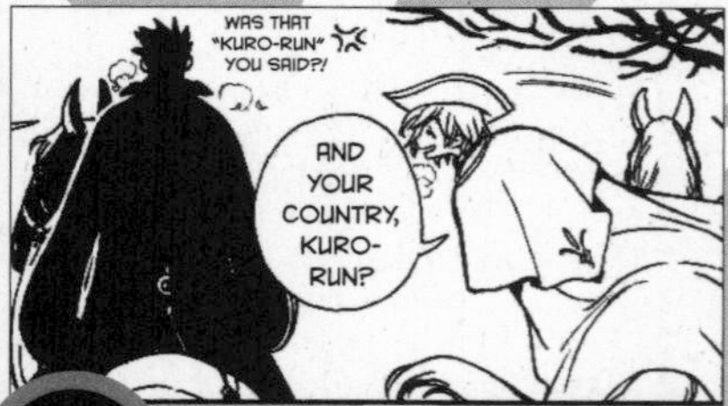
AND YOUR COUNTRY, KURO-RUN?
WAS THAT "KURO-RUN" YOU SAID?!

Kuro-run
Vol. 4, P. 99
Anger: 10%

His words show some anger, but otherwise, he is a lot less affected by the nickname than he has been before. Could it be that he's gotten used to all the nicknames after so long?

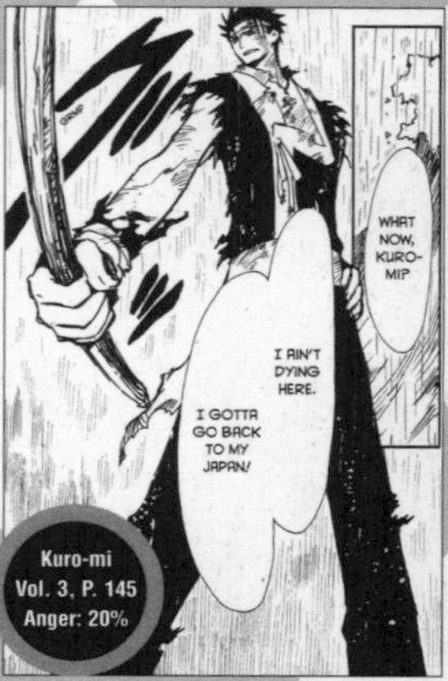
WHAT NOW, KURO-MI?
I AIN'T DYING HERE.
I GOTTA GO BACK TO MY JAPAN!
GRIP

Kuro-mi
Vol. 3, P. 145
Anger: 20%

Even in a rough spot, Fai gives Kurogane a nickname as if he didn't have a care in the world. But it may be because he was concentrating on his battle with the Kiishim, but he didn't seem to mind this time.

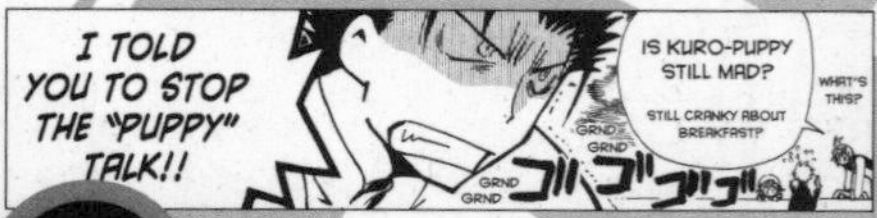
WHAT'S THIS?
IS KURO-PUPPY STILL MAD?
STILL CRANKY ABOUT BREAKFAST?
GRND GRND
I TOLD YOU TO STOP THE "PUPPY" TALK!!

Kuro-puppy
Vol. 6, P. 23
Anger: 100%

Kurogane had been becoming less and less angry at Fai's nicknames as time went on, but when he hears this one he becomes enraged. He probably doesn't like being treated like a dog.

AUTHOR INTRODUCTION

This section contains an interview in which a member of CLAMP talks about the story; an exclusive Tsubasa story drawn just for this book; and there are special tributes drawn by Oh!great-sensei and Kazuki Yamamoto-sensei.

WE'RE GOING TO WRITE A BOOK.

CLAMP GUIDE

Five Works that Can Be Summarized as "S"

Sensitive
Suspenseful
Sweet
Stylish
Strange

The authors of Tsubasa, a group of four creative women called CLAMP, have put out many hit series. Here we present the distinctive charms of five works that would be fascinating for the readers of Tsubasa.

Sensitive

A love story between a university ronin (a young man who has failed his college entrance exams), Hideki Motosuwa, and a personal computer in human form, Chii. Although Chii should only behave as she is programmed, the series warmly illustrates Hideki's emotional progress as he falls in love with her as a girl. It's as if the feelings playing on the faces of Sakura and Syaoran were repeated in the ways that CLAMP thoroughly displays the play of emotions across the lead characters' faces.

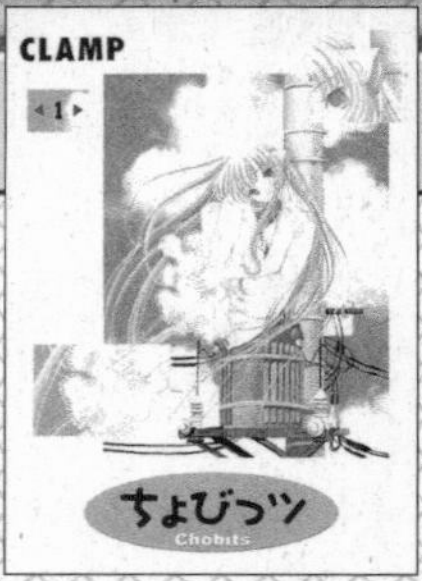
CLAMP
1
ちょびっツ
Chobits

CHOBITS
Total 8 Volumes
Kodansha / KC Deluxe

Suspenseful

Entering an entirely new world on an adventure must be a thrilling experience. The priest Zagato has captured the Princess Emeraude, and to help, three young girls are called into the strange world of Cephiro. As the three become the Magic Knights Rayearth, they find themselves in the middle of thrilling adventures. The unusual scenery in the alternate world and the shocking plot developments keep us turning the pages of this amazing work!

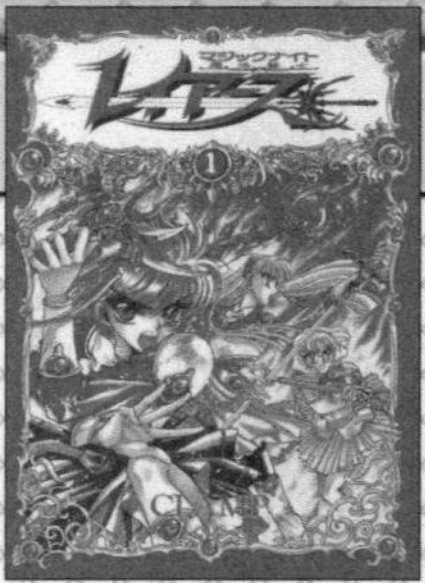

MAGIC KNIGHT RAYEARTH, 2 SERIES
Each series, total 3 volumes
Kodansha / KC Deluxe

Sensitive

An avant-garde series with its movie-style use of dialogue and the innovative full-page layouts, Clover is a work that has a distinctly adult feel. A young girl with deep scars on her heart has a simple wish—to be happy—and stylish Kazuhiko risks his life in an effort to fulfill her wish. Adult characters like him are a specialty of CLAMP works.

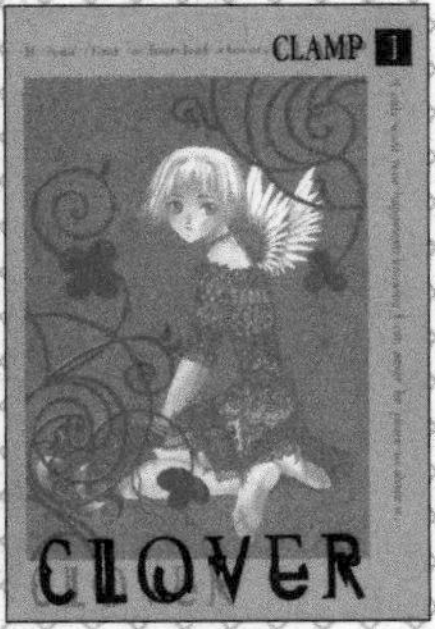
CLAMP 1
CLOVER

CLOVER
Currently 4 Volumes
Kodansha / Amie KC

Sweet

There is no main character more thoughtful, kind, and able to move the readers as much as this one. Cardcaptor Sakura is a series that warms the heart with its overwhelming sweetness. When you see Sakura, who is hardworking and undiscouraged no matter what happens, just about anybody would feel good. The heartfelt aspect of this series is something that Tsubasa has inherited.

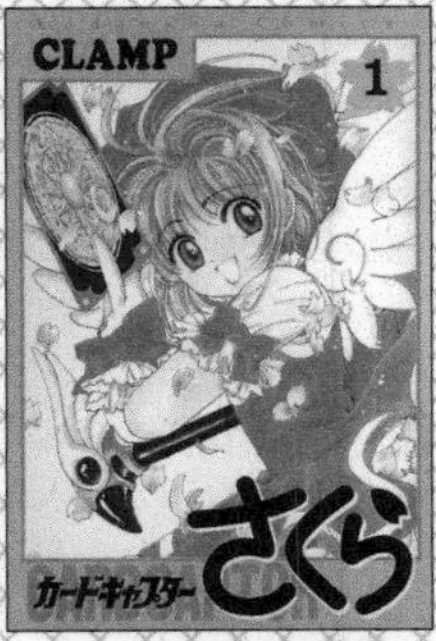
CLAMP
1
カードキャプターさくら

CARDCAPTOR SAKURA
Total 12 Volumes
Kodansha / KC Deluxe

Strange

CLAMP, who specialize in strange worlds, present their eighteenth work in the series xxxHolic. Our guide is Yûko Ichihara, who also appears in Tsubasa, as she takes the readers on a journey through the strange world that lies just beneath the surface of our normal lives. With all of the worlds that Syaoran and his group have traveled, what new worlds will be visited in both Tsubasa and xxxHolic? We think you will be surprised at the upcoming developments!

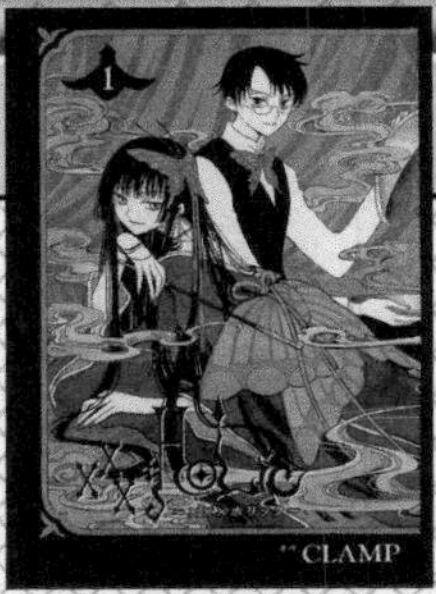
1
CLAMP

XXXHOLIC
Currently 8 Volumes
Kodansha / KC Deluxe

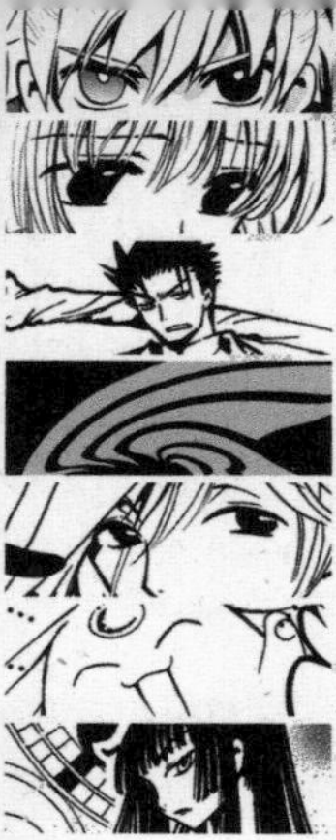

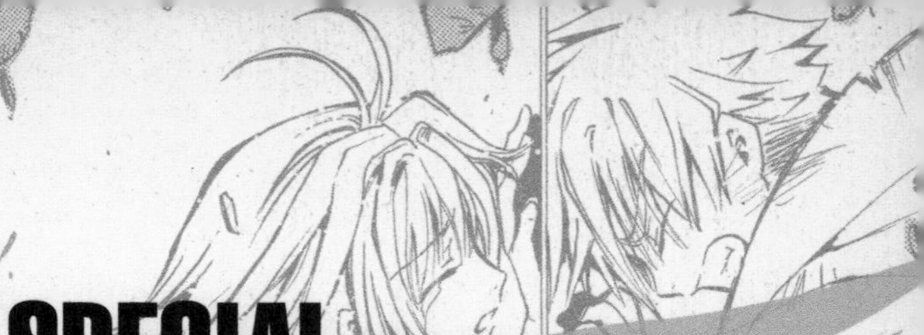

SPECIAL INTERVIEW

AGEHA OHKAWA
KIICHIRO SUGAWARA

スペシャルインタビュー

Ageha Ohkawa (CLAMP)
Kiichiro Sugawara (Weekly Shonen Magazine Editorial Department)

A long-form interview with Clamp's leader, Ageha Ohkawa-sensei and CLAMP's editor, Kiichiro Sugawara of Weekly Shonen Magazine's Editorial Department. All sorts of topics are discussed, including the stories behind the continuing story and what might be coming up in the future.

Tsubasa is CLAMP's very first continuing series published in a weekly shônen magazine setting. Do you see many differences between this and when CLAMP was working on monthly magazines, shôjo magazines, or on your work with series in seinen magazines?

OHKAWA: We're still doing our best to get used to the weekly series schedule, but now the monthly series pace seems very slow. It's so different in ways like how quickly we get reactions from the fans and the pace in which the publications come out. Sometimes we find ourselves asking, "Hasn't the graphic novel come out yet?!" (laughter) The time I really felt that this was a shônen publication was when I saw the results of Weekly Shonen Magazine's character popularity polls (listed on page 148 of this book). Syaoran, who doesn't have much to do in most action sequences, gets number one on the list!

SUGAWARA: I think a standard part of shônen manga is that the main character is very popular.

OHKAWA: I also think the fact that it's a shônen manga is what made Kurogane more popular than Fai. The people who take part in the fight scenes are very popular, and that's a part of it being a shônen manga too. That's very much what I'd expect from Shônen Magazine. If this were published in a magazine with mainly a female readership, Syaoran may remain number 1, but Fai would rank much, much higher—maybe even number 2. At the same time, Kurogane would have been much lower, and someone like Seishirô might have gotten enough votes to place pretty high.

SUGAWARA: To a shônen-manga fan, the most important thing is who is the strongest of the characters. In the fan letters, phrases like, "Character XX is so strong and cool!" come along all the time.

OHKAWA: When the series was just starting out, we relied on fans of our previous work or fans of Cardcaptor Sakura for their kind support, but now a huge percentage of the people we hear from are elementary school students.

SUGAWARA: That's very true. Among the series being run in Shônen Magazine, Tsubasa is the title with the youngest readership. The magazine itself is aimed at middle school and high school age-group readers, so this is really unusual for our magazine.

OHKAWA: There are many readers who learned of CLAMP from Tsubasa, and they wonder just who this CLAMP guy is. I'm sure there are quite a few who think he's some kind of foreigner. (laughter)

TSUBASA AS A PART OF SHÔNEN MAGAZINE

When you're drawing your pages, is there a part of you that keeps in mind that this is running in Shônen Magazine?

OHKAWA: We're very conscious of the fact that it's Shônen Magazine when we draw the way Fai lounges around. (laughter) I mean, Shônen Magazine is known for all of its biker-gang-style manga, right? So in this magazine, I want at least one character who sits like a gang member! (laughter) Also, I think that maybe Sorata Arisugawa from the Hanshin Republic is very much like the normal

characters in the magazine. Sure, he's a character that appeared in a different work of ours, but he has such an open-hearted personality that he's such an exemplary manga character. But he wasn't quite right for this story, so instead we introduced another very manga-like character, Shôgo Asagi to the story…

SUGAWARA: As an editor in the Shônen Magazine editorial department, all I could think of was, now this is a shônen manga magazine! Among the editorial department, most knew of Sakura as the main character of Cardcaptor Sakura, but they had no idea who Syaoran was. When Tsubasa was starting, one thing I heard a lot was, "That's weird! And who's that guy beside her?" (laughter)

OHKAWA: Yeah, in the editorial department of a shônen manga magazine, you'll certainly find a lot of people who only know the title and main character of (the shôjo manga series) Cardcaptor Sakura! (laughter) Also, there are the times when Sugawara-san said to me that I have to decide on how to foreshadow the events of the next week's installment. Or when I haven't wrapped up a particular plot line, and try to stretch it out a little, Sugawara-san tells me that the readers are going to forget (that plot line) pretty soon! (laughter) That's very much like a weekly shônen manga magazine—that and the really quick pace.

Then what do you think about the fact that your readers are very young? Have you ever done things differently because of it?

OHKAWA: We're a little careful of what language we use. We're careful to use words and phrases that elementary school students can easily understand. And some of the time when I change something, Sugawara-san might say, "Things do change, don't they?" I've been told to avoid difficult phrasing, and if a sword breaks, they just say it straight, "Damn, my sword broke!" In a shôjo manga, if you say, "I wanted to tell you that I...," and leave it there, the readers will understand that the next words are, "love you," without having to

come out and say it. But in a shônen manga, you have to come out and say, "I love you," or they don't get it. (laughter) And for that reason, the words we use in Tsubasa are in some ways different from previous CLAMP shôjo-style manga that readers have seen before.

AND TO MAKE A SHÔNEN MANGA-STYLE STORY...

Have you had story conferences with Sugawara-san about the plot?

OHKAWA: We have the conferences, but the story hardly ever changes because of them. The only time the story changed was in the Country of Jade. At the first, I wanted it to be a horror story with vampires, but in the conference we changed it to a detective mystery. Syaoran acts like a certain manga elementary-student detective in that he deduces who the culprit is, chases him, and the criminal confesses his motive to everybody. (laughter) I also had TV suspense stories in mind. In those dramas, the criminal falls from a cliff to his death in the end—that seems to happen a lot. So I wanted a scene that was very much like that. (laughter)

Are there any parts of Tsubasa where you thought, "I wish I had drawn the story this way instead"?

OHKAWA: In the Country of Koryo, I really wanted to have more battle scenes, but we drew it that way so we could have the entire fight in one chapter. Now, thinking it over, I keep coming to the conclusion that we should have had more enemies in that fight. I'm not talking about Bruce Lee's Game of Death or anything, but in every part of the castle, there should have been an enemy and the final and greatest enemy should have been the Kiishim or something. (laughter) Or maybe in the Country of Ôto, I wish I had a few more battles. I get the feeling we didn't draw enough of Syaoran's and Ryûô's friendship.But up to that point, the Country of Ôto was the longest episode we had drawn, so we really didn't have the room to make it much longer. When you think of it in graphic-novel terms, it took up about two full volumes, and when you add in Edonis, it comes out closer to three volumes. Up until then, all of the worlds took maybe 1 volume each, so I thought that it wouldn't do to make it too long. But we felt that the Country of Ôto had some interesting developments in it, so that's why we stretched it out as long as we did.

SUGAWARA: Don't say that! All you have to do is get used to the pace of Shônen Magazine! In the magazine, we have one race or one ball game that may take a half a year to play out! (laughter)

OHKAWA: I don't know if I want to get used to that kind of pace. . . . (laughter) But I have come to the point where I think more battle scenes would be good. We like having battles within our stories, but I was thinking that if you only have battle scenes, the story isn't moving forward and it gets boring. And if the story isn't progressing at a good tempo, we get sick of drawing it. (laughter) But in the case of shônen manga, it's probably the right thing to do to have battle after battle.

I WANT TO LEAVE A FAMOUS CATCH PHRASE TO POSTERITY!

The graphic novels have two different formats, the deluxe edition and normal edition, what brought about that result?

SUGAWARA: At first, there was the idea of adding character goods to the releases as well, but when we were thinking of what the most interesting things for that would be, we hit on the idea of a deluxe edition. This doesn't just apply to CLAMP-sensei's work, but novels get hardcover releases. Why don't manga get them, too? I've wondered about that for a very long time now.

OHKAWA: From our point of view, the two editions on sale, the deluxe edition and the regular edition, mean that for the two editions, we have to draw two different covers. And although on the one side we're very happy doing that, on the other, we have twice the hard work! (laughter) Now that you mention it, on the case of the first deluxe edition, the illustration was reversed left-to-right by mistake. So the case had the image going one way, and the book inside had the same image going the other, but nobody noticed. So we switched the image out for a brand-new image that we drew, so there were two different image versions of that book.

SUGAWARA: And I had never worked on a case before, so it was an unexpected problem. And beyond the images, there were all sorts of work that had to be done on it. We had no experience working on it, so that kind of mistake happened a lot!

In the deluxe editions on the frontispieces (chapter title illustrations), you left the text and catch phrases that were used in the magazine. That isn't done very often...

OHKAWA: Sugawara-san's wonderful catch phrases come one right after the other. We'd be sad to just see them disappear along with the magazines, and we wanted to leave them for posterity! (laughter) The catch phrases that Sugawara-san makes up aren't like any of the ones we've had on our works before. The catch phrases any normal editor comes up with are something like, "Once again today, XX-san is full of energy!" or "The rival arrives!" or something like that. Harmless little phrases that you see all of the time. But Sugawara-san uses lines like, "I'll protect you! You, the one I love..." He writes phrases that match both the characters and the illustration. We've never had an editor quite like that before.

SUGAWARA: No, I'm nothing special. Everyone who works on Shônen Magazine are fanatics about catch phrases. When I was the new guy on the job, I'd write some fifty catch phrases for one manga installment.

OHKAWA: Kind of like the way a baseball team runs a new guy through the ringer, huh? Like batting at a thousand pitches a day. (laughter)

SUGAWARA: I consider it a blessing that my magazine allows us to polish our catch phrase skills more than other magazines do.

EVEN IF IT'S ONLY IN ONE AREA, WE WANT A WELL ORGANIZED STORY...

While Tsubasa is running, at the same time you have another series running in Young Magazine, xxxHolic, and the two series are linked. When did this idea come up?

OHKAWA: The idea itself started when we first presented our written series plan (to the editorial department).

And when that happened, Sugawara-san, as an editor, what did you think of it?

SUGAWARA: I was wondering if something like that could actually be done in reality. I thought it might make for a lot of extra work for the artists if that was tried at a weekly pace. But I was convinced that if it could be done, it would turn out great!

OHKAWA: I'm sure that if we tried to link the series every week, we'd have big continuity problems. Especially when Syaoran and Yûko of xxxHolic are working on stories with completely different influences, it'd be incredibly difficult to link them. For example, when

Yûko sent them the Valentine's Day chocolate, Syaoran and the group know nothing about returning the favor on White Day, right? But Yûko is starting to hold a grudge on Syaoran's party because they haven't given her anything back. If that plot thread got too much out of hand, then the stories wouldn't stand on their own, right? In the scene where Mokona shoots an arrow out of its mouth (Volume 7, page 144), that was one link. As far as the story goes, Mokona shot "something" out of it's mouth, and that didn't have much of a deep meaning. If we were to give it a deep meaning, that means that the readers who don't know xxxHolic would be

lost. In the Country of Ôto, when they all got some Fondant au Chocolat from Yûko that was sent through Mokona (Volume 5, page 156), that is pretty much the same thing. We're careful to arrange it so that even though you don't read the work that it's linked to, you still have no problem following the story.

We'd like to hear what you have in store for us in the future.

OHKAWA: What I'd like to do is make Tsubasa more like the other stories that run along with ours in Shônen Magazine, with thick lines and simple page layouts. The page layouts on shônen manga are quite a bit different from shôjo manga, so we'd like to be more like shônen manga with very easy-to-read layouts. We also had a problem such that when we made the lines in the drawings too thin, it didn't have the impact that it needed. We've already started drawing the story with more thought toward the fact that it's running in a shônen manga magazine. But we used our normal style to get those initial readers to pick up the story, and after, we began to walk them through the changes. When they've accustomed themselves to the new style, we're thinking of slowly returning to our previous style. I think there are some people who have noticed, but somewhere around the Country of Ôto, the art style has been changing. The mood of our present images should be quite different compared to the way it was in volume one. As far as the story is concerned, it's basically the story of a young man's journey, so we can't make it too complicated.

THE ROAD TO SYAORAN'S GOAL IS LITTERED WITH A THOUSAND CORPSES?

What about you, Sugawara-san? Is there any particular direction that you'd like to see Tsubasa take as the editor in charge of the work?

SUGAWARA: So far, Syaoran hasn't had very much go right for him, so I'd like to see him be happy. Other than that, I'd like to see him get stronger. I'd like him to get the kind of skills

that are normal for Shônen Magazine, but . . . For example, on the left-hand page, you have Syaoran facing several thousand enemies, then you turn the page and all of them are defeated. Then Kurogane says, "Hm. So you've managed to get a little better, huh?" That's the kind of strength I'd like to see. (laughter)

OHKAWA: Several thousand? Don't hold your breath. (laughter).

Do you have the end of the series completely decided already?

OHKAWA: The story from here on out is a secret, even from the other members of CLAMP.

Kurogane's and Fai's past, and the end of the series, too. I've answered the questions to the staff of the anime version that's coming out in April, but other than that, I'm making sure that nobody else knows. But since this is such a good opportunity, I'll let a little slip. In reality, Mokona is the heroine of the entire story. In the Country of Koryo, didn't you think that Syaoran's reaction to when Mokona was in danger was pretty violent (Volume 3, page 153)? So our plans for the end of the story is to turn Tsubasa into a huge romance between Syaoran and Mokona. I've got the final scenes firmly in mind, so you can just relax. (laughter)

An original manga
that you can only read
in this guide book!

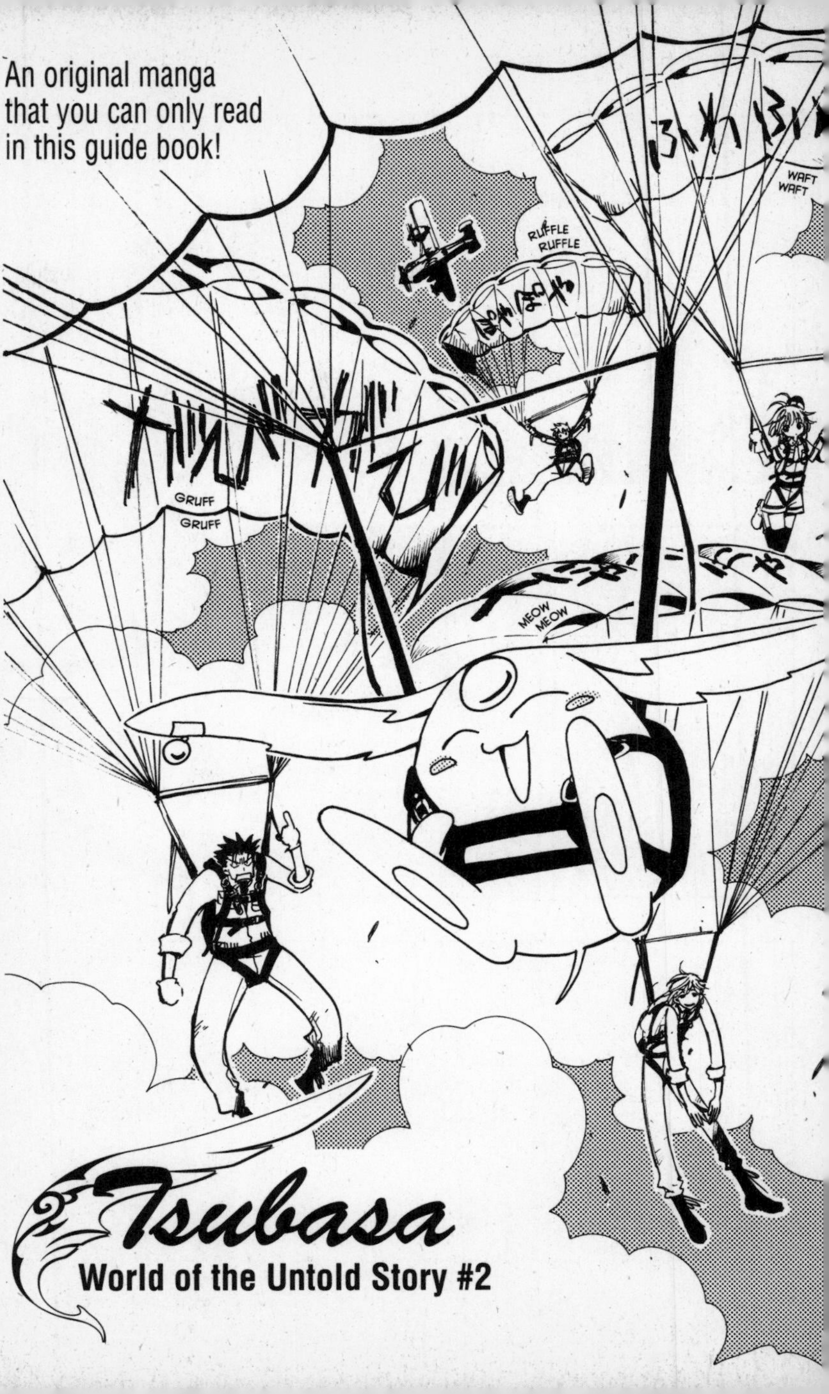
WAFT WAFT
RUFFLE RUFFLE
GRUFF GRUFF
MEOW MEOW

Tsubasa
World of the Untold Story #2

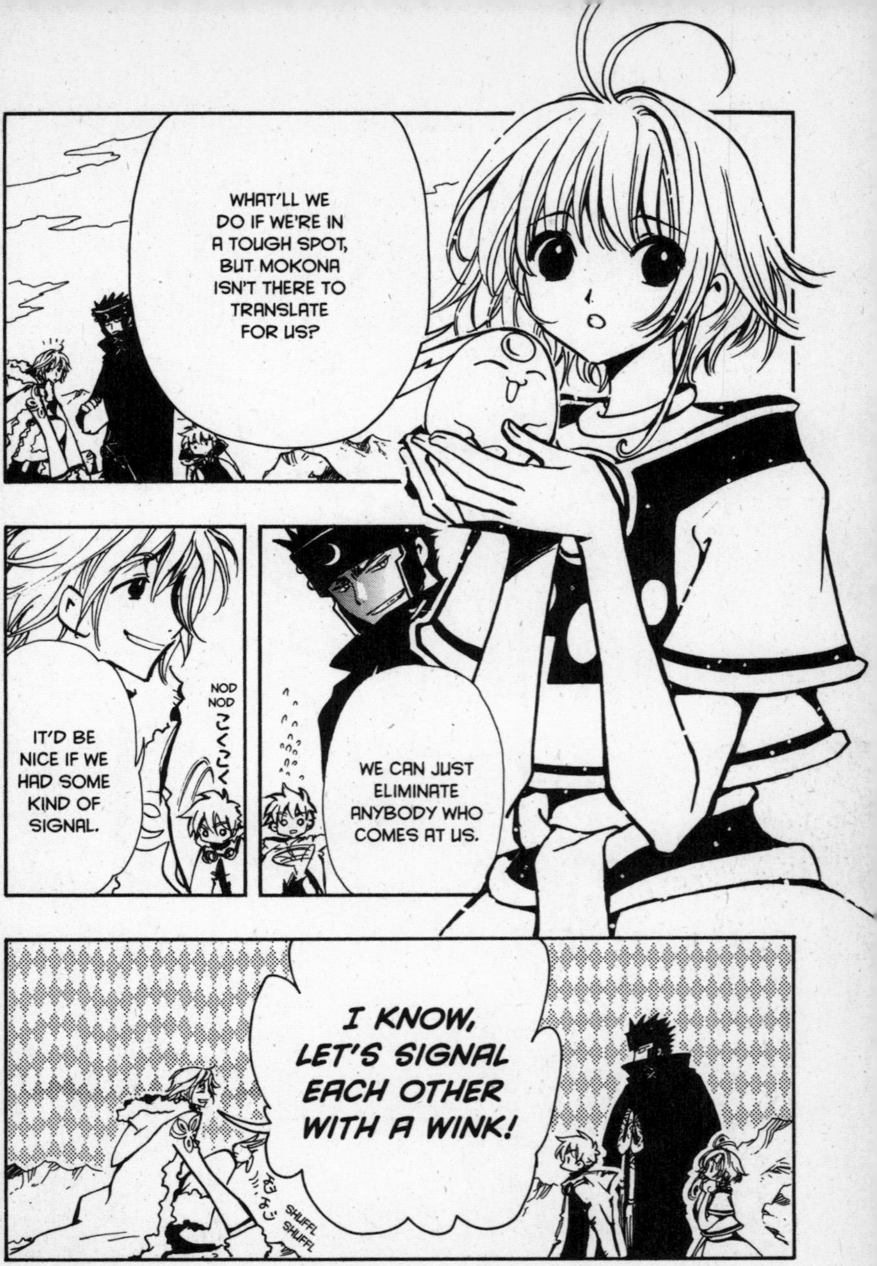
WHAT'LL WE DO IF WE'RE IN A TOUGH SPOT, BUT MOKONA ISN'T THERE TO TRANSLATE FOR US?
WE CAN JUST ELIMINATE ANYBODY WHO COMES AT US.
NOD NOD
IT'D BE NICE IF WE HAD SOME KIND OF SIGNAL.
I KNOW, LET'S SIGNAL EACH OTHER WITH A WINK!
SHUFFL SHUFFL

WHAT IS A WINK?
THIS IS STUPID!
YOU CLOSE JUST ONE EYE.
ぱちん
POINK
ぱちん
POINK
LIKE SO! ♥
SHAKK
JUST WHILE WE'RE DISCUSSING IT?!
WHOOSH
HYAA!
HYAA!
HYAA!
ちょ
こん。。。
KATHUNK
WE'VE BEEN CAUGHT...!

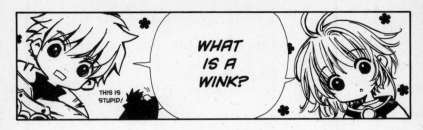

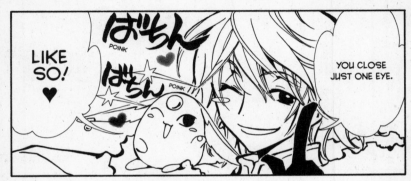

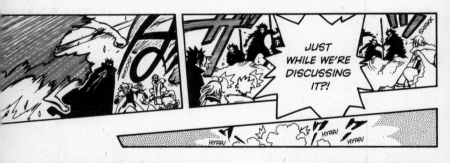

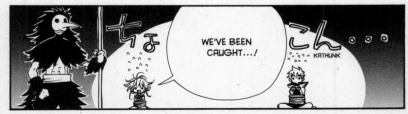

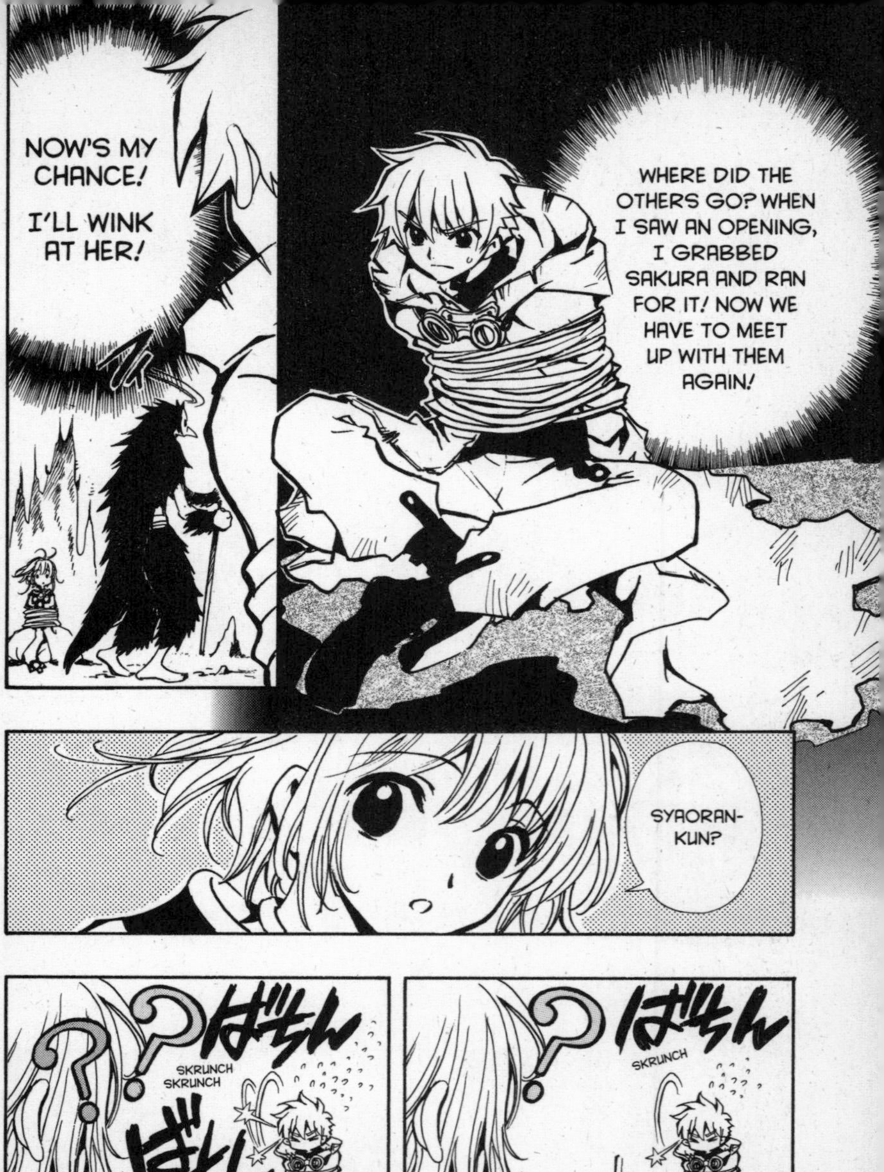
WHERE DID THE OTHERS GO? WHEN I SAW AN OPENING, I GRABBED SAKURA AND RAN FOR IT! NOW WE HAVE TO MEET UP WITH THEM AGAIN!
NOW'S MY CHANCE!
I'LL WINK AT HER!
SYAORAN-KUN?
ぱちん
SKRUNCH
ぱちん
ぱちん
SKRUNCH SKRUNCH

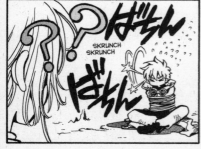

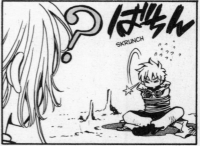

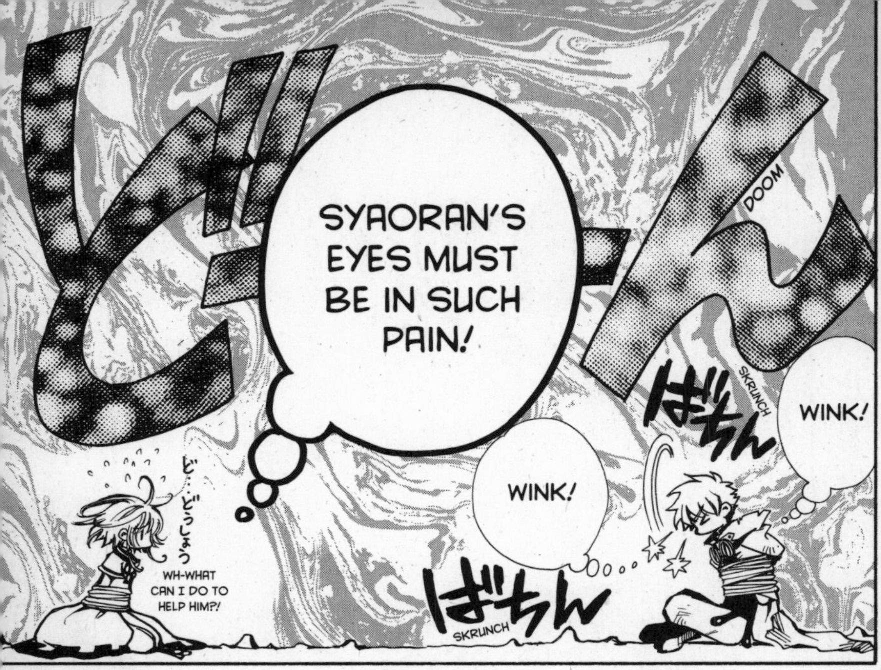
どーん
DOOM
SYAORAN'S EYES MUST BE IN SUCH PAIN!
WINK!
ばちん
SKRUNCH
WINK!
ばちん
SKRUNCH
ど…どうしよう
WH-WHAT CAN I DO TO HELP HIM?!

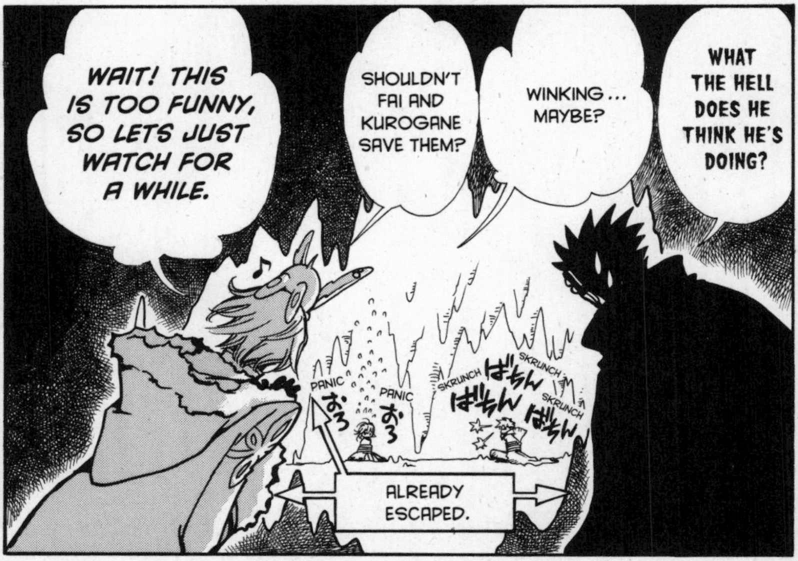
WHAT THE HELL DOES HE THINK HE'S DOING?
WINKING… MAYBE?
SHOULDN'T FAI AND KUROGANE SAVE THEM?
WAIT! THIS IS TOO FUNNY, SO LETS JUST WATCH FOR A WHILE.
SKRUNCH ばちん
SKRUNCH ばちん
SKRUNCH ばちん
ばちん
PANIC おろ
PANIC おろ
ALREADY ESCAPED.

SYAORAN, WHEN YOU GET SOME TIME, ASK FAI TO TEACH YOU HOW TO WINK!

★ THE END. ★

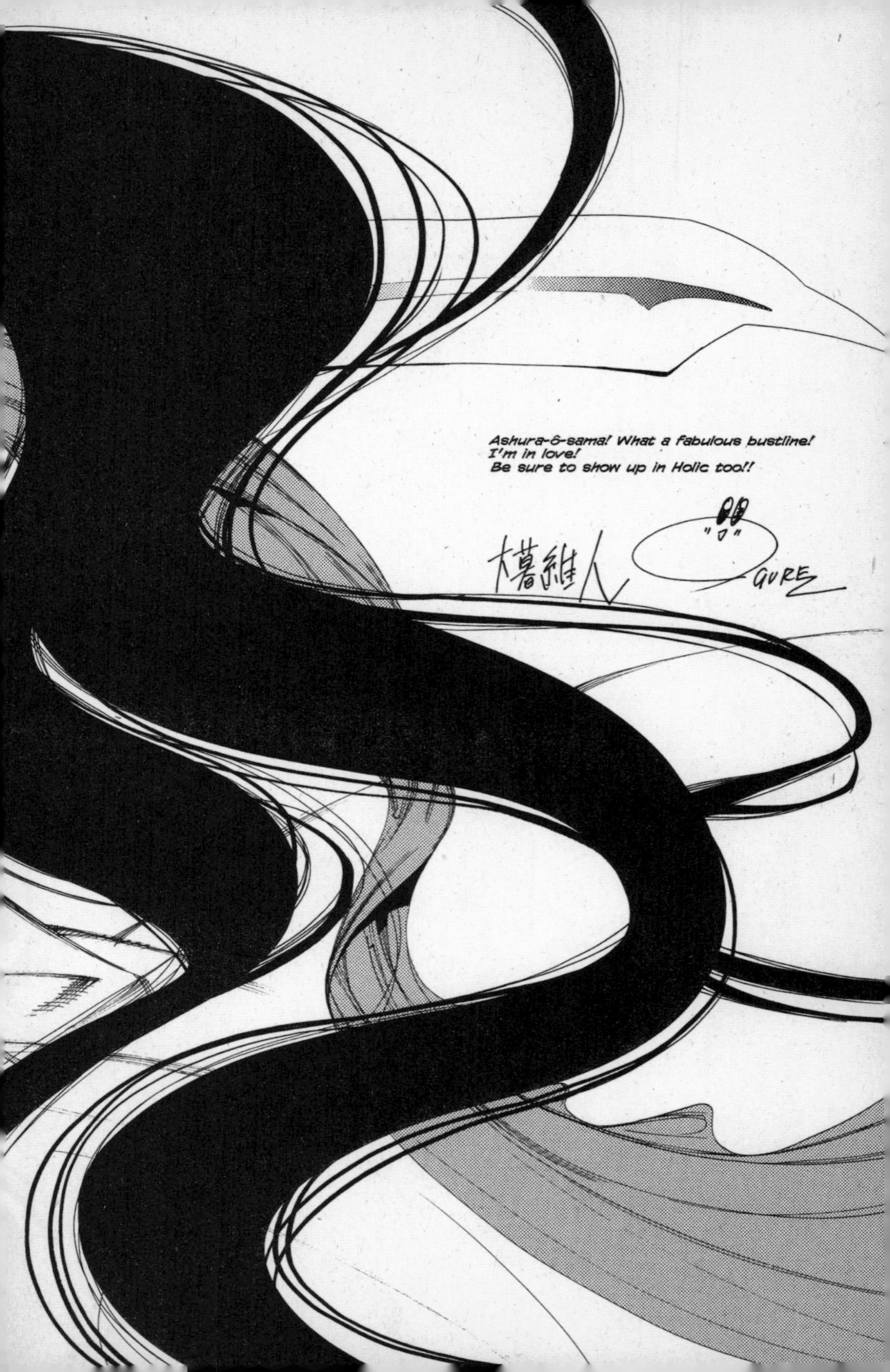
Ashura-ô-sama! What a fabulous bustline!
I'm in love!
Be sure to show up in Holic too!!
大暮維人
GURE

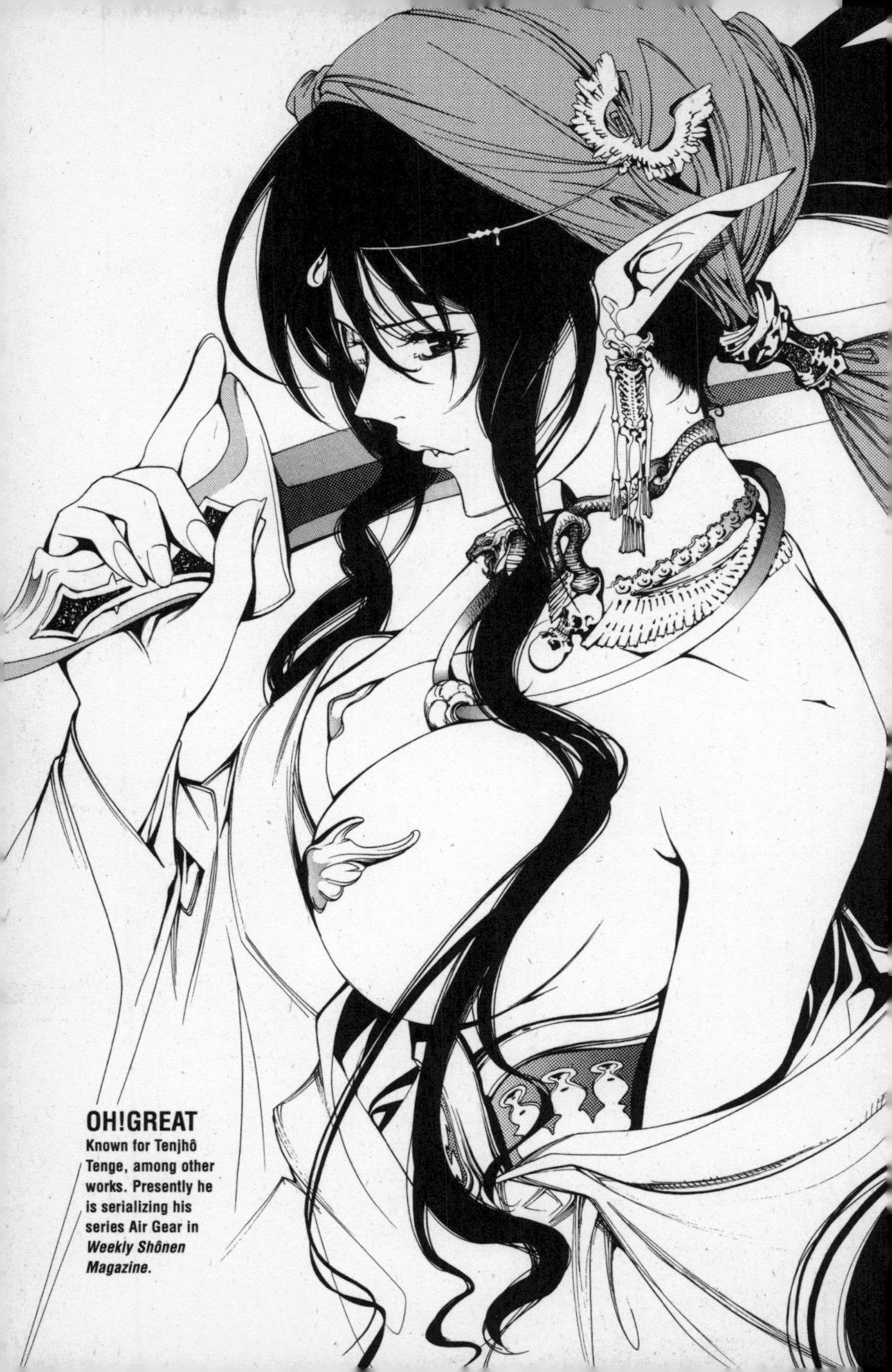

OH!GREAT
Known for Tenjhô Tenge, among other works. Presently he is serializing his series Air Gear in *Weekly Shônen Magazine*.

I love Tsubasa!!

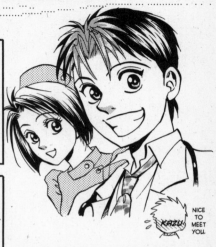

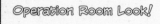

Operation Room Look!
Yamamoto's Manga is a medical manga, so you see plenty of operations.
CAP →
MASK →
GOWN →
IT MUST BE DIFFICULT TO DRAW FEMALE-ORIENTED MANGA IN AN OPERATING ROOM.
TRUE. ALL YOU CAN SEE ARE THE EYES.
IT'S SEEMS LIKE IT'D BE DIFFI-CULT.
MEMBERS OF CLAMP
KAZU
On the other hand, it's possible that the sensei of CLAMP might have a different person draw each character?!
Among 10 people, or even 20 people!
...
Look at all the different types of characters!
But they're so cute!

KAZU
NICE TO MEET YOU.

Hello. This is Kazuki Yamamoto, the author of God Hand Teru (presently serialized in Weekly Shônen Magazine). I'd like to use this chance to make friends with the members of CLAMP. Personally, Tsubasa is a work that I just love!! The guys are cool, the girls are cute. But more than anything else, I love the story—I have no idea what's going to happen and the speed at which everything occurs! What's going to happen between Syaoran and Seishirô? Is Subaru ever going to appear? I read it every week with great excitement!

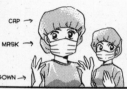

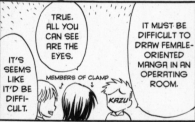

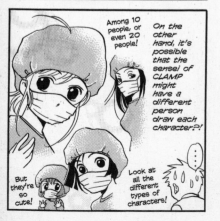

KAZUKI YAMAMOTO

Known for Kaze Densetsu Hikoza among others. Current series, God Hand Teru, is being serialized in *Weekly Shônen Magazine*.

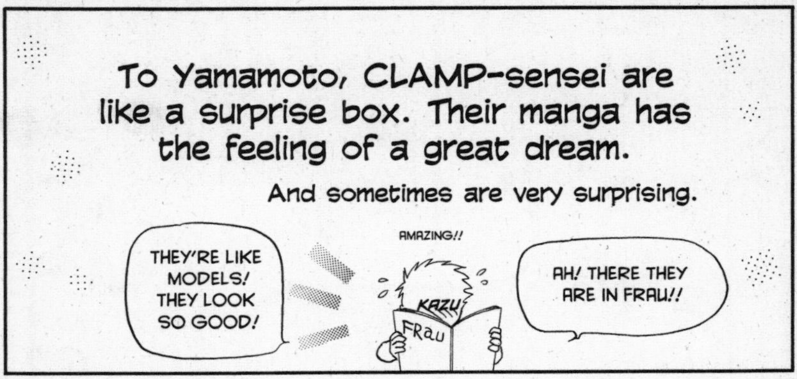
To Yamamoto, CLAMP-sensei are like a surprise box. Their manga has the feeling of a great dream.
And sometimes are very surprising.
AH! THERE THEY ARE IN FRAU!!
AMAZING!!
KAZU
FRau
THEY'RE LIKE MODELS! THEY LOOK SO GOOD!

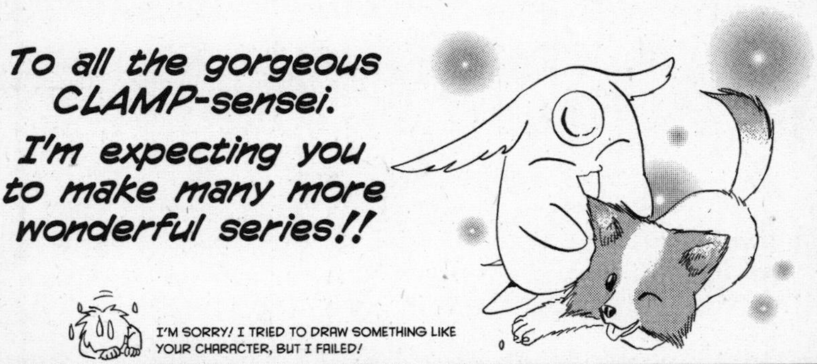
To all the gorgeous CLAMP-sensei.
I'm expecting you to make many more wonderful series!!
I'M SORRY! I TRIED TO DRAW SOMETHING LIKE YOUR CHARACTER, BUT I FAILED!

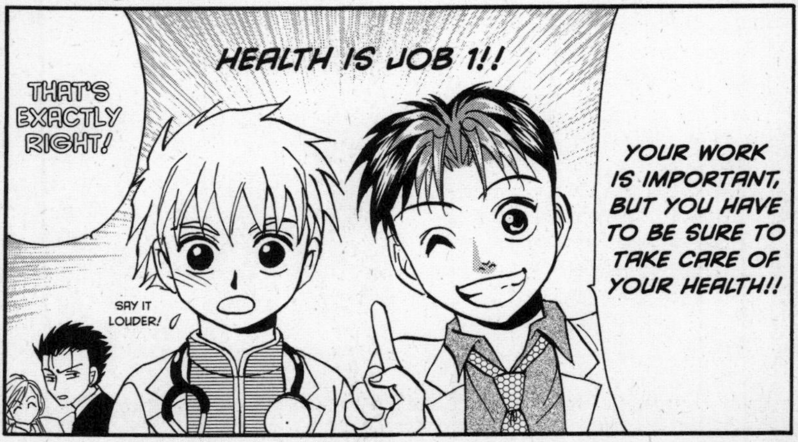
HEALTH IS JOB 1!!
YOUR WORK IS IMPORTANT, BUT YOU HAVE TO BE SURE TO TAKE CARE OF YOUR HEALTH!!
THAT'S EXACTLY RIGHT!
SAY IT LOUDER!

DIMENSION TRAVEL Q&A

Syaoran, Sakura, and Mokona's

You have all sorts of questions, and now is the time to ask. Syaoran, Sakura and Mokona answer the questions.

"Here is where we'll tell you all we know about dimension travel!"

"If you know the facts, it'll make a big difference if you ever find yourselves traveling between dimensions."

Q1   What do you need to travel dimensions?

A   You need to pay a price.

Sakura: "I was sleeping at the time. Are you talking about the Time-Space Witch?"

Syaoran: "That's right. Kurogane-san, Fai-san and I flew to the place where the Time-Space Witch was. But to go from there, to any other world she required us to pay a price."

Sakura: "A price? What kind of price?"

Syaoran: "For example, Kurogane had to turn over his own sword, Ginryû, to her. But he said he'd be back to claim it again."

Sakura: "How could he do that?"

Syaoran: "He'd probably have to pay a price that's the same as it's worth . . . maybe?"

Mokona: "Oh, yeah! Mokona remembers Yûko saying that she wants somebody to help out doing the housework!"

Syaoran: "(I don't know if Kurogane would want to be a live-in servant at the Time-Space Witch's house doing cleaning...)"

WHAT WILL YOU DO?

Syaoran: "Kurogane was pretty unwilling, but in the end he grudgingly handed the sword over."

Q2 I'm a little worried whether the language I speak will be understood in the world I'm going to.

A Be sure to take Mokona with you.

Sakura: "Come to think of it, it's a little strange, isn't it? Why can we understand everyone on the new worlds? There were times when I couldn't understand the writing at all."

Mokona: "Mokona does it!! Mokona translates the language in everybody's head!"

Syaoran: "As long as we have Mokona close by, everyone speaks just as if we were hearing it in our own country's language."

Sakura: "That's amazing!"

Syaoran: "(But if it's inside our head, does that mean that Mokona can hear our thoughts . . .)"

Sakura: "Syaoran, what's wrong? You've gone pale all of a sudden."

Syaoran: "Nothing. It was just a thought . . ."

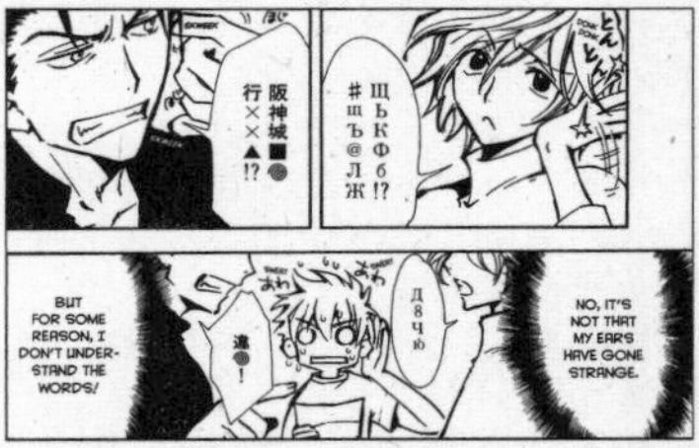
NO, IT'S NOT THAT MY EARS HAVE GONE STRANGE.
BUT FOR SOME REASON, I DON'T UNDERSTAND THE WORDS!

Syaoran: "When Mokona was kidnapped, we found that we couldn't communicate at all."

Q3 Will there be any danger in the world I'm going to?

A Traveling is dangerous business.

Sakura: "When we travel, we've been to all sorts of worlds, but we always seem to end up fighting someone and involved in some trouble."

Syaoran: "Yeah, but we're looking for Princess Sakura's memory feathers, and those carry enormous powers."

Sakura: "But we've even gone to worlds without any people. Maybe we'll find ourselves in a world that's all water with no dry land . . . ?"

Mokona: "Don't worry! Trust Mokona! Mokona will find a place to land that's not dangerous!"

Syaoran: "(If you can do that, why don't you take us to worlds that are certain to have feathers . . .)"

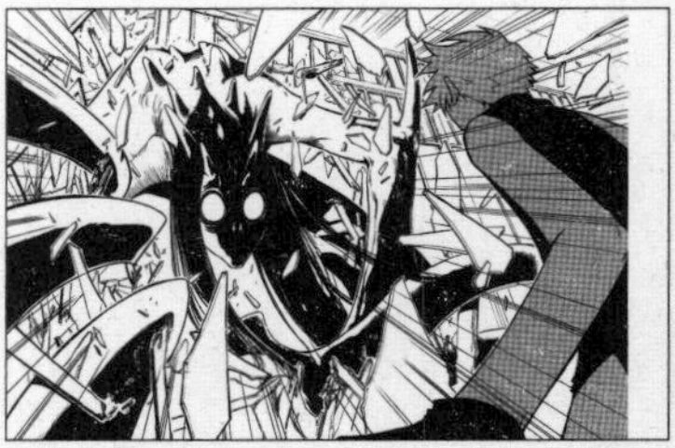

Sakura: "There so many times when we were suddenly attacked by monsters. Be careful everybody!"

Q4 Can I use the money that I have now?

A Odds are you won't be able to.

Sakura: "Money has always been a problem. We can't exchange it."

Syaoran: "(I wonder if we could stick money in Mokona's mouth and get it exchanged . . . ?)"

Mokona: "Syaoran, why do you stare at Mokona so hard? Could it be love?"

Syaoran: "N-No! It couldn't!"

Sakura: "In the Country of Ôto, we all worked in a café and made money."

Syaoran: "And we were able to use Princess Sakura's great luck and made some bets to get cash."

Sakura: "I don't know . . . I get the feeling that I did something bad when I did that . . ."

Syaoran: "W-Well, it isn't like we were cheating or anything . . ."

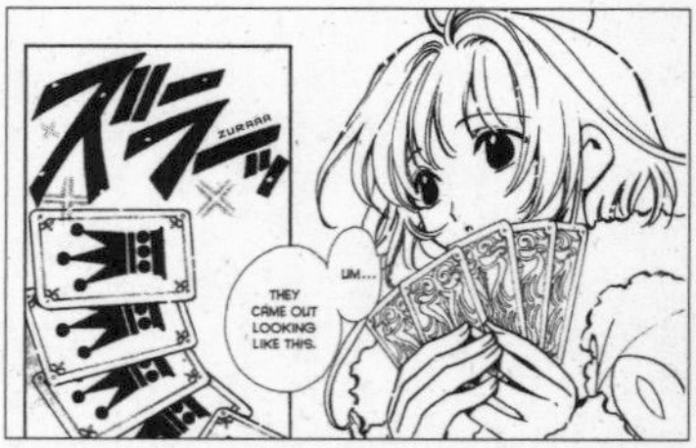
UM...
THEY CAME OUT LOOKING LIKE THIS.
ZURAAA

Sakura: "Whenever they gave me my cards, they always looked so pained."

Q5 I'm not good in weather that's too cold or too hot.

A Buy your clothes when you get to where you're going.

Syaoran: "It'd be nice if you could prepare in advance, but so long as you don't know what country you're going to, the best thing to do is get your supplies when you get there."

Sakura: "I have a coat, but it does no good to pull it out in a hot country."

Mokona: "And it's a problem to bring too much baggage!"

Syaoran: "There's another reason to buy your clothes where you end up that has nothing to do with climate. When you buy clothes at your destination, you blend in more with the world. And sometimes, that's necessary."

Sakura: "Sometimes the people of that world would say, 'Look at those people in the strange clothes.'"

Syaoran: "It's difficult when you're in an odd culture."

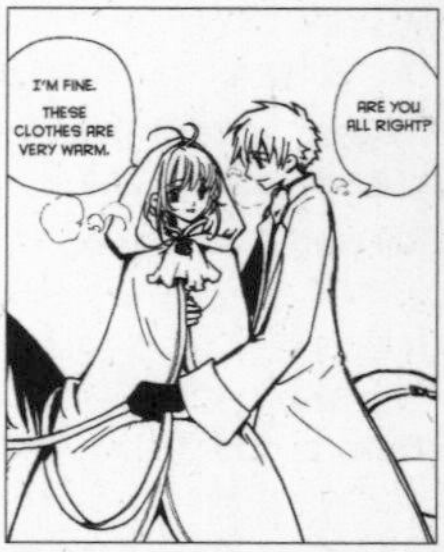
ARE YOU ALL RIGHT?
I'M FINE. THESE CLOTHES ARE VERY WARM.

Sakura: "There's something very fun when you go to all kinds of worlds and try on all sorts of clothes!"

Q6 There aren't all that many bad people, are there?

A Actually, there are plenty.

Syaoran: "There are quite a few people who think only of themselves; don't care about the feelings of others; and are willing to put others in danger."

Mokona: "The son of the Ryanban was very, very mean to Mokona in the Country of Koryo!"

Sakura: "They weren't very nice to the people of the town either."

Syaoran: "On the other hand, there are people like Dr. Kyle in the Country of Jade who acted like a nice man, but actually was plotting very bad things. So when you get to a new dimension, you're going to have to be more than just cautious!"

Sakura: "So when everybody goes traveling worlds, be very, very careful!"

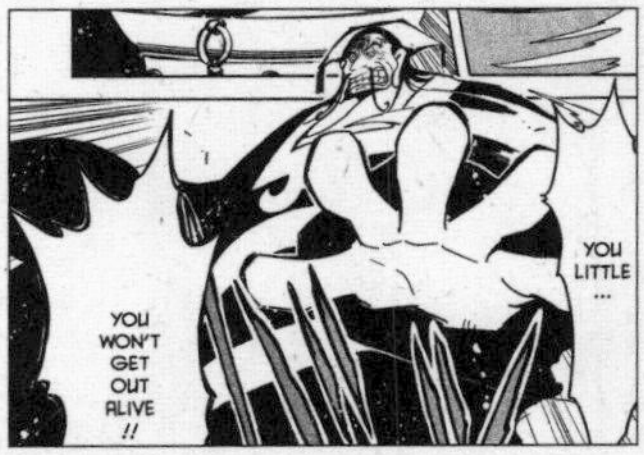
YOU LITTLE ...
YOU WON'T GET OUT ALIVE !!

Syaoran: "After the bad Ryanban was removed, I hope the people found some peace."

Q7 Is it fun to travel between worlds?

A Yes, it's very fun!

Syaoran: "We've gathered a few of Princess Sakura's feathers, but we'll need to gather a lot more. Isn't this journey very hard on you, Your Highness?"

Sakura: "Nope! I'm with Kurogane-san, Fai-san, and you, Syaoran-kun! So everything's just fine!"

Syaoran: "Your Highness . . ."

Sakura: "We go to lots of worlds and meet all sorts of people! We have to part with them so soon, and that's too bad, but in the next world, there's always somebody wonderful there to meet! So it's just fine!"

Syaoran: "Thank you, Princess."

Mokona: "Then it's time to get going to the next world! Here, Mokona will lead the way!"

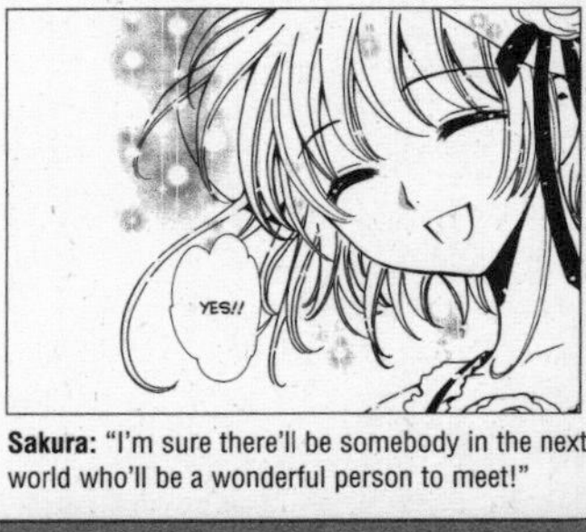
YES!!

Sakura: "I'm sure there'll be somebody in the next world who'll be a wonderful person to meet!"

TSUBASA MINI REPORT ④

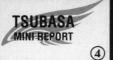

Mysterious Crests and Marks

MINI REPORT

One can see quite a few crests and marks in various worlds of Tsubasa. What will their meaning turn out to be? Could they hold the key that reveals the secrets to entire worlds?

There is a certain mark on Sakura's memory feathers. They all are the same, so it may be a mark for Sakura herself.

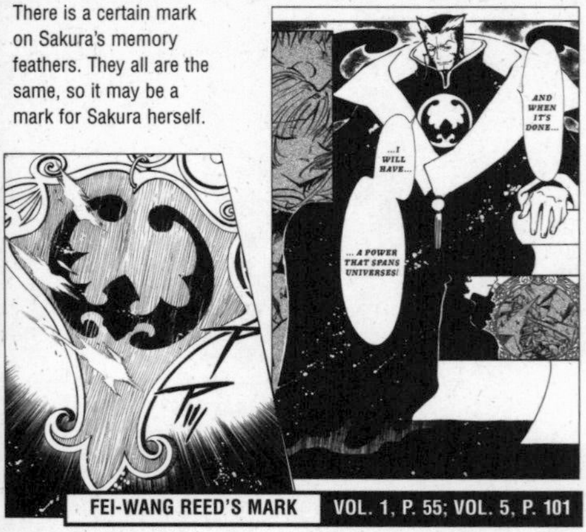
AND WHEN IT'S DONE...
...I WILL HAVE...
...A POWER THAT SPANS UNIVERSES!

FEI-WANG REED'S MARK VOL. 1, P. 55; VOL. 5, P. 101

Right after Sakura touched this crest, the feathers of her memory were scattered to the different worlds. The crest itself looks like feathers, but is that just coincidence?

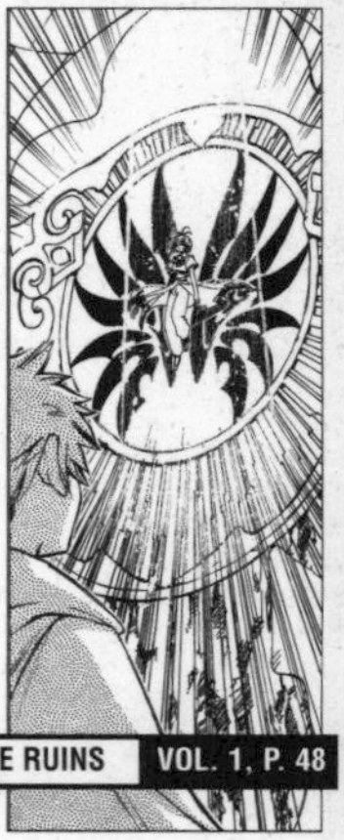

CREST IN THE RUINS VOL. 1, P. 48

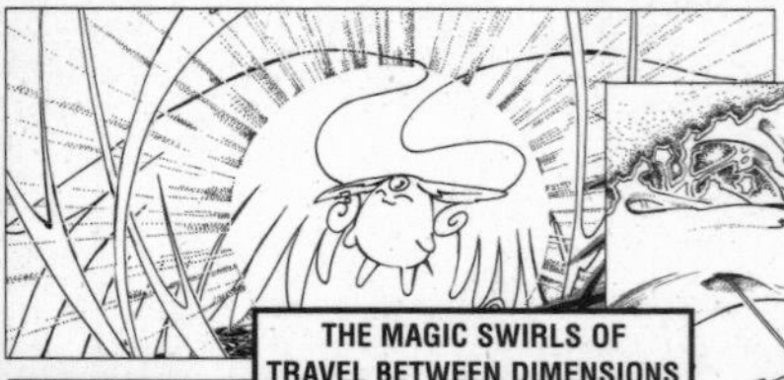

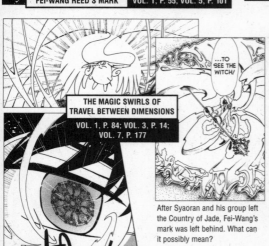

THE MAGIC SWIRLS OF TRAVEL BETWEEN DIMENSIONS

VOL. 1, P. 84; VOL. 3, P. 14; VOL. 7, P. 177

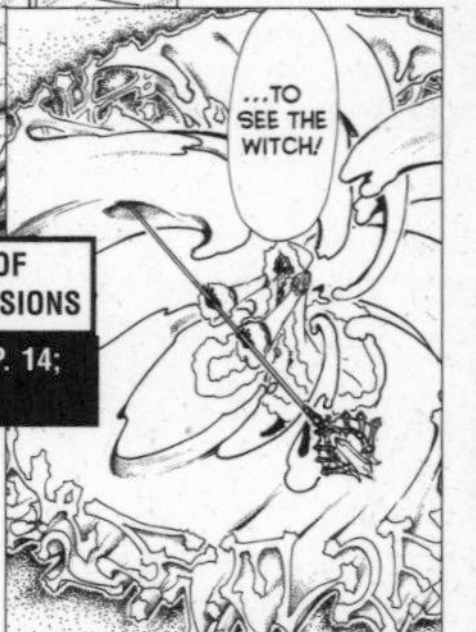
...TO SEE THE WITCH!

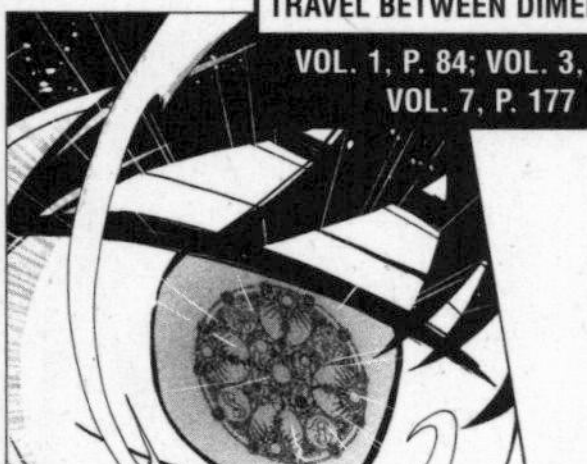

After Syaoran and his group left the Country of Jade, Fei-Wang's mark was left behind. What can it possibly mean?

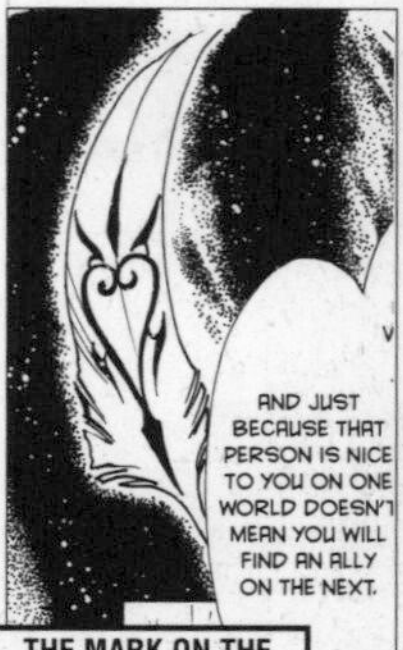
AND JUST BECAUSE THAT PERSON IS NICE TO YOU ON ONE WORLD DOESN'T MEAN YOU WILL FIND AN ALLY ON THE NEXT.

THE MARK ON THE MEMORY FEATHER

VOL. 1, P. 111

The way magic swirls when someone is traveling between worlds is different depending on who controls the power. It looks like there's more than one way to travel dimensions.

FAN'S SQUARE

Shônen Magazine (from 2005, Vols. 1, 4, & 5) put out polls and illustrations, and they received a tremendous response. So who was the most popular character?

Did your vote make the difference? Turn the page and find out!

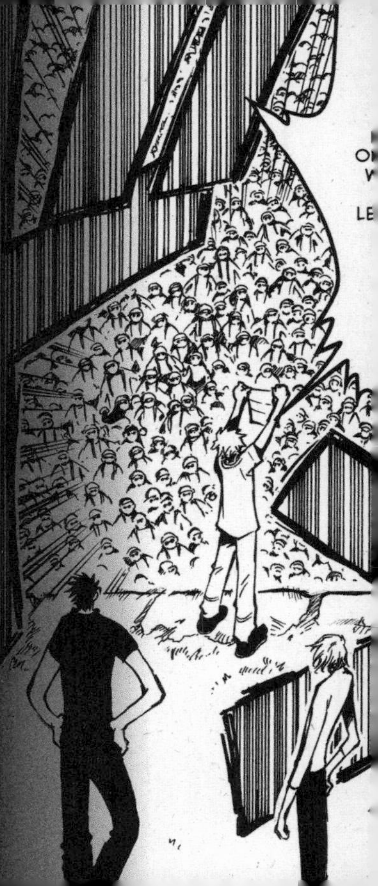

THE READERS CHOSE

Who Is Your Favorite Character?!

In Tsubasa, there are plenty of excellent characters. But which character will get the most votes for favorite character? Here are the results you've been waiting for!!

第1位

Character

2553 VOTES

SYAORAN

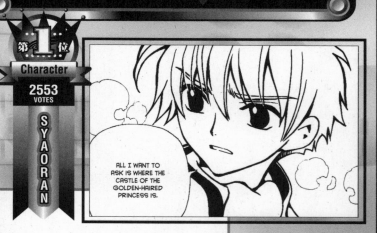

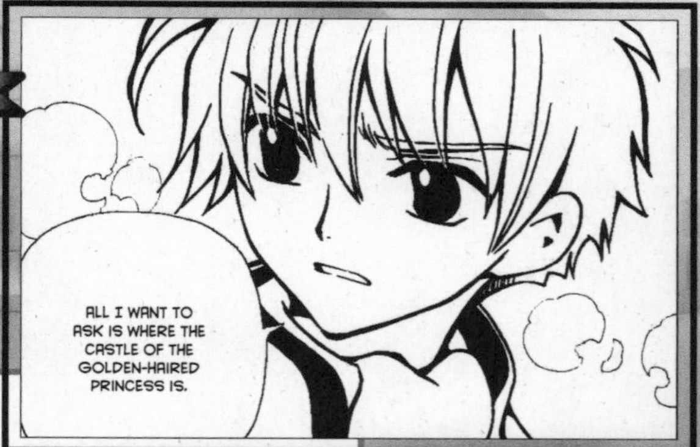
ALL I WANT TO ASK IS WHERE THE CASTLE OF THE GOLDEN-HAIRED PRINCESS IS.

What you'd expect from the hero, he won first place fair and square. The guy who protects Sakura as he quickly grows up has won the sympathy of quite a lot of people. • I love the way he does his best for Sakura's sake! (Chizu Maeda/Kyoto) /I just flat-out root for him wholeheartedly! (Ikumi Narahara/Osaka)

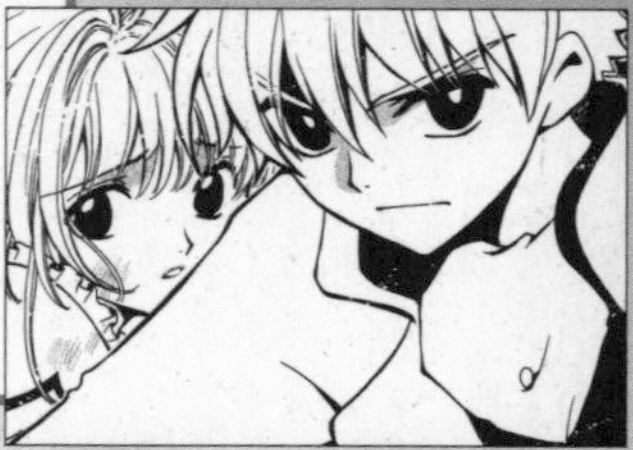

▲ The coolest thing about him is how he protects Sakura. (Kazuko Niiyama/Gunma Prefecture)

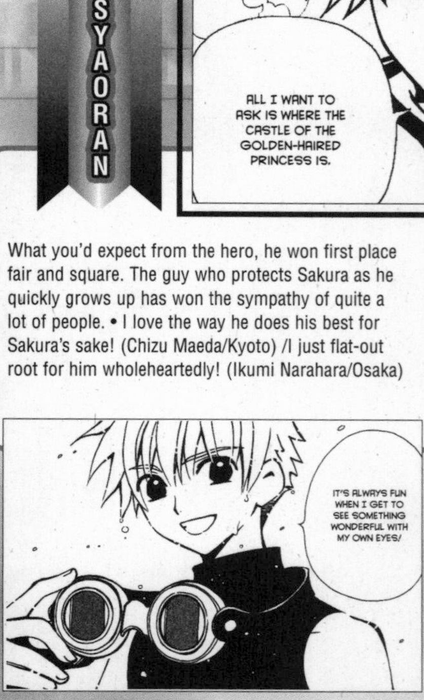
IT'S ALWAYS FUN WHEN I GET TO SEE SOMETHING WONDERFUL WITH MY OWN EYES!

◀ He's got this sensitive side that's so cute it makes me want to keep him safe. (Saeko Tamura/Chiba Prefecture)

第2位
Character
1617
VOTES
SAKURA

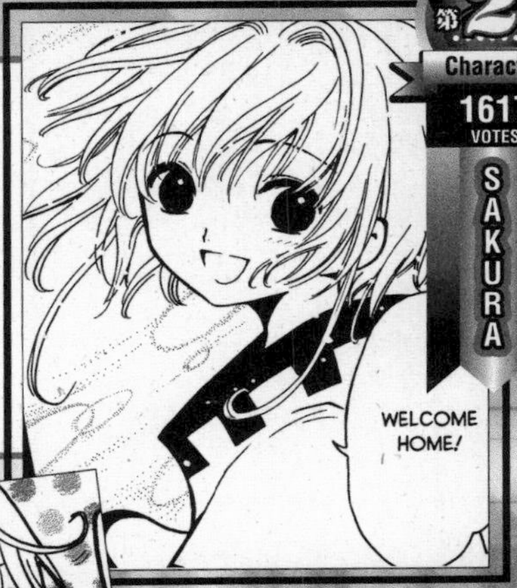
WELCOME HOME!

With her cute smile, everybody's head-over-heels for her. • I was just knocked out by her smile! (Shôji Mizono/Saitama Prefecture) /She has a certain spontaneity and lightness that make her irresistible! (Yurika Kuno/Aichi Prefecture)

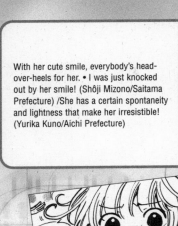

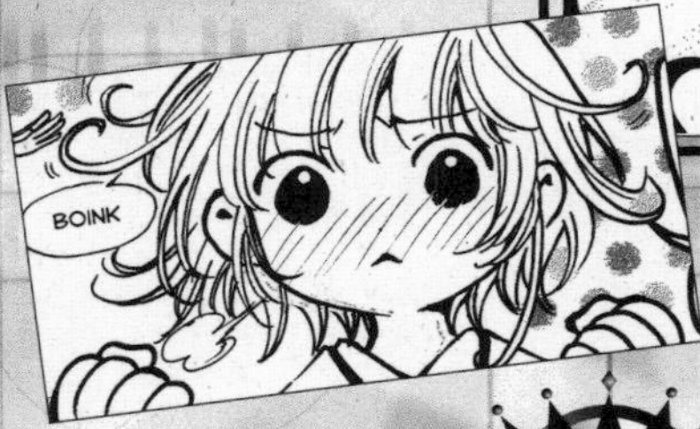
BOINK

◀ I love the way she's always trying to do her best to help out. (Yuki Endo/Fukushima Prefecture)

第3位
Character
1268
VOTES
KUROGANE

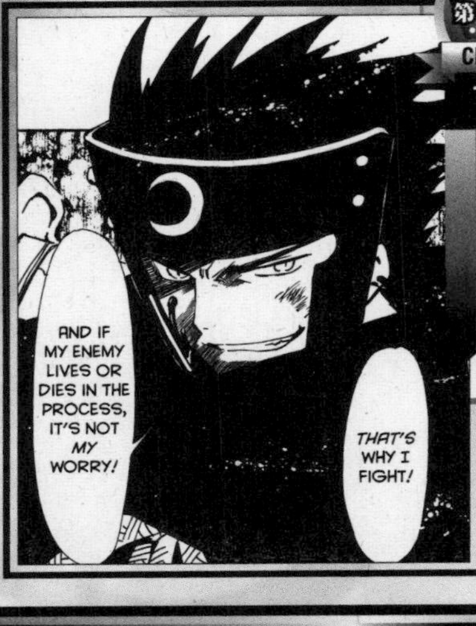
THAT'S WHY I FIGHT!
AND IF MY ENEMY LIVES OR DIES IN THE PROCESS, IT'S NOT *MY* WORRY!

Complete with strength and a hidden kindness, he's a man among men. • He's silent and quick to anger, but he's also unusually gentle. What can I say? I really like him! (Asuka Konno/Chiba Prefecture) /He's fun as the angry guy, but his skill with the sword is just too cool! (Shuhei Saito/Miyazaki Prefecture)

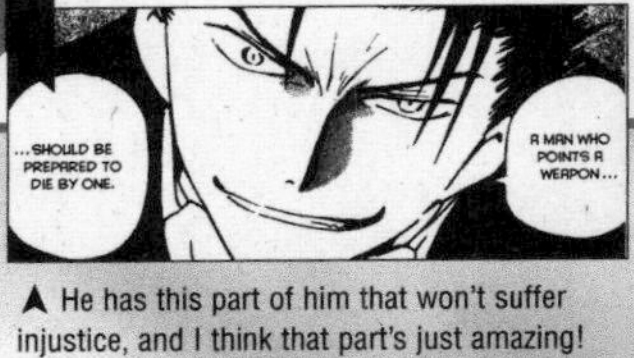
A MAN WHO POINTS A WEAPON...
...SHOULD BE PREPARED TO DIE BY ONE.

▲ He has this part of him that won't suffer injustice, and I think that part's just amazing! (Naoko Sugimoto/Tokyo)

1250 VOTES

Character 4 — FAI

What kind of secrets are hiding behind his smile? • He is usually grinning, but when he isn't grinning are the times when he's really cool! (Megumi Sato/Akita Prefecture) /I love that darkness that we sometimes see! (Maya Kitanaka/Hyogo Prefecture)

571 VOTES

Character 5 — MOKONA

Tsubasa's mascot is so cute and adorable! • The way Mokona talks and looks are really cute, but the 108 secret techniques are the best!! (Shuji Nishihara/Gifu Prefecture) /The real top skilled "person"? (Masami Yamaguchi/Hokkaido)

163 VOTES

Character 6 — SEISHIRÔ

His style captured the imaginations of reader after reader. • It doesn't matter, he's cool! Please bring him back soon! (Shusuke Fujinaga/Hokkaido) /Because he acts so high and mighty . . . (laughter) (Yuko Saeki/Tokyo)

96 VOTES
Character 7 — ASHURA-Ô & YÛKO

Yûko and Ashura-ô received the same number of votes so both wound up at 7th. • I like watching Yûko because her sense of fun makes reading about her a joy! (Shinji Ishikuchi/Niigata Prefecture) /Ashura-ô was very courageous when fighting and very sexy when dancing! ♥ (Yumiko Nakamichi/Oita Prefecture)

10 — Character TOMOYO

There's a gap between her princess-like dignity and her devilish smile that people just ♥! • She's pretty, cute and mysterious. (Yumi Takeuchi/Gunma Prefecture) /What a woman for Kurogane to swear eternal allegiance to! (Namiko Hirano/Saitama Prefecture)

9 — 85 VOTES
Character TÔYA

A collection of votes for the ideal big brother! • He's a little malicious, but I just love how much he cares for his sister. (Akie Shigeno/Kanagawa Prefecture) /Oh, his kind eyes! ♥ (Mariko Takahashi/Iwate Prefecture)

TOP 11>>>19

No. 11	56 Votes	Yukito	No. 14	13 Votes	Watanuki
No. 12	32 Votes	Sorata Arisugawa	No. 17	12 Votes	Sôma
No. 13	29 Votes	Black Mokona	No. 17	12 Votes	Subaru
No. 14	13 Votes	Chii	No. 19	10 Votes	The Three Amen'osa
No. 14	13 Votes	Chu'nyan	No. 19	10 Votes	Shôgo Asagi

THE READERS CHOSE

Who Could Be Your Ideal Friend or Lover?!

If a character that you really like was close by in your life, would you try to make that person a friend or lover? Would you go on an adventure with this person? Or a romantic date? What would you do?

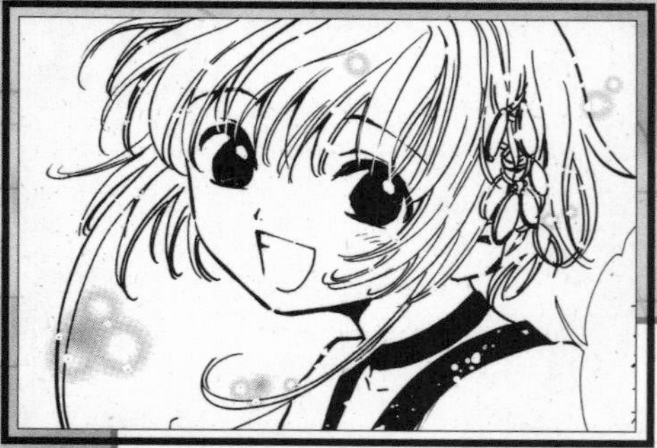

第1位

Friends & Lovers

2507 VOTES

SAKURA

The top vote getter by a large margin regardless of gender! • I want to learn from Sakura and become a wonderful girl myself! (Yuma Sato/Hokkaido)

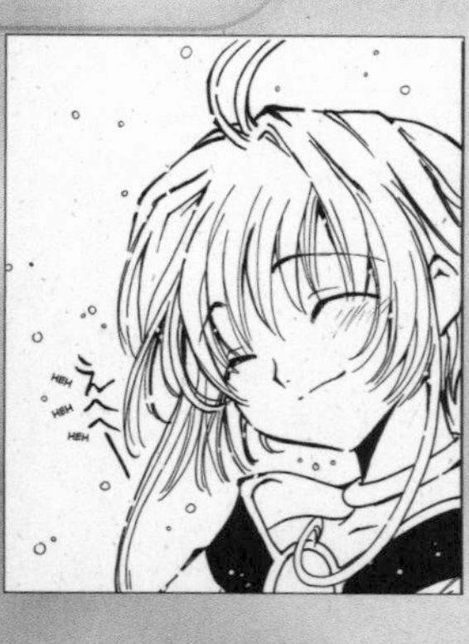
HEH
HEH
HEH

➤ If Sakura were with me, I could even become kinder myself. I have the feeling that I'd become a lot more optimistic. (Natsuko Yanagisawa/Hokkaido)

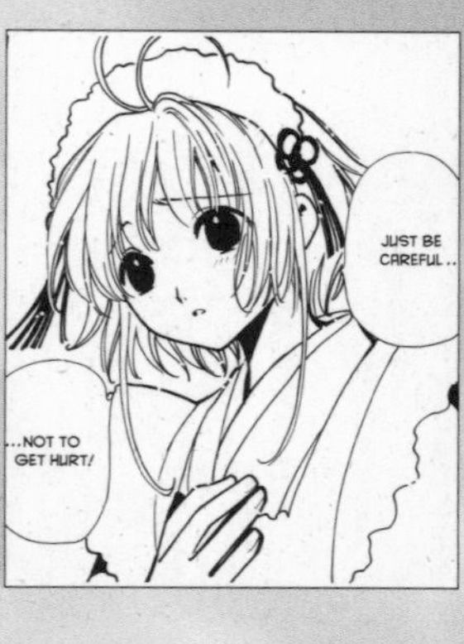
JUST BE CAREFUL...
...NOT TO GET HURT!

➤ If I had a great best friend like her, I'd love every day of my life! (Ayumi Kiyama/Kagawa Prefecture) /I'm so envious of Syaoran! (Yoshikazu Shiraishi/Tochigi Prefecture)

Just like Sakura, Syaoran got votes from both guys and girls. • He's giving his all to be strong and reliable, and he is never one to complain! (Ayano Nishimura/Kagoshima Prefecture) /I want him by my side protecting me. (Ayumi Miura/Hiroshima Prefecture)

第2位
Friends & Love
1619 VOTES

SYAORAN

SURE!

WE MAY HAVE GROWN UP TOGETHER ...

...BUT SHE'S STILL A PRINCESS.

◄ I think the part of him that wants to protect people is his best part. (Miki Tamura/Chiba Prefecture)

第3位
Friends & Lovers
1526 VOTES

FAI

With an overwhelming press of female fans, Fai becomes number 3! • I get the feeling he'd treat me better than any other. (Aiko Saga/Iwate Prefecture) /He looks like he wouldn't mind lending his advice no matter what I might ask. (Mari Sugimoto/Aichi Prefecture)

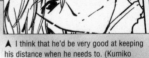

▲ I think that he'd be very good at keeping his distance when he needs to. (Kumiko Koyano/Saitama Prefecture)

第4位 **785 VOTES**

Friends & Lovers

KUROGANE

Maybe you'd like him as a big brother or mentor? • He seems like the kind of guy who could teach you to go beyond your basic abilities. (Fumiaki Sobue/Aichi Prefecture) /He's strong with an offhand-style kindness. (Hiromi Shintani/Fukuoka Prefecture)

第5位 **683 VOTES**

Friends & Lovers

TÔYA

All the ingredients to make a great big brother. • He's a little mean, but he's so nice! ♥ (Yuki Maura/Nagasaki Prefecture) /I want a big brother like him! He's my ideal! (Saki Masaoka/Niigata Prefecture)

第6位 **239 VOTES**

Friends & Lovers

MOKONA

With a friend like this, you'd certainly never be bored! • Because Mokona could take me to all kinds of worlds! (Emi Yoshino/Chiba Prefecture) /Mokona would make half of a great comedy pair. (Tatsuya Horio/Osaka)

THEY'RE
A
SECRET!

第7位 **137 VOTES**

Friends & Lovers

RYÛÔ

The type of guy who could be friends with anyone. • I couldn't help but think that this is one good guy. (Aki Shimada/Kanagawa Prefecture) /I get the feeling that if we were together, he could make me feel good. (Tadashi Deguchi/Mie Prefecture)

I'M RYÛÔ!

第9位 **111 VOTES**
Friends & Lovers **YUZURIHA NEKOI**

We figured this open-hearted girl would get a lot of girls who want to be her friend. • I'd love to go shopping and talk with her! It'd be so fun!! (Ayumi Kawase/Chiba Prefecture)

第8位 **130 VOTES**
Friends & Lovers **TOMOYO**

Just about anybody would fall for this princess. • I fell for the kindness that makes her abhor the taking of life. (Yuji Wada/Osaka) /I've always wanted a princess as a friend! (Takako Hoshino/Tokyo)

TMP
TMP

IT'S AL-MOST...
...AS IF THE STORMS PROTECT WHATEVER IS INSIDE.

第10位 **106 VOTES**
Friends & Lovers **YUKITO & YÛKO**

A tie for number ten! • Yukito-san is the definition of gentility. (Kayo Takaoka/Mie Prefecture) /I'd love to have tea with Yûko and become friends. (Sari Takada/Tokyo)

TOP 12>>>21

No. 12	55 Votes	Watanuki
No. 13	45 Votes	Shôgo Asagi
No. 14	41 Votes	Sôma
No. 15	38 Votes	Seishirô
No. 16	36 Votes	Chu'nyan
No. 17	35 Votes	Arashi Arisugawa
No. 18	34 Votes	Fujitaka
No. 19	31 Votes	Masayoshi Saito
No. 20	26 Votes	Chii
No. 21	21 Votes	Caldina

THE READERS CHOSE

Countries You Most Want to Go to or Live in

Among the countries that Syaoran and the group have visited so far, which one would you most like to go to? Is there one you'd like to live in, or you think would be a real adventure? What's the most popular country?

第1位

World

2577 VOTES

HANSHIN REPUBLIC

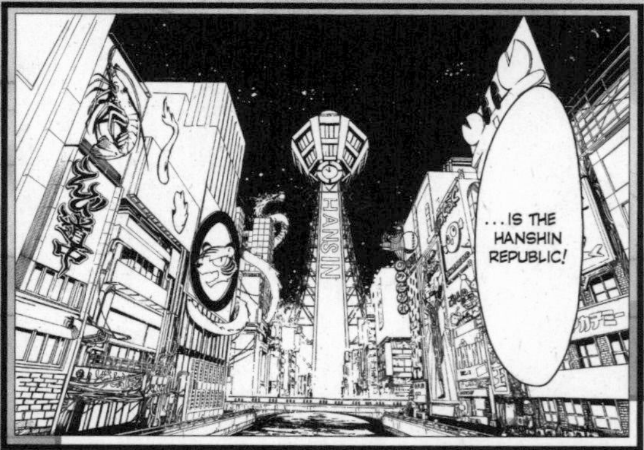

HANSIN
...IS THE HANSHIN REPUBLIC!

"I want to see my own Kudan!" is what a lot of voters said. • It's so full of life and fun! (Nao Matsumoto/Hyogo Prefecture) /I want to live in Sorata's and Arashi's apartment building! (Remika Watanabe/Fukuoka Prefecture)

第2位

World

1690 VOTES

COUNTRY OF EDONIS

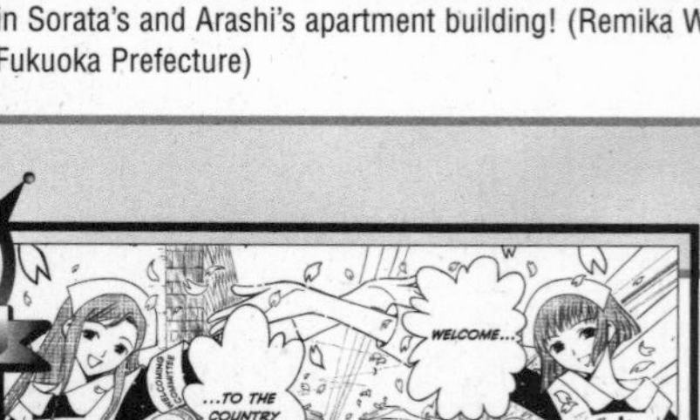

WELCOME...
...TO THE COUNTRY OF ŌTO! ♥

In this country you could have the fun of playing a game! • I want to get strong and take up work as an Oni hunter! (Maho Abe/Hyogo Prefecture) /I want to be welcomed like that. (Tatsunori Mori/Ishikawa Prefecture)

第3位 World — 533 VOTES

COUNTRY OF ÔTO

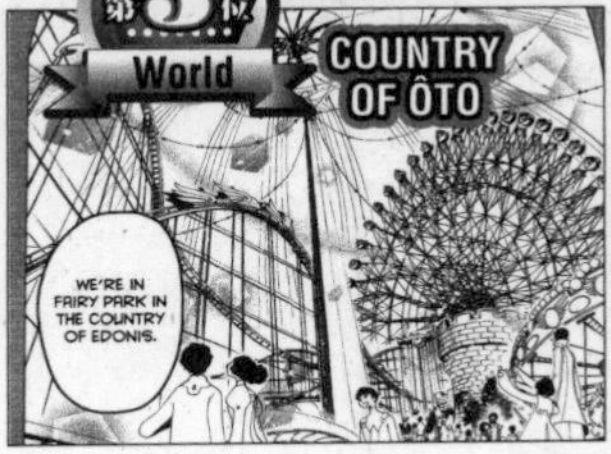
WE'RE IN FAIRY PARK IN THE COUNTRY OF EDONIS.

If you're going to the Country of Ôto, your first stop is here! • I want to have some fun in Fairy Land Park! (Yumiko Endo/Osaka)

第4位 World — 388 VOTES

KINGDOM OF CLOW

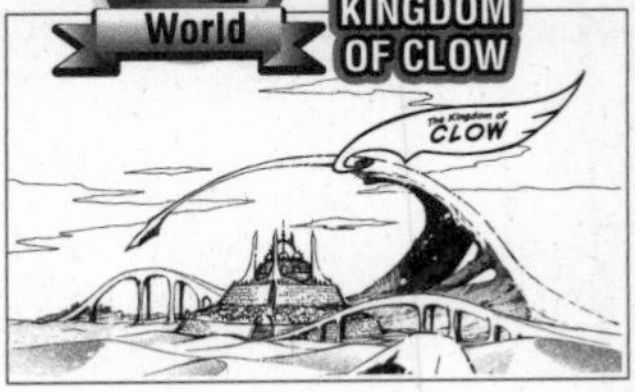
The Kingdom of CLOW

Let's visit Sakura's and Syaoran's homeland! • I'd like to see those ruins with my own eyes. (Michiko Sato/Aichi Prefecture)

第5位 World — 222 VOTES

COUNTRY OF JAPAN

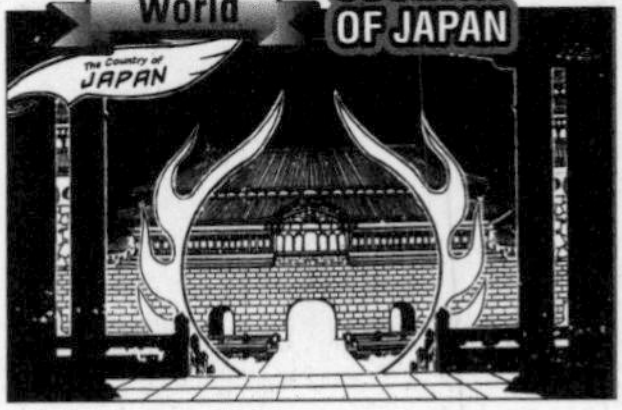
The Country of JAPAN

This country is perfect for Japanophiles. • I want to see the castle where Princess Tomoyo lives. (Yoko Kurogawa/Iwate Prefecture)

第6位 World — 137 VOTES

COUNTRY OF JADE

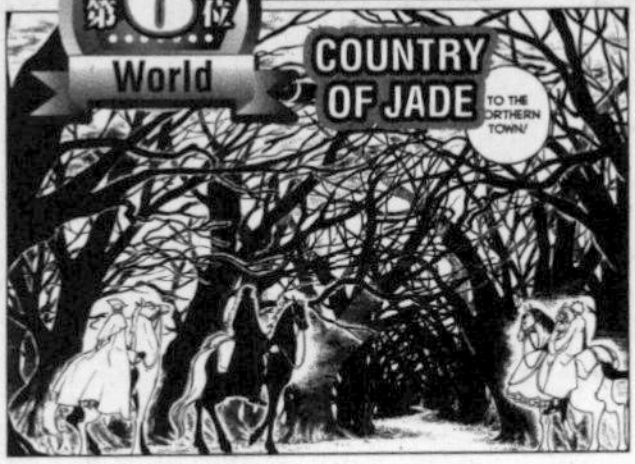

A country painted in beautiful scenery. • It may be cold, but I love the feel of the West in ages past. (Mariya Kawada/Tokyo)

第7位 World — 107 VOTES

COUNTRY OF KORYO & COUNTRY OF SERESU

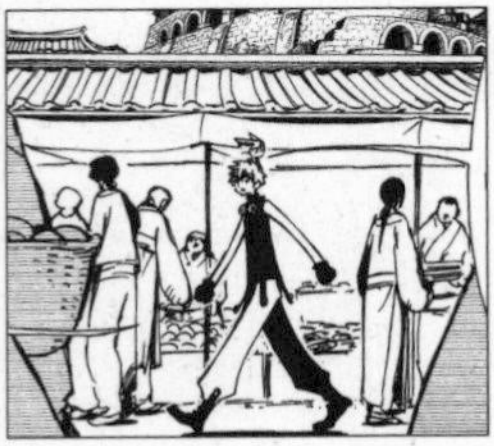

Lots of people said they'd like to see this country after it became peaceful • I'd love to meet an adult Chu'nyan. (Eichu Sakarai/Tokyo)

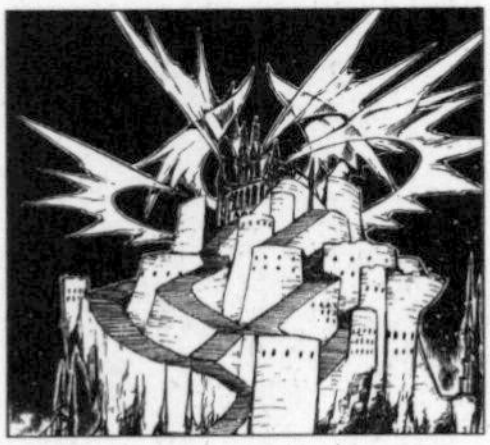

Fai's Homeland. • I'm a little worried about Chii as she sleeps!! (Tomohiro Watanabe/Aichi Prefecture)

THE READERS CHOSE Most Memorable Lines of Dialog and Scenes

In Tsubasa, with its many moving moments, there are those scenes and lines of dialog that the readers remember most. Those moments you close your eyes and remember. Let's replay those chosen best.

Dialog

第1位 I WILL NOT LET SAKURA DIE!

Speech **1045** VOTES

The words Syaoran says after he has decided that he will pay Yûko's price. • Both Yûko and Syaoran are so cool! (Yuna Masuda/Tokushima Prefecture)

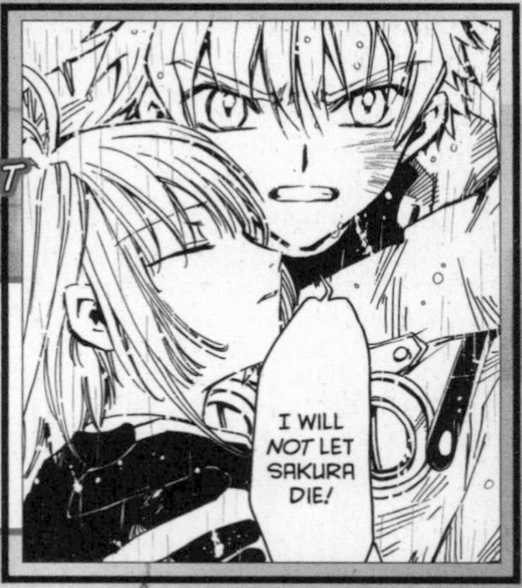
I WILL *NOT* LET SAKURA DIE!

第2位 WHEN I DECIDE TO DO SOMETHING, I DO IT!

Speech **331** VOTES

Even with painful wounds on his legs, Syaoran fights on. • A sentence that shows his iron will!! (Yumiko Kawai/Osaka)

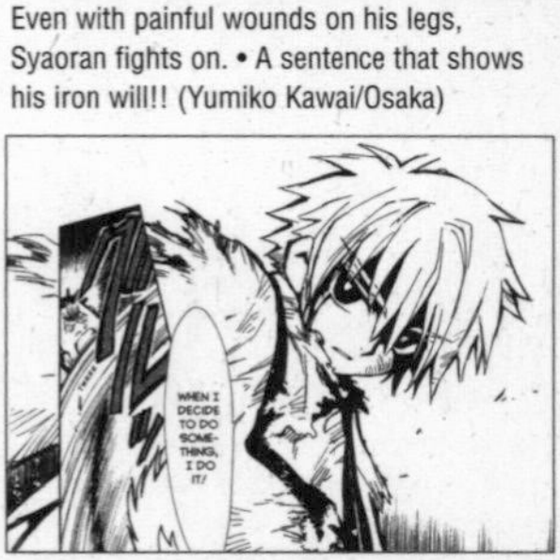
WHEN I DECIDE TO DO SOME-THING, I DO IT!

第3位 LISTEN, IN MY LIFE, I'VE ONLY SERVED UNDER ONE PERSON!

Speech **239** VOTES

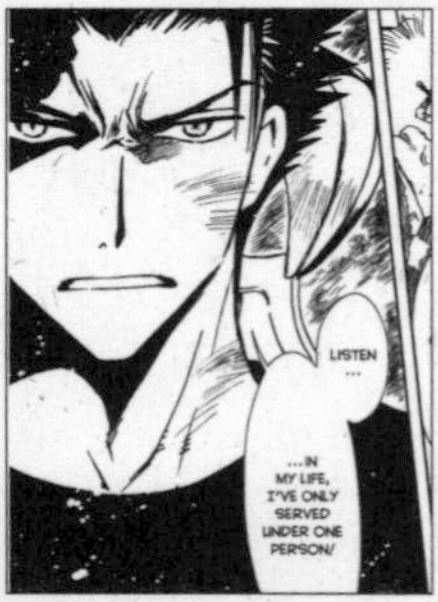
LISTEN ...
...IN MY LIFE, I'VE ONLY SERVED UNDER ONE PERSON!

A line of dialog that shows a part of Kurogane's heart. • You don't know how jealous I've been of Tomoyo! (Mizuki Shinozaki/Nagano Prefecture)

第5位 Speech

DON'T EVER GIVE UP! GET STRONGER! MUCH STRONGER!

152 VOTES

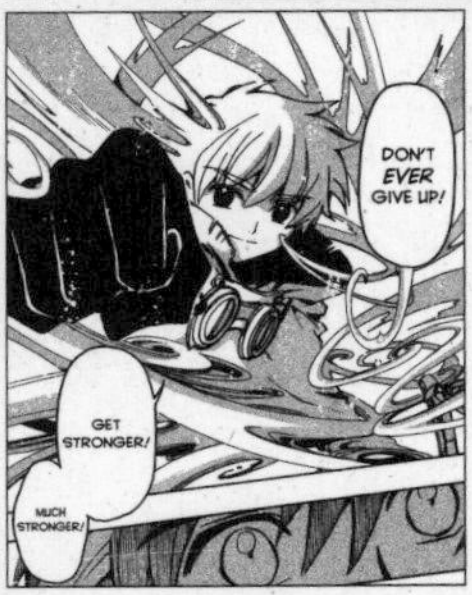
DON'T EVER GIVE UP!
GET STRONGER!
MUCH STRONGER!

The parting words between Ryûô and Syaoran as he leaves the Country of Ôto. • Those words really got across Syaoran's strength of heart! (Mai Tanaka/Nara Prefecture)

第4位 Speech

I NEED YOU TO SAVE SAKURA!

165 VOTES

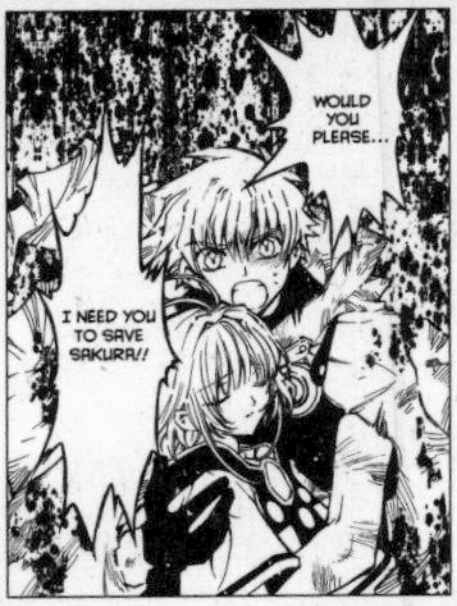
WOULD YOU PLEASE...
I NEED YOU TO SAVE SAKURA!!

The first thing Syaoran says when he meets Yûko. • This is where Syaoran's journey began. (Koki Aijima/Yamaguchi Prefecture)

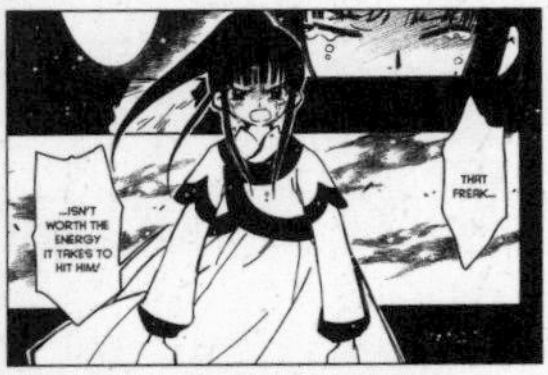
THAT FREAK...
...ISN'T WORTH THE ENERGY IT TAKES TO HIT HIM!

THAT FREAK ISN'T WORTH THE ENERGY IT TAKES TO HIT HIM!

I think this is how Chu'nyan managed to grow up. (Manako Watanabe/Chiba Prefecture)

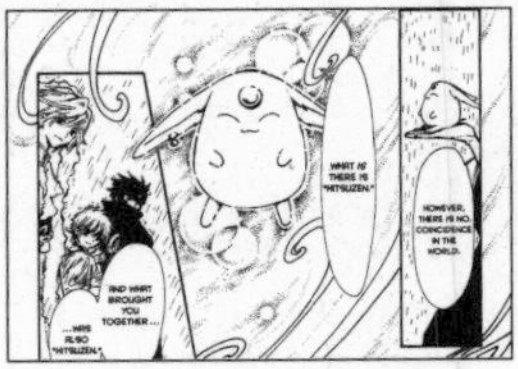
HOWEVER, THERE IS NO COINCIDENCE IN THE WORLD.
WHAT IS THERE IS "HITSUZEN."
AND WHAT BROUGHT YOU TOGETHER...
...WAS ALSO "HITSUZEN."

THERE IS NO COINCIDENCE IN THE WORLD. WHAT IS THERE IS "HITSUZEN."

I like this line of Yûko's better than any other. (Makoto Kasuga/Tokyo)

REMEMBER THESE OTHER GREAT LINES!

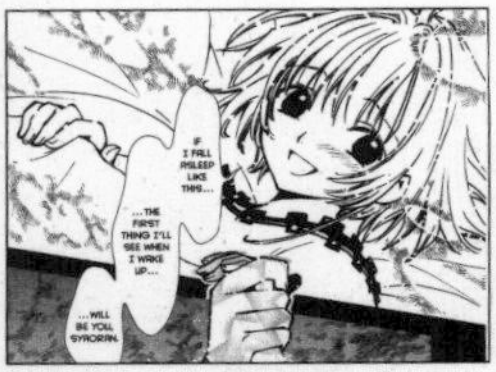
IF I FALL ASLEEP LIKE THIS...
...THE FIRST THING I'LL SEE WHEN I WAKE UP...
...WILL BE YOU, SYAORAN.

IF I FALL ASLEEP LIKE THIS THE FIRST THING I'LL SEE WHEN I WAKE UP WILL BE YOU, SYAORAN.

It's heartbreaking to see those days that will never return. (Akira Yuki/Yamaguchi Prefecture)

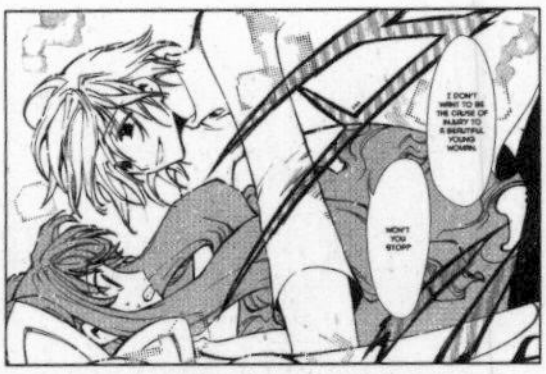
I DON'T WANT TO BE THE CAUSE OF INJURY TO A BEAUTIFUL YOUNG WOMAN.
WON'T YOU STOP?

I DON'T WANT TO BE THE CAUSE OF INJURY TO A BEAUTIFUL YOUNG WOMAN.

When Fai said that, I completely fell for him! (Shoko Fujimura/Hokkaido)

Scene

第1位 THE FLASHBACK SCENES BETWEEN SYAORAN AND SAKURA

Scene **2415** VOTES

Remember the two as they were with tears . . . and more tears . . . • I want the two of them to go back to the way they were! (Miho Katazari/Fukuoka Prefecture)

...I JUST HAD TO SHOW YOU, SYAORAN-KUN!

第2位 THE PARTY AT CAT'S EYE!

Scene **1267** VOTES

Witness the characters in a scene you rarely see, entirely free of cares. • That was just . . . cute! (IzumiYuka/Tokushima Prefecture) /Kurogane as the only sober one, was really fun! (Kaoru Takayama/ Gunma Prefecture)

ISN'T IT PERFECT? THE EYE OF A KITTY! MEOOOW!
MEOOOW!
......

第3位 THE SCENE WHERE SYAORAN'S GROUP GATHERS TOGETHER BEFORE YŪKO.

Scene **864** VOTES

The inaugural scene where Kurogane and Fai join Syaoran and Sakura for the first time. • No matter how many times I read it, I always get shivers down my spine. (Satsuki Aoyama/Kanagawa Prefecture) /This scene is the point of launch for Tsubasa!! (Kanae Mizuno/ Aichi Prefecture)

第5位 THE PARTING SCENE BETWEEN SYAORAN AND RYÛÔ.

Scene 668 VOTES

Ranked the same as the dialog section. • I thought it was good at showing friendship between guys. (Ayaka Agata/Fukuoka Prefecture)

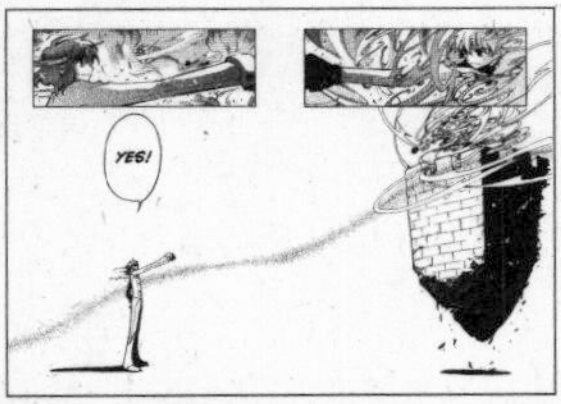
YES!

第4位 THE SCENE WHERE SAKURA VISITS SYAORAN AT HIS HOUSE!

Scene 748 VOTES

A moment of peace in the Kingdom of Clow. • It was heartwarming and always makes me smile. (Akira Sugihara/Saitama Prefecture)

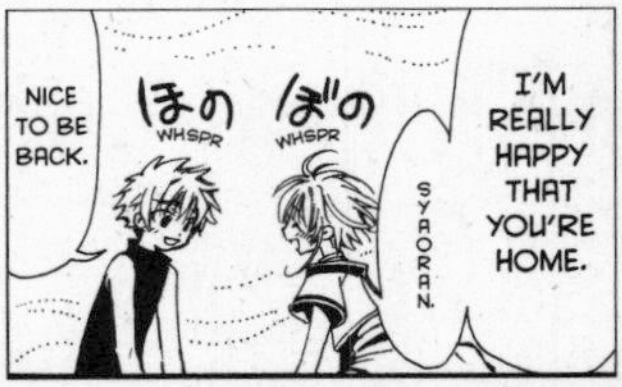
I'M REALLY HAPPY THAT YOU'RE HOME.
SYAORAN.
ぼの
WHSPR
ほの
WHSPR
NICE TO BE BACK.

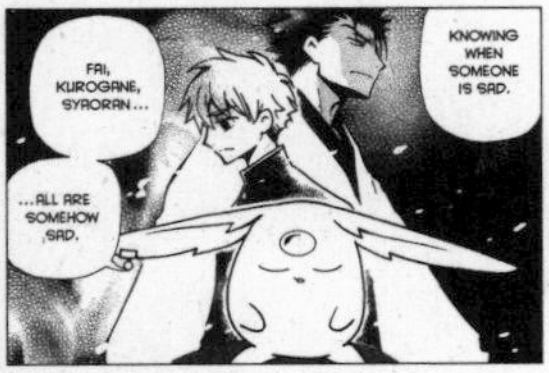
KNOWING WHEN SOMEONE IS SAD.
FAI, KUROGANE, SYAORAN...
...ALL ARE SOMEHOW SAD.

THE SCENE WHERE MOKONA WORRIES OVER THE GROUPS SADNESS.

Even Mokona can be thoughtful, huh? (Kumiko Hiiragi/Osaka)

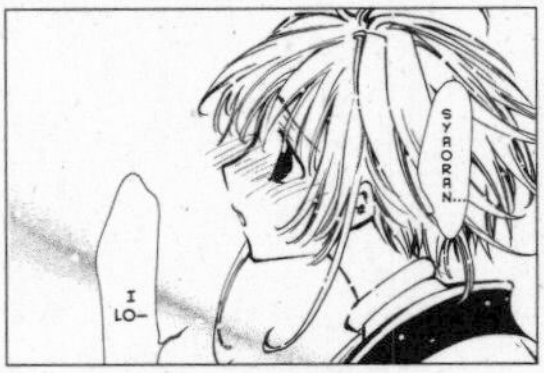
SYAORAN...
I LO—

THE SCENE WHERE SAKURA TRIES TO TELL SYAORAN HER FEELINGS.

She's so cute when she blushes! (Yumi Sakai/Niigata Prefecture)

OTHER GREAT SCENES YOU MIGHT THINK OF.

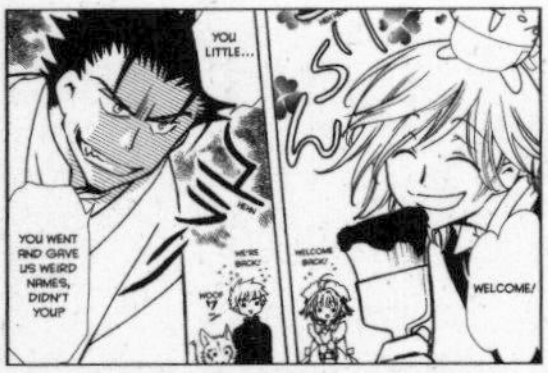
WELCOME!
WELCOME BACK!
WE'RE BACK!
YOU LITTLE...
YOU WENT AND GAVE US WEIRD NAMES, DIDN'T YOU?

THE SCENE WHERE EVERYONE FINDS OUT THAT FAI NAMED THEM BIG PUPPY AND LITTLE PUPPY.

I loved the contrast between Kurogane's and Fai's expressions. (Yayoi Nagashima/Saitama Prefecture)

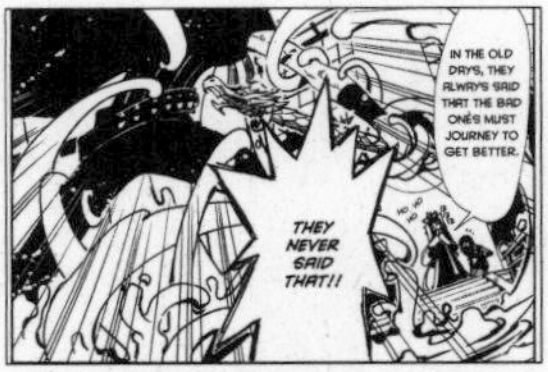
IN THE OLD DAYS, THEY ALWAYS SAID THAT THE BAD ONES MUST JOURNEY TO GET BETTER.
THEY NEVER SAID THAT!!

TOMOYO SENDS KUROGANE AWAY IN THIS SCENE.

I think that Princess Tomoyo's smile is so nice! (Tatsuro Wakamatsu/Tokyo)

THE READERS CHOSE

Best Couple and Best Pairing

1+1 can equal 2, but it can also mean more than that! If one great character teams up with another as two parts of a team, it can made both much better!! So which two do you most like to see together?

第1位 Couple & Pair

SYAORAN & SAKURA

4682 VOTES

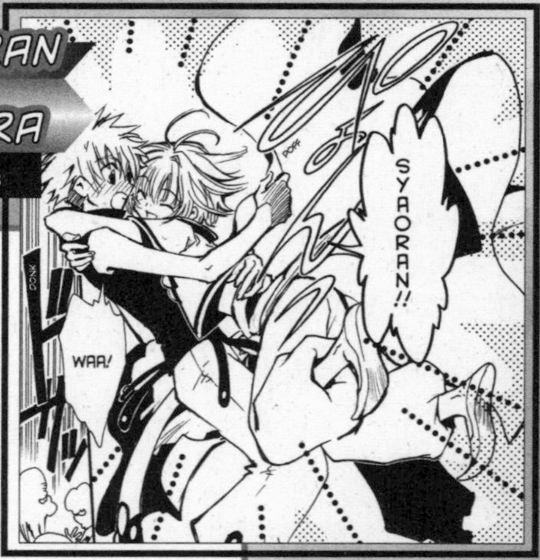
SYAORAN!!
WAA!
DONK

Of course Number 1 are these two!! • Maybe it's innocence, but the way the two care for each other is so cute!! (Kaori Tajima/Saitama Prefecture) /Their love scenes are so fresh, it almost makes me blush. (Noriko Iwata/Gifu Prefecture) /Watching the two is almost painful. I really think it'd be great to have a love relationship like that!! (Emi Kubozuka/Kagoshima Prefecture)

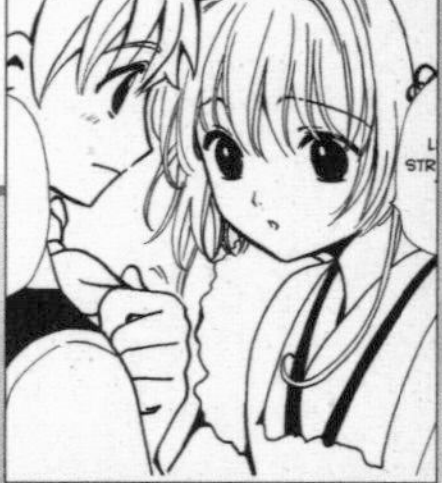

➤ I think childhood sweethearts are the best!! (Moe Ohara/ Yamaguchi Prefecture) /They both have personalities that think of the other one first. (Yuki Fujimura/ Iwate Prefecture)

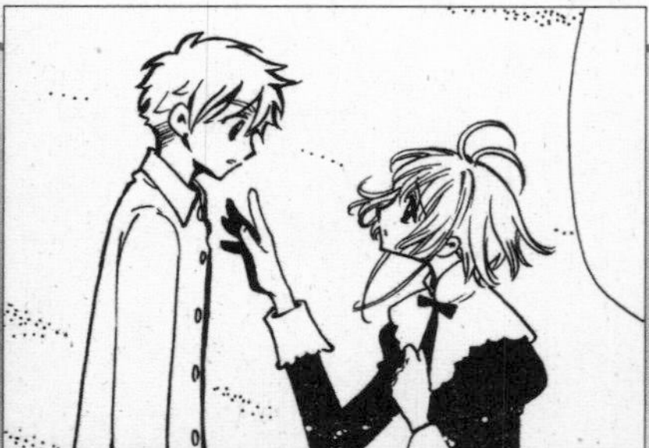

➤ I knew that I couldn't come up with a better couple than them. Those two are just too nice and kind!! (Hiromasa Shoji/Miyazaki Prefecture)

第2位 KUROGANE & FAI

Couple & Pair **2435** VOTES

A combination made of polar opposites. • I love combos made of the sword and magic!! (Saori Takahashi/Miyazaki Prefecture) /I love the nicknames that Fai gives Kurogane. (Akiko Iijima/Ibaraki Prefecture)

THIS WATER... HURTS, DOESN'T IT?
THAT'S 'CAUSE WHATEVER IT HITS, IT MELTS.
CLOTHES... SKIN...

THIS IS NO LAUGHING MATTER!
WHY NOT? IT'S CUTE!
THE PUPPY PAIR!
EVEN THE INFORMANT LADY KNEW THE NAME!!

第3位 KUROGANE & MOKONA

Couple & Pair **1064** VOTES

Maybe they're in charge of laughter in Tsubasa? • They've found a strange harmony between the angry guy and the dumb guy. (Mitsuki Baba/Hyogo Prefecture) /I love their interplay! (Masami Imai)

BEH HEH!
MOKONA HAS MANY GIRLFRIENDS!
BLUSH BLUSH
VSSH
THEY AREN'T GIRLFRIENDS!!

WHO ARE YOU CALLING KUROGANE?!

TÔYA & YUKITO

第4位 Couple & Pair **430** VOTES

Whether in the Kingdom of Clow or in the Hanshin Republic, they're still together. • They both treat the other as immensely important. (Kaori Inose/ Ibaraki Prefecture) /They're great partners no matter what world they're in. (Hitomi Tenri/Chiba Prefecture)

YOU NEVER GIVE UP...
...DO YOU, TÔYA?

SAKURA & FAI

第5位 Couple & Pair **344** VOTES

PWOIT
BIG KITTY AND...
...LITTLE KITTY!

Don't you think Fai is better than expected at looking after people? • I love that feeling of a great brother-sister relationship that they give off!! (Yurie Kibizuka/Saitama Prefecture) /Their meowing during the party was so cute! (Akane Ishihara/Kanagawa Prefecture)

SORATA & ARASHI

第6位 Couple & Pair **316** VOTES

The happily married couple, forever living in peace. • I think her shy attitude in front of Sorata-san is so precious! (Mayu Shioiri/Fukui Prefecture) They seem happy, and that's the most important thing. (Chiaki Sugawara/Tokyo)

KA-KLAK
SO YOU'RE ALL AWAKE NOW!

第9位 KUROGANE & TOMOYO

Couple & Pair **130** VOTES

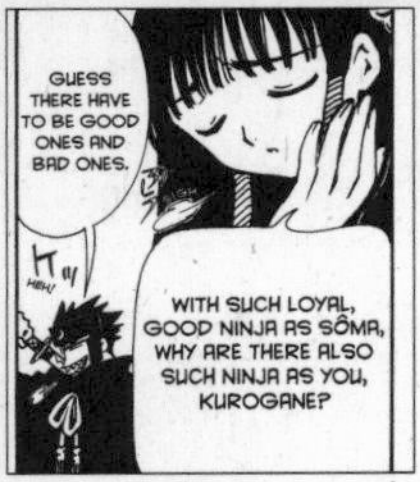
GUESS THERE HAVE TO BE GOOD ONES AND BAD ONES.
WITH SUCH LOYAL, GOOD NINJA AS SÔMA, WHY ARE THERE ALSO SUCH NINJA AS YOU, KUROGANE?
HEH!

A master/servant relationship with strong bonds between them. • I think it's so cute how Kurogane can't get fully angry with her. (Ryoko Ota/Kagawa Prefecture)

第7位 SYAORAN & KUROGANE

Couple & Pair **299** VOTES

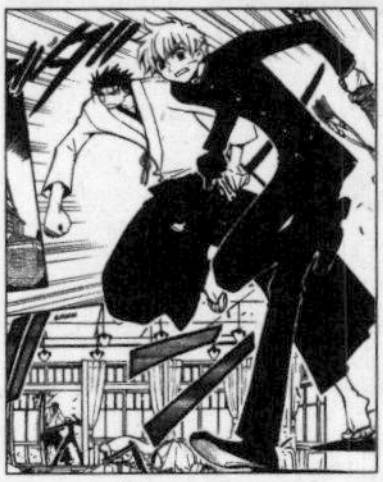

Teacher and pupil make a strong pair which is just getting stronger. • They look like they could beat even the strongest enemy. (Naoto Kanja/Hiroshima Prefecture)

第10位 YUZURIHA & KUSANAGI

Couple & Pair **98** VOTES

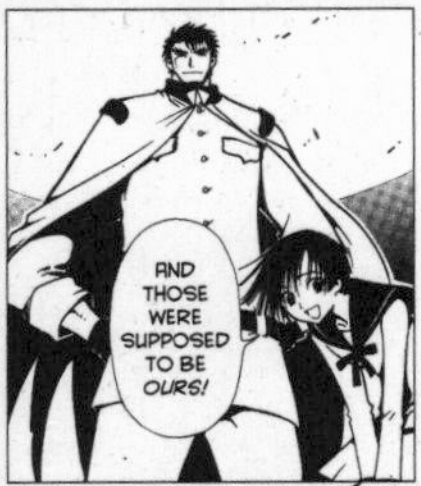
AND THOSE WERE SUPPOSED TO BE OURS!

The famous Oni hunting combo. • I'd love to go to the Country of Ôto and go Oni hunting with them! (Ryoko Furuya/Ishigawa Prefecture)

第8位 FAI & MOKONA

Couple & Pair **245** VOTES

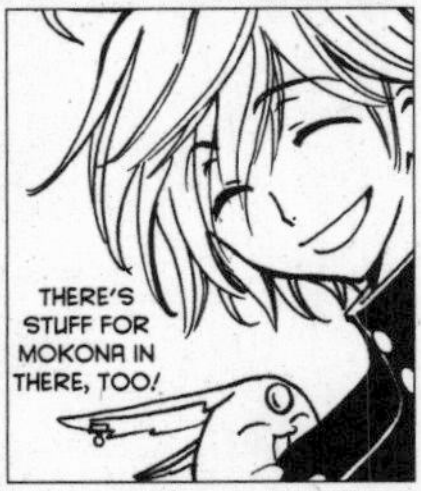
THERE'S STUFF FOR MOKONA IN THERE, TOO!

The chuckling pair. • When these two tease Kurogane, nothing's better! (Maki Sato/Fukushima Prefecture)

MORE GREAT COUPLES AND COMBOS!

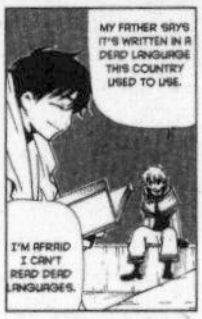
MY FATHER SAYS IT'S WRITTEN IN A DEAD LANGUAGE THIS COUNTRY USED TO USE.
I'M AFRAID I CAN'T READ DEAD LANGUAGES.

SYAORAN & SEISHIRÔ

They aren't a pair now, but... • If those two combine, no enemy stands a chance! (Madoka Hokin/Tokyo)

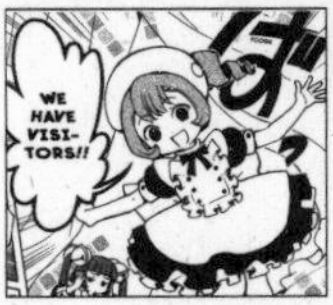
WE HAVE VISITORS!!

SUMOMO & KOTOKO

Probably the most lively pair. • Their size was amazing! (Ryo Horii/Tokyo)

KUROGANE & SÔMA

The ninja combo from the Country of Japan. • I want to see them fight together! (Kaoru Tsukishima/Fukushima Prefecture)

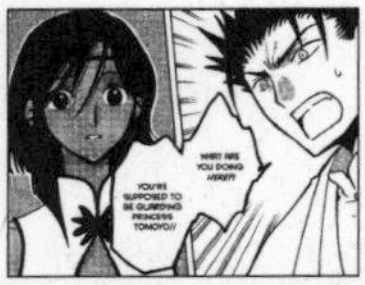
WHAT ARE YOU DOING HERE?!
YOU'RE SUPPOSED TO BE GUARDING PRINCESS TOMOYO!!

FAI & CHII

Ever wonder what's in their past? • A beautiful guy and a beautiful girl as a couple! (Satomi Matsuda/Saitama Prefecture)

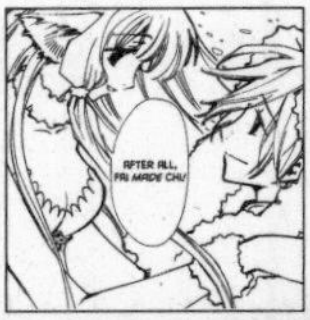
AFTER ALL, FAI MADE CHII!

What Would Be the Best Wish for the Time-Space Witch to Grant?

Is there some wish you would make of the incredibly powerful Time-Space Witch Yûko? Wish for anything from the tiny to the enormous. But be sure you pay close attention to what the price is.

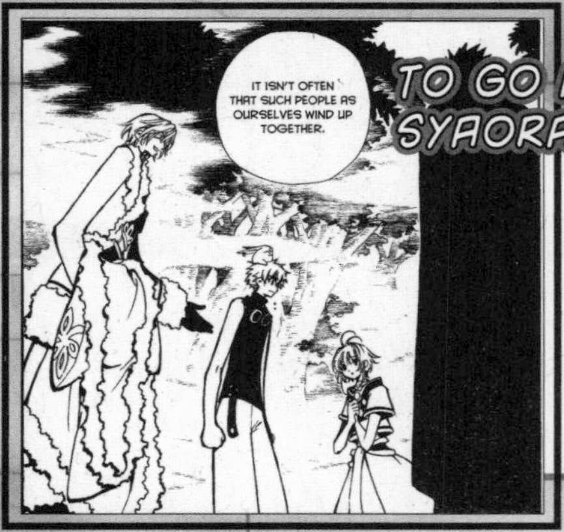
IT ISN'T OFTEN THAT SUCH PEOPLE AS OURSELVES WIND UP TOGETHER.

TO GO ALONG WITH SYAORAN AND HIS GROUP!

Any Tsubasa fan would have wished this at one time or other. • The price is my memories up to this point... (Ryoko Hashiguchi/Kumamoto Prefecture) /Once I'm an adult, I'll buy as many drinks as Yûko wants! (Nanami Takahashi/Kanagawa Prefecture)

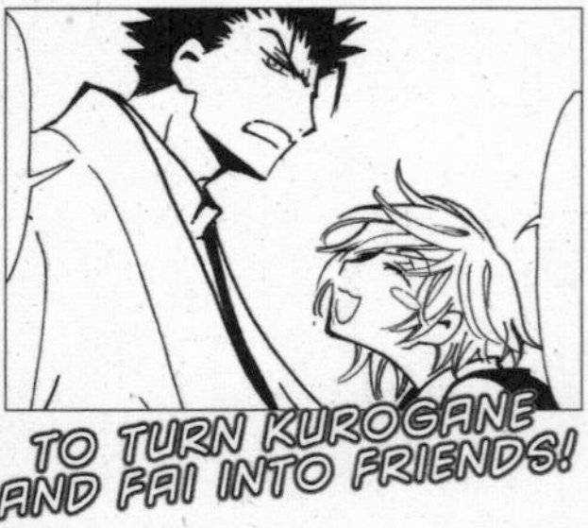

TO TURN KUROGANE AND FAI INTO FRIENDS!

If those two were together, could you stand the excitement?! • As a price, I'd pay my hair... maybe? (Nozomi Okuda/Hiroshima Prefecture)

TO LET SYAORAN AND SAKURA HAVE HAPPINESS TOGETHER.

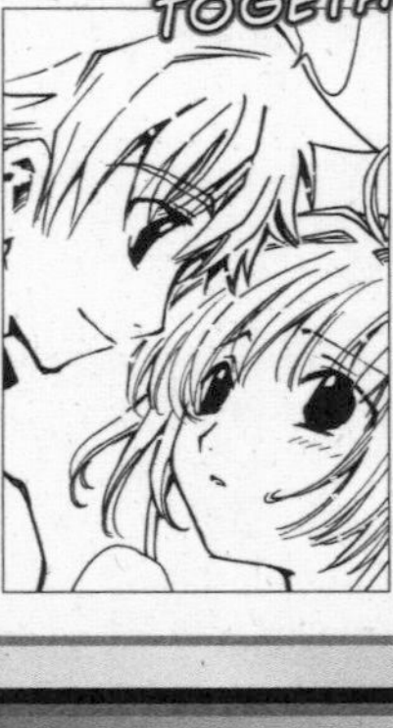

Seeing the two together, who wouldn't wish that? • I want to watch over them! (Janki Miwa/Osaka)

IT'S CALLED FONDANT AU CHOCOLAT!
THERE'S CHOCOLATE INSIDE!
YOU EAT IT HOT.
REALLY!
HER TIMING IS PERFECT!
LET'S ALL HAVE SOME!
THE TEA IS READY, TOO!

TO EAT SOME FONDANT AU CHOCOLAT!!

Wouldn't you like the ultimate flavor just once? • I'd pay for it with some really delicious tea!! (Rumi Kobayashi/Gunma Prefecture)

TO BECOME GOOD FRIENDS WITH YÛKO!

One would see some amazing things. • I'd pay by working hard, just like Watanuki. (Takumi Sato/Wakayama Prefecture)

THERE ARE OTHER WISHES TOO!

I'd like to be able to fly. Walking would be my payment. But if I did that, and I had to fly forever, it would be pretty hard on me. (laughter) (Naoko Okawa/Tokyo) /I'm not very courageous, so I'd want the courage to tell the one I love how I feel! For payment, I'd give the memories of my first love. I've got enough courage to get rid of those. (Kyo Fujimura/ Fukuoka Prefecture) /I want my stuffed toys to be able to talk to me! I'd pay for it with my pendant. (Saori Murase/Mie Prefecture) /I'd like about 5 extra cm in height. As a price, I'm willing to pay with our famous local liquor. (Asuka Yokota/Aichi Prefecture) /I would like my father to stop making his bad puns and dirty jokes to any other human being. For payment, I'd give away my pictures of my first love. ♥ (Mario Urano/Tokyo) /I want to be a voice actor on the anime version of Tsubasa! For a price, you could even have my . . . soul! (Yui Suehiro/Chiba Prefecture) I want to be able to teleport! That way I wouldn't need to pay to commute! (laughter) I'm willing to become Yûko's maid. I'd work really hard! (Yuki Fukumoto/Hiroshima Prefecture) /I want the resurrection of the Osaka Kintetsu Buffaloes! ★ I'll clean Yûko's house as payment. (Kazuko Watanabe/Aichi Prefecture) I need to pass my entrance exams. I'll pay with my favorite stuffed toy. (Manami Yasunaka/Nara Prefecture) /I want to know what happens in the last installment of Tsubasa. To pay for it, I'll work off my debt by working alongside Watanuki. (Hitomi Kanai/Chiba Prefecture)

These Would Be Great Clothes for the Characters to Wear!! The Contributor's Fashion Contest!

When Syaoran and his friends go to a new country, they wear that country's clothes. And because we received so many great submissions, we'll just have the characters wear them. There are many stylish clothes and some that one would just call weird. Take a look!!

さくら
Sakura

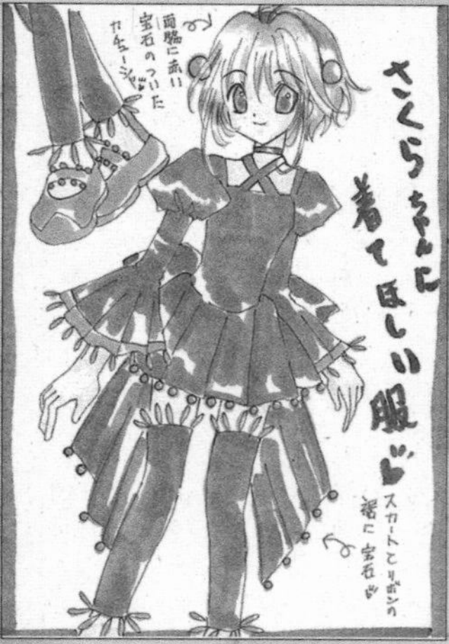
さくらちゃんに着てほしい服

◄ Maki Sato/Fukushima Prefecture • Her Katyusha hairband and the hem of her skirt are set with jewels in this original design. Just like a princess!

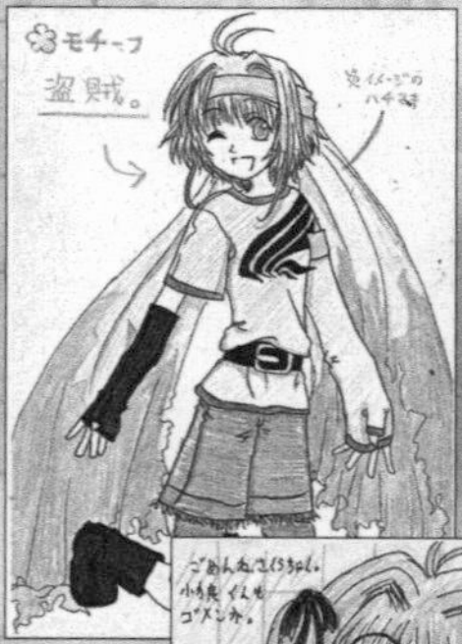
モチーフ
盗賊。

◄ Hono Arashiyama/Ehime Prefecture • The motif is "Pirate"! What would a tomboyish princess do with pirate's treasure?

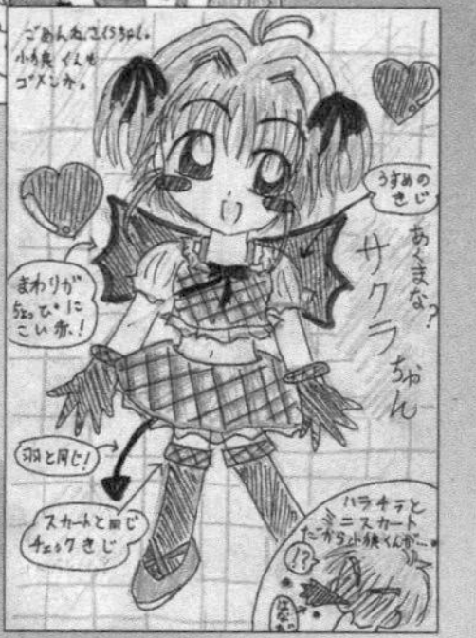
サクラちゃん
あくまな?
羽と同じ!

Narumi Shinohara/Saitama Prefecture • The devilish Sakura. The checkered miniskirt is so cute!

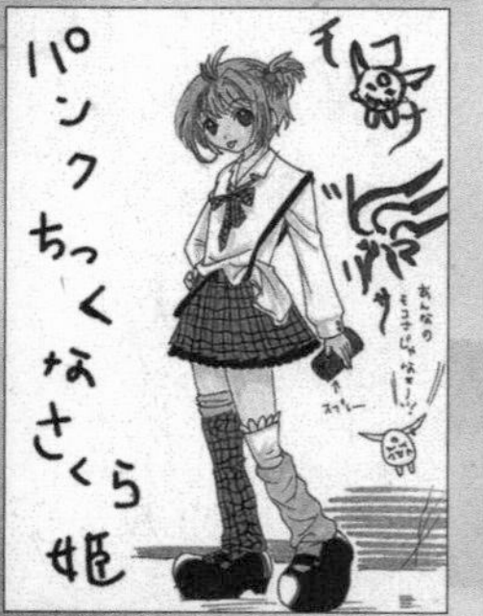
パンクちっくなさくら姫
モコ

Mitsuki/Hyogo Prefecture • A Punk Chick, of course! ★ And she's sticking her tongue out at us! Cute!! ♥

Kokeshi/Hokkaido • Sakura and Mokona have turned into magicians! How'd you like to see an illusion?

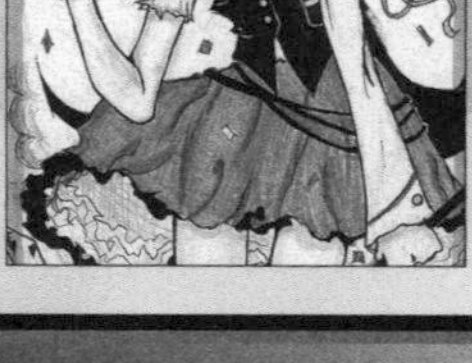
マジシャンさくら&モコナ

小狼 (シャオラン)
Syaoran

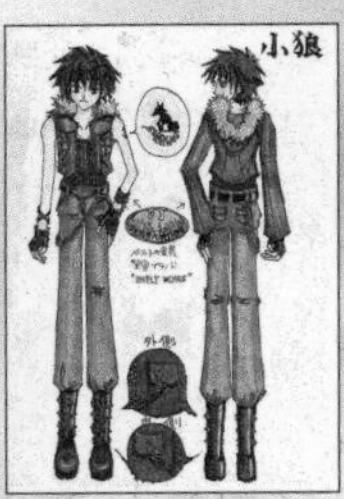
小狼

➤ Ren Kobayashi/Tokyo • The tattoos and metal belt buckle are casually eye-catching.

◀ Raimei/Toyama Prefecture • The concept is "The Wolf"! Doesn't it remind you of the two Puppies?

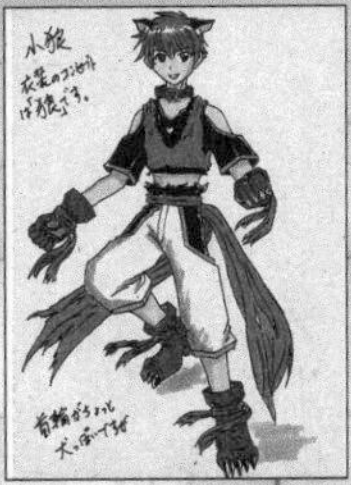

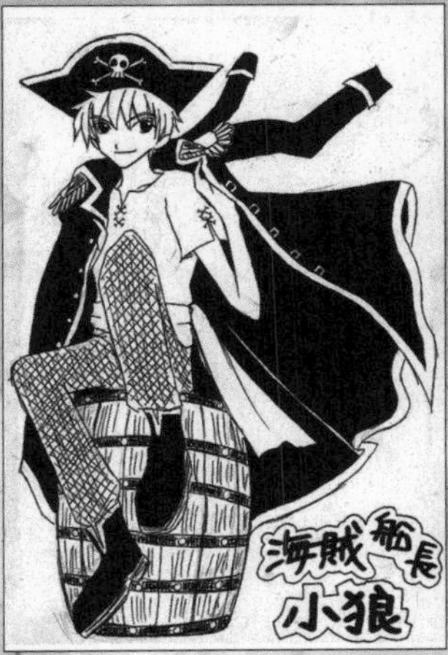
海賊船長
小狼

◀ Midori Yoneyam Chiba Prefectur Syaoran's become captain o a pirate ship! It's so sweet to see th courageo captain head out the open sea!!

さくら & 小狼 (シャオラン)
Sakura & Syaoran

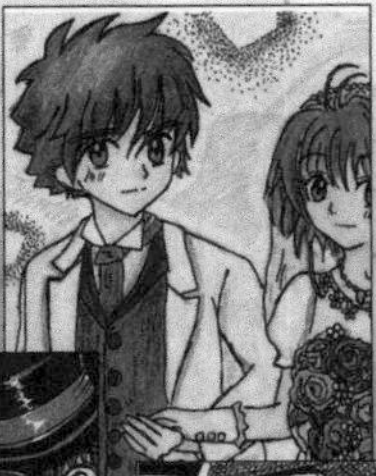

◀ Lucky/ Wakayama Prefecture • The newlywed couple. Maybe that day will come someday.

▼ Kotori Makura/Saitama Prefecture • Sakura in Wonderland. Mokona is unusually large, though.

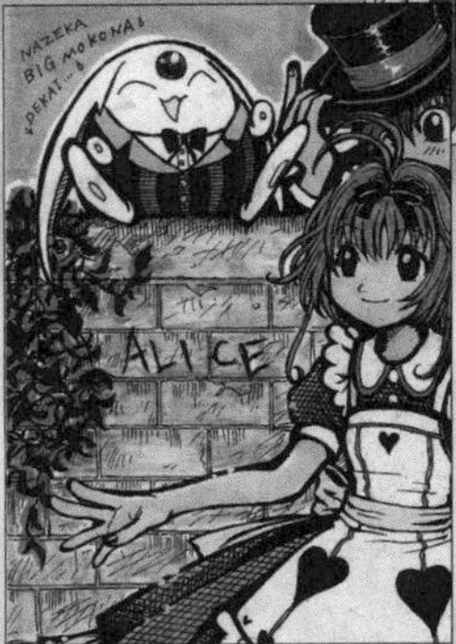
NAZEKA BIG MOKONA!
ALICE

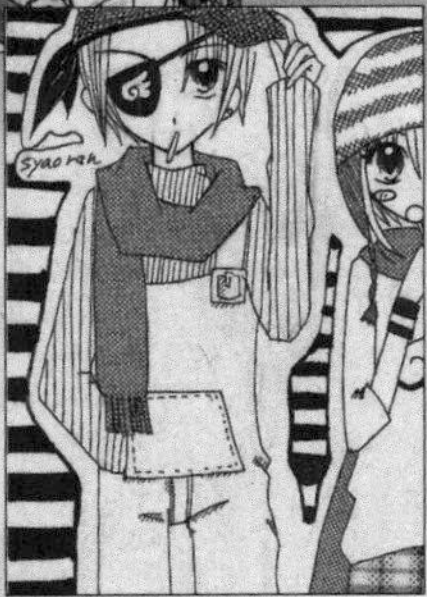
Syaoran

◀ Panda/Yamagata Prefecture • They look a little delinquent, but the energy in the picture is OK!

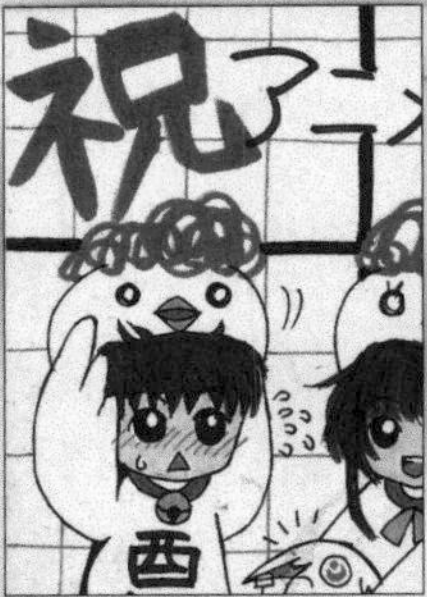
祝
西

◀ Aoko Juo/Ibarak Prefecture This has the couple wearing rooster costumes celebratio of Tsubasa becoming an anime and of 200 zodiac sig

ファイ
Fai

◀ Mami/Kanagawa Prefecture • The vampire that appeared in the town at night was Fai? It might be fun to fall into darkness!

▼ Sato/Tokyo • He's good looking, so it's OK for him to wear a cat costume!

◀ Papa Ricky • A cloak with pink leopard spots with an interior lining of tiger stripes! Well, it's Fai, so we can forgive it.

◀ Ruru/Gifu Prefecture • I'm sure he looks good in Japanese clothes, but why the costume of a *miko* priestess?

黒鋼
Kurogane

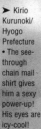

➤ Kirio Kurunoki/ Hyogo Prefecture • The see-through chain mail shirt gives him a sexy power-up! His eyes are icy-cool!

◀ Kei Izumi/ Hyogo Prefecture • We ♥ the pendant on his open-shirted chest.

黒鋼 & ファイ
Kurogane & Fai

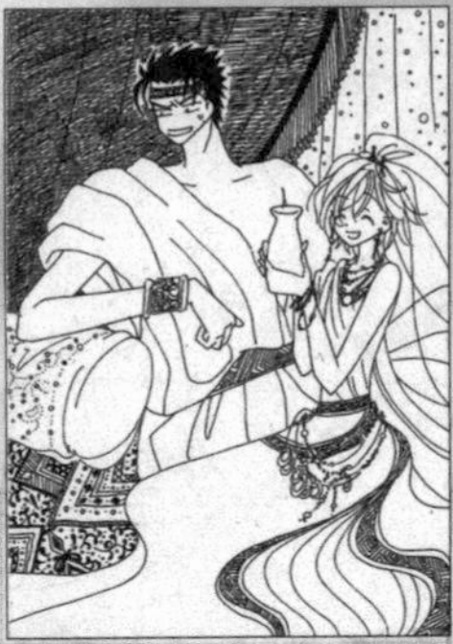

➤ Ginka/Osaka • It's almost a scene out of a myth with a beautiful goddess serving liquor! She isn't female, though . . .

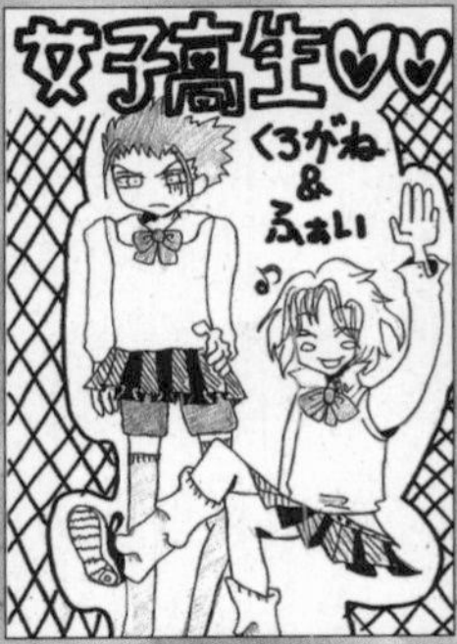
女子高生♥♥
くろがね
&
ふぁい

➤ Ikuko/Aichi Prefecture • For some reason, Kurogane and Fai are in girls' high-school uniforms! Fai's the only one enjoying it! (laughter)

モコナ
Mokona

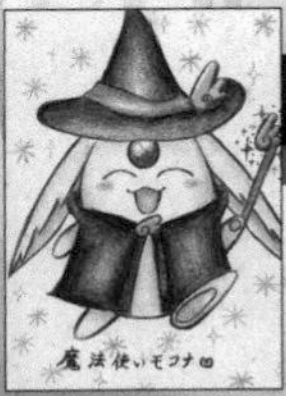
魔法使いモコナ

➤ Yuka Matsue/Kumamoto Prefecture • Witch Mokona. What is your wish?

さくら&知世姫
Sakura & Tomoyo

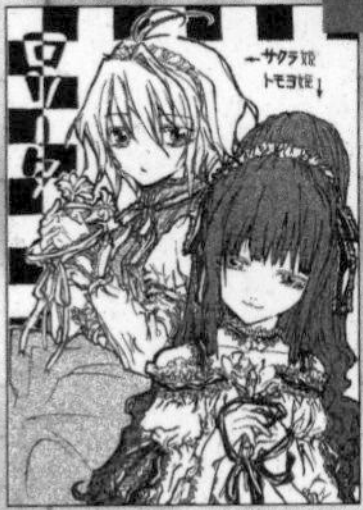

▲ Umu Kayo/Yamagata Prefecture • Goth-Lolita twins! ♥

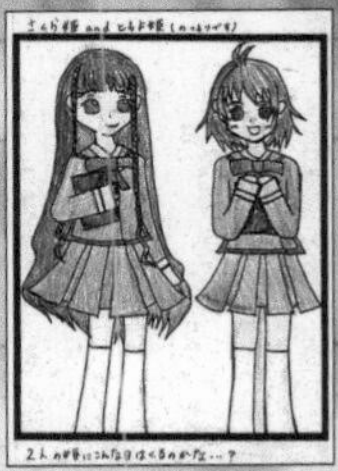

▲ Chiroro/Kanagawa Prefecture • Best friends.

チィ
Chii

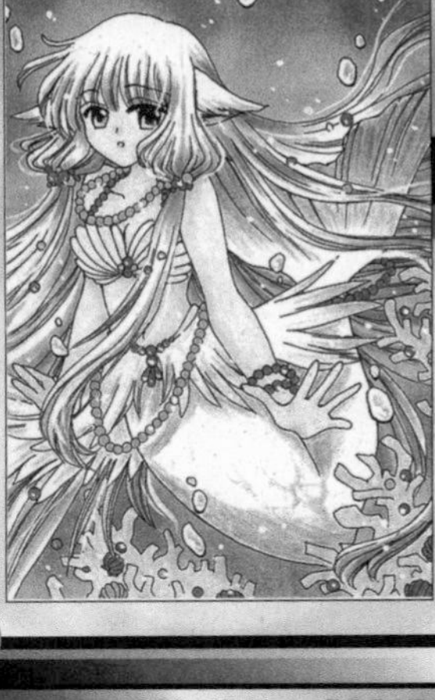

➤ Tethys/Chiba Prefecture • Chii has become a mermaid princess! When will her happiness come?

知世姫
Tomoyo

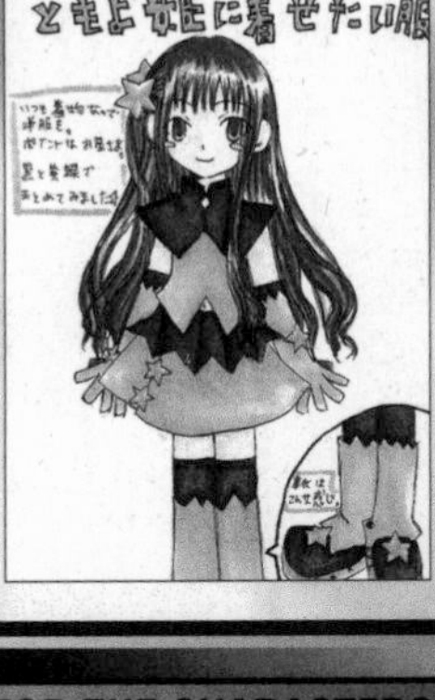
ともよ姫に着せたい服

➤ Yuki Fujiwara/Osaka • She's normally in Japanese kimono, so here she is in Western-style clothes! The main point are the stars.

What if Tsubasa's Characters Were in Real-Life Japan . . . ?

Amid all of the travels of Syaoran, Sakura, Kurogane and Fai, there should be a time when they make a stop in Japan of the world we live in. So what would they do while they were here? You wonder that too, right?

◀ Yuko Sato/Chiba Prefecture • The image of a student during class. Even in learning his *kanji*, Syaoran's personality comes into play.

▶ Nekoyanagi/Kanagawa Prefecture • Syaoran's a soccer goalie! Do your best to join the Japan National Team!

▲ Kiyoshi/Tochigi Prefecture • Of course, school clothes are the basic thought. Are Kurogane and Fai high-school age?

YOUTH AT ITS BEST!

◀ Rie/Fukuoka Prefecture • Genius (?) Scientist Fai. Maybe science is the magic of the real world!!

◀ Ikuse/Aichi Prefecture • This Is Swing Boys? It's almost like you can hear the music!

FAN SQUARE • WHAT IF . . . REAL-LIFE JAPAN . . . ? 172

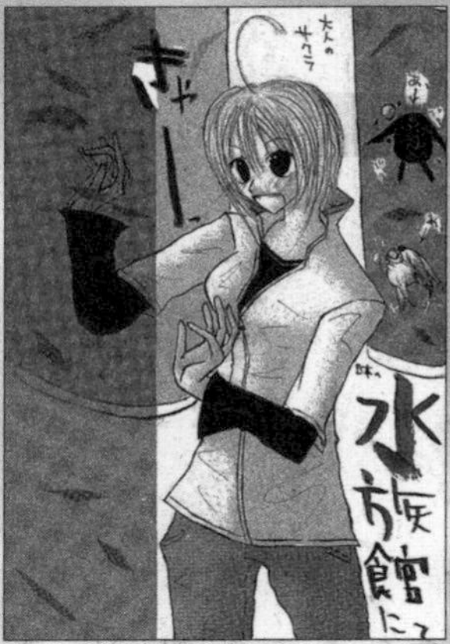
大人のサクラ
水族館にて

➤ Shinichi Takada/Aichi Prefecture • An adult Sakura visiting an aquarium. Her outside looks like an adult, but she still seems to be childlike inside.

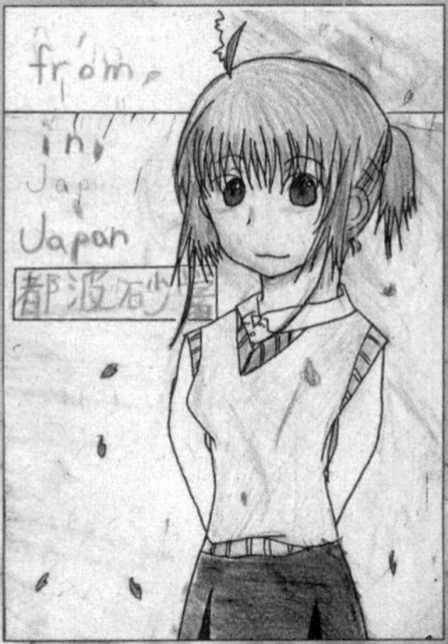
from in Japan

➤ Aosora/Hiroshima Prefecture • During Spring when the cherry blossoms go dancing toward the ground, Sakura starts a new life, but in modern Japan, what grade would she be in?

➤ Aoino-Sora/Chiba Prefecture • Their first picture in a photo machine. It's cute to see Syaoran so nervous!

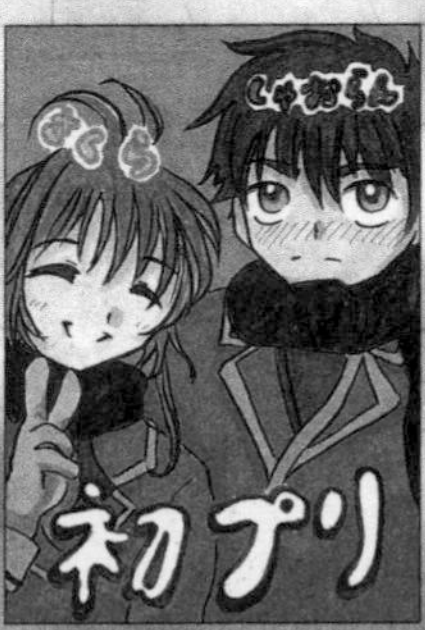
初プリ

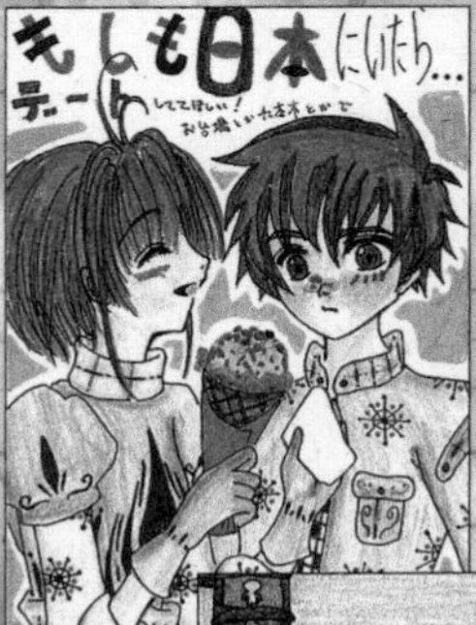
もしも日本にいたら…
デート

➤ Setsuna Hiiragi/Okinawa Prefecture • A date between Syaoran and Sakura. ♥ Apparently Sakura said, "I want to go to a fun place like Odaiba or Roppongi!"

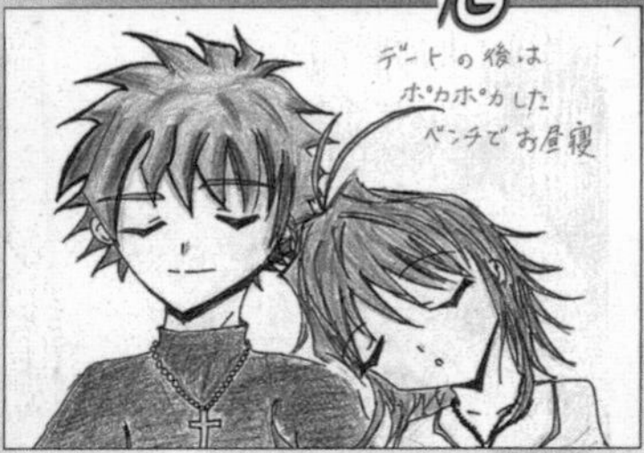
デートの後は
ポカポカした
ベンチでお昼寝

➤ Icho/Kanagawa Prefecture • The end of a long date! ♥ Sleeping warmly on a bench.

➤ Sasa-Batta/Kanagawa Prefecture • The couple coming home from shopping. They seem less like a dating couple and more like newlyweds.

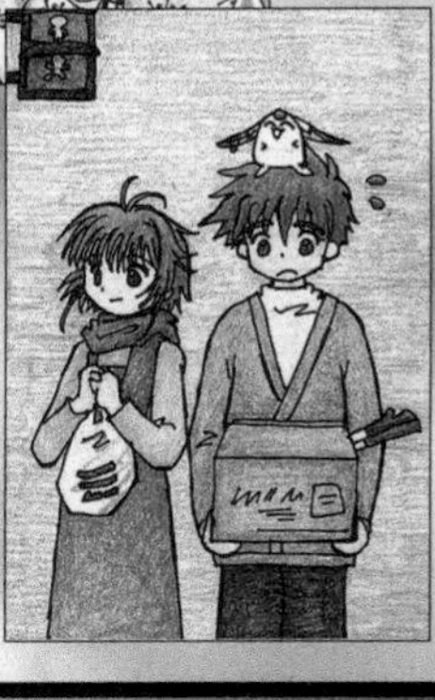

AT WORK!

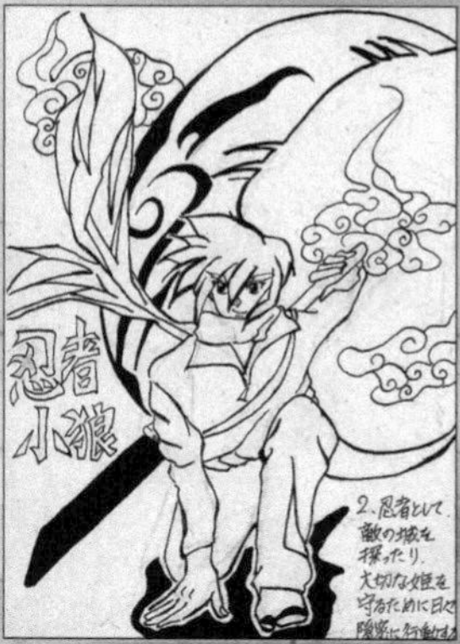
忍者小狼
2. 忍者として敵の城を探ったり、大切な姫を守るために日々

➤ Hisako Ito/Hokkaido • Even in modern Japan, there are ninja living in secret out there. Here's the young ninja who is protecting the princess, Syaoran!!

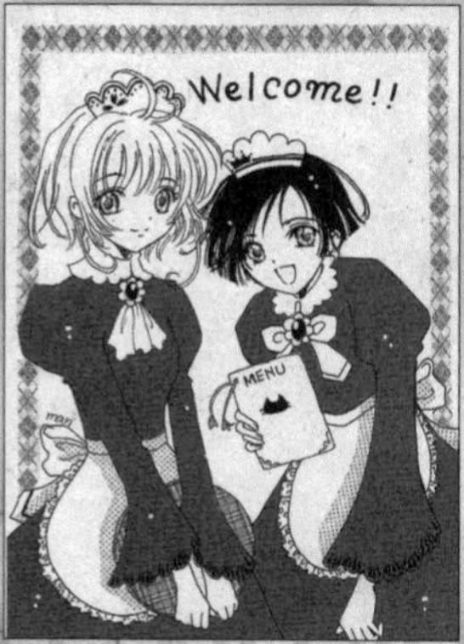
Welcome!!
MENU

➤ Nekomari/Gunma Prefecture • Sakura and Yuzuriha make such cute waitresses! ♪

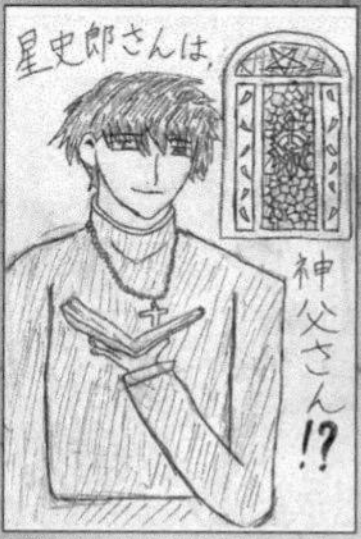
星史郎さんは、
神父さん!?

➤ Takeshi Yamana/Nara Prefecture • Mysterious Seishirô as a priest.

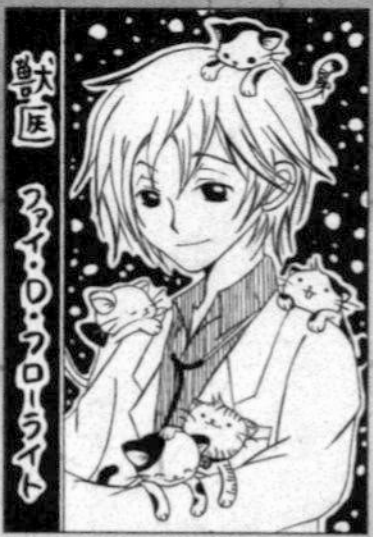
獣医
ファイ・D・フローライト

➤ Kohana/Saitama Prefecture • A veterinarian who is loved by all the animals! ♥

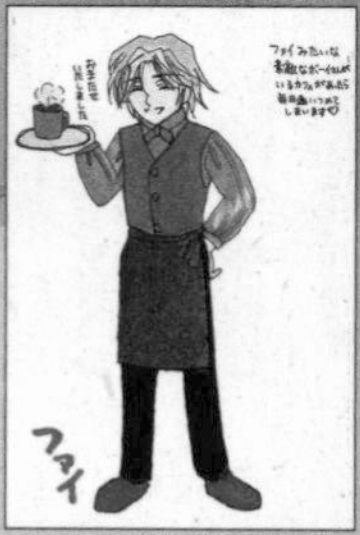
ファイ

➤ Keiko Takeda/Tokyo • Fai uses his experience from the Country of Ôto and takes up work as a waiter.

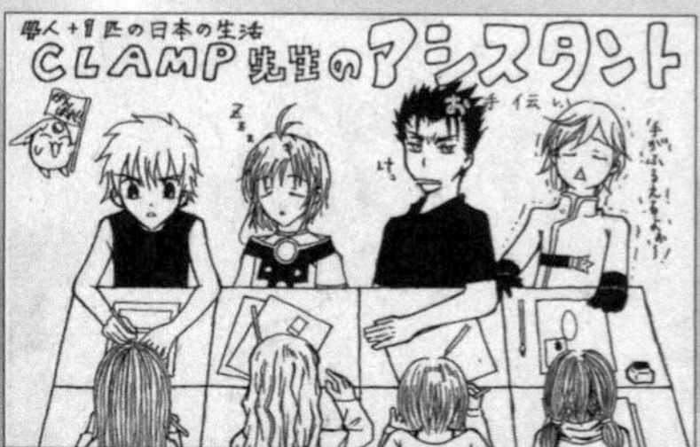
CLAMP先生のアシスタント

➤ Mikan Hoshizuki/Gifu Prefecture • Please, we're begging! Do the best work you can...!! (laughter)

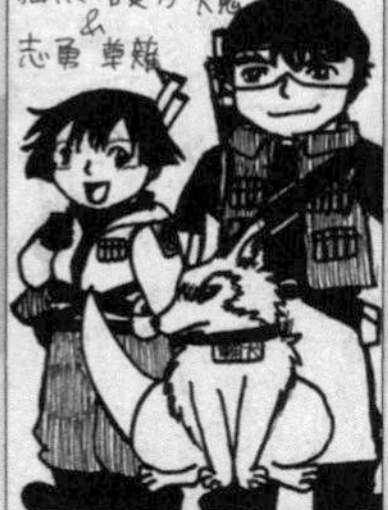
猫依 護刃 & 志勇 草薙

➤ Mabu/Saitama Prefecture • The Yuzuriha and Kusanagi combo as rangers. More than a job, it's a calling.

FUN ALL TOGETHER! ♥

おいしいおにぎり
おにぎり
しゃけ
うめ
おかか

◄ Maki Fukuoka/ Tokyo • To raise cash for the coming campaign, the entire group opens an onigiri rice-ball stand.

◄ Tetsuro Taira/Aichi Prefecture Everybody heads out on a drive toward fun times together! By the way, does Kurogane even have a license?

早食い大会
日本

◄ Morimo/ Aomori Prefecture • Challenged to a food fight!

◄ Chiyori Morikawa/ Tokyo • Everybody's getting into a night of Karaoke.

◄ Miuri Nishizu/ Okayama Prefecture On Sunda there's time to go planting in the garden or play with birds in the birdhouse. Such a happy feeling!

◄ Supineru/ Saitama Prefecture • If the four of them were a family, Mom would be Kurogane?! Sounds like a lot of work! (laughter)

EVERYONE THOUGHT UP

Original Kudan

All the people of the Hanshin Republic have a Kudan attached. If you all went to the Hanshin Republic, what kind of Kudan would appear to you? Here we present the Kudan the readers came up with!!

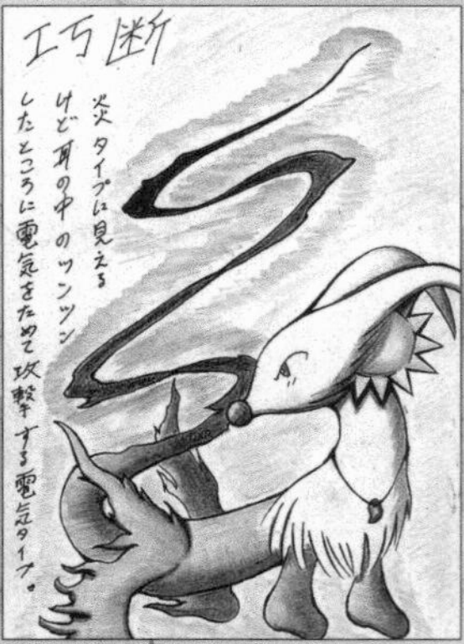
炎タイプに見える
けど耳の中のツンツン
したところに電気をためて
攻撃する電気タイプ。

➤ K3/Aichi Prefecture • Although it looks like at fire-type on the outside, its specialty is to build up electrical energy in its ears and attack with it.

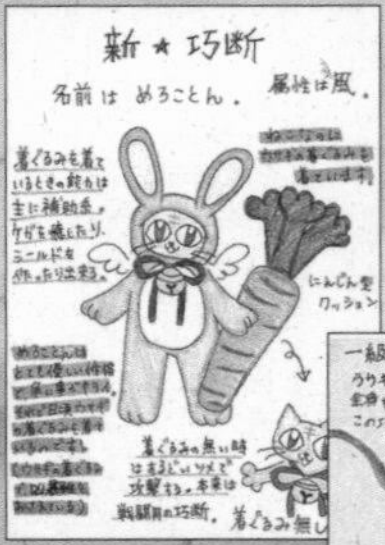
新★巧断
名前は めろことん。 属性は風。

◀ Miruuto/Saitama Prefecture • Its name is Merukoton. Its totem is wind and it can heal wounds or make shields. It has a very gentle nature.

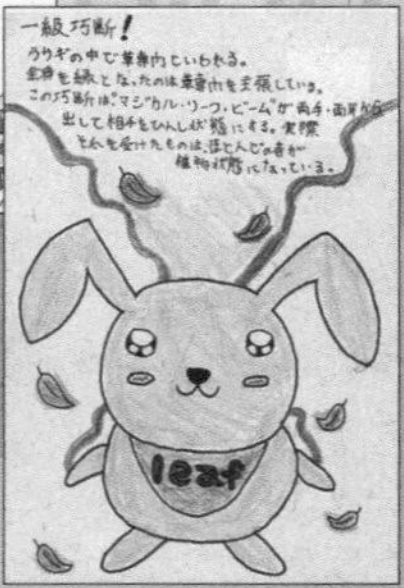
一級巧断!
leaf

➤ Miyu Nakazawa/Ishikawa Prefecture • It's a first-level Kudan that can control plants. It can shoot off its ultimate attack, Magical Leaf Beam, from both of its ears and both of its hands.

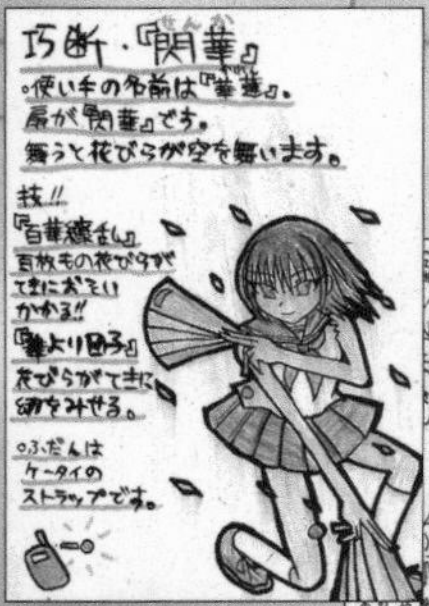
巧断・『閃華』
使い手の名前は『華蓮』。
扇が『閃華』です。
舞うと花びらが空を舞います。

◀ Mokona Tare/Osaka • The owner is a young girl called Karen, and her Kudan is named Senka.

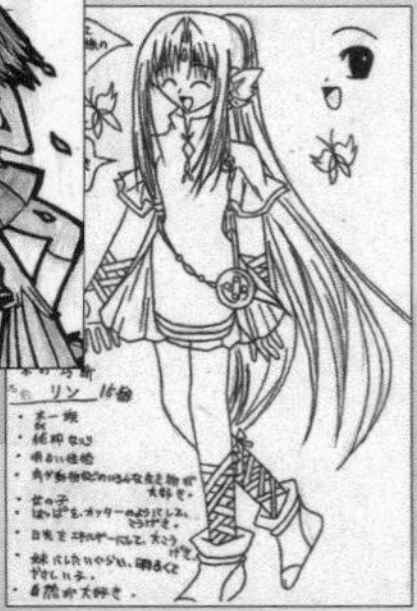

➤ Rika Miyazaki/Gifu Prefecture • It's a tree-type Kudan, and its name is Rin. She's a bright and kind girl.

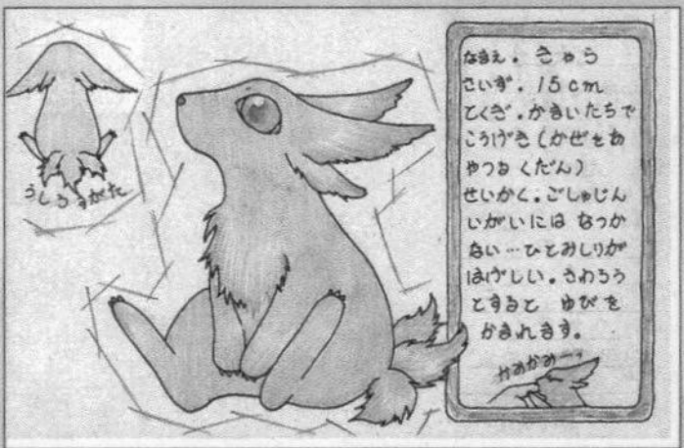
なまえ、きゃら
さいず。15cm
とくぎ、かまいたちで
こうげき(かぜをあやつるくだん)
せいかく、ごしゅじん
いがいには なつか
ない…ひとみしりが
はげしい。さわろう
とすると ゆびを
かまれます。

▲ Aoki Tenjin/Hokkaido • This wind-controlling Kudan's name is Kyara. It's cute, but they say it's very shy of strangers.

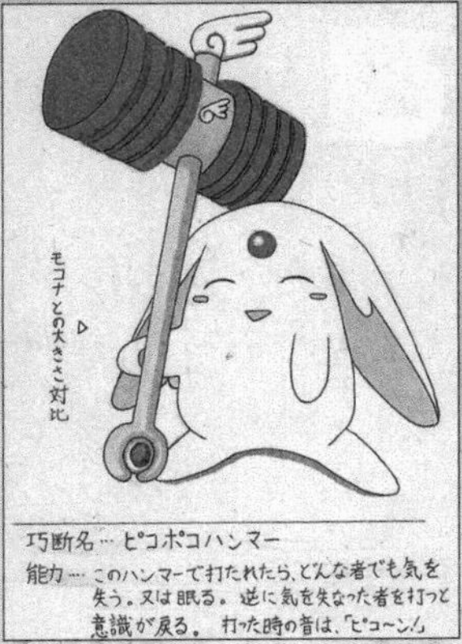
モコナとの大きさ対比
巧断名…ピコポコハンマー
能力…このハンマーで打たれたら、どんな者でも気を失う。又は眠る。逆に気を失なった者を打つと意識が戻る。打った時の音は、「ピコ～ン!」

◄ Oze Shin/ Kanagawa Prefecture • Not Mokona, the hammer is the Kudan. Its name is the Pikopoko Hammer.

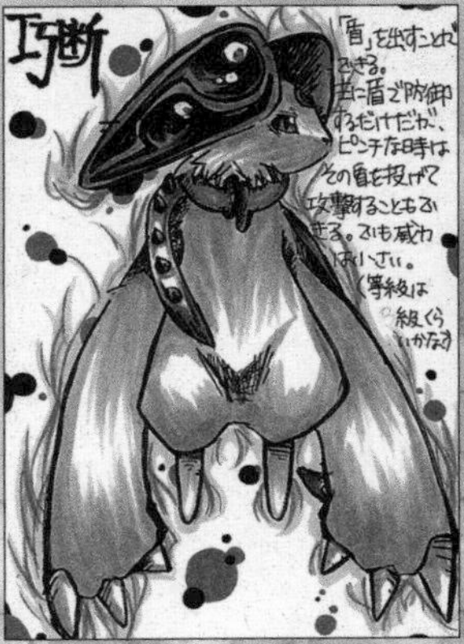
巧断
「盾」を出すことができる。
主に盾で防御するだけだが、ピンチな時はその盾を投げて攻撃することもできる。でも威力は小さい。

◄ Yukkiyo/ Nara Prefecture • As it has the ability to put up a shield, and is a Kudan that specializes in protection. It seems not very good at attacks.

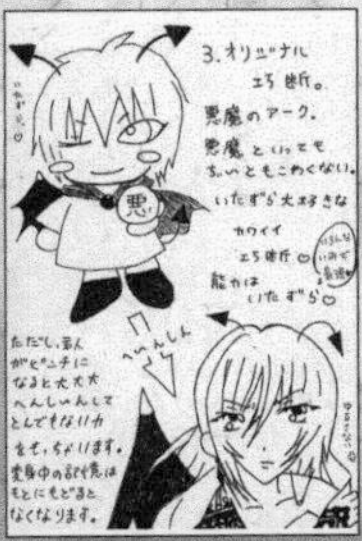
3. オリジナル巧断。
悪魔のアーク。

◄ Kai Fuzuki/ Chiba Prefecture • This is Aaku, a cute Kudan who loves to play practical jokes.

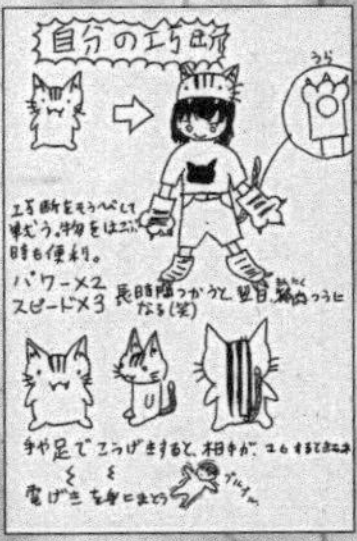
自分の巧断
パワー×2
スピード×3

◄ Dokuro (Lone Wolf)/ Kanagawa Prefecture • Prepare yourself with the stuffed cat (?) and battle!

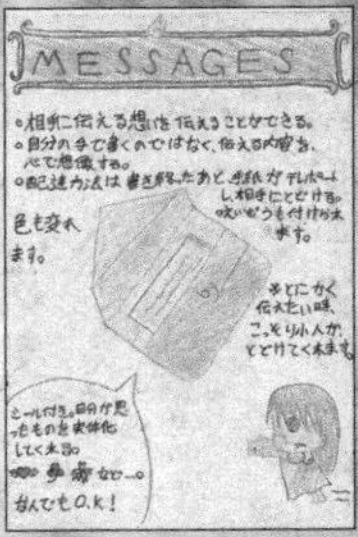
MESSAGES
○相手に伝える想いを伝えることができる。
なんでもO.K!

◄ Yuri Shiotani/ Hokkaido • This is a letter-type Kudan that can communicate the feelings of others.

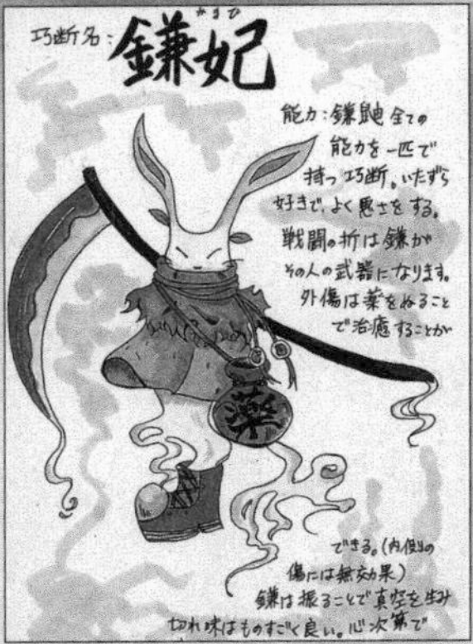
巧断名:鎌妃
能力:鎌鼬全ての能力を一匹で持つ巧断。いたずら好きで、よく悪さをする。
戦闘の折は鎌がその人の武器になります。
外傷は薬をぬることで治癒することができる。(内側の傷には無効果)
鎌は振ることで真空を生み切れ味はものすごく良い。心次第で
薬

◄ Koku'u/ Osaka • Its name is Kamahi, and it is a strong Kudan versed in all methods of the rapid cut.

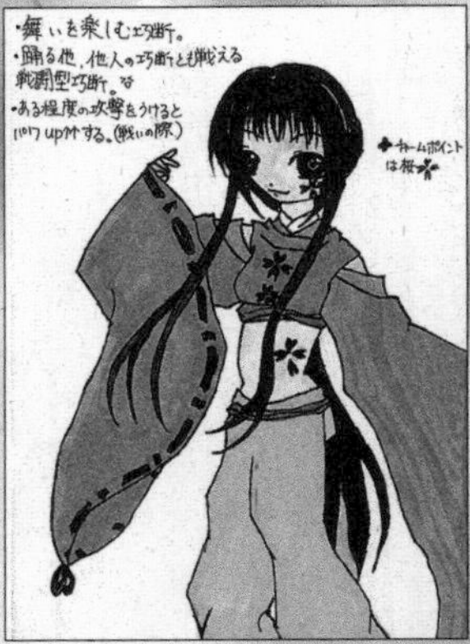
・舞いを楽しむ巧断。
・踊る他、他人の巧断と戦える戦闘型巧断。
・ある程度の攻撃をうけるとパワーupする。(戦いの際)
チャームポイントは桜

◄ Hisui/ Tokushima Prefecture • An elegant Kudan who loves to dance. But it's not just dancing, it's excellent in battle too!

EVERYONE'S WORKS

Illustration Exhibition

To adorn the final installment of our illustration corner, here's a large exhibition of illustrations with the artists' free choice of theme. Every entry was drawn with care, so it's too bad we didn't have the space to show them all. But we'll do our best to introduce the ones we were able to print.

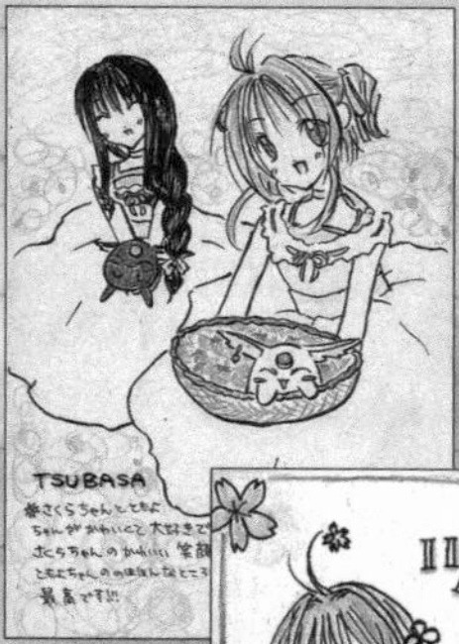
TSUBASA

◀ Sugina/Kumamoto Prefecture • Princesses Sakura and Tomoyo. Both princesses are so cute with perfect smiles!

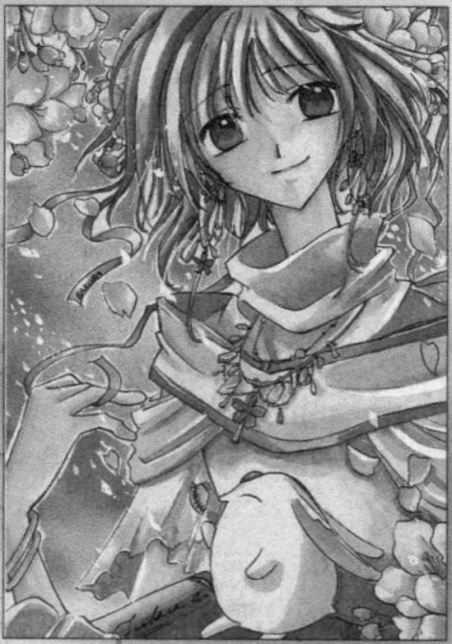

◀ Yoko Heguri/Hyogo Prefecture • Sakura's warm smile. She and Mokona are good friends! ♪

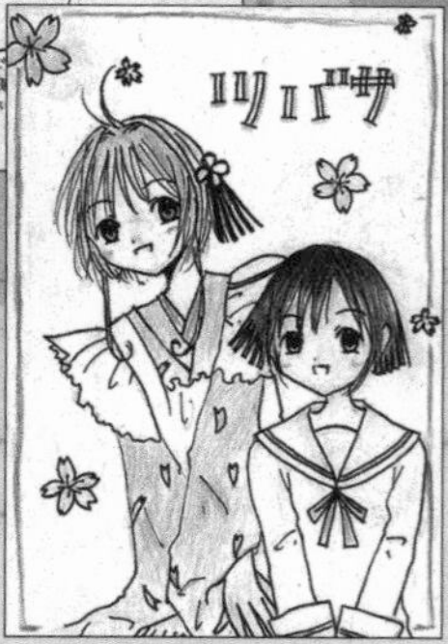
ツバサ

➤ Candy/Saitama Prefecture • Two people who became good friends in the Country of Ôto. It's like they've met in the real world.

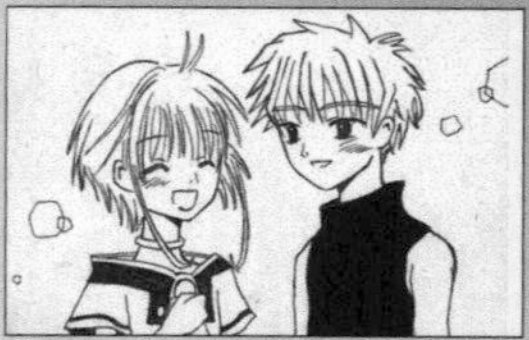

➤ Misaki/Tokyo • Is this from the time the couple lived in the Kingdom of Clow? A precious memory.

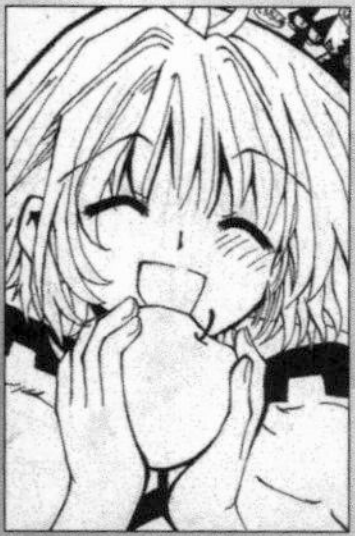

◀ Manami Nakamura/Aichi Prefecture • Yeah, Sakura looks best with a big smile!

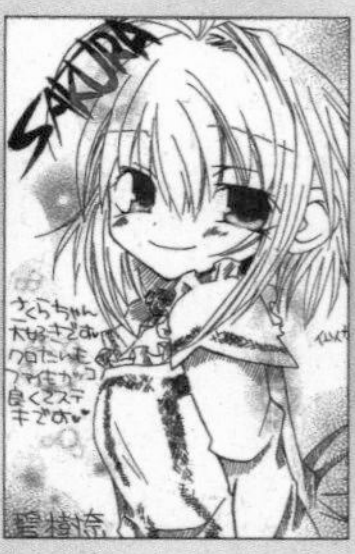
SAKURA

◀ Juna Heki/Mie Prefecture • This is a picture that demonstrates just how much the artist loves Sakura!

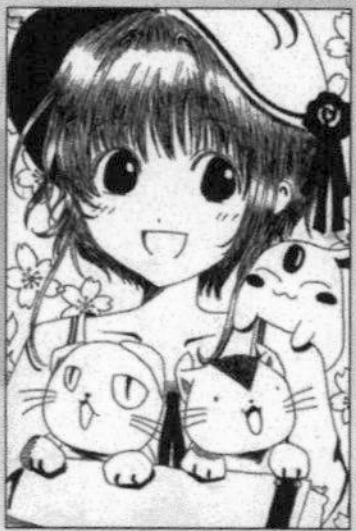

◀ Sachiko Ideura/Saitama Prefecture • Sakura, kitties, and Mokona! ♥

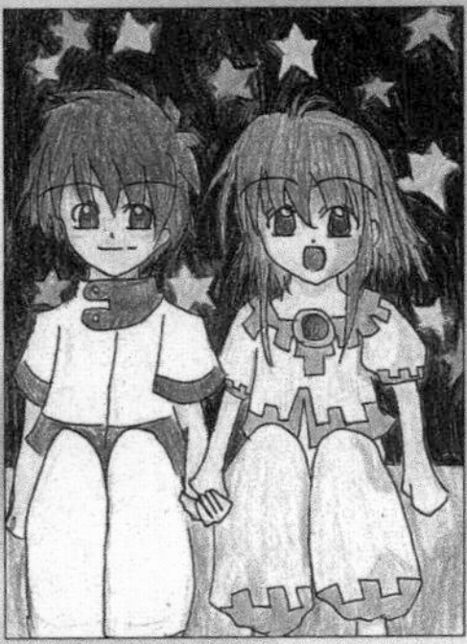

➤ Tsurugi/ Saitama Prefecture • What do the two wish when the first stars came out in that starry sky? We think it will come true.

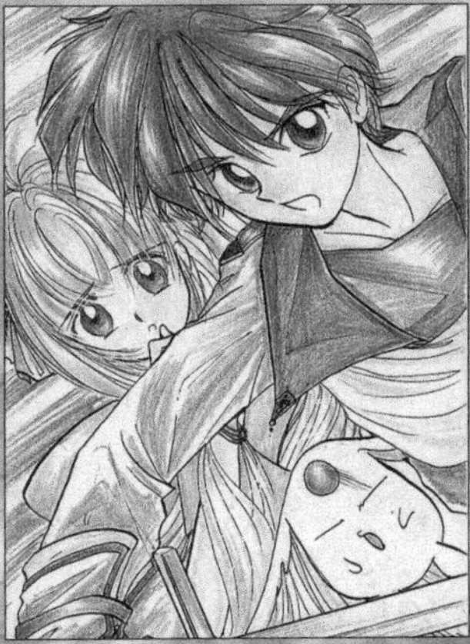

➤ Kaumi/ Gunma Prefecture • Syaoran battling to protect Sakura. Nobody has their hearts bound together more than these two.

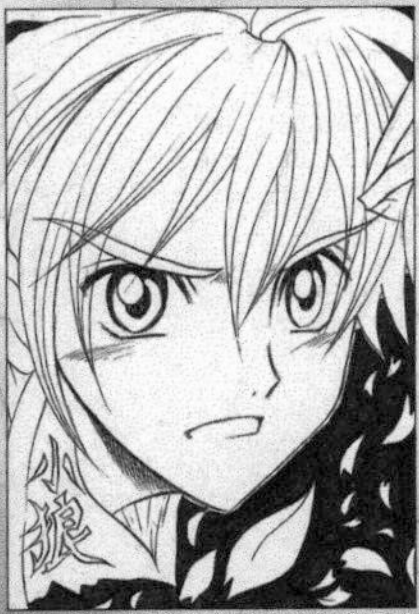
小狼

◄ Taku Murakami/ Kanagawa Prefecture • Syaoran looking gallant. What can those eyes be looking at?

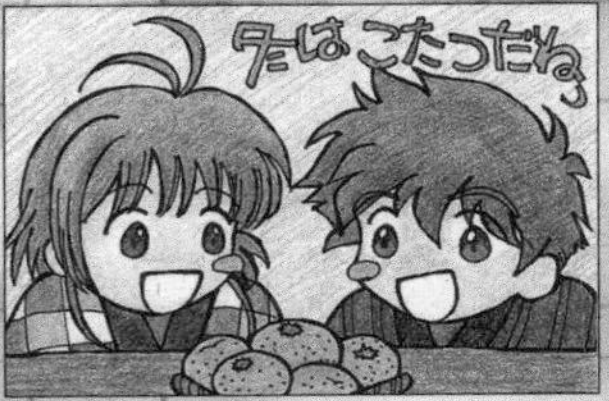
冬はこたつだね

◄ Godzilla Meme/ Kanagawa Prefecture • The best thing in winter is eating mikan while sitting at a kotatsu heated table! Warms the body and soul!

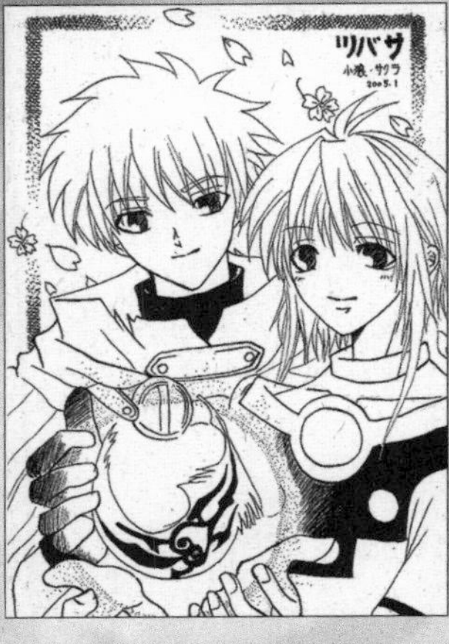
ツバサ
小狼・サクラ
2005.1

◄ Maho Tachibana/ Ibaraki Prefecture • Syaoran and Sakura, and in their hands is a feather glowing with a warm light that will never go out.

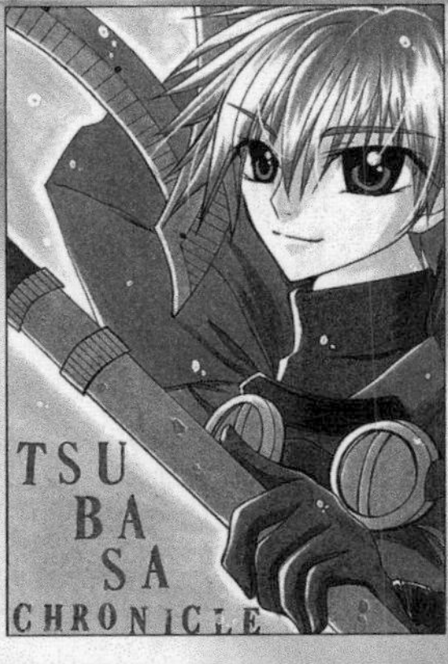
TSU
BA
SA
CHRONICLE

◄ Makoto Ryuo/ Hyogo Prefecture • Calm, and very cool, Syaoran looks very much the hero. How strong will he be able to become?

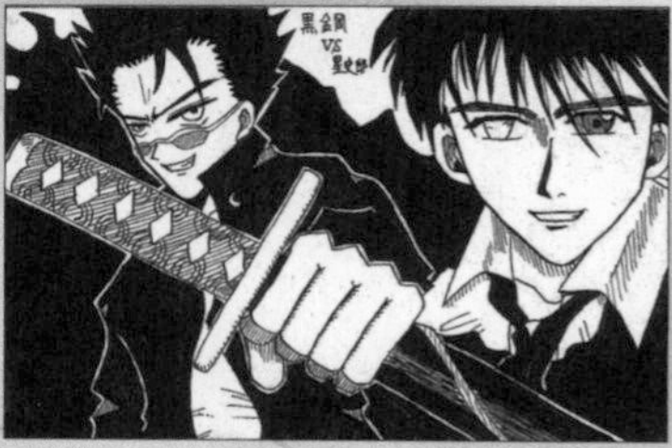
黒鋼 VS 星史郎

▲ Motoki Tsuruya/Oita Prefecture • One gets a little anxious over the showdown between Kurogane and Seishirô.

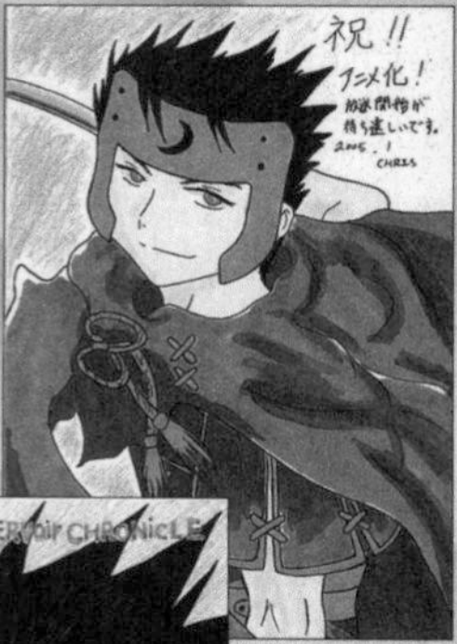
祝!!
アニメ化!
CHRIS

➤ Chris/ Hyogo Prefecture • A really good man in a pinch.

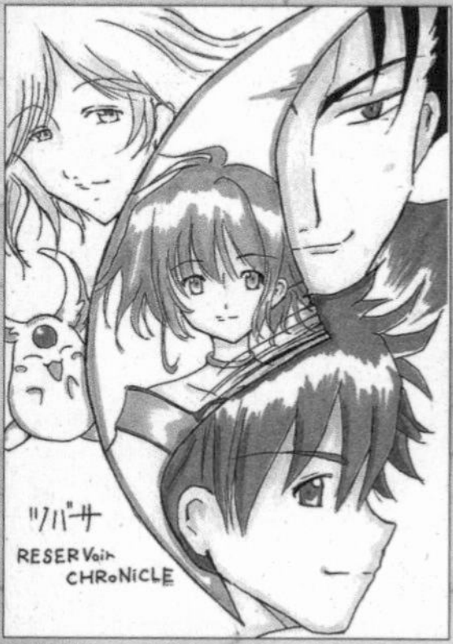
ツバサ
RESERVoir CHRoNICLE

◀ Mitsuki/ Niigata Prefecture • Syaoran's journey goes on and on in search of Sakura's scattered feathers.

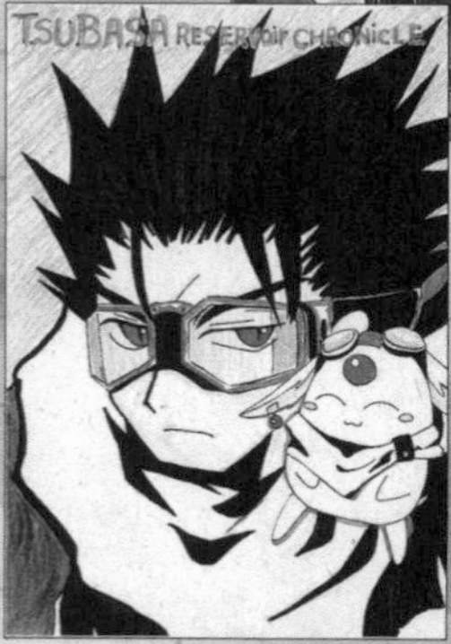
TSUBASA RESERVoir CHRoNICLE

◀ Shoka Amano/ Fukuyama Prefecture • Where is Kurogane trying to go with Mokona on his shoulder like that?

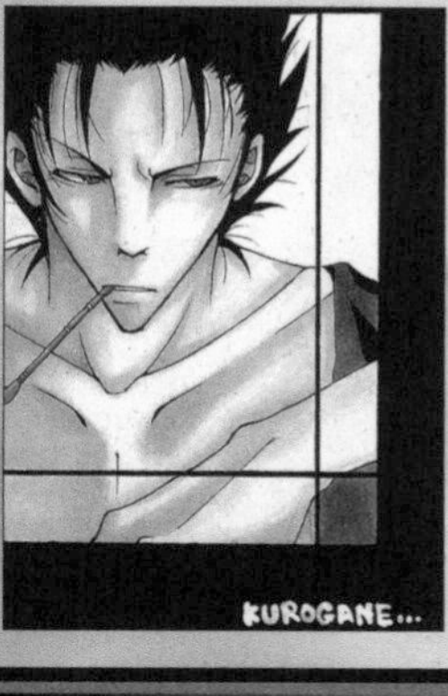
KUROGANE...

◀ Tonbo/ Fukushima Prefecture • Kurogane in a Japanese setting. It's saying that the man has an adult allure.

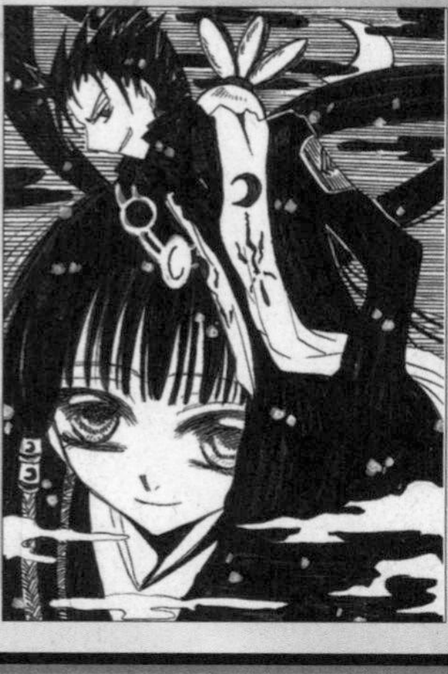

◀ Senka Kojo/ Kagoshima Prefecture • He talks rough and has a bad attitude. But even so, his loyalty to Princess Tomoyo is absolute.

➤ Yuki Okuma/Chiba Prefecture • Fai looking away, as he is engrossed in some thought. The look of ennui is charming.

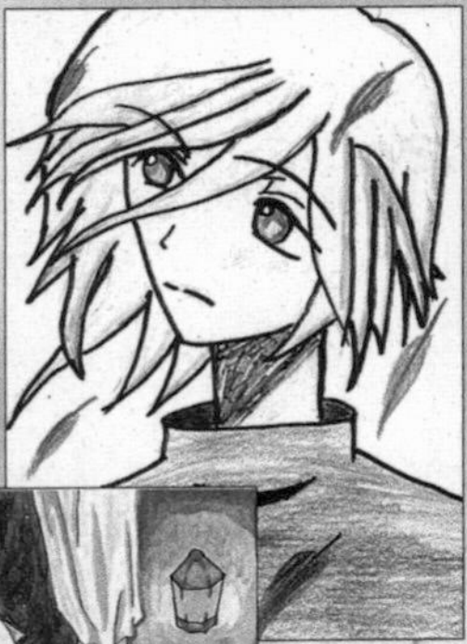

➤ Teru/Chiba Prefecture • Fai, the sexiest guy in Tsubasa. He looks great in the stylish suit.

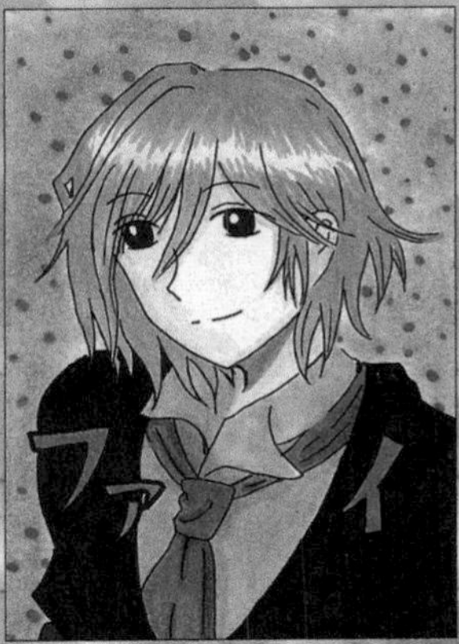

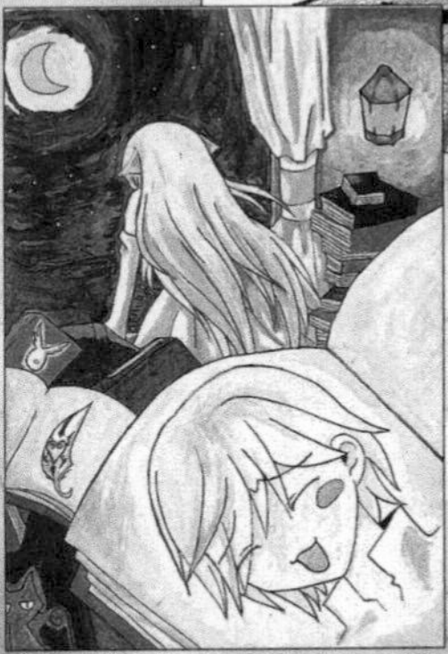

◄ Yui Tanaka/Fukuyama Prefecture • The one Chii is thinking of would have to be Fai. But who is Fai thinking of?

➤ Really Big Kitty/Shiga Prefecture • A picture of everyone all together. ★ Kurogane was taken out of the picture by Mokona's kick. (laughter)

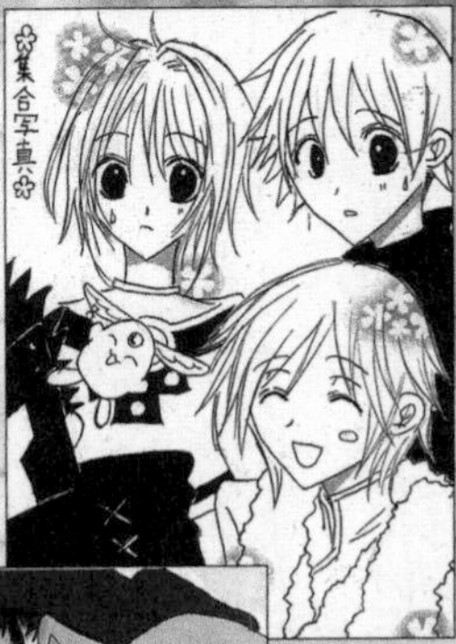

➤ Rai Kusanagi/Mie Prefecture • In weather so cold it could freeze, Fai is wearing an unusually serious face. His translucent eyes show beauty.

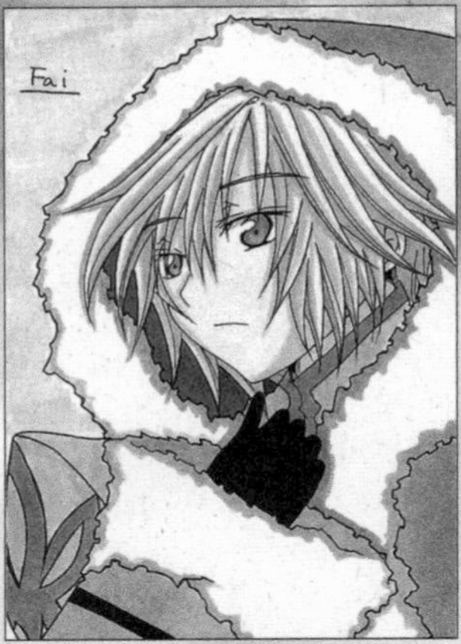
Fai

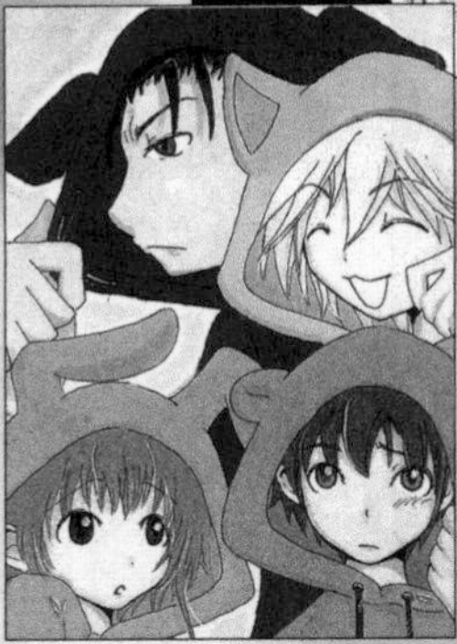

◄ Manami Mizuno/Aichi Prefecture • Everyone wearing hoods with animal ears attached. The only one into the idea is Fai.

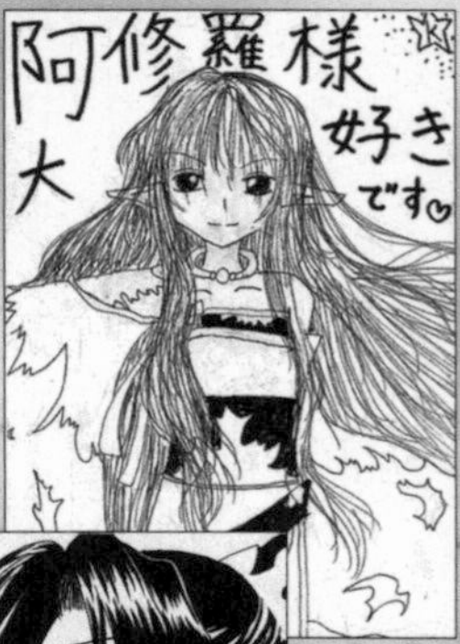
阿修羅様
大好きです

➤ Mana ★ Kasumi/ Kanagawa Prefecture • Gallant and stylish Ashura-ô's popularity is presently rocketing skyward!!

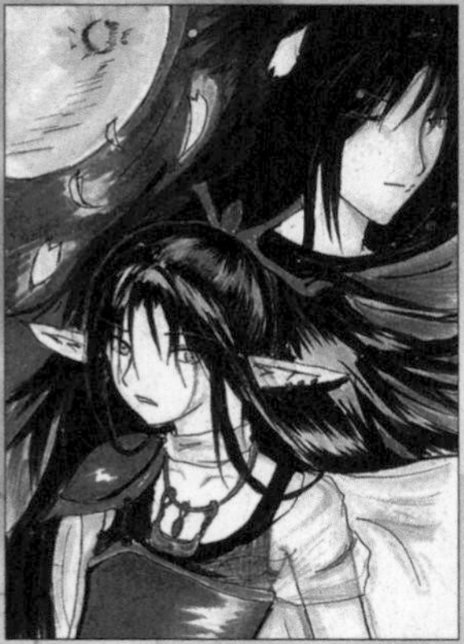

➤ Yu Kotona/ Niigata Prefecture • Ashura-ô and Yasha-ô. Their story will still be told, not over the next years, but into the next epochs.

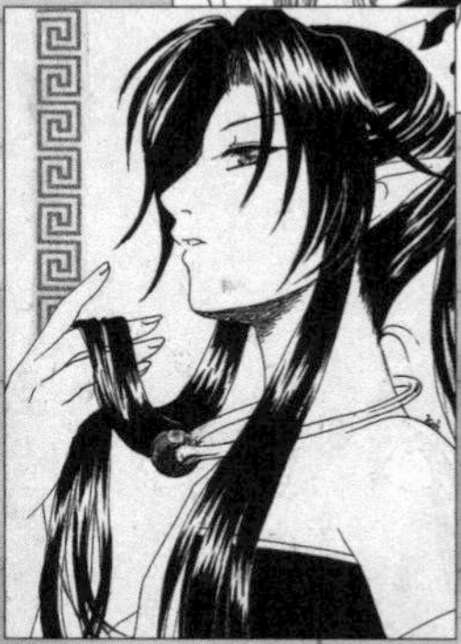

◄ Ryuren Kurenai/ Tokyo • Don't you wish you had that long, wispy black hair? Another attraction is the Chinese-style cut clothes.

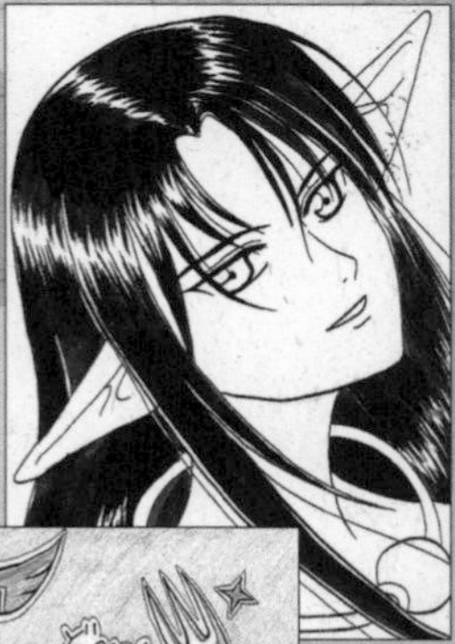

➤ Marusu/ Fukuoka Prefecture • It isn't just bravery, this erotic smile is another of Ashura-ô's charms.

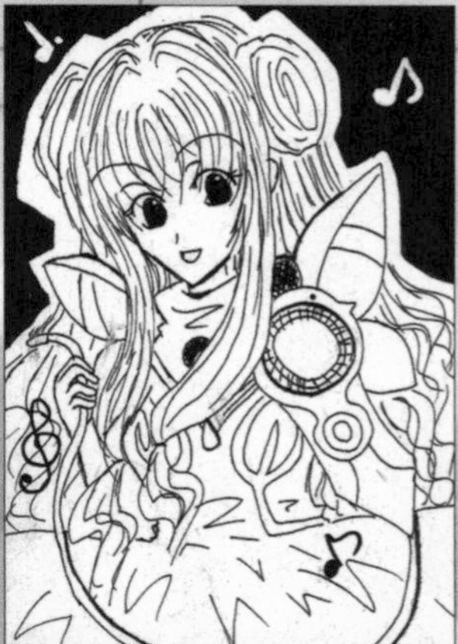

➤ Yaon Tsubakino/ Saitama Prefecture • Our idol, Primela! She's got her mike in hand, and she's ready for the start of her concert!

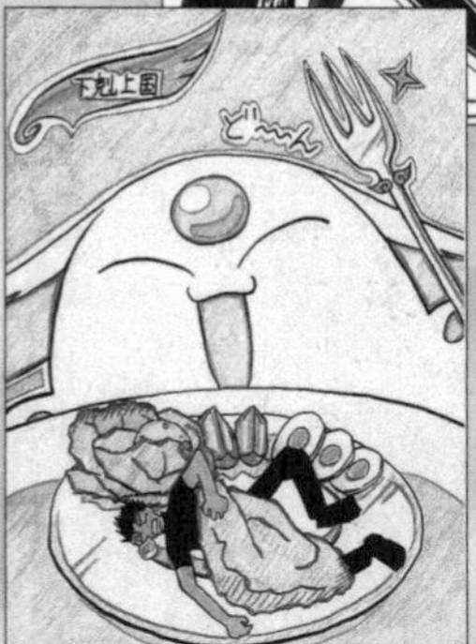

◄ Naofumi Mori/Fukuoka Prefecture • Upside-Down Country! Kurogane is about to get eaten by Mokona! It's life or death!! (laughter)

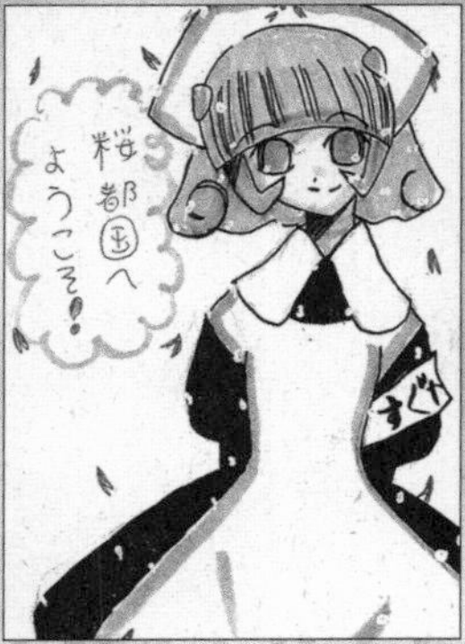
桜都国へようこそ!

◄ Kurosaki/ Saitama Prefecture
• If you are ever having any trouble in the Country of Ôto, you can always ask the girl at the information booth.

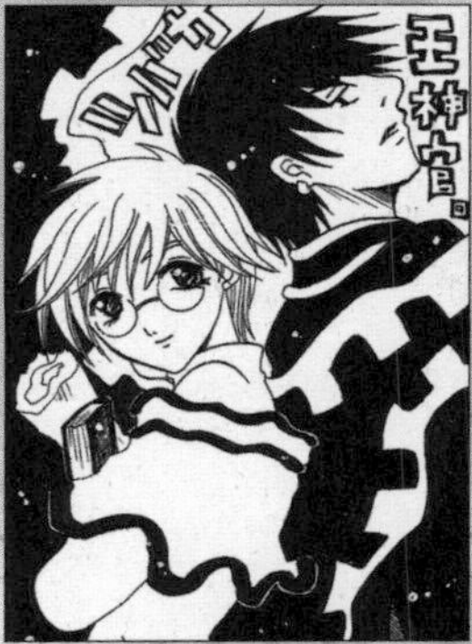

◄ Yukito Love/ Kanagawa Prefecture
• Whether they're the King and the High Priest or two waiters at an *Okonomiyaki* restaurant, these two are always together.

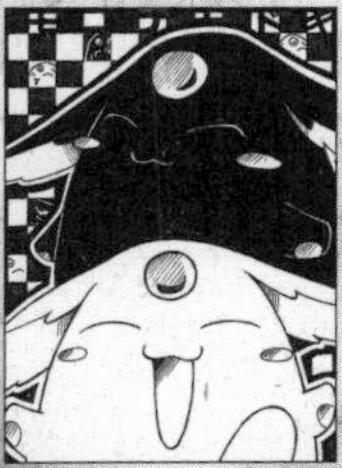

Kayui/Kanagawa Prefecture
• Mokona times two! With double the fun!

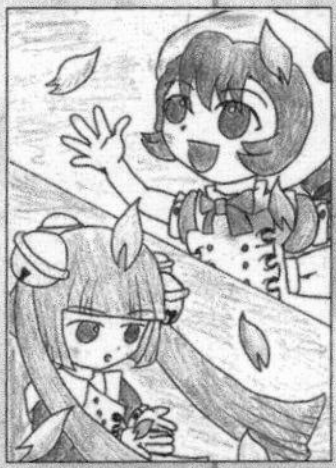

Furyuga/Saitama Prefecture
• Sumomo and Kotoko are so pretty! ♥

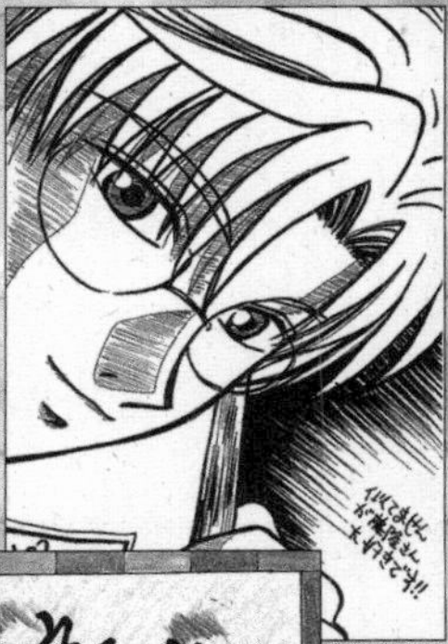

◄ Hisaki/ Nara Prefecture
• The always gentle Fujitaka may just be the ideal father figure.

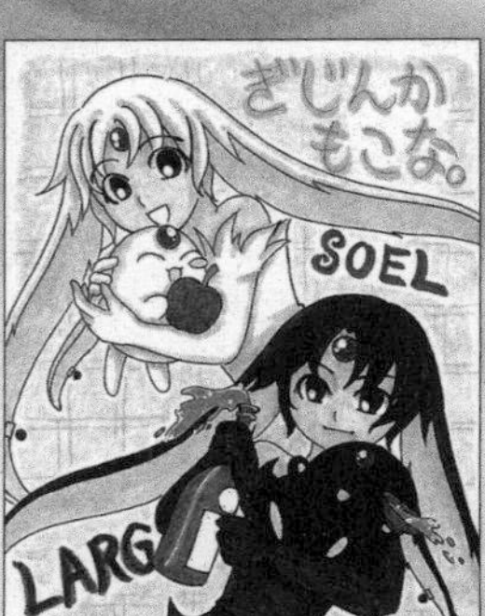
ぎじんか
もこな。
SOEL
LARG

◄ Koni Naniwa/ Osaka
• Personifications of the two Mokona. Light Soel and the somewhat strong-willed Larg.

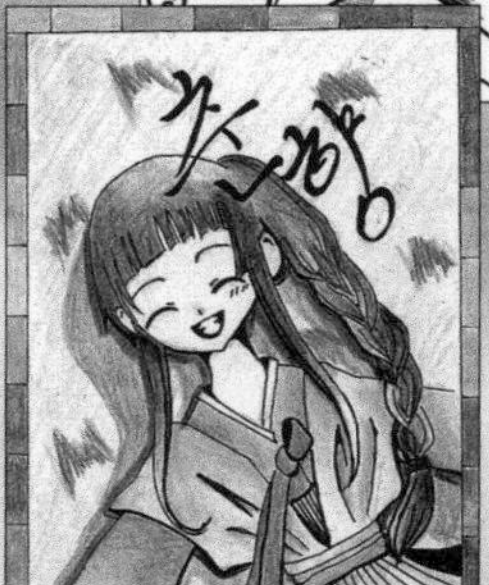

◄ China Fujii/ Tokyo
• Chu'nyan must be living with a smile these days.

TRY TO GET 100%

TSUBASA QUIZ

Let's check just how well you know Tsubasa! If you've read it a number of times, you may just get a score of 100%!

Character Quiz

Syaoran and his friends are on a multi-dimensional journey. Our first set of questions cover their experiences up to this point.

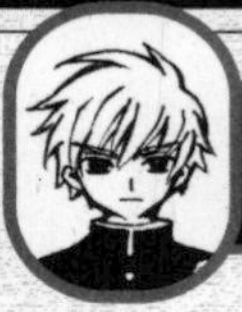

Questions from Syaoran

There may be some hard questions in here, but if you have all of the graphic novels, you should be able to answer them. Good luck!

Q01. Which of the four people below is the one who found lonely, young Syaoran and raised him?

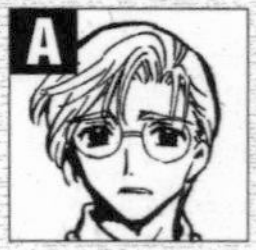
A

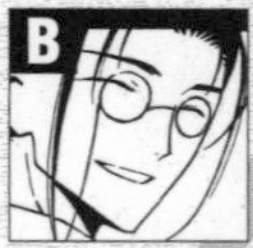
B

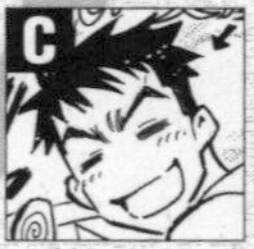
C

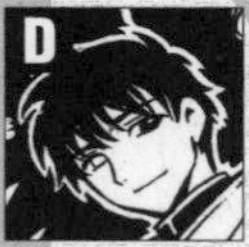
D

Q02. In the Hanshin Republic, what kind of power did the Kudan attached to Syaoran control?

A. Earth **B.** Water **C.** Fire **D.** Wind

Q03. In the town of Ryonfi, which place on Syaoran's body did he injure in battle in the Ryanban's castle?

A. Right Hand **B.** Left Hand **C.** Right Foot **D.** Left Foot

Q04. In the Country of Ôto when he went into the weapon shop with Kurogane, what is the name the sword that Syaoran obtained?

A. Hien **B.** Kamui **C.** Sôhi **D.** Fûma

Q05. When Sakura disappeared, to what building of those below did Syaoran go to search for her?

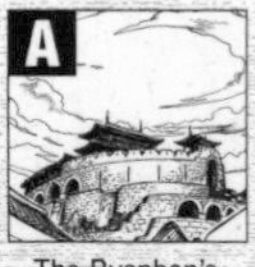
A
The Ryanban's Castle

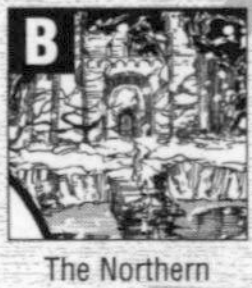
B
The Northern Castle

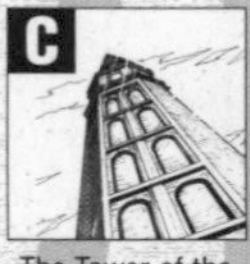
C
The Tower of the Little People

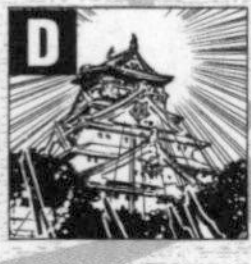
D
Hanshin Castle

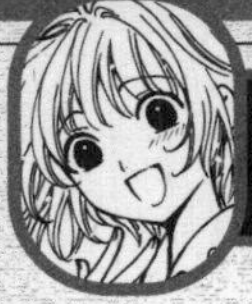

Questions from Sakura

I was asleep through a lot of what happened, but try to remember the scenes where I was awake, okay?

Q06. **What day is Sakura's birthday?**

A. Jan. 1st **B.** Apr. 1st **C.** Sep. 1st **D.** Oct. 1st

Q07. **At the point when the group left the Country of Ôto, how many of Sakura's feathers were returned to her?**

A. 3 feathers **B.** 4 feathers **C.** 5 feathers **D.** 6 feathers

Q08. **Using the images, A–D, to the right, which of those images represent the clothes Sakura wore in the Country of Ôto?**

Q09. **Using the same images, A–D, to the right, which of those images represent the clothes Sakura wore in the Country of Jade?**

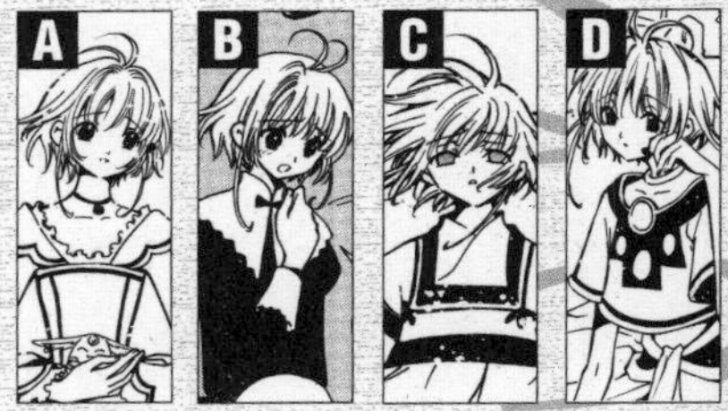
A
B
C
D

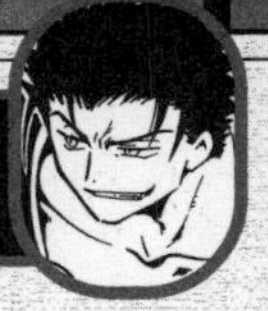

Questions from Kurogane

You think you can get stronger than me? If you can't at least answer these questions, you're out of luck! Well, give it your best shot.

Q10. **What was the name of the sword that Kurogane paid to Yûko as her price?**

A. Rairyû **B.** Jinryû **C.** Hyôryû **D.** Ginryû

Q11. **When he was serving Tomoyo, what castle was Kurogane protecting?**

A. Shirasaki Castle **B.** Shachihoko Castle **C.** Kanedori Castle **D.** Maizuru Castle

Q12. **In the image to the right, what technique is Kurogane trying to use?**

A. Ha-ma: Ryû-ô-jin

B. Chi-ryû: Jin-en-bu

C. Ten-ma: Jô-ryû-sen

D. Sen-ryû: Hi-kô-geki

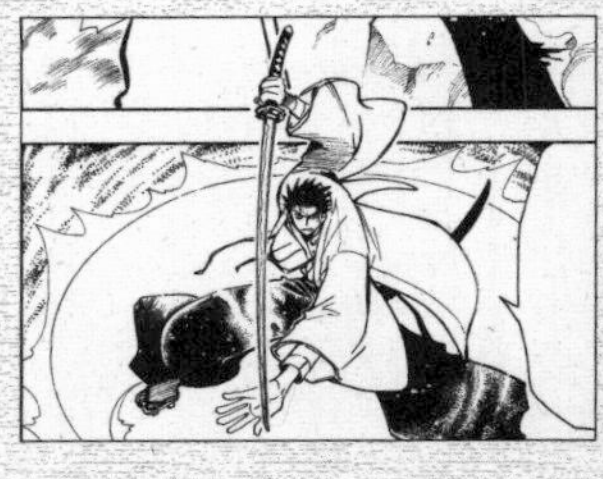

Q13. **What was the issue number of the Shônen Maganyan that Kurogane took with him as he left the Hanshin Republic?**

A. Weekly 24 **B.** Weekly 25 **C.** Weekly 26 **D.** Weekly 27

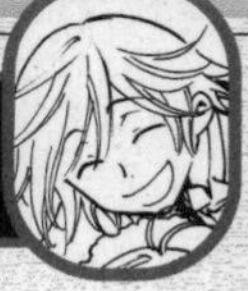

Questions from Fai

I'm a such nice guy. I wouldn't even know how to give you hard questions! I'd just feel sorry for you!

Q14. **What is the full name that Fai gave to Yûko?**

A. Fai A. Flowright **B.** Fai B. Flowright **C.** Fai C. Flowright **D.** Fai D. Flowright.

Q15. **What is the name of Fai's original country where King Ashura is sleeping?**

A. Regaria **B.** Reyearth **C.** Windam **D.** Seresu

Q16. **What was the name of the café that Fai opened in the Country of Ôto?**

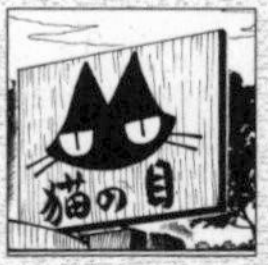
猫の目

A. Cat's Claw **B.** Cat's Eye

C. Cat's Paw **D.** Cat's Tail

Q17. **In the Country of Ôto, what did Fai use as weapons when he and Kurogane were attacked by Oni?**

A. Forks **B.** Coins **C.** Billiard Balls **D.** Darts

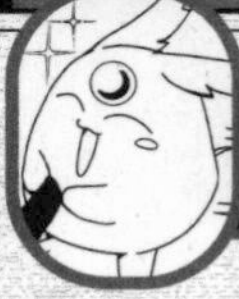

Questions from Mokona

Mokona's found you!! They asked Mokona to make a quiz, and Mokona did a great job! Maybe it's a new Secret Technique!

Q18. **How many Secret Techniques does Mokona have?**

A. 18 **B.** 48 **C.** 108 **D.** 1999

Q19. **What does Kurogane call Mokona?**

A. White Pork Bun **B.** White Marshmallow **C.** White Rice Cake **D.** White Dumpling

Q20. **What part of Mokona's body becomes the entrance to the next world when traveling through dimensions?**

A. Tail **B.** Ears **C.** Eyes **D.** Mouth

Q21. **In what country was Syaoran's group when Mokona delivered Yûko's gift of Chocolat au Fondant pictured on the right?**

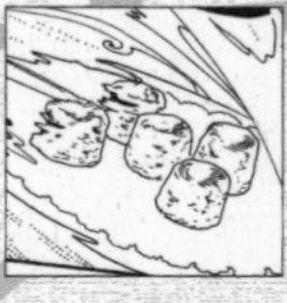

A. Hanshin Republic **B.** Country of Koryo

C. Country of Jade **D.** Country of Ôto

Country Quiz

These questions cover the many worlds visited within the story. If you haven't read the graphic novels thoroughly, you may not know the answers.

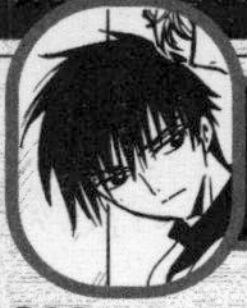

Questions about the Kingdom of Clow

It'd be a pain if you made Sakura cry because you got the questions wrong, so I came up with questions even she could answer.

Q22. **What is Yukito's position in the Country of Clow?**

A. Master of Magic Weapons **B.** High Wizard
C. High Priest **D.** Master Summoner

Q23. **On what other world did Tôya and Yukito appear?**

A. Hanshin Republic **B.** Country of Koryo **C.** Country of Jade **D.** Country of Ôto

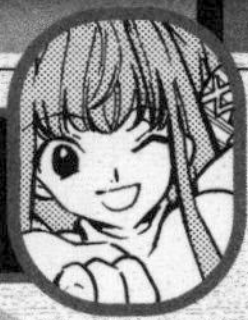

Questions about the Hanshin Republic

These are questions about my country and the man I love, Shôgo Asagi! If you don't get the answers right, you have no right to be my fan!

Q24. **What kind of food did Masayoshi say was a staple of the Hanshin Republic's diet?**

A. *Takoyaki* **B.** *Ikayaki* **C.** *Okonomiyaki* **D.** *Yakisoba*

Q25. **What kind of family shop does Shôgo help out in?**

A. Rice Shop **B.** Fish Shop **C.** Liquor Shop **D.** Noodle Shop

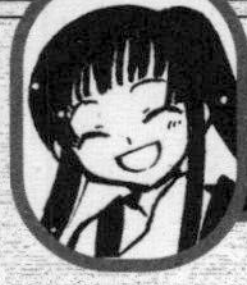

Questions about the Country of Koryo

I guess there's no magic you can use to answer quiz questions! Well, give them a lot of thought so you get the right answers!

Q26. **What was Chu'nyan's mother's line of work?**

A. Baban **B.** Renkonban **C.** Euban **D.** Shinban

Q27. **How many years ago did Sakura's feather come and suddenly make the evil Ryanban extremely powerful?**

A. 1 year ago **B.** 2 years ago **C.** 3 years ago **D.** 4 years ago

Q28. **In the images to the right, which isn't a member of Amen'osa?**

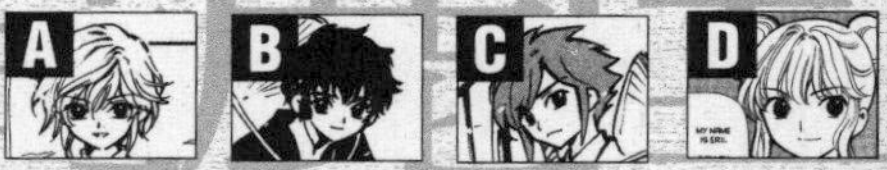
A
B
C
D

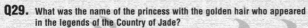

Questions about the Country of Jade

Huh? We're supposed to work on a quiz? Hm, I must admit that it isn't a specialty of mine. How about these? Are they too easy?

Q29. What was the name of the princess with the golden hair who appeared in the legends of the Country of Jade?

A. Princess Tomoyo   **B.** Princess Sakura

C. Princess Emerald   **D.** Princess Shirahime

Q30. At the time when Syaoran's group arrived in Spirit, how many children had vanished?

A. 10 children   **B.** 15 children   **C.** 20 children   **D.** 30 children

Questions about the Country of Ôto

Won't you join me at Clover for a drink? And if you pick up the bill, I'll tell you the answers to these questions.

Q31. Among the pairs of Oni hunters below, which pairing is mistaken?

Q32. Where in Edonis are the Dream Capsules in which you can go to the Country of Ôto?

A. Time-Space Park   **B.** Fairy Park   **C.** Illusion Park   **D.** Magic Park

Questions about the Other Countries

All you readers have watched over the journeys of Syaoran and his crew with great care, so you should answer these questions easily.

Q33. What was the first variety of special sword attack techniques that Kurogane used after leaving the Country of Japan?

A. Tenma   **B.** Fûma   **C.** Hama   **D.** Sôma

Q34. What is the fruit on Fai's home world that is a pale yellow color?

A. Raki seed   **B.** Ruki seed   **C.** Reki seed   **D.** Roki seed

Q35. In the Kingdom of Clow, Yukito said that Yûko, "like me, carries the power of the _____." What is in the blank?

A. Sun   **B.** Moon   **C.** Stars   **D.** Light

Answers

Q.01	A	(2 Points)	Q.13	C	(4 Points)	Q.25	C	(3 Points)
Q.02	C	(2 Points)	Q.14	D	(3 Points)	Q.26	D	(2 Points)
Q.03	C	(3 Points)	Q.15	D	(2 Points)	Q.27	A	(3 Points)
Q.04	A	(3 Points)	Q.16	B	(3 Points)	Q.28	D	(3 Points)
Q.05	B	(4 Points)	Q.17	D	(2 Points)	Q.29	C	(2 Points)
Q.06	B	(3 Points)	Q.18	C	(2 Points)	Q.30	C	(3 Points)
Q.07	B	(3 Points)	Q.19	A	(2 Points)	Q.31	D	(2 Points)
Q.08	B	(3 Points)	Q.20	D	(2 Points)	Q.32	B	(4 Points)
Q.09	B	(3 Points)	Q.21	D	(3 Points)	Q.33	C	(4 Points)
Q.10	D	(3 Points)	Q.22	C	(2 Points)	Q.34	A	(4 Points)
Q.11	A	(4 Points)	Q.23	A	(2 Points)	Q.35	B	(4 Points)
Q.12	B	(4 Points)	Q.24	C	(2 Points)			

80–100 Points

YOU ARE AN ACCOMPLISHED TSUBASA PROFESSOR.

Congratulations! You will find very few people in your world who know more about Tsubasa than you do. We hope you keep rooting for Syaoran and his group as you have been.

60–79 Points

YOU ARE A HOT-BLOODED, AVID TSUBASA FAN.

Well done! You received a respectably high score. You scored high, but there are higher levels to go. You might want to give your graphic novels another read.

40–59 Points

LET'S TRY FOR A HIGHER SCORE NEXT TIME!

Your score wasn't too bad, but you can do better. Talk with your friends about Tsubasa, and you should be able to pick up more details.

39 Points or Less

THIS NEEDS SOME EFFORT.

Tsubasa is a wonderful adventure with many fun details. If you read it a little closer, we guarantee that you'll enjoy all of the great details you find in it.

CHASING THE SEVEN MYSTERIES

Have Even More Fun With the Coming Story

There are many mysteries in Tsubasa that haven't been solved yet. Any fan would be interested in the answers to at least some of these. So let's investigate the most important seven of them. The following are integral to the enjoyment of Tsubasa.

> NOW, TO THE NEXT PLAN...

▲ In an effort to interfere with Syaoran and his group, he attempts several different plans.

MYSTERY 01

WHO IS THIS MYSTERIOUS FEI-WANG REED?

Fei-Wang Reed has been watching Syaoran and his group from the start. In the Country of Jade, he sent his underlings to keep an eye on them. Reed seems to be after the power of Sakura's feathers, and he's attempted to interfere with Syaoran's efforts. But why does he want that kind of power? Up to this point in the story, one could say that Reed is the greatest mystery.

> HOWEVER, THE PRICE FOR INTERFERENCE IS THE SAME FOR HER AS FOR ME.

> ANOTHER GAMBIT FROM THE "WITCH," I THINK.

▲ Fei-Wang Reed seems to know about the Time-Space Witch, but in what way?

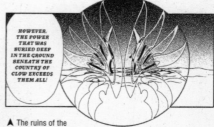

> HOWEVER, THE POWER THAT WAS BURIED DEEP IN THE GROUND BENEATH THE COUNTRY OF CLOW EXCEEDS THEM ALL!

▲ The ruins of the Kingdom of Clow may have a lot to do with his plans, but...

CHASING THE SEVEN MYSTERIES • MYSTERY 1   190

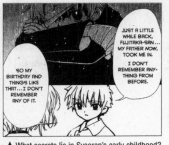

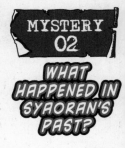

MYSTERY 02

WHAT HAPPENED IN SYAORAN'S PAST?

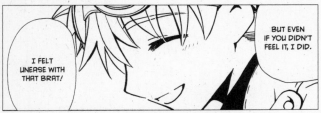

Syaoran has no memory of the time before he met his adoptive father, Fujitaka. He doesn't even remember why he can't see out of his right eye. He also never smiled and seemed completely emotionless until he finally met Sakura. The reasons should be hidden somewhere in Syaoran's past, but . . .

JUST A LITTLE WHILE BACK, FUJITAKA-SAN... MY FATHER *NOW*, TOOK ME IN.
I DON'T REMEMBER ANY-THING FROM BEFORE.
SO MY BIRTHDAY AND THINGS LIKE THAT... I DON'T REMEMBER ANY OF IT.

▲ What secrets lie in Syaoran's early childhood?

BUT EVEN IF YOU DIDN'T FEEL IT, I DID.
I FELT UNEASE WITH THAT BRAT!

▲ Does the unease that Tôya felt in Syaoran also have to do with Syaoran's past?

MYSTERY 03

WHAT IS THE SECRET POWER OF SAKURA'S?

Yukito said that Princess Sakura has enough power to change the world, but it will bring on great adversity. What can those words possibly mean? Can it have a connection to the fact that Sakura's feathers were scattered among the many worlds, and each have a great deal of magical power themselves?

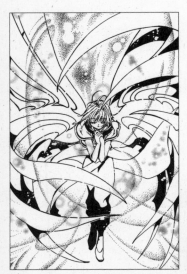

▲ Sakura is greatly affected by the markings in the ruins in the Kingdom of Clow. Why did something like that happen?

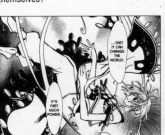

...THAT IT CAN CHANGE THE WORLD.
IT'S THAT MUCH POWER.

◄ Will the day come when the power within Sakura will awaken and change her world?

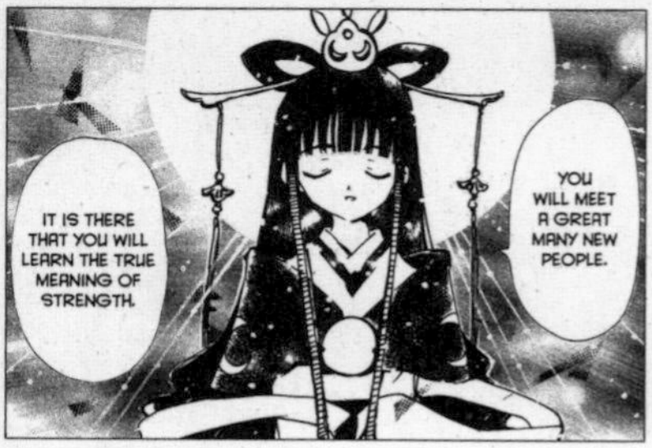
YOU WILL MEET A GREAT MANY NEW PEOPLE.
IT IS THERE THAT YOU WILL LEARN THE TRUE MEANING OF STRENGTH.

➤ When will Kurogane come to realize the true meaning of strength that Princess Tomoyo talked about?

MYSTERY 04

WHAT IS THE REAL REASON PRINCESS TOMOYO SENT KUROGANE ON HIS JOURNEY?

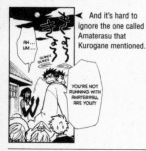

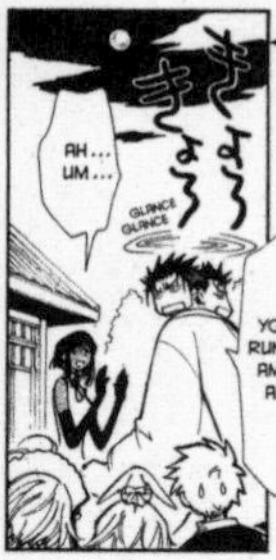
AH... UM...
GLANCE GLANCE
YOU'RE NOT RUNNING WITH AMATERASU, ARE YOU?!

➤ And it's hard to ignore the one called Amaterasu that Kurogane mentioned.

In his quest to become stronger, Kurogane never had anything against killing his opponent in battle. But Princess Tomoyo placed a curse on him such that his skills lessen for every person he kills, then sent him out across the dimensions. One could surmise from Princess Tomoyo's words that she did it hoping for Kurogane's personal growth. But is that really the only reason? Or could there be some other hidden reason behind her actions?

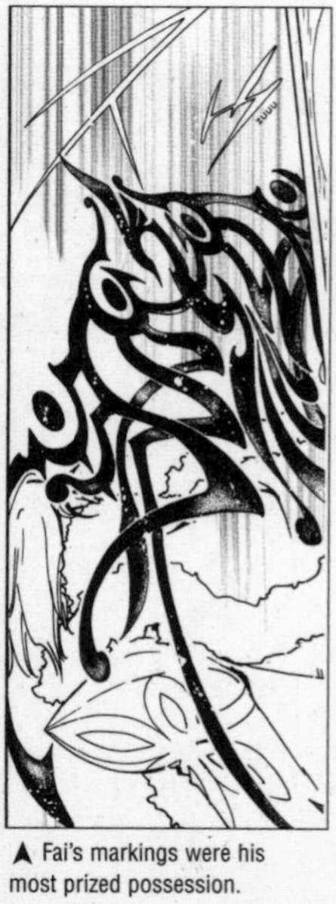

▲ Fai's markings were his most prized possession.

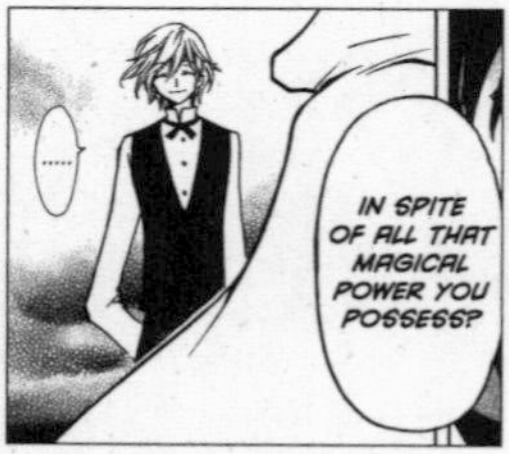
......
IN SPITE OF ALL THAT MAGICAL POWER YOU POSSESS?

▲ Seishirô can tell that Fai has enormous magical powers.

MYSTERY 05

WHY DOESN'T FAI USE HIS MAGIC?

Fai paid the price of the markings on his back to the Time-Space Witch. According to the Witch, Fai's markings were to suppress his magical power, so it shouldn't be that losing his markings made him lose his power. Fai has stated that without his markings, he decided never to use magic, and later, even though his life was on the line, he never has used his magic. One thought is that it has something to do with King Ashura who Fai left sleeping in the Country of Seresu, but . . .

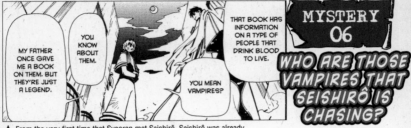

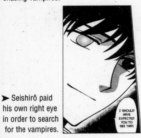

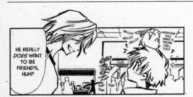

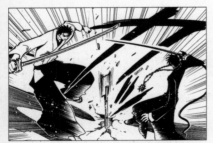

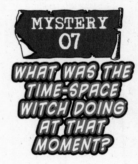

MYSTERY 06

WHO ARE THOSE VAMPIRES THAT SEISHIRÔ IS CHASING?

THAT BOOK HAS INFORMATION ON A TYPE OF PEOPLE THAT DRINK BLOOD TO LIVE.
YOU MEAN VAMPIRES?
YOU KNOW ABOUT THEM.
MY FATHER ONCE GAVE ME A BOOK ON THEM. BUT THEY'RE JUST A LEGEND.

▲ From the very first time that Syaoran met Seishirô, Seishirô was already chasing vampires.

I SHOULD HAVE EXPECTED YOU TO SEE THAT.

➤ Seishirô paid his own right eye in order to search for the vampires.

Long ago, Seishirô told Syaoran that the hunt of vampires is his calling, and although the reason hasn't been revealed, he has continuously been searching for a pair of twin vampires. The name he mentioned in the Country of Ôto, Subaru, may be the name of one of them. Perhaps the next time Seishirô's story coincides with the story we're following, we may be treated to some new revelations.

MYSTERY 07

WHAT WAS THE TIME-SPACE WITCH DOING AT THAT MOMENT?

MOKONA WILL MAKE A PHONE CALL, TOO!
HELLOP HELLOP HELLOP
HE REALLY DOES WANT TO BE FRIENDS, HUH?
TMP TMP TMP

▲ There are times when the white and black Mokona talk to each other without Yûko even knowing.

GATCH

▲ An arrow shot from Yûko puts an unexpected stop to Kurogane's and Seishirô's duel.

As you may know, the Time-Space Witch, Yûko, also appears in the manga xxxHolic. Some of her actions in xxxHolic have repercussions on the events and characters in Tsubasa. So finding some of those scenes is a part of the fun found in Tsubasa. If you keep your eyes on Mokona, the scenes may be easier to spot than you think.

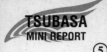

TSUBASA MINI REPORT ⑤

MINI REPORT

HERE'S WHERE Mokona Goes Boink

When Mokona senses the power of one of Sakura's memory feathers, Mokona's eyes get very big and go, "Boink." But it seems that the boink can come at other times too.

▼ Nobody noticed Mokona's eye "boink" at the reception of feather power waves, and so Mokona becomes upset. Mokona's angry face is still cute.

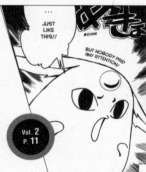

GAK!
AND MOKONA WILL BE LIKE...
...THIS!!

Vol. 1 P. 127

▲ In the instant of the first time that the "boink" of Mokona's eyes is demonstrated, Kurogane is shocked by the sudden change of expression.

... JUST LIKE THIS!!
BOINK
BUT NOBODY PAID ANY ATTENTION!

Vol. 2 P. 11

Vol. 3 P. 7

I'M SORRY TO HAVE INTERRUPTED YOUR BATTLE.
BOW
BOINK
YAAAAAH!
IT'S OKAY.
IT WAS THE ONLY THING YOU COULD DO, CIRCUMSTANCES BEING WHAT THEY WERE.

◀ When nearly fried while sitting on a griddle, Mokona goes "boink" without knowing it. Maybe Mokona goes "boink" when surprised?

▼ The scene where Mokona delivered the Fondant au Chocolat. The "boink" may also happen when Mokona is about to receive something.

Vol. 5 P. 155

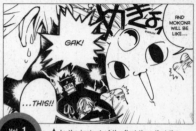

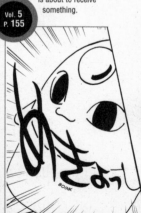

BOINK

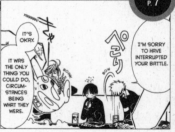

▼ This is the scene where Fai sent his staff to Yûko. It seems that when sending items back and forth to Yûko, Mokona goes "boink."

Vol. 3 P. 85

GULP
ARE YOU SURE?
YES... I'M SURE.
BOINK

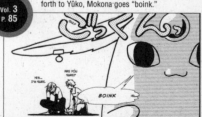

MATERIAL GALLERY

Original character designs, Name (pronounced nehmu, the word is taken from the English word name, but refers to a preliminary, sketchy version of the comic with all dialog drawn as a first draft of the manga for the editors and artists to see and make changes if necessary), and other items. Here is a special look at those important elements that fans never see, but go to make up a manga! If you want to know more about Tsubasa, you should not miss these materials

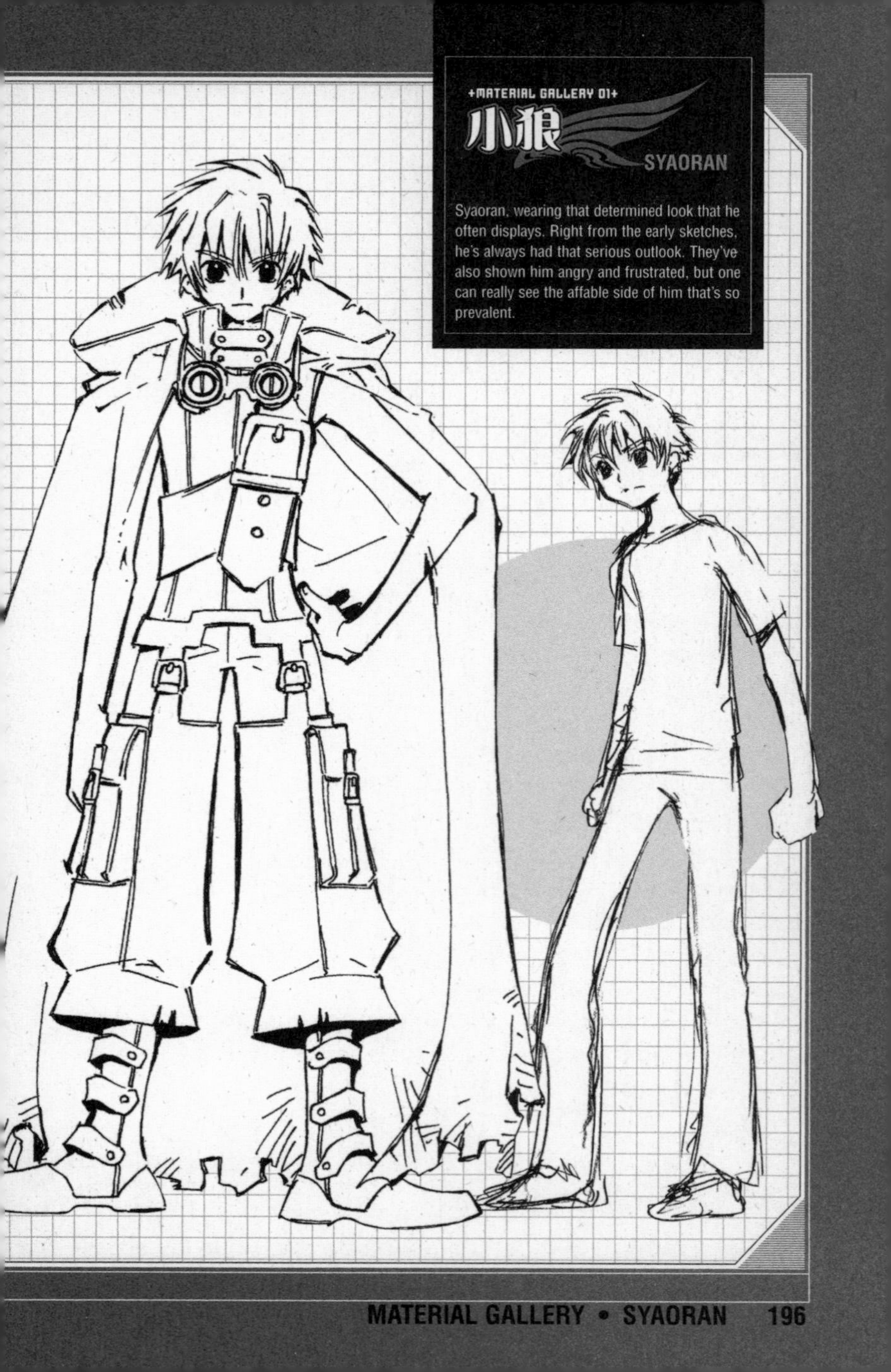

+MATERIAL GALLERY 01+

小狼 SYAORAN

Syaoran, wearing that determined look that he often displays. Right from the early sketches, he's always had that serious outlook. They've also shown him angry and frustrated, but one can really see the affable side of him that's so prevalent.

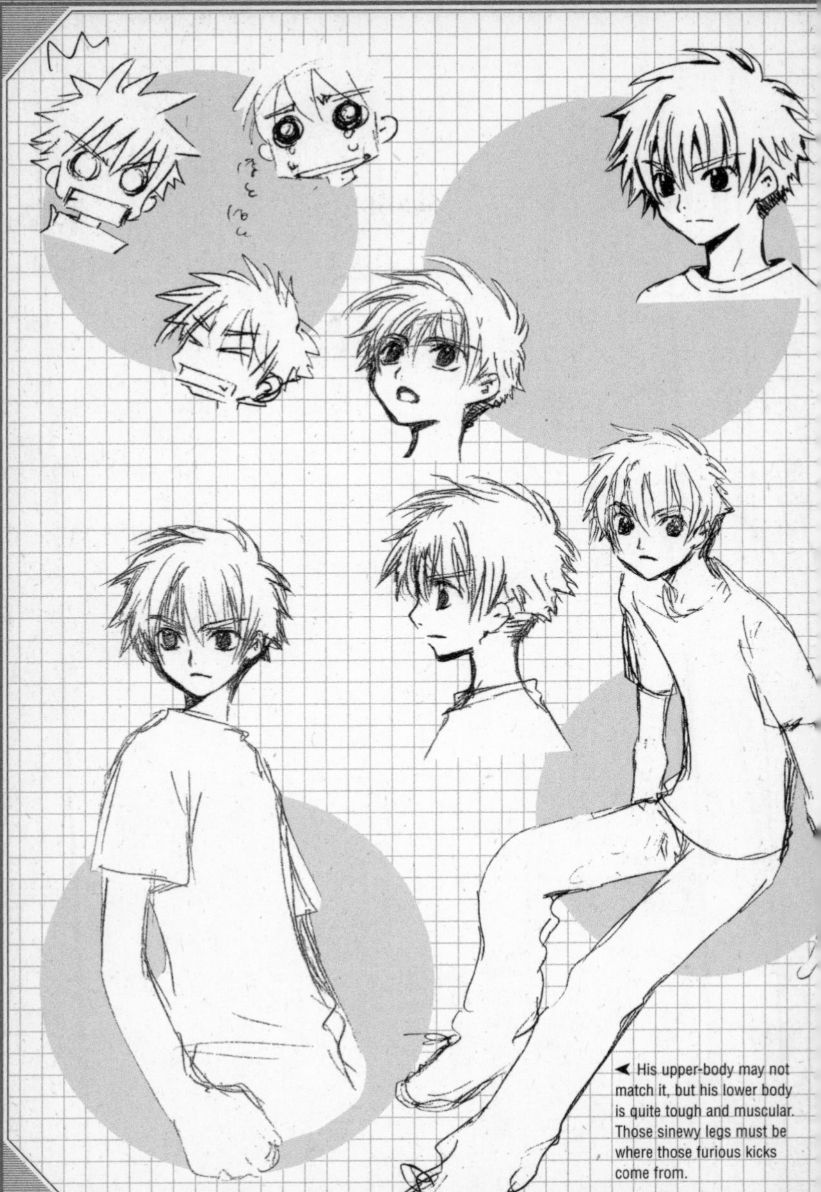

◀ His upper-body may not match it, but his lower body is quite tough and muscular. Those sinewy legs must be where those furious kicks come from.

+MATERIAL GALLERY 02+

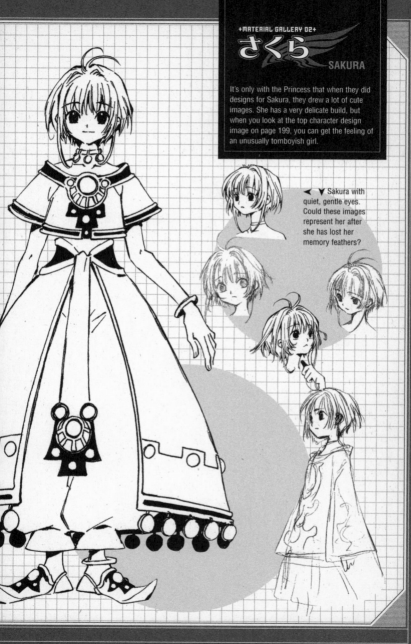

さくら SAKURA

It's only with the Princess that when they did designs for Sakura, they drew a lot of cute images. She has a very delicate build, but when you look at the top character design image on page 199, you can get the feeling of an unusually tomboyish girl.

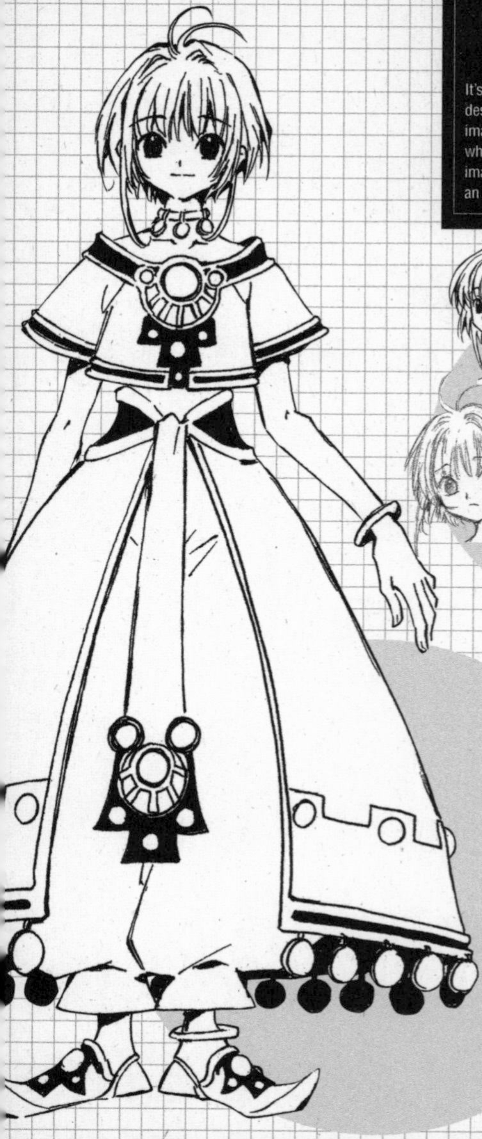

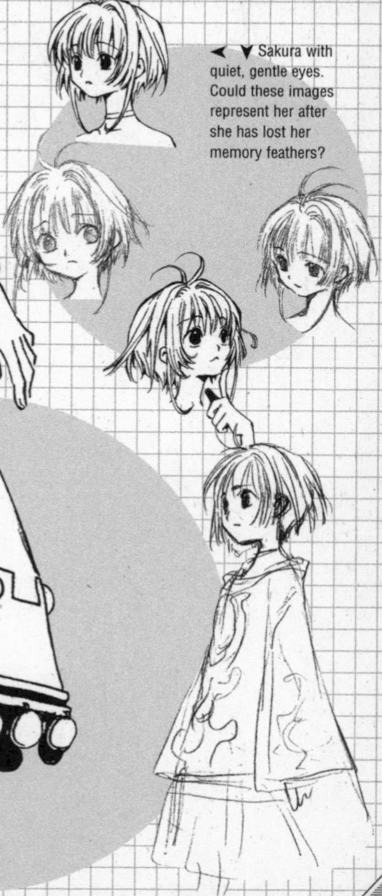

◀ ▼ Sakura with quiet, gentle eyes. Could these images represent her after she has lost her memory feathers?

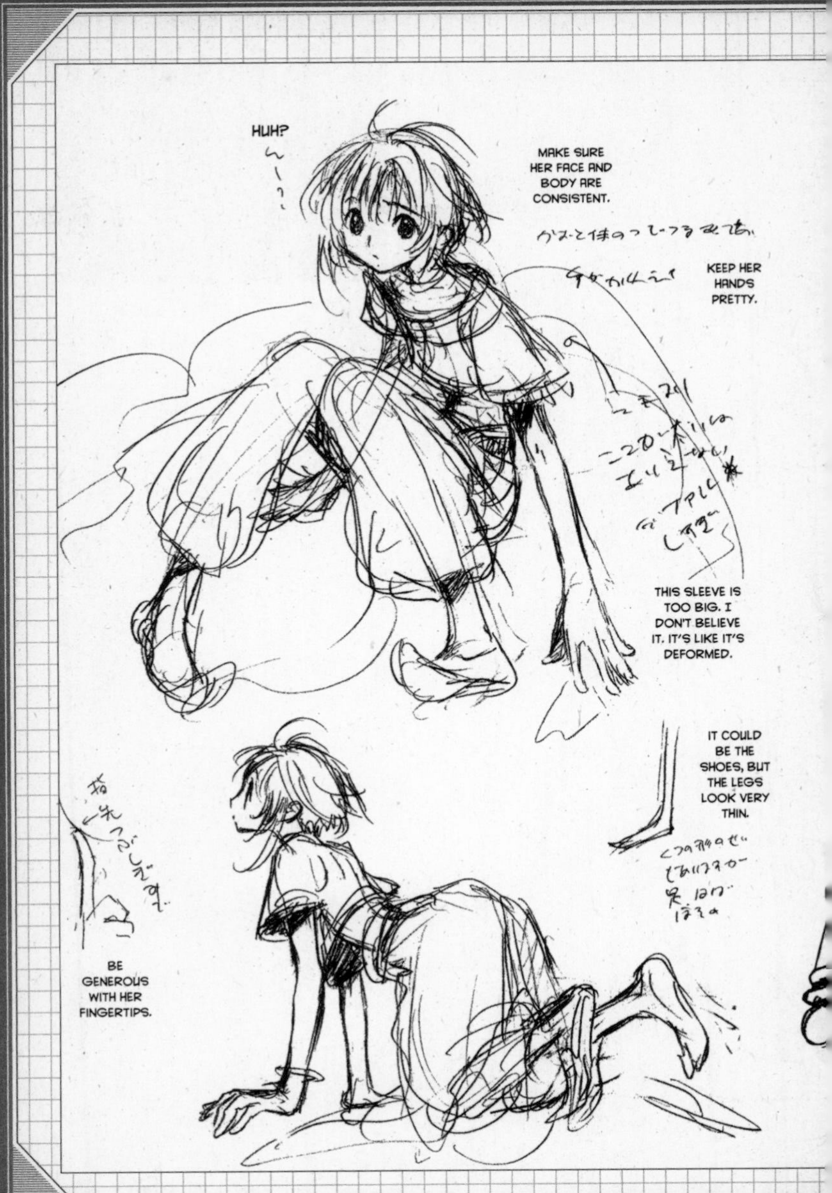
HUH?
MAKE SURE HER FACE AND BODY ARE CONSISTENT.
KEEP HER HANDS PRETTY.
THIS SLEEVE IS TOO BIG. I DON'T BELIEVE IT. IT'S LIKE IT'S DEFORMED.
IT COULD BE THE SHOES, BUT THE LEGS LOOK VERY THIN.
BE GENEROUS WITH HER FINGERTIPS.

+MATERIAL GALLERY 03+

黒鋼 KUROGANE

Kurogane with an abundance of expressions. Angry, laughing, all sorts of facial patterns. Take a look at the image of Kurogane with Ginryû on his hip. When you compare the sword to his height, you get a feeling of how long the sword is.

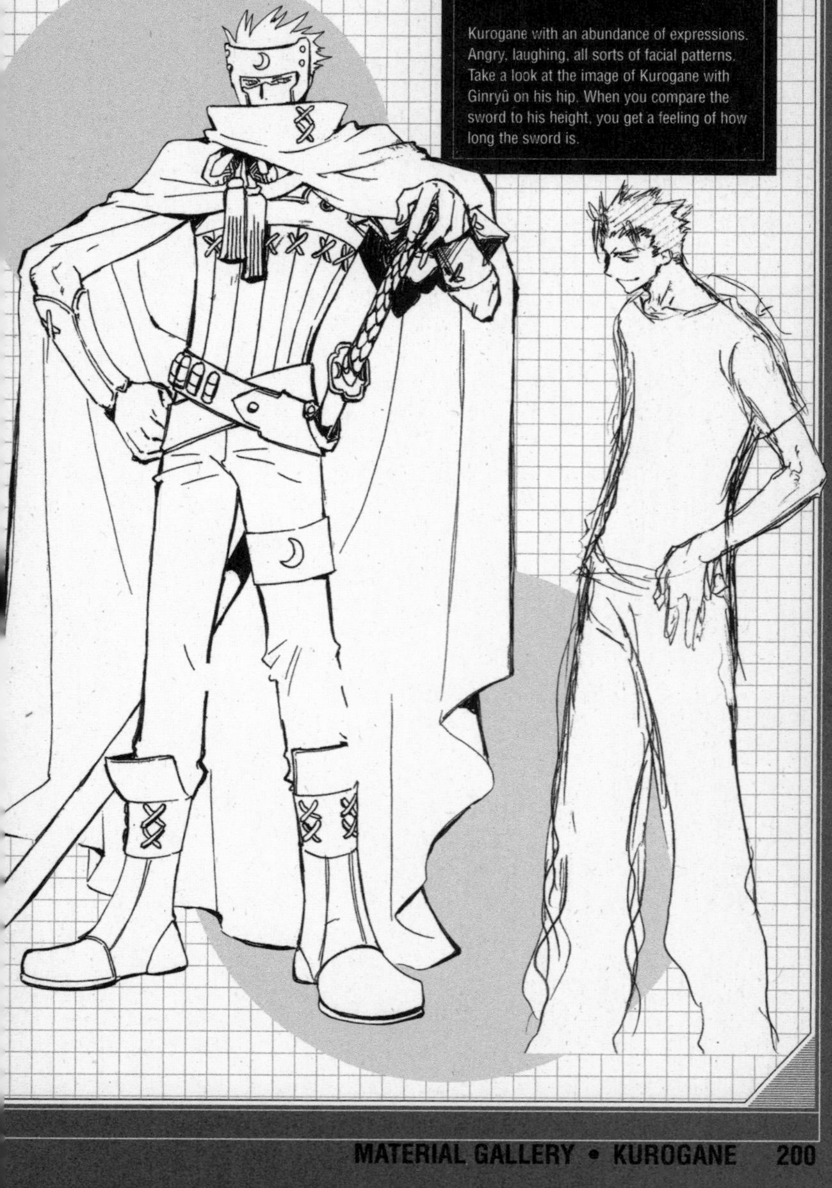

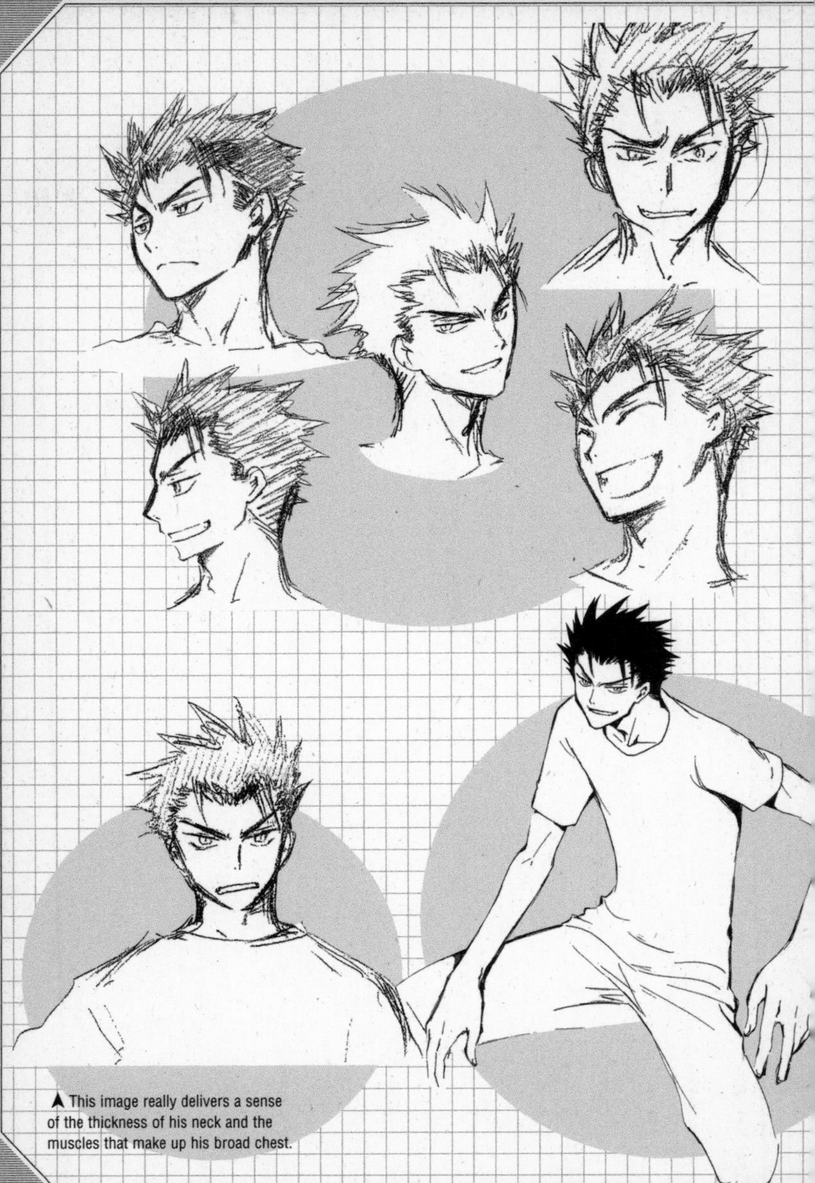

➤ This image really delivers a sense of the thickness of his neck and the muscles that make up his broad chest.

+MATERIAL GALLERY 04+

ファイ

FAI

In Fai's expressions, which make one suspect an intelligence under the aloof exterior, there's also a hint of hidden power. If you take a look at the left character design image on page 202, it looks like he was originally less of a magic user and more of a cleric.

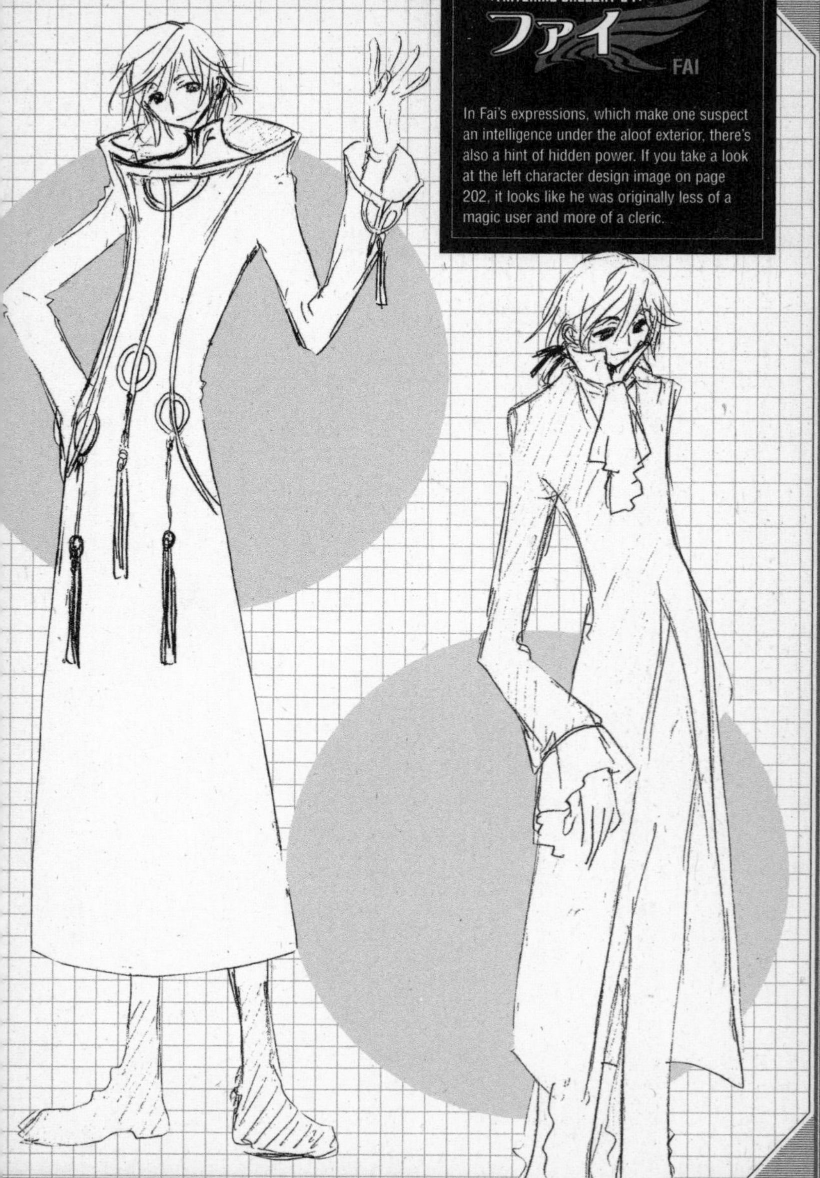

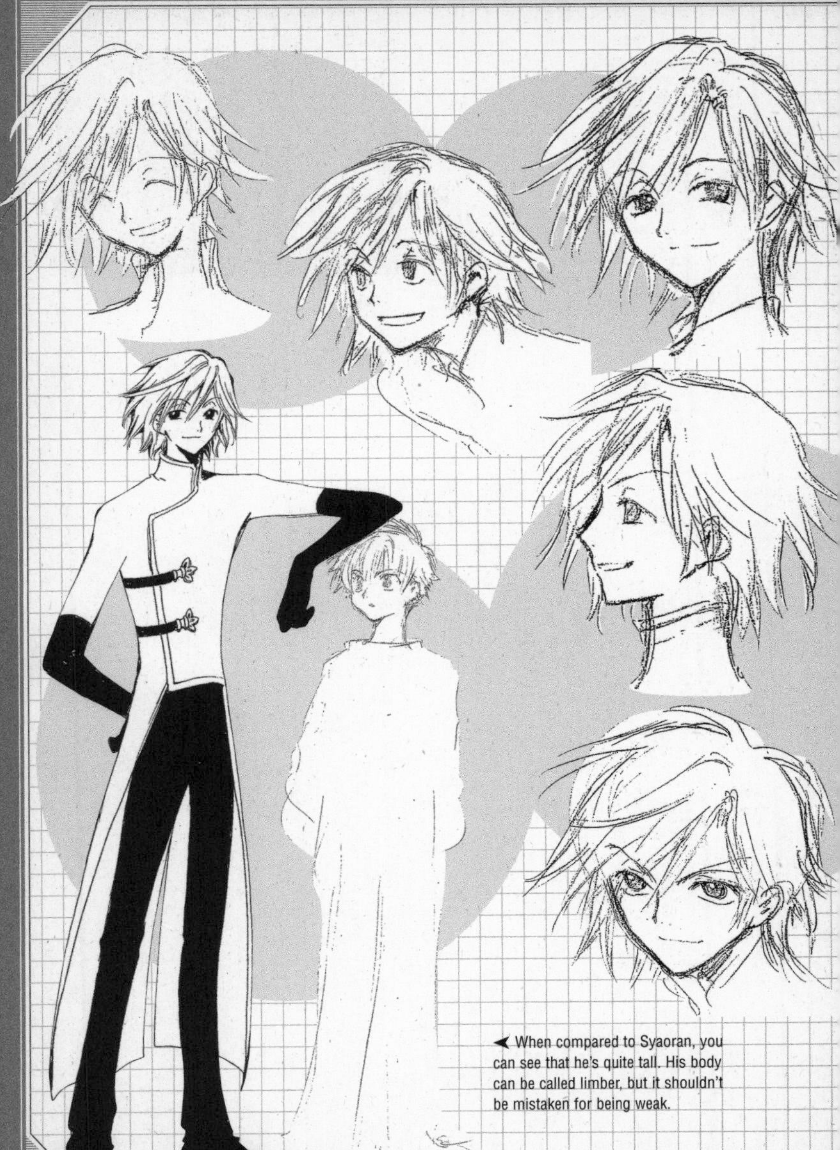

➤ When compared to Syaoran, you can see that he's quite tall. His body can be called limber, but it shouldn't be mistaken for being weak.

+MATERIAL GALLERY 05+

ポーズ集 POSE

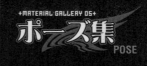

This isn't about the Character's personalities, expressions or the way they talk. This is about what the way they walk and sit says about them. You may be surprised at the detail in which these features were designed.

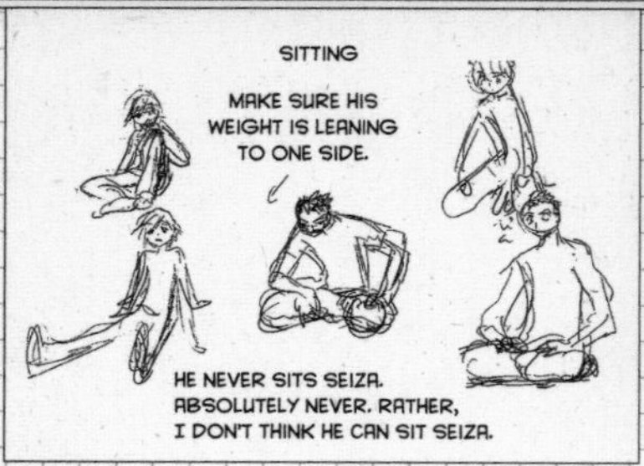

SITTING
MAKE SURE HIS WEIGHT IS LEANING TO ONE SIDE.
HE NEVER SITS SEIZA. ABSOLUTELY NEVER. RATHER, I DON'T THINK HE CAN SIT SEIZA.

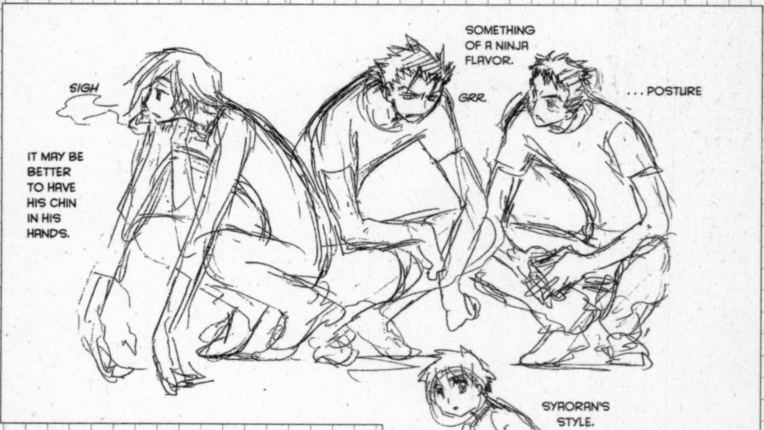

SIGH
IT MAY BE BETTER TO HAVE HIS CHIN IN HIS HANDS.
SOMETHING OF A NINJA FLAVOR.
GRR.
. . . POSTURE
SYAORAN'S STYLE.

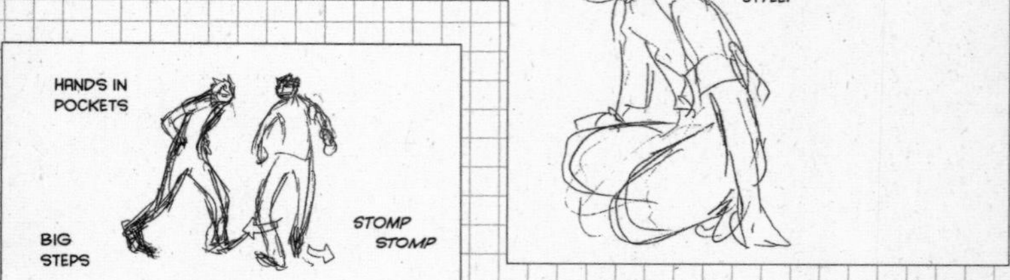

HANDS IN POCKETS
BIG STEPS
STOMP STOMP

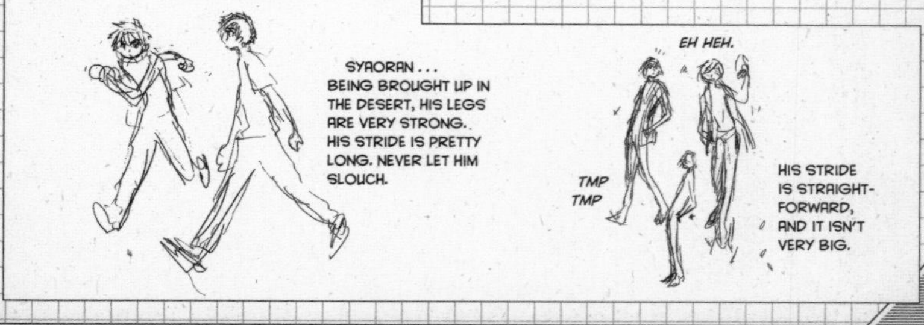

SYAORAN . . . BEING BROUGHT UP IN THE DESERT, HIS LEGS ARE VERY STRONG. HIS STRIDE IS PRETTY LONG. NEVER LET HIM SLOUCH.
EH HEH.
TMP TMP
HIS STRIDE IS STRAIGHT-FORWARD, AND IT ISN'T VERY BIG.

+MATERIAL GALLERY 06+

初期設定
EARLY MATERIAL

What we have here are some of the drawings done when the series was originally proposed. Although his face is slightly different, Kurogane was a hard man from the very beginning. Is that young man holding the wrench Syaoran?

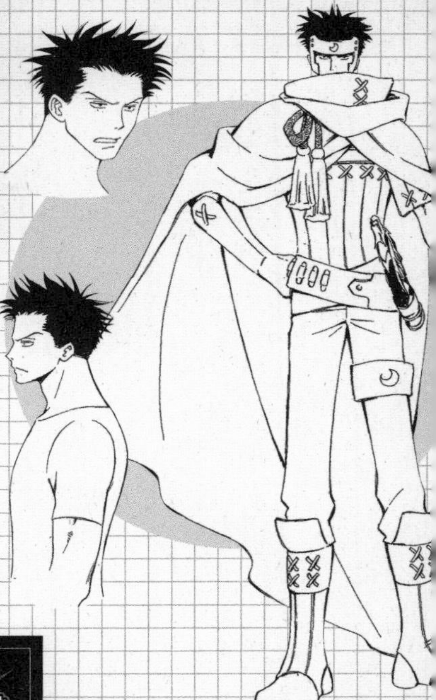

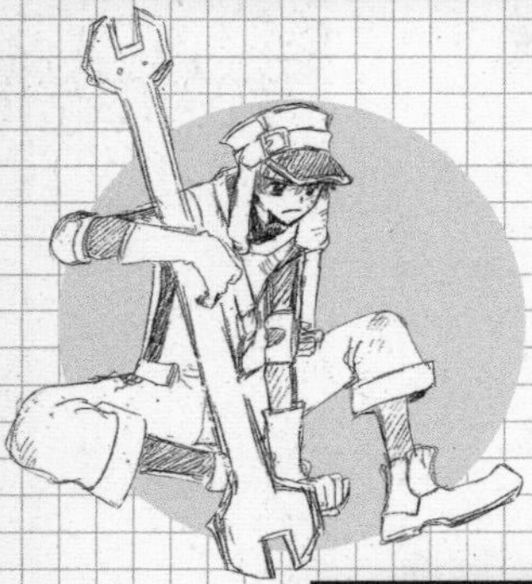

+MATERIAL GALLERY 08+

蘇摩と謎の女性
SOUMA & MYSTERIOUS LADY

To the left is the design for Sôma. The low-cut top is so sexy! CLAMP fans may recognize the woman to the right.

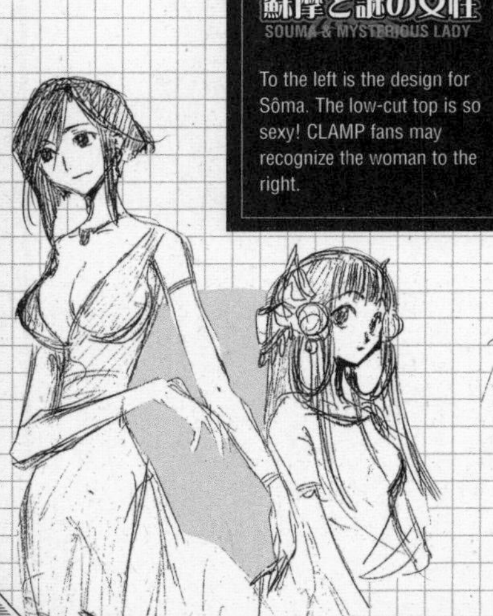

+MATERIAL GALLERY 07+

小狼と藤隆
SYAORAN & FUJITAKA

Fujitaka teaching young Syaoran his lessons. This image really gets across their warm relationship.

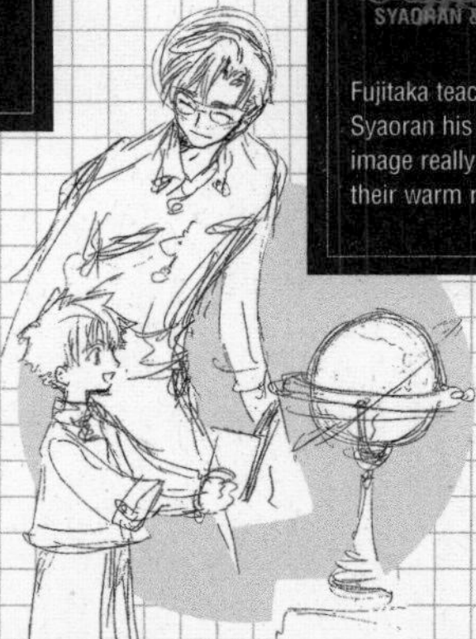

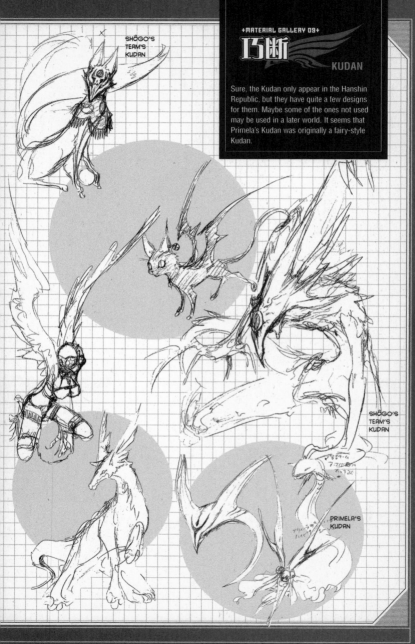

+MATERIAL GALLERY 09+

巧断 KUDAN

Sure, the Kudan only appear in the Hanshin Republic, but they have quite a few designs for them. Maybe some of the ones not used may be used in a later world. It seems that Primela's Kudan was originally a fairy-style Kudan.

SHÔGO'S TEAM'S KUDAN
SHÔGO'S TEAM'S KUDAN
PRIMELA'S KUDAN

+MATERIAL GALLERY 10+

背景 BACKGROUND

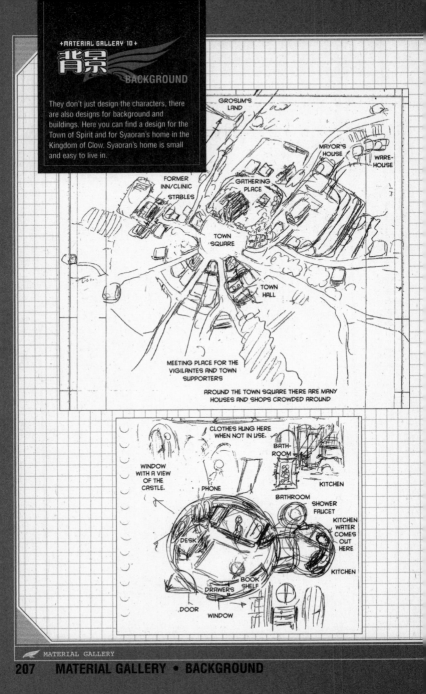

They don't just design the characters, there are also designs for background and buildings. Here you can find a design for the Town of Spirit and for Syaoran's home in the Kingdom of Clow. Syaoran's home is small and easy to live in.

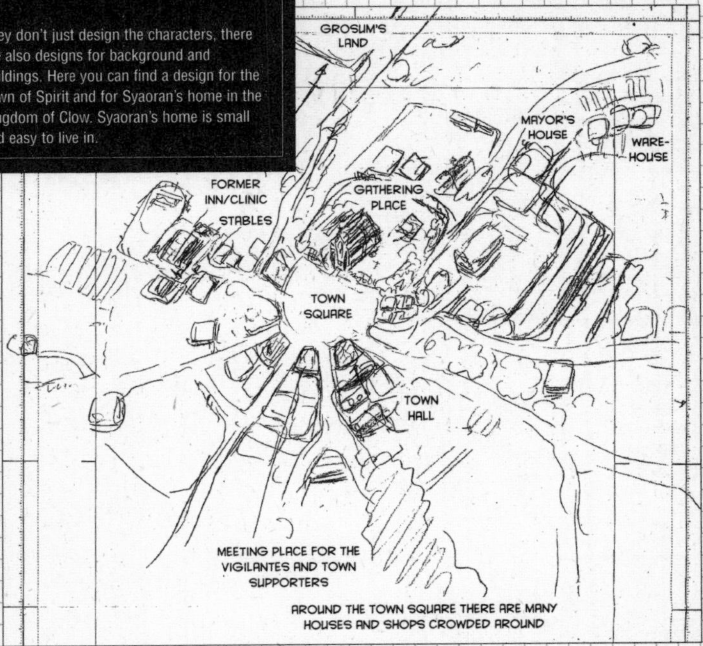
GROSUM'S LAND
MAYOR'S HOUSE
WARE-HOUSE
FORMER INN/CLINIC
STABLES
GATHERING PLACE
TOWN SQUARE
TOWN HALL
MEETING PLACE FOR THE VIGILANTES AND TOWN SUPPORTERS
AROUND THE TOWN SQUARE THERE ARE MANY HOUSES AND SHOPS CROWDED AROUND

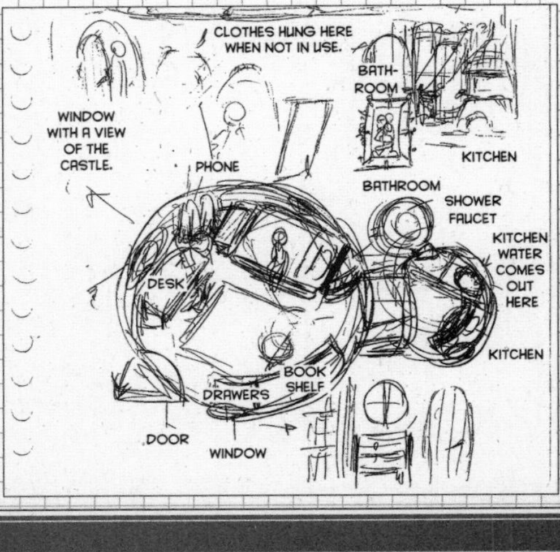
CLOTHES HUNG HERE WHEN NOT IN USE.
BATH-ROOM
WINDOW WITH A VIEW OF THE CASTLE.
PHONE
KITCHEN
BATHROOM
SHOWER FAUCET
KITCHEN WATER COMES OUT HERE
DESK
KITCHEN
BOOK SHELF
DRAWERS
DOOR
WINDOW

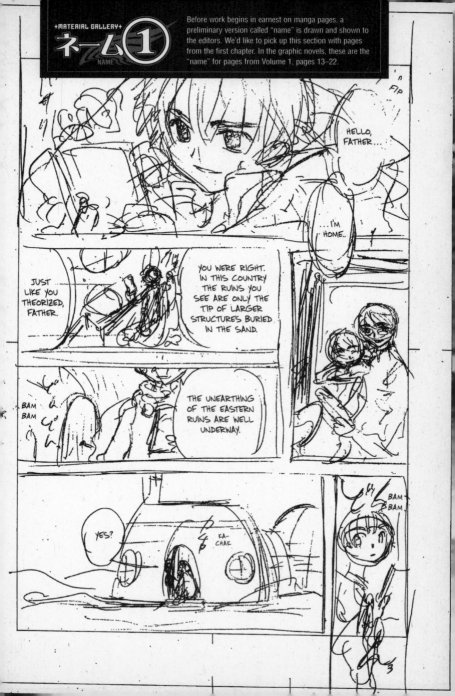

+MATERIAL GALLERY+

ネーム 1

NAME

Before work begins in earnest on manga pages, a preliminary version called "name" is drawn and shown to the editors. We'd like to pick up this section with pages from the first chapter. In the graphic novels, these are the "name" for pages from Volume 1, pages 13–22.

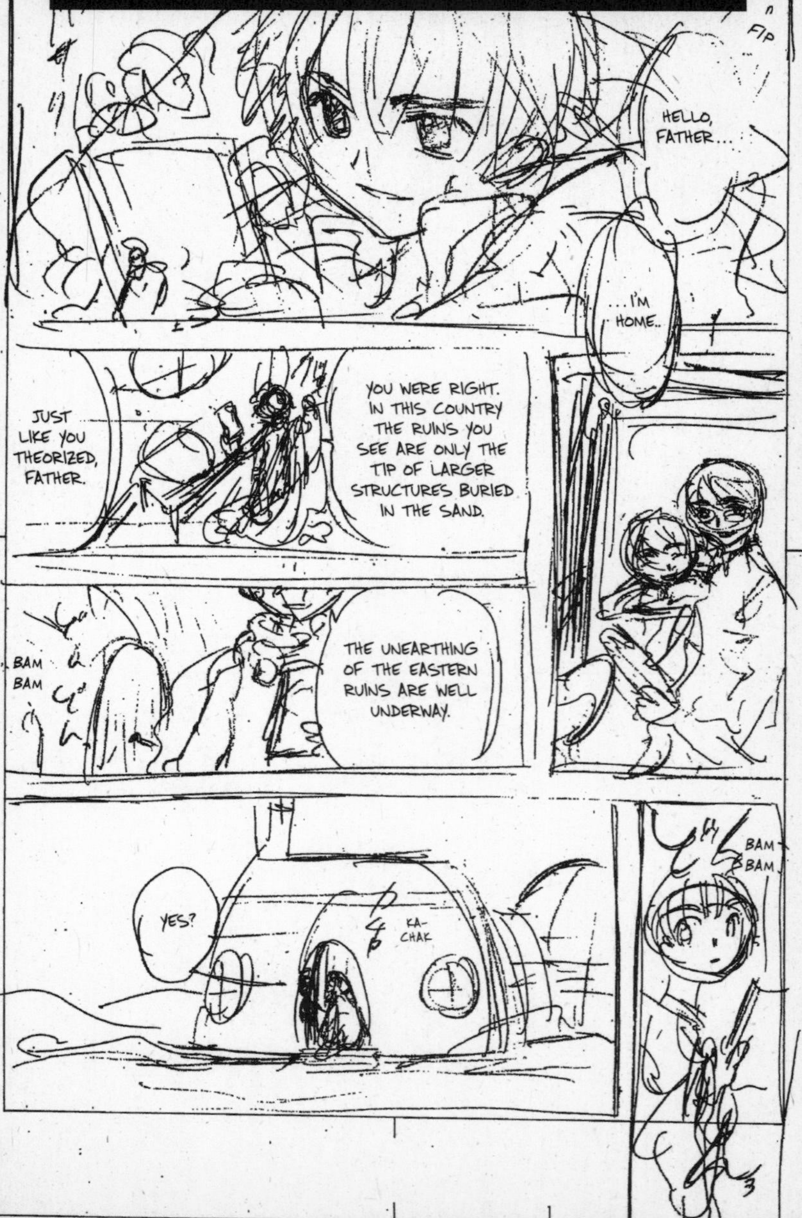
HELLO, FATHER...
...I'M HOME.
YOU WERE RIGHT. IN THIS COUNTRY THE RUINS YOU SEE ARE ONLY THE TIP OF LARGER STRUCTURES BURIED IN THE SAND.
JUST LIKE YOU THEORIZED, FATHER.
THE UNEARTHING OF THE EASTERN RUINS ARE WELL UNDERWAY.
BAM BAM
BAM BAM
KA-CHAK
YES?

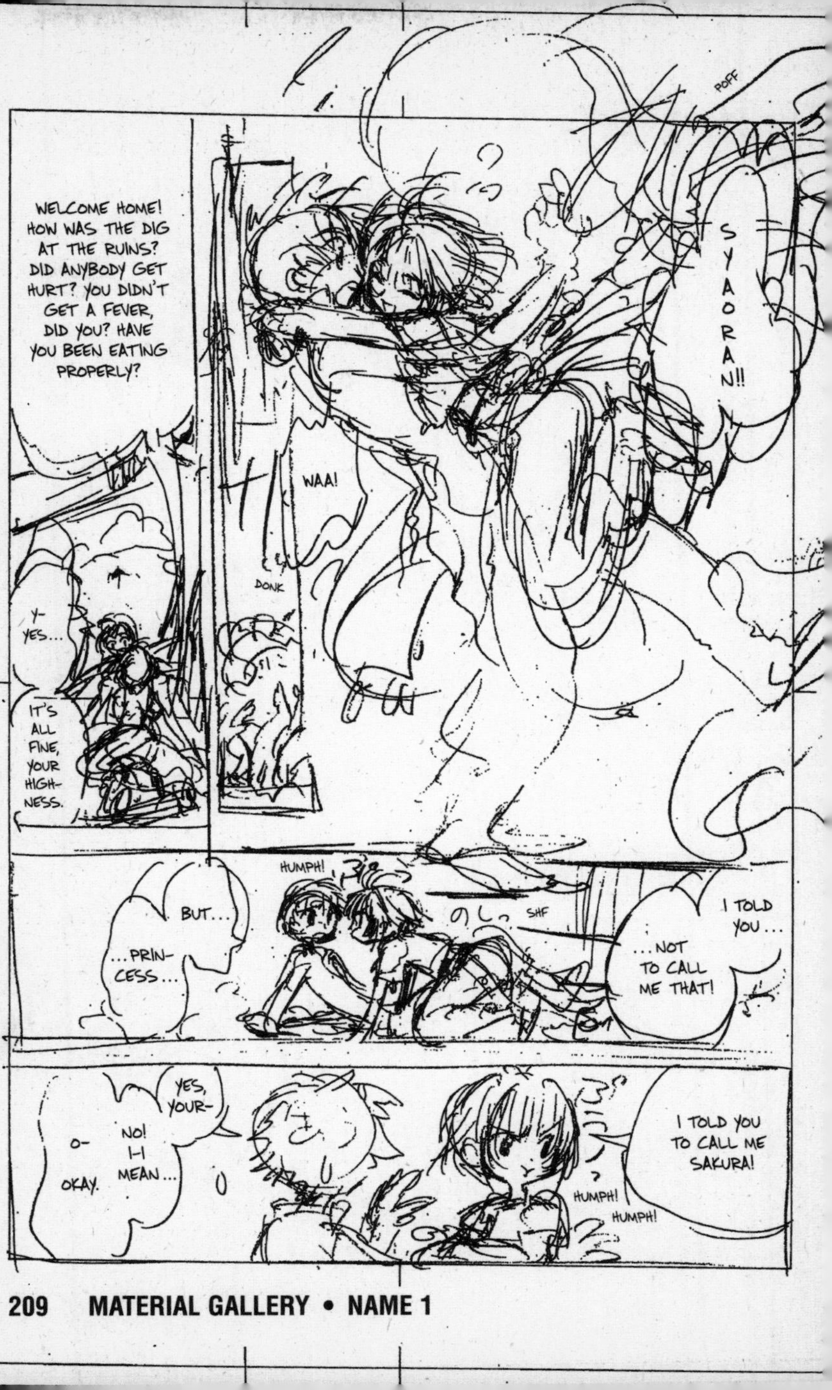

POFF
SYAORAN!!
WAA!
DONK
WELCOME HOME! HOW WAS THE DIG AT THE RUINS? DID ANYBODY GET HURT? YOU DIDN'T GET A FEVER, DID YOU? HAVE YOU BEEN EATING PROPERLY?
Y-YES...
IT'S ALL FINE, YOUR HIGHNESS.
I TOLD YOU...
...NOT TO CALL ME THAT!
SHF
HUMPH!
BUT...
...PRINCESS...
I TOLD YOU TO CALL ME SAKURA!
HUMPH!
HUMPH!
YES, YOUR-
NO! I-I MEAN...
O-OKAY.

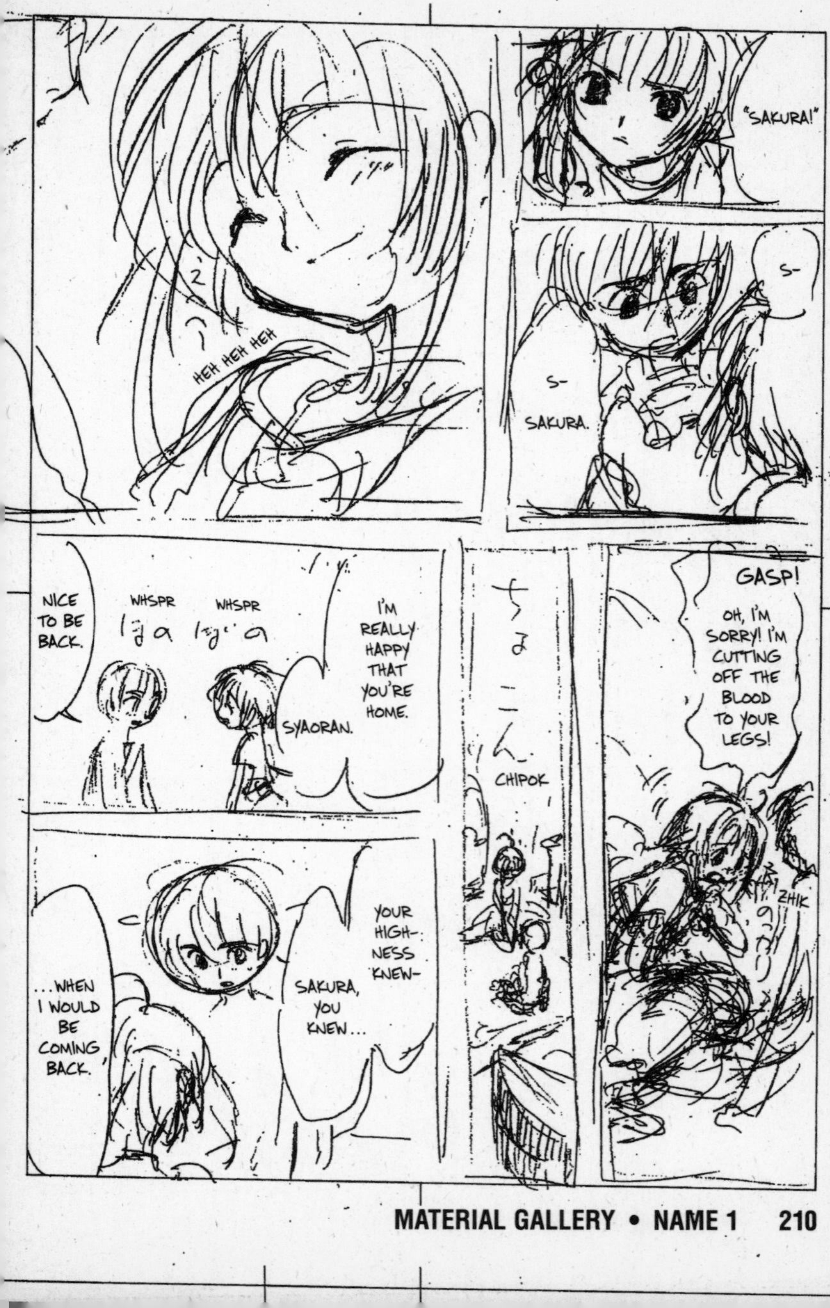
"SAKURA!"
S-
S-
SAKURA.
HEH HEH HEH
GASP!
OH, I'M SORRY! I'M CUTTING OFF THE BLOOD TO YOUR LEGS!
ZHIK
ちょこん
CHIPOK
I'M REALLY HAPPY THAT YOU'RE HOME.
SYAORAN.
WHSPR
WHSPR
NICE TO BE BACK.
YOUR HIGHNESS KNEW-
SAKURA, YOU KNEW...
...WHEN I WOULD BE COMING BACK.

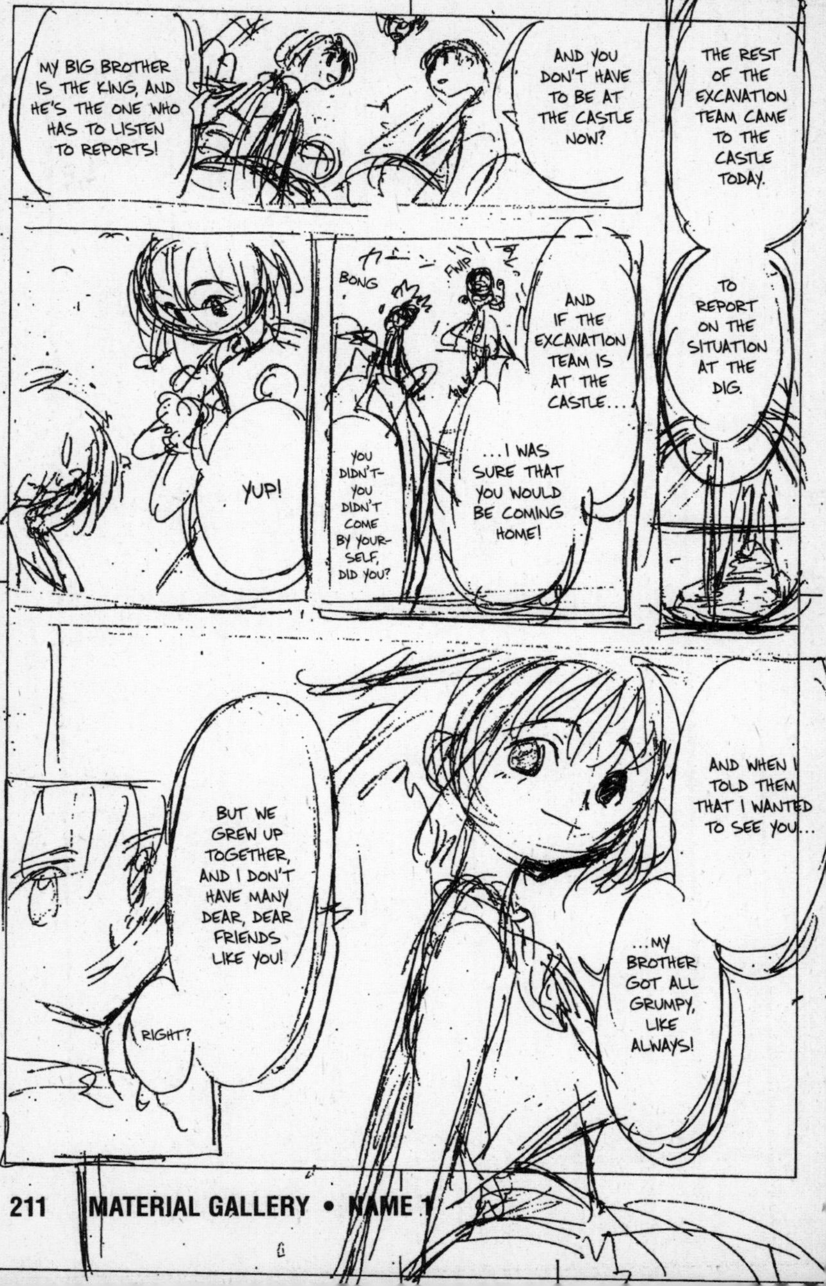
THE REST OF THE EXCAVATION TEAM CAME TO THE CASTLE TODAY.
TO REPORT ON THE SITUATION AT THE DIG.
AND YOU DON'T HAVE TO BE AT THE CASTLE NOW?
MY BIG BROTHER IS THE KING, AND HE'S THE ONE WHO HAS TO LISTEN TO REPORTS!
FWIP
BONG
AND IF THE EXCAVATION TEAM IS AT THE CASTLE...
...I WAS SURE THAT YOU WOULD BE COMING HOME!
YOU DIDN'T- YOU DIDN'T COME BY YOUR-SELF, DID YOU?
YUP!
AND WHEN I TOLD THEM THAT I WANTED TO SEE YOU...
...MY BROTHER GOT ALL GRUMPY, LIKE ALWAYS!
BUT WE GREW UP TOGETHER, AND I DON'T HAVE MANY DEAR, DEAR FRIENDS LIKE YOU!
RIGHT?

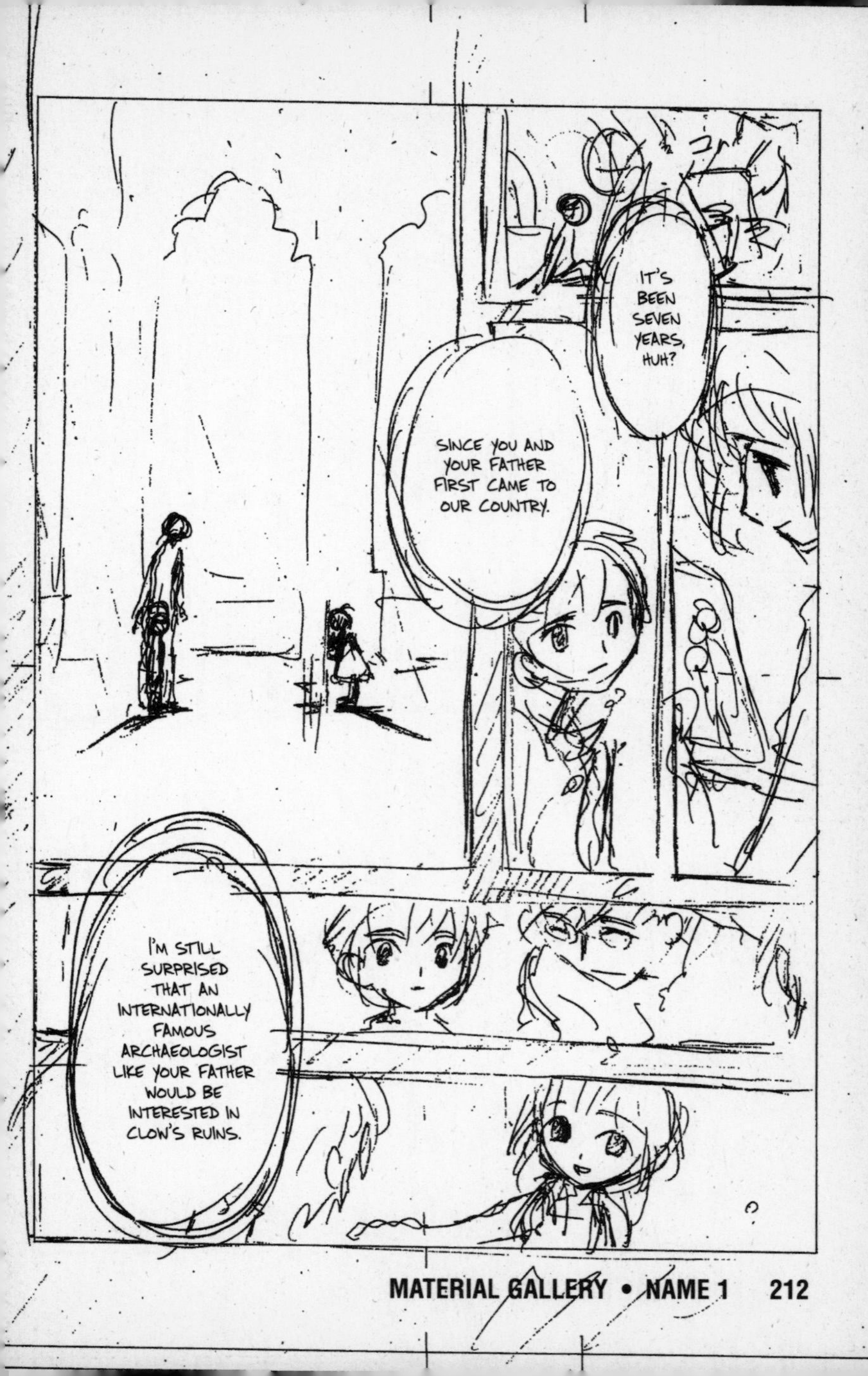
IT'S BEEN SEVEN YEARS, HUH?
SINCE YOU AND YOUR FATHER FIRST CAME TO OUR COUNTRY.
I'M STILL SURPRISED THAT AN INTERNATIONALLY FAMOUS ARCHAEOLOGIST LIKE YOUR FATHER WOULD BE INTERESTED IN CLOW'S RUINS.

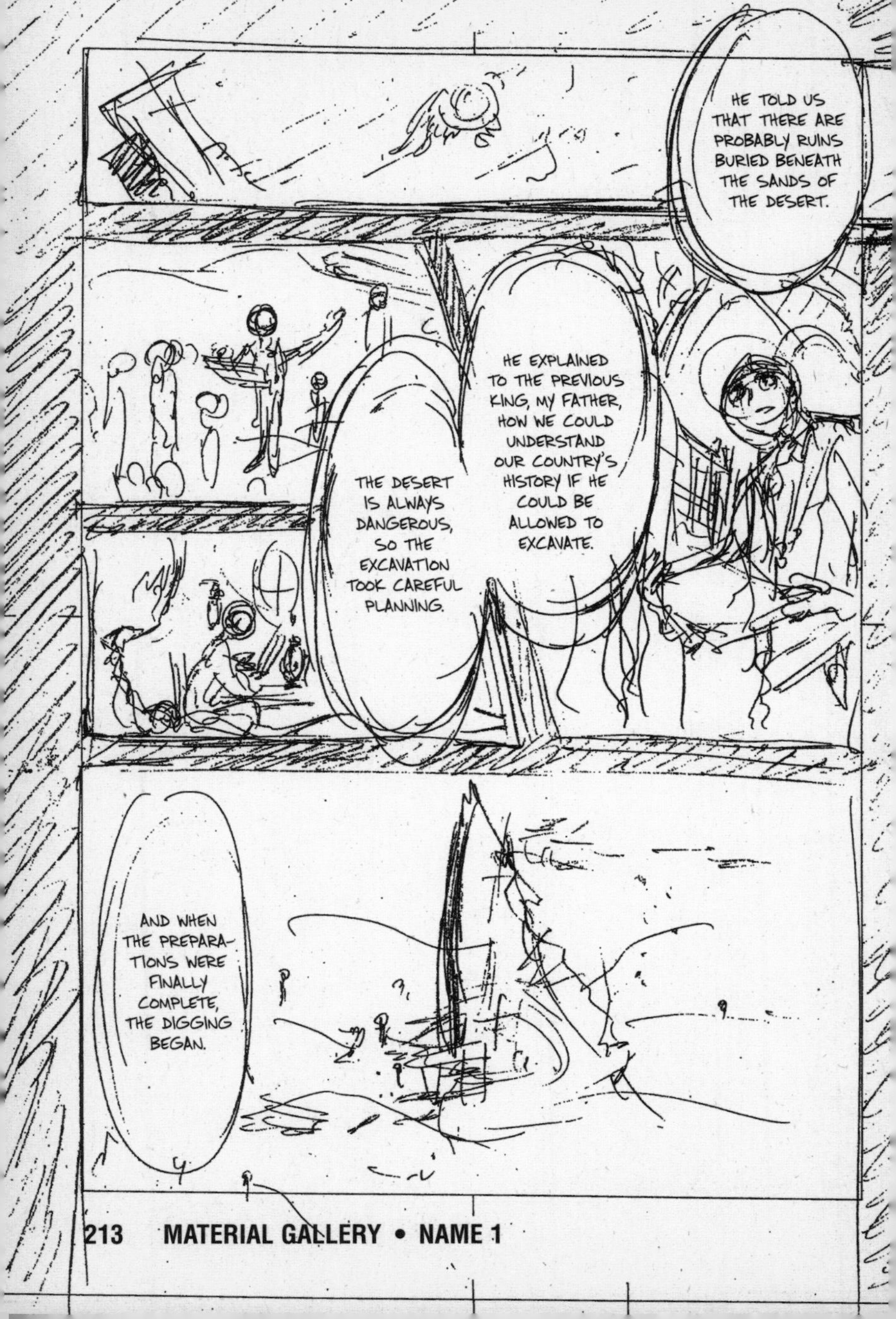
HE TOLD US THAT THERE ARE PROBABLY RUINS BURIED BENEATH THE SANDS OF THE DESERT.
HE EXPLAINED TO THE PREVIOUS KING, MY FATHER, HOW WE COULD UNDERSTAND OUR COUNTRY'S HISTORY IF HE COULD BE ALLOWED TO EXCAVATE.
THE DESERT IS ALWAYS DANGEROUS, SO THE EXCAVATION TOOK CAREFUL PLANNING.
AND WHEN THE PREPARA-TIONS WERE FINALLY COMPLETE, THE DIGGING BEGAN.

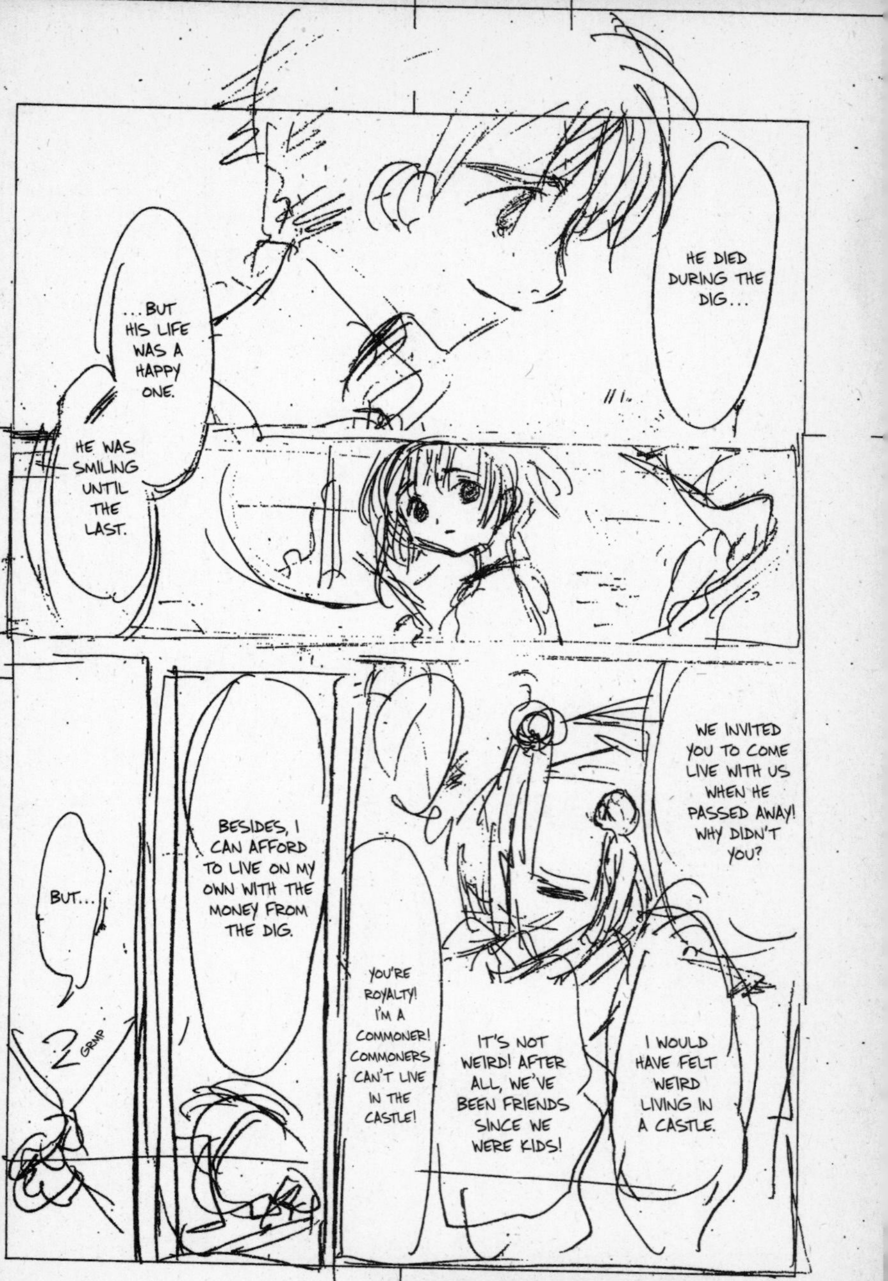
HE DIED DURING THE DIG...
...BUT HIS LIFE WAS A HAPPY ONE.
HE WAS SMILING UNTIL THE LAST.
WE INVITED YOU TO COME LIVE WITH US WHEN HE PASSED AWAY! WHY DIDN'T YOU?
I WOULD HAVE FELT WEIRD LIVING IN A CASTLE.
IT'S NOT WEIRD! AFTER ALL, WE'VE BEEN FRIENDS SINCE WE WERE KIDS!
YOU'RE ROYALTY! I'M A COMMONER! COMMONERS CAN'T LIVE IN THE CASTLE!
BESIDES, I CAN AFFORD TO LIVE ON MY OWN WITH THE MONEY FROM THE DIG.
BUT...
GRMP

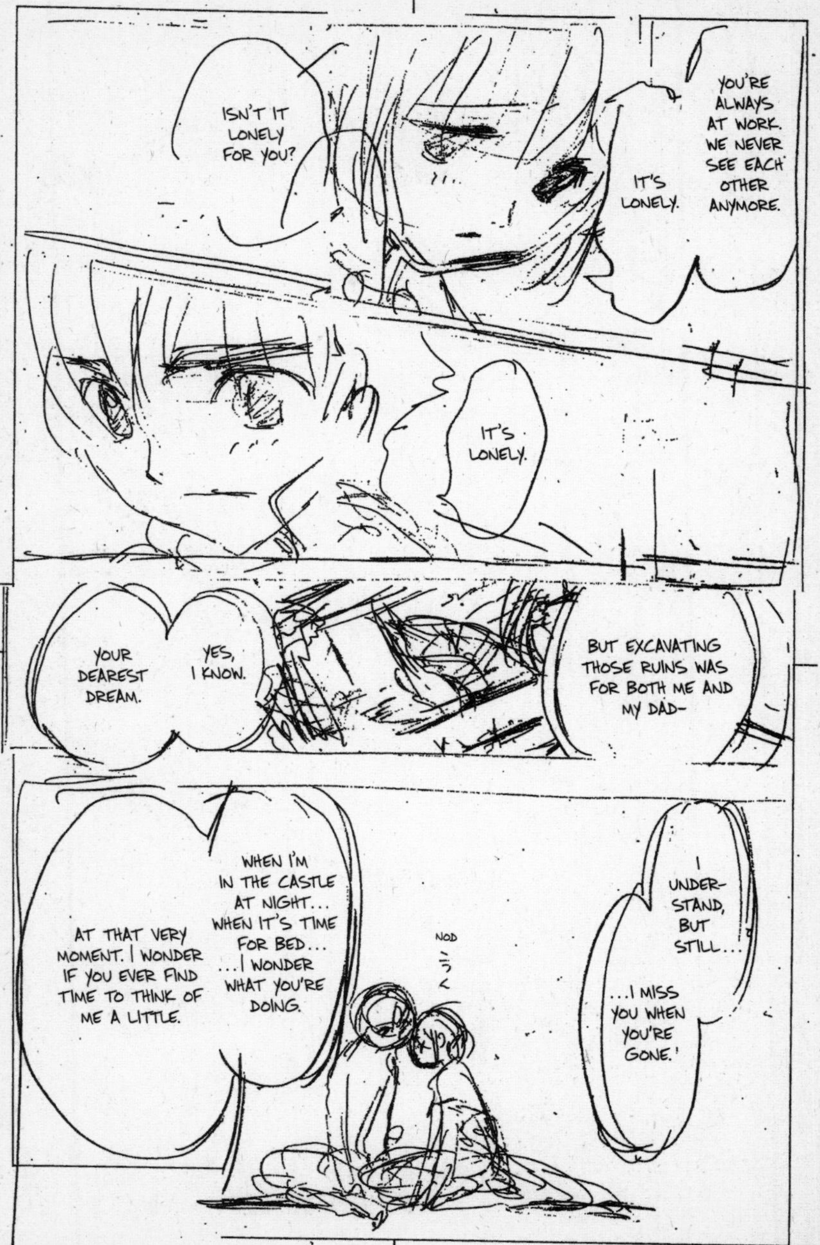
YOU'RE ALWAYS AT WORK. WE NEVER SEE EACH OTHER ANYMORE.
IT'S LONELY.
ISN'T IT LONELY FOR YOU?
IT'S LONELY.
BUT EXCAVATING THOSE RUINS WAS FOR BOTH ME AND MY DAD-
YES, I KNOW.
YOUR DEAREST DREAM.
I UNDER-STAND, BUT STILL...
...I MISS YOU WHEN YOU'RE GONE.
NOD
WHEN I'M IN THE CASTLE AT NIGHT... WHEN IT'S TIME FOR BED... ...I WONDER WHAT YOU'RE DOING.
AT THAT VERY MOMENT. I WONDER IF YOU EVER FIND TIME TO THINK OF ME A LITTLE.

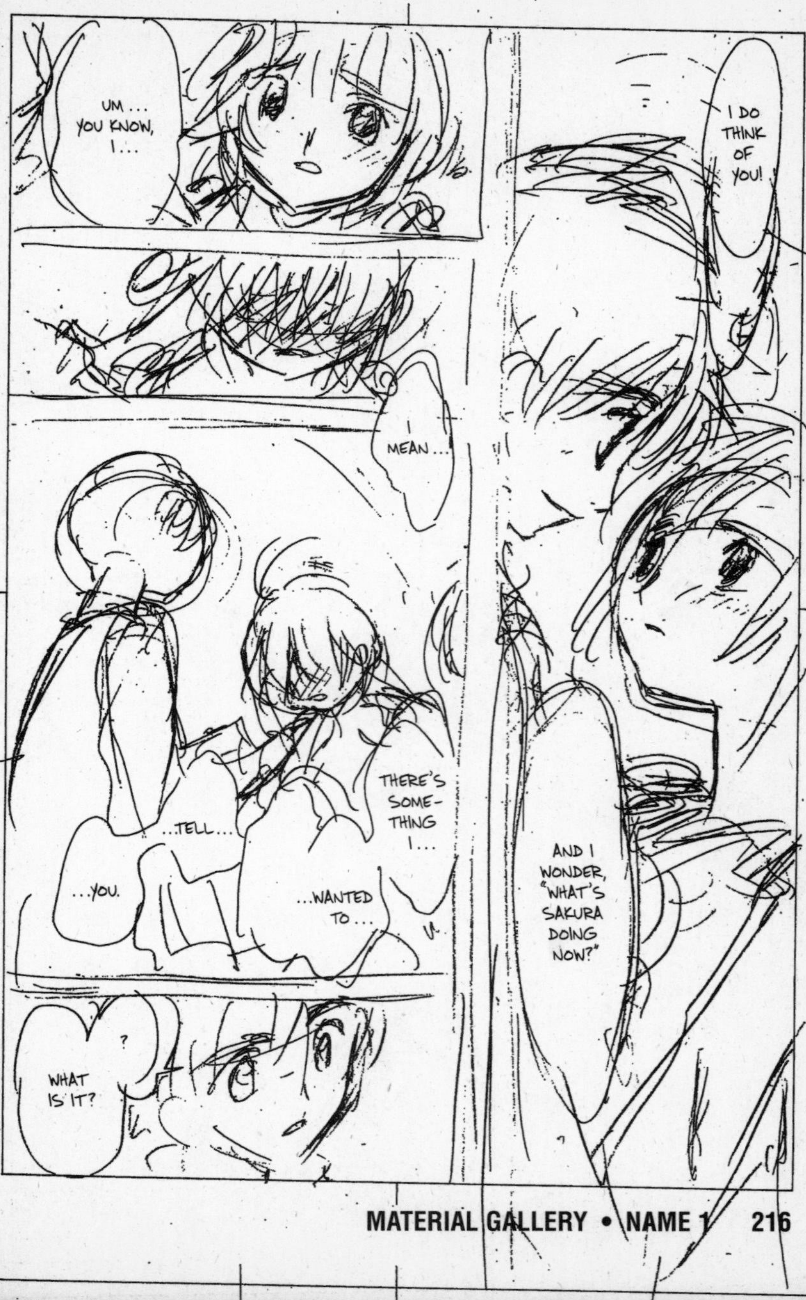
I DO THINK OF YOU!
AND I WONDER, "WHAT'S SAKURA DOING NOW?"
UM … YOU KNOW, I …
I MEAN …
THERE'S SOME-THING I …
…WANTED TO …
…TELL…
…YOU.
?
WHAT IS IT?

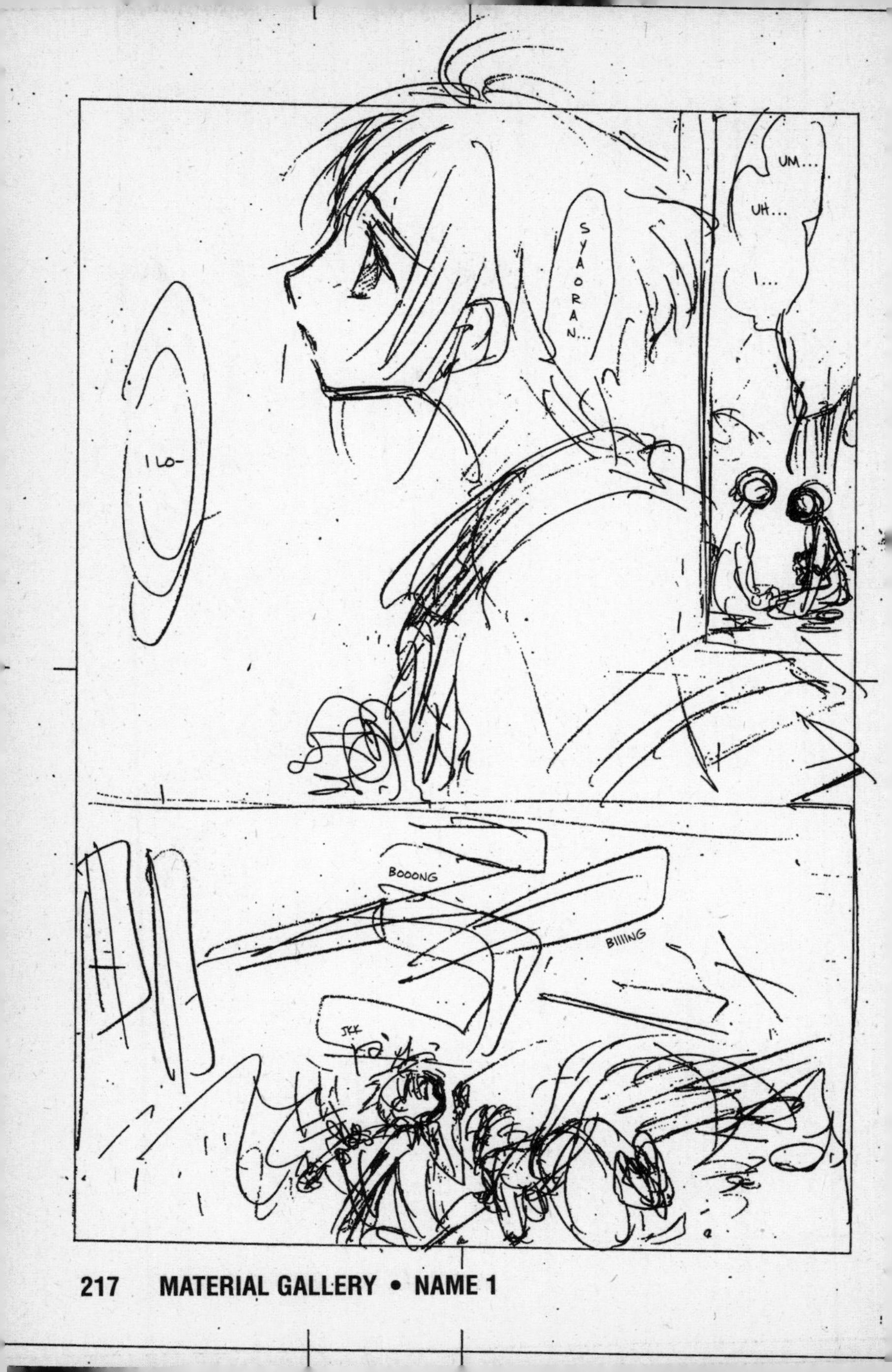
UM...
UH...
I...
SYAORAN...
I LO-
BOOONG
BIIIING
JKK

+MATERIAL GALLERY+

ネーム 2

NAME

Here is the name that corresponds to the graphic novel volume 1, pages 27–32. The fight between Tōya and Sakura is drawn as a lively exchange. You can see how much fun the group of CLAMP-sensei put into their drawings.

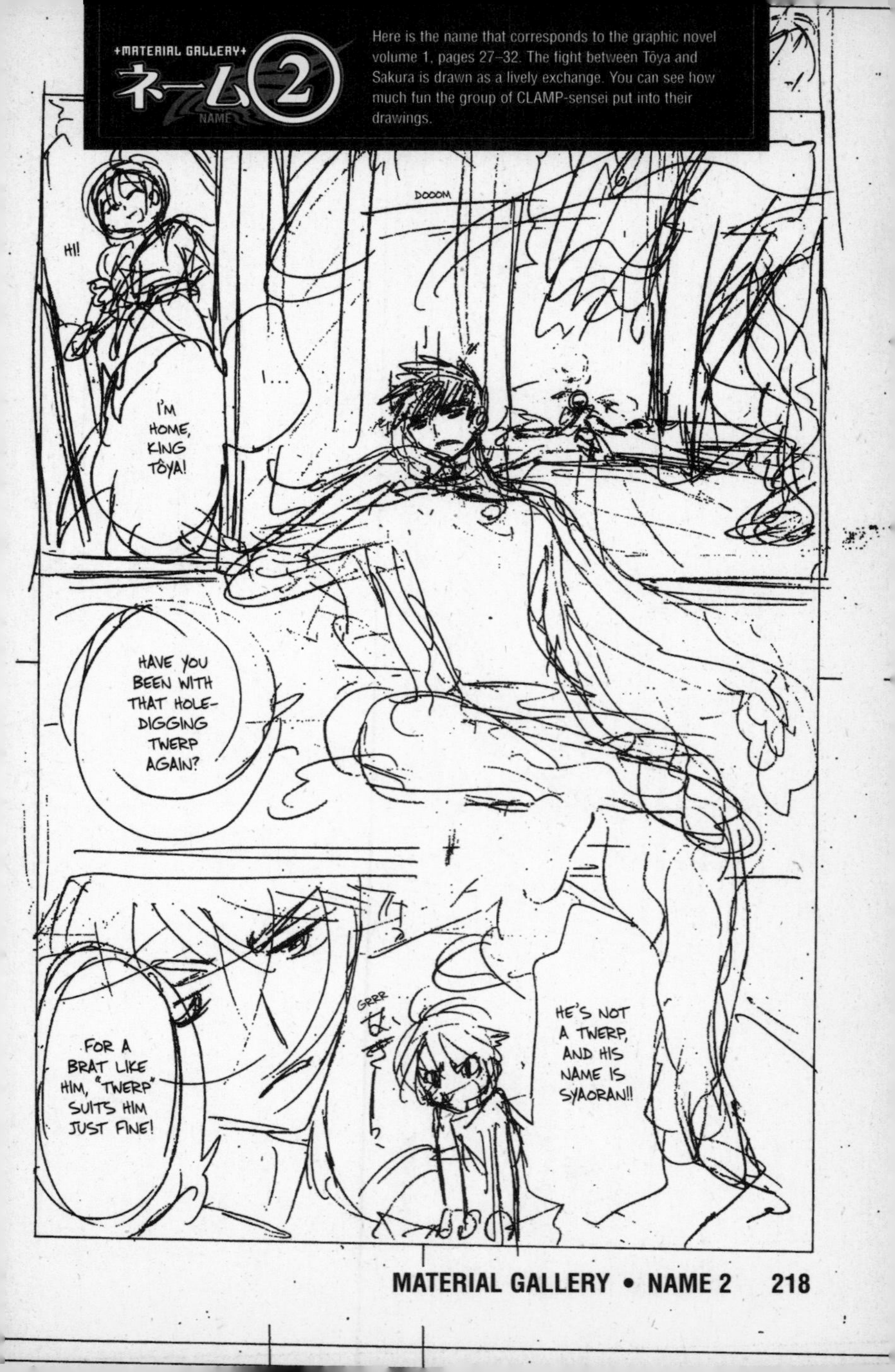

DOOOM
I...
I'M HOME, KING TŌYA!
HI!
HAVE YOU BEEN WITH THAT HOLE-DIGGING TWERP AGAIN?
HE'S NOT A TWERP, AND HIS NAME IS SYAORAN!!
GRRR
FOR A BRAT LIKE HIM, "TWERP" SUITS HIM JUST FINE!

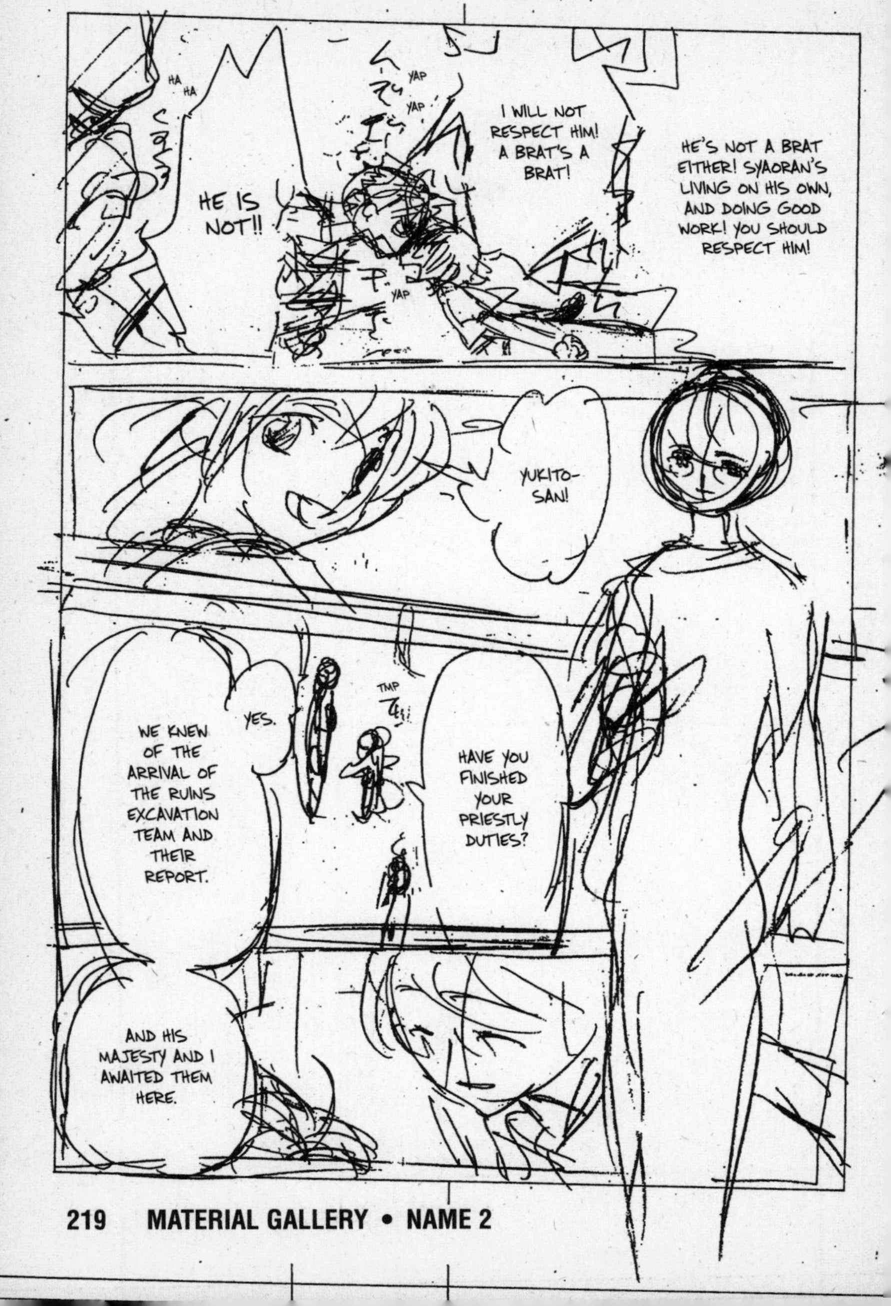
HE'S NOT A BRAT EITHER! SYAORAN'S LIVING ON HIS OWN, AND DOING GOOD WORK! YOU SHOULD RESPECT HIM!
I WILL NOT RESPECT HIM! A BRAT'S A BRAT!
YAP YAP
YAP
HE IS NOT!!
HA HA
YUKITO-SAN!
HAVE YOU FINISHED YOUR PRIESTLY DUTIES?
TMP
YES.
WE KNEW OF THE ARRIVAL OF THE RUINS EXCAVATION TEAM AND THEIR REPORT.
AND HIS MAJESTY AND I AWAITED THEM HERE.

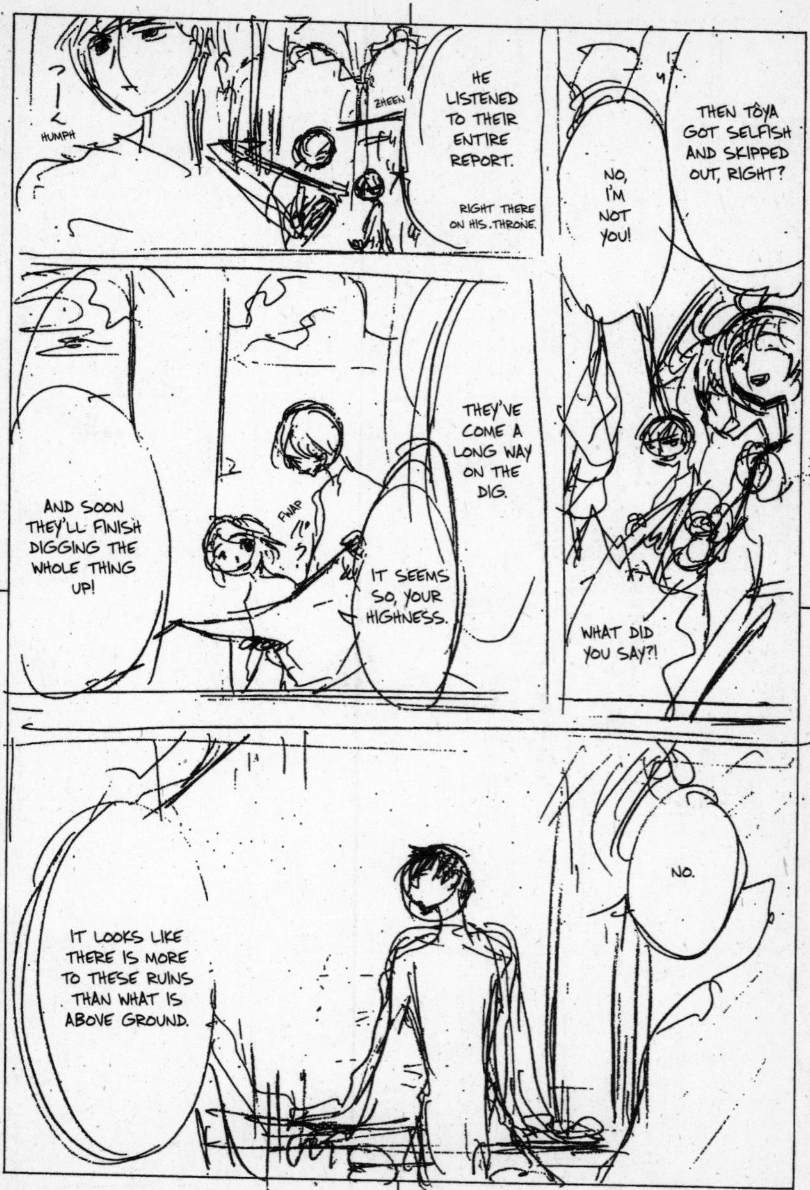
THEN TÔYA GOT SELFISH AND SKIPPED OUT, RIGHT?
NO, I'M NOT YOU!
WHAT DID YOU SAY?!
HE LISTENED TO THEIR ENTIRE REPORT.
ZHEEN
RIGHT THERE ON HIS THRONE.
HUMPH
THEY'VE COME A LONG WAY ON THE DIG.
IT SEEMS SO, YOUR HIGHNESS.
FWAP
AND SOON THEY'LL FINISH DIGGING THE WHOLE THING UP!
NO.
IT LOOKS LIKE THERE IS MORE TO THESE RUINS THAN WHAT IS ABOVE GROUND.

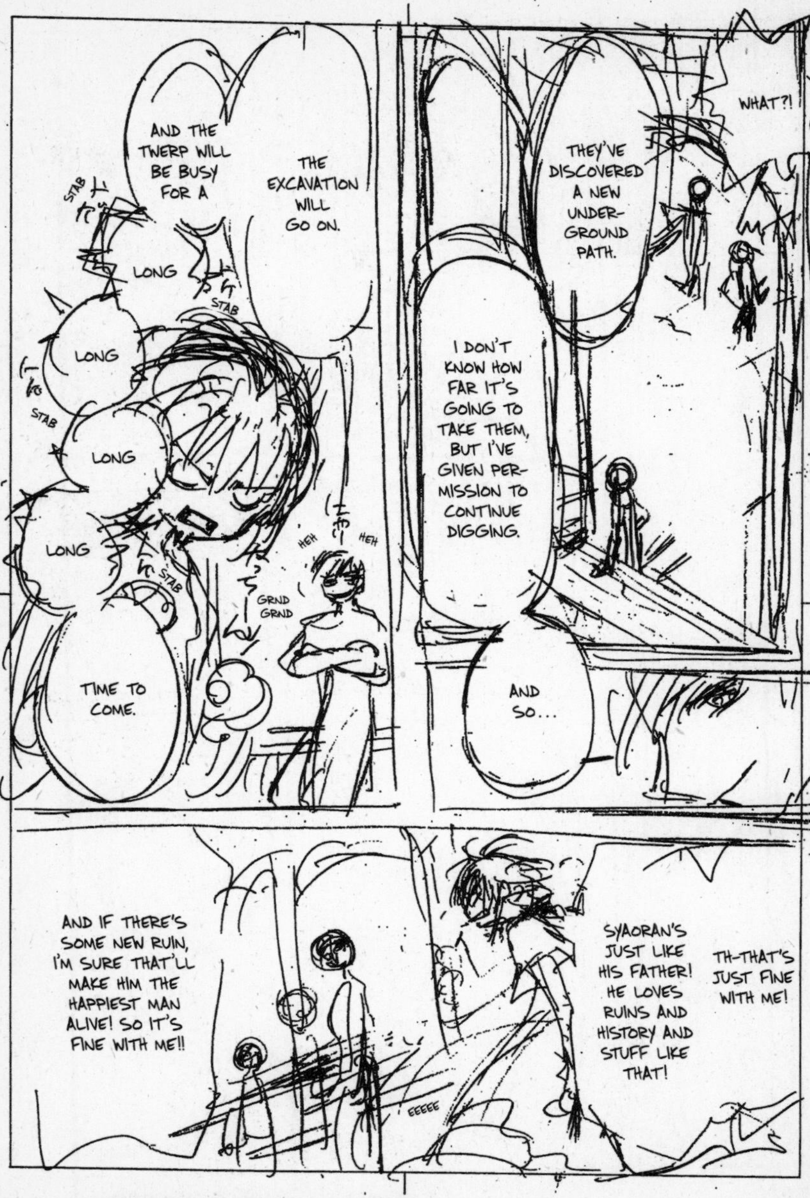
WHAT?!
THEY'VE DISCOVERED A NEW UNDER-GROUND PATH.
I DON'T KNOW HOW FAR IT'S GOING TO TAKE THEM, BUT I'VE GIVEN PER-MISSION TO CONTINUE DIGGING.
AND SO...
THE EXCAVATION WILL GO ON.
AND THE TWERP WILL BE BUSY FOR A
LONG
LONG
LONG
LONG
TIME TO COME.
STAB
STAB
STAB
STAB
HEH
HEH
GRND GRND
TH-THAT'S JUST FINE WITH ME!
SYAORAN'S JUST LIKE HIS FATHER! HE LOVES RUINS AND HISTORY AND STUFF LIKE THAT!
EEEEE
AND IF THERE'S SOME NEW RUIN, I'M SURE THAT'LL MAKE HIM THE HAPPIEST MAN ALIVE! SO IT'S FINE WITH ME!!

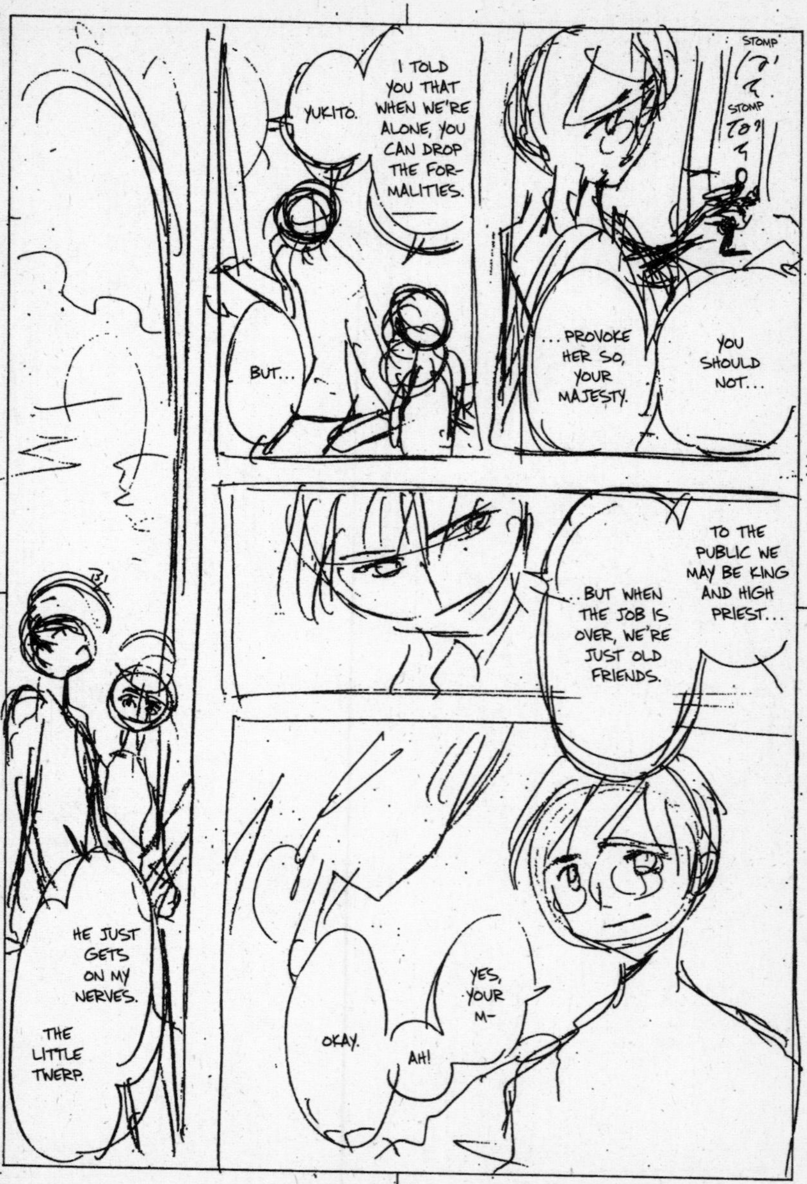
STOMP
STOMP
YOU SHOULD NOT...
...PROVOKE HER SO, YOUR MAJESTY.
I TOLD YOU THAT WHEN WE'RE ALONE, YOU CAN DROP THE FORMALITIES.
YUKITO.
BUT...
TO THE PUBLIC WE MAY BE KING AND HIGH PRIEST...
...BUT WHEN THE JOB IS OVER, WE'RE JUST OLD FRIENDS.
YES, YOUR M-
AH!
OKAY.
HE JUST GETS ON MY NERVES.
THE LITTLE TWERP.

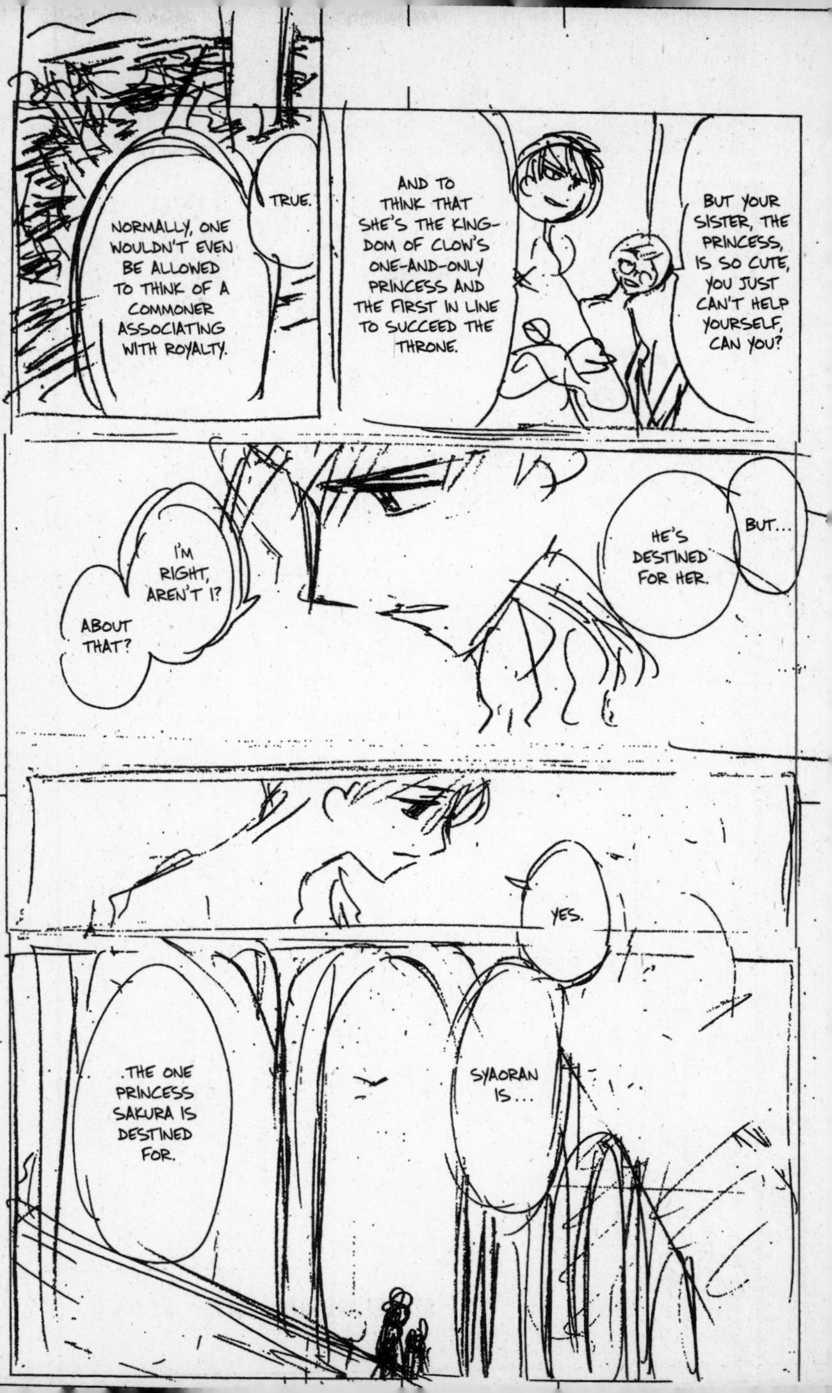
BUT YOUR SISTER, THE PRINCESS, IS SO CUTE, YOU JUST CAN'T HELP YOURSELF, CAN YOU?
AND TO THINK THAT SHE'S THE KING-DOM OF CLOW'S ONE-AND-ONLY PRINCESS AND THE FIRST IN LINE TO SUCCEED THE THRONE.
TRUE.
NORMALLY, ONE WOULDN'T EVEN BE ALLOWED TO THINK OF A COMMONER ASSOCIATING WITH ROYALTY.
BUT...
HE'S DESTINED FOR HER.
I'M RIGHT, AREN'T I?
ABOUT THAT?
YES.
SYAORAN IS...
.THE ONE PRINCESS SAKURA IS DESTINED FOR.

+MATERIAL GALLERY+

ネーム 3 NAME

The last name we have comes from the graphic novel volume 1, pages 43–50. Any would-be manga artists should notice that, even though the details aren't drawn in, it's surprising just how much the emotion of the characters is communicated.

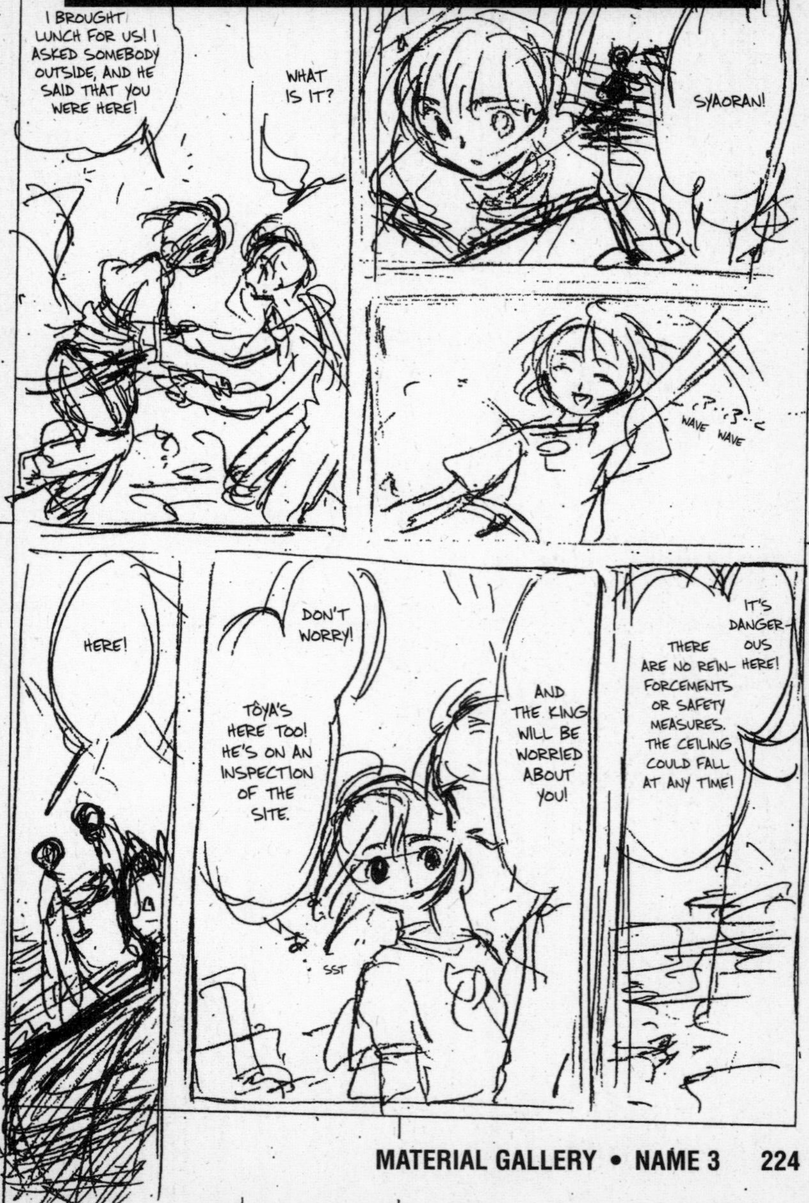

SYAORAN!
WAVE WAVE
WHAT IS IT?
I BROUGHT LUNCH FOR US! I ASKED SOMEBODY OUTSIDE, AND HE SAID THAT YOU WERE HERE!
IT'S DANGER-OUS HERE!
THERE ARE NO REIN-FORCEMENTS OR SAFETY MEASURES. THE CEILING COULD FALL AT ANY TIME!
AND THE KING WILL BE WORRIED ABOUT YOU!
DON'T WORRY!
TÔYA'S HERE TOO! HE'S ON AN INSPECTION OF THE SITE.
SST
HERE!

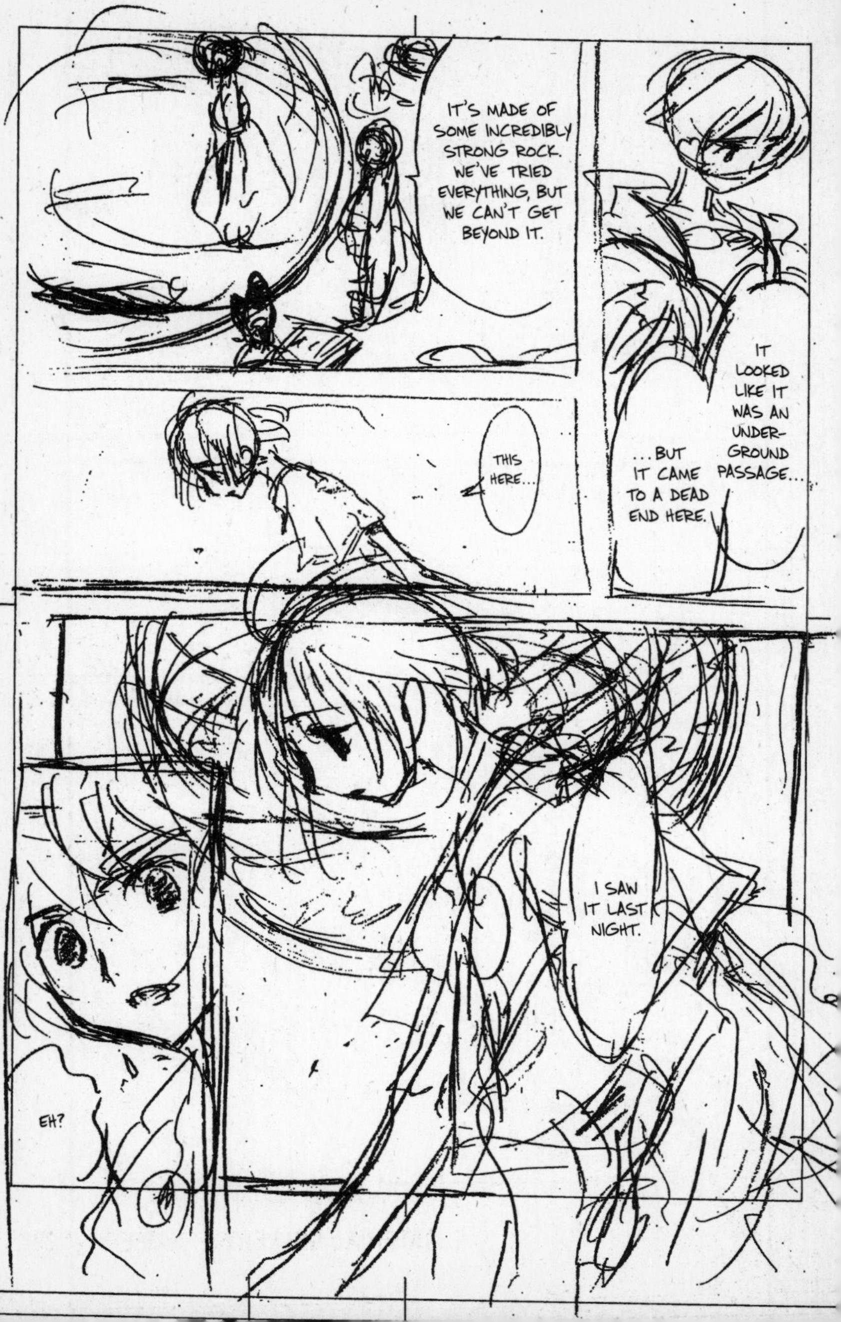
It looked like it was an under-ground passage...
...but it came to a dead end here.
It's made of some incredibly strong rock. We've tried everything, but we can't get beyond it.
This here...
I saw it last night.
Eh?

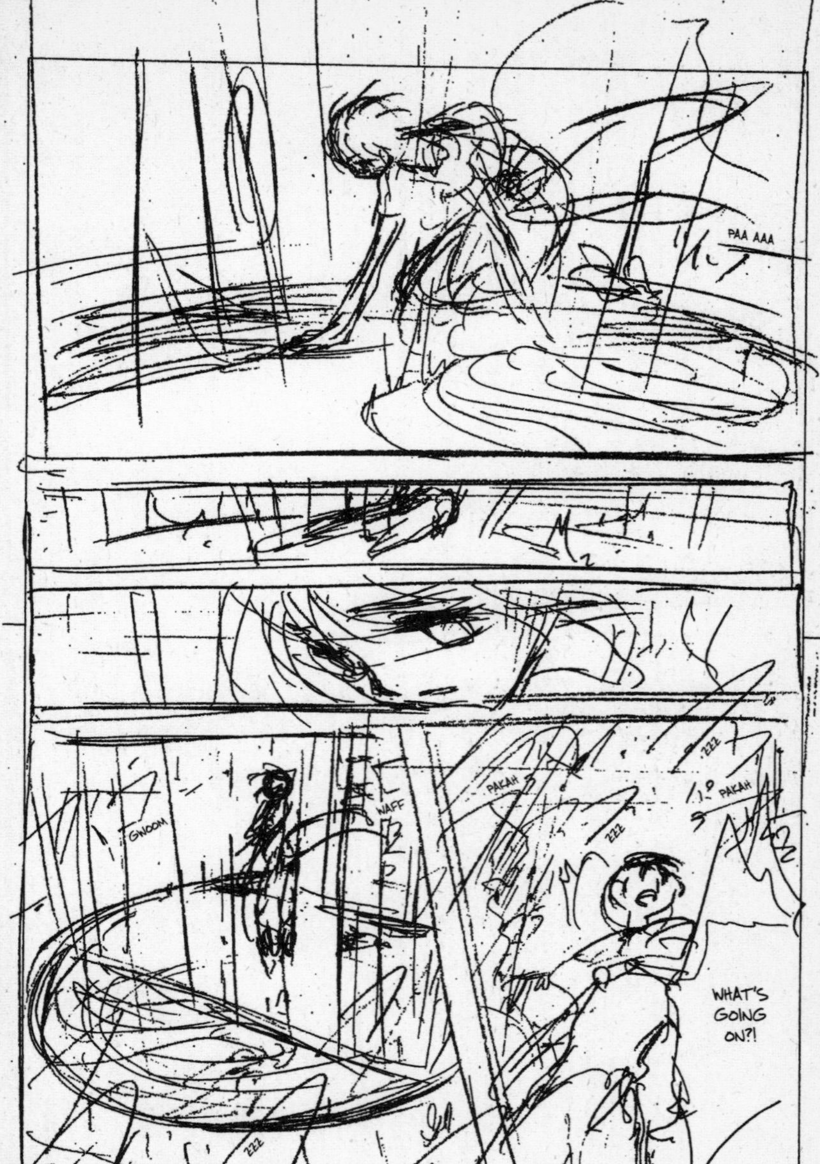
PAA AAA
ZZZ
PAKAH
PAKAH
ZZZ
WAFF
GWOOM
WHAT'S GOING ON?!
ZZZ
ZZZZ

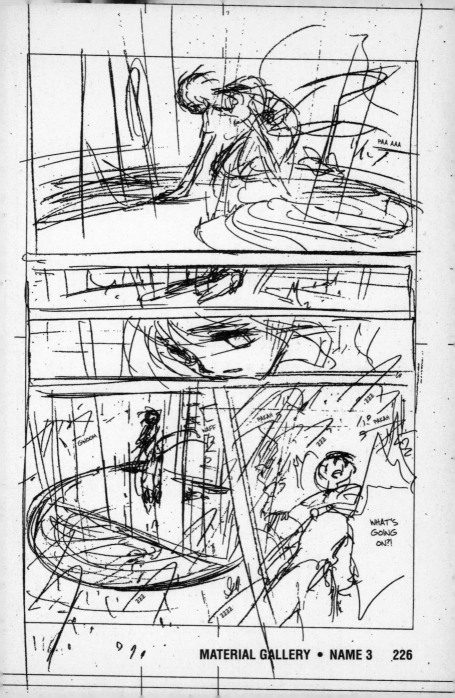

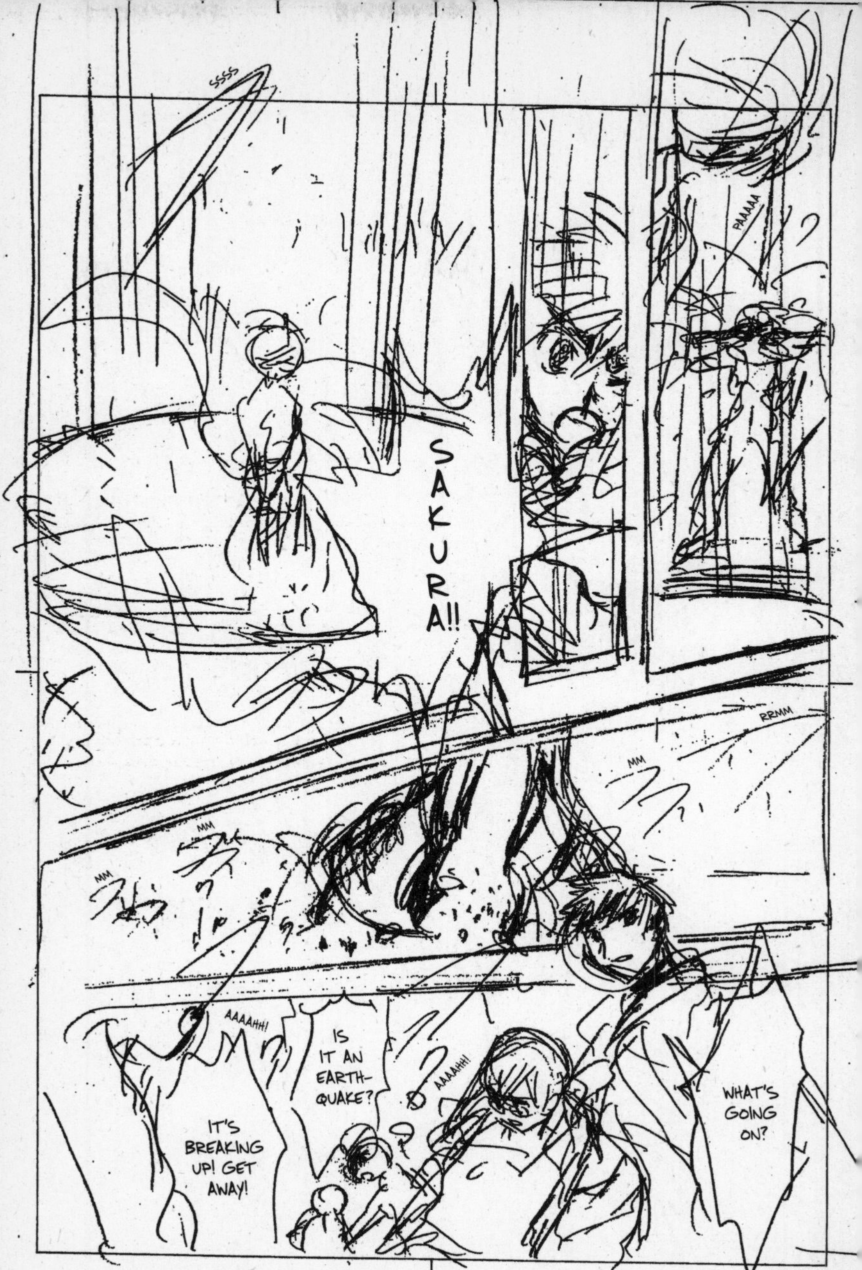
PAAAAA
SAKURA!!
SSSS
RRMM
MM
MM
MM
WHAT'S GOING ON?
AAAAHH!
IS IT AN EARTHQUAKE?
AAAAHH!
IT'S BREAKING UP! GET AWAY!

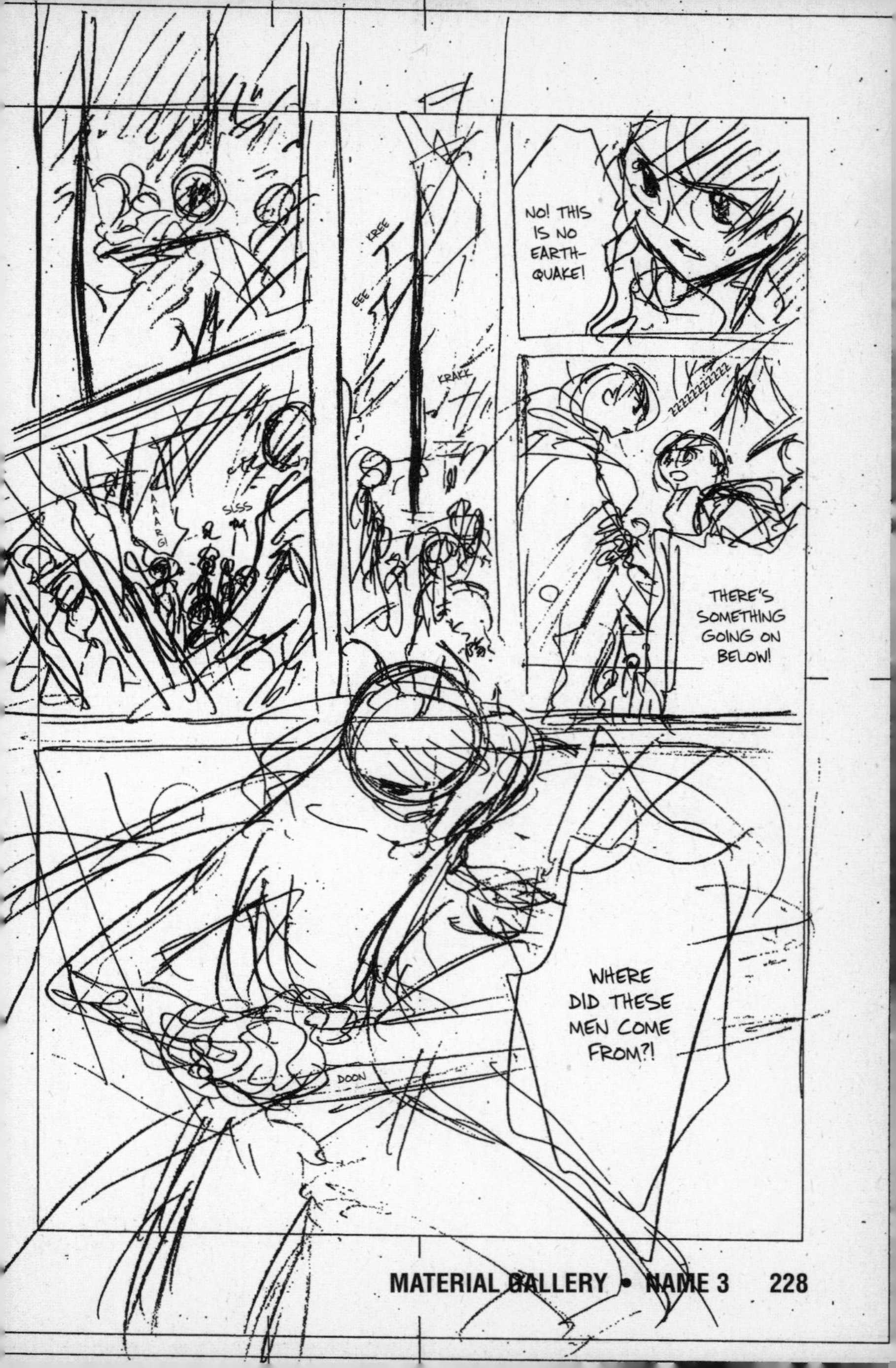
NO! THIS IS NO EARTH-QUAKE!
THERE'S SOMETHING GOING ON BELOW!
KREE
EEE
KRAKK
AAARG!
SLSS
WHERE DID THESE MEN COME FROM?!
DOON

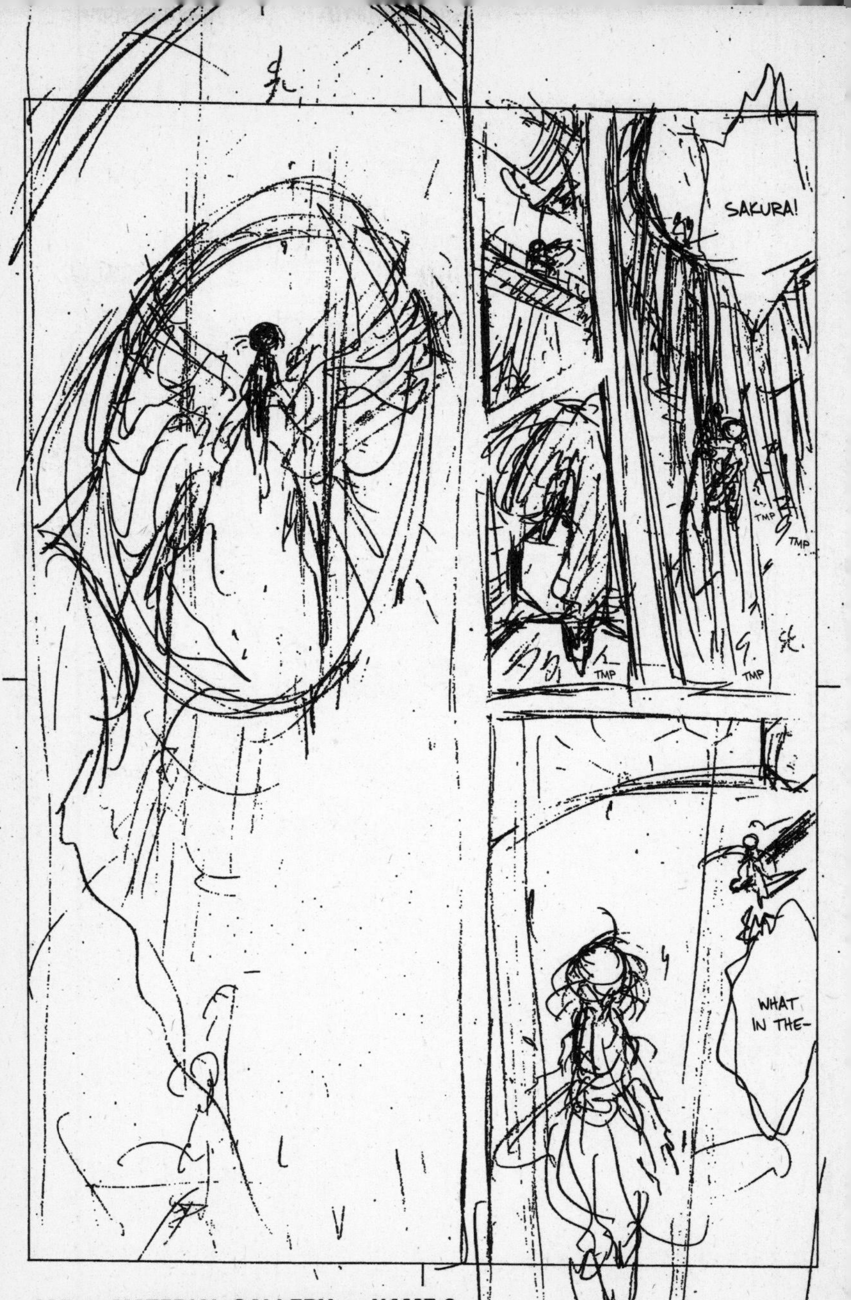
SAKURA!
TMP
TMP
TMP
TMP
WHAT IN THE-

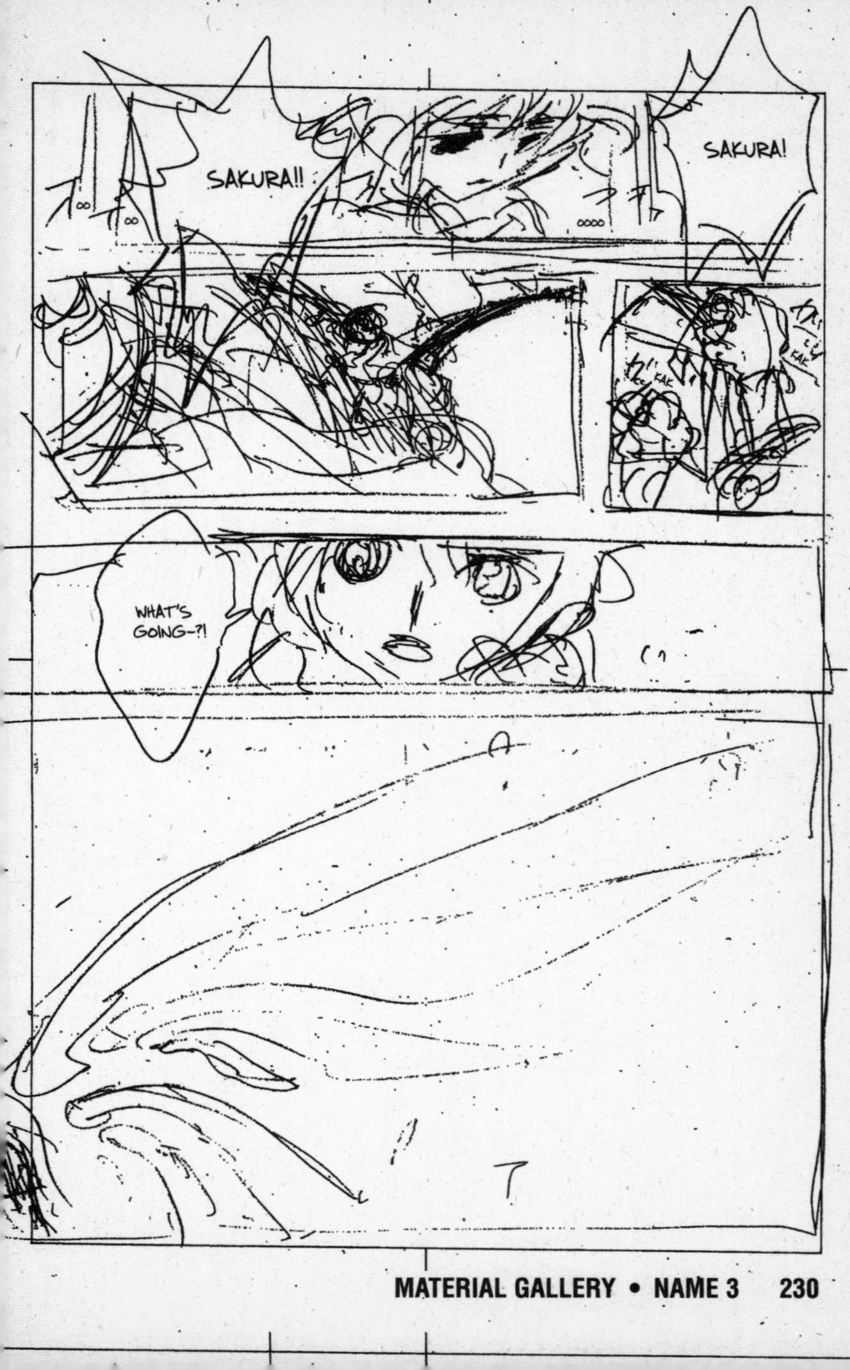
SAKURA!
SAKURA!!
KAK
KAK
WHAT'S GOING-?!

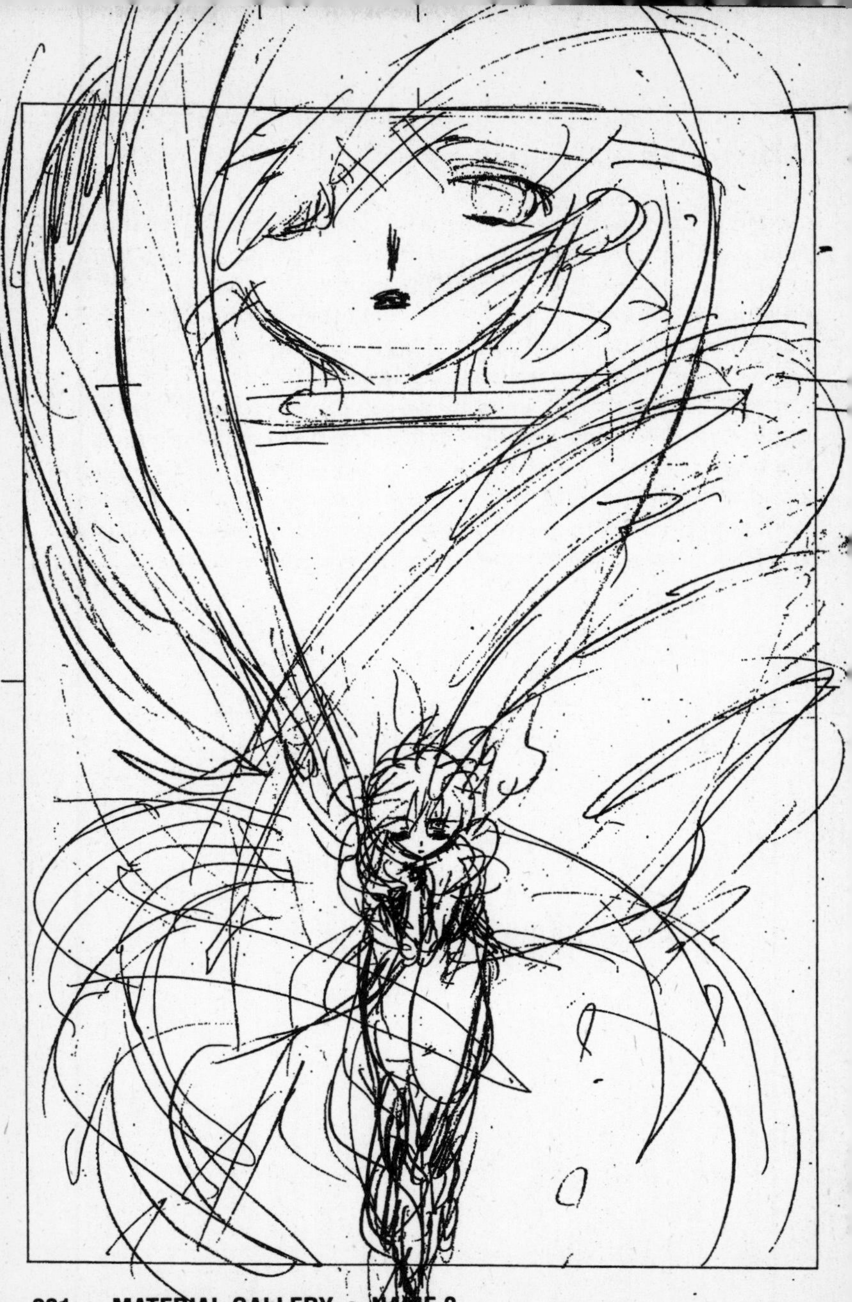

About the Creators

CLAMP is a group of four women who have become the most popular manga artists in America—Ageha Ohkawa, Mokona, Satsuki Igarashi, and Tsubaki Nekoi. They started out as doujinshi (fan comics) creators, but their skill and craft brought them to the attention of publishers very quickly. Their first work from a major publisher was *RG Veda*, but their first mass success was with *Magic Knight Rayearth*. From there, they went on to write many series, including Cardcaptor Sakura and Chobits, two of the most popular manga in the United States. Like many Japanese manga artists, they prefer to avoid the spotlight, and little is known about them personally.

CLAMP is currently publishing three series in Japan: Tsubasa and xxxHOLiC with Kodansha and Gohou Drug with Kadokawa.

BY CLAMP

Watanuki Kimihiro is haunted by visions. When he finds himself irresistibly drawn into a shop owned by Yûko, a mysterious witch, he is offered the chance to rid himself of the spirits that plague him. He accepts, but soon realizes that he's just been tricked into working for the shop to pay off the cost of Yûko's services! But this isn't any ordinary kind of shop . . . In this shop, Yûko grants wishes to those in need. But they must have the strength of will not only to truly understand their need, but to give up something incredibly precious in return.

Ages: 13+

Special extras in each volume! Read them all!

VISIT WWW.DELREYMANGA.COM TO:
- View release date calendars for upcoming volumes
- Sign up for Del Rey's free manga e-newsletter
- Find out the latest about new Del Rey Manga series

KURO GANE

BY KEI TOUME

AN EERIE, HAUNTING SAMURAI ADVENTURE

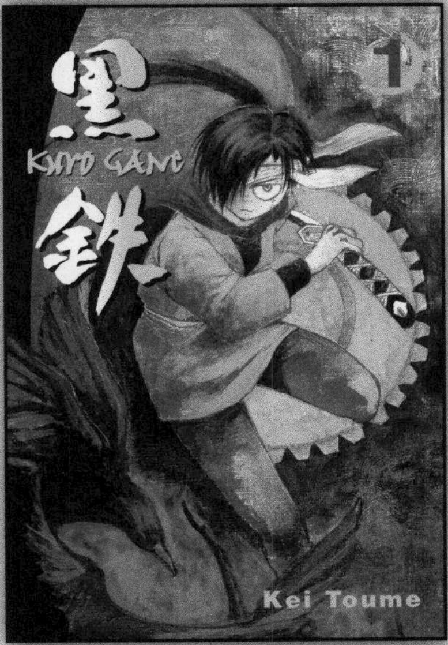

黒
KURO GANE
鉄
1
Kei Toume

Teen: Ages 13 +

Avenging his father's murder is a matter of honor for the young samurai Jintetsu. But it turns out that the killer is a corrupt government official—and now the powers that be are determined to hunt Jintetsu down. There's only one problem: Jintetsu is already dead.

Torn to pieces by a pack of dogs, Jintetsu's ravaged body has been found by Genkichi, outcast and master inventor. Genkichi gives the dead boy a new, indestructible steel body and a talking sword—just what he'll need to face down the gang that's terrorizing his hometown and the mobster who ordered his father's hit. But what about Otsuki, the beautiful girl he left behind? Steel armor is defense against any sword, but it can't save Jintetsu from the pain in his heart.

Special extras in each volume! Read them all!

DEL REY

VISIT WWW.DELREYMANGA.COM TO:
- Read sample pages
- View release date calendars for upcoming volumes
- Sign up for Del Rey's free manga e-newsletter
- Find out the latest about new Del Rey Manga series

TOMARE!

[STOP!]

You're going the wrong way!

Manga is a completely different type of reading experience.

To start at the *beginning*, go to the *end*!

That's right! Authentic manga is read the traditional Japanese way—from right to left. Exactly the *opposite* of how American books are read. It's easy to follow: Just go to the other end of the book, and read each page—and each panel—from right side to left side, starting at the top right. Now you're experiencing manga as it was meant to be.